GERD THEISSEN is Professor of New Testament at the University of Heidelberg, West Germany. Among his other works are *The Social Setting of Pauline Christianity, The Sociology of Early Palestinian Christianity,* and *A Critical Faith: A Case for Religion,* all published by Fortress Press.

John Riches is Lecturer in New Testament Language and Literature at the University of Glasgow.

Francis McDonagh, an editor at the Catholic Institute of International Relations, London, has translated several works including part of Schnackenburg's *Commentary on John's Gospel* and Pannenberg's *Theology and the Philosophy of Science.*

Studies of the New Testament and its World

EDITED BY JOHN RICHES

The Miracle Stories of the Early Christian Tradition

by
GERD THEISSEN

translated by
FRANCIS McDONAGH

edited by
JOHN RICHES

FORTRESS PRESS
PHILADELPHIA

Translated by Francis McDonagh from the German
Urchristliche Wundergeschichten: Ein Beitrag zur formgeschichtlichen
Erforschung der synoptischen Evangelien, © 1974 by
Gütersloher Verlaghaus Gerd Mohn, Gütersloh,
Federal Republic of Germany.

English Language Copyright © 1983 by T. & T. Clark Ltd.,
Edinburgh, Scotland.

First Fortress Press Edition 1983

Library of Congress Cataloging in Publication Data

Theissen, Gerd.
  The miracle stories of the early Christian tradition.

  Translation of: Urchristliche Wundergeschichten.
  Includes bibliographical references.
  1. Miracles. 2. Bible. N.T. Gospels — Criticism,
Form. I. Riches, John Kenneth. II. Title.
BS2555.2.T4613   1983   226'.70663   82–48546
ISBN 0–8006–0700–7

9613J82   **Printed in Great Britain by Clark Constable (1982) Ltd., Edinburgh**   *1–700*

Contents

Author's Foreword

The present form-critical study of primitive Christian miracle stories was accepted for the degree of *Habilitation* by the Evangelical Theological Faculty of Bonn University in the summer of 1972. It was written while I was Director of Studies at the Evangelical Theological *Stift* at Bonn University. Its completion was made possible because Professor P. Vielhauer allowed me a great deal of time for my own studies while I was working as his assistant. Above and beyond this he substantially contributed to its progress by his tolerance and understanding of new literary critical questions, and for this I am most grateful. For this published version the Introduction, Chapter IV of Part I, Chapter II of Part II and the whole of Part III were rewritten. In so doing I was able to take account of criticisms and suggestions for which I am grateful to Professors L. Delekat, W. Schrage and G. Klein.

Where certain fundamental criticisms of a theological nature are concerned I have had of course to restrict myself to offering a more detailed exposition of the concept of the holy (pp. 35-39) which is taken from the phenomenology of religion and which raises related issues. I am aware that the problems which await attention here are too serious and important to be dealt with adequately in an excursus of this kind.

I would like to thank the editors of the series *Studien zum Neuen Testament* for accepting this work for inclusion, the *Deutsche Forschungsgemeinschaft* for a grant towards the cost of publication and Dr. H. Kühne and G. Tinne as well as other staff and employees at the publishers and printers for their care and work.

I owe particular thanks to my wife, not only for accepting the usual distribution of roles in the family and the consequent restriction in her own profession, but because she has discussed each chapter critically with me and has allowed me to benefit from her professional skills in psychology and sociology.

Gerd Theissen
Bonn, October 1973

Technical Points

In the notes each publication at its first mention is given with the full title (without sub-title) and date, thereafter with an abbreviated title. Page references after the title are given without a preceding 'p' or 'pp'. The bibliography makes no claims to comprehensiveness. I have given further literature to individual miracle stories in part in the supplement to R. Bultmann, *Geschichte der synoptischen Tradition*, 4th ed., 1971. The abbreviations follow the 3rd edition of *Die Religion in Geschichte und Gegenwart*. I also used the abbreviations in the *Lexikon der Antiken Welt*, Zürich–Stuttgart 1965. For Rabbinic writings, Lucian of Samosata and Philo I have used abbreviations which follow various conventional systems. As well as this I have used the following abbreviations.

AH	O. Weinreich: Antike Heilungswunder 1909.
BL	Bibel und Leben.
EHPhR	Études d'histoire et de philosophie religieuses.
Epidauros W	Inscriptions from Epidauros in R. Herzog's listing: *Die Wunderheilungen von Epidauros* 1931.
Fab	Fabula. Zeitschrift für Erzählforschung.
FE	M. Dibelius: Die Formgeschichte des Evangeliums 1933.
GRM	Germanisch-romanische Monatsschrift.
GST	R. Bultmann: Geschichte der synoptischen Tradition 1921.
IJR	Internationales Jahrbuch für Religionssoziologie.
JAF	Journal of American Folklore.
LB	Linguistica Biblica. Interdisziplinäre Zeitschrift für Theologie und Linguistik.
PGM	K. Preisendanz: Papyri Graecae Magicae 1928/1931.
PSI	Pubblicazioni della Societa Italiana: Papiri Greci et Latini I-IX 1912-1935.
Q	Logienquelle.
rde	Rowohlts deutsche Enzyklopädie.
SBM	Stuttgarter Biblische Monographien.
SBS	Stuttgarter Bibelstudien.
StANT	Studien zum Alten und Neuen Testament.
StNT	Studien zum Neuen Testament.
StudGen	Studium Generale.
StUNT	Studien zur Umwelt des Neuen Testaments.
ThomEv	Thomas-Evangelium.
VA	Philostratus: vita Apollonii.
WF	Wege der Forschung.

Part Three: Miracle Stories as Symbolic Actions

Editor's Foreword

Until recently publication in English of Professor Theissen's work has been restricted to his shorter study of the sociology of earliest Christianity, *The First Followers of Jesus,* and his systematic treatise, *On Having a Critical Faith.* At the same time he has published in German a series of more detailed articles and studies which have earned him the reputation both of being a rigorous *Neutestamentler* in the great tradition, and also of being one of the most creative and innovative of the present generation of German scholars in that field, willing and well qualified to apply the insights from more recent literary critical and sociological studies to New Testament historiography.

The work here presented constitutes a sustained attempt to develop the insight of an earlier generation of form critics as it seeks to examine (1) the constraints and possibilities which the miracle story form imposed on and offered to its narrator; (2) the way in which such constraints and possibilities might influence the development of a particular tradition as it reproduced such stories; (3) the way in which such stories function: in regard to existing social conditions, to the development of religious movements and traditions and to individual self-consciousness. The result is a fascinating study of the Synoptic miracle stories which forms a fitting counterpart to his studies of *The Social Setting of Pauline Christianity* and which opens up a rich field of enquiry for students of the Synoptic Gospels.

John Riches
Glasgow, 1982

Introduction

TASK AND METHOD

After half a century of New Testament scholarship the form-critical approach has become established as a classical method of exegesis. The adjective 'classical' here expresses not just a certain distance from the 'classical' examples of the method, but also an historical and technical distance, which obliges us to develop our own approach. The present study has therefore set itself the task of developing the methods of classical form criticism by way of an analysis of one Synoptic literary form.[1] For this purpose we distinguish in the following discussion three aspects of form-critical enquiry, synchronic, diachronic and functional.[2]

Form criticism contains a synchronic element. It analyses literary forms or genres, which is to say that it classifies similarities and connections between texts whose contemporaneity in a cultural area makes possible a methodological (not a fundamental) bracketing of their historical succession. When, for example, texts

---

[1] 'Classical form criticism' here means notably the works of Rudolf Bultmann (*The History of the Synoptic Tradition,* Oxford, 2nd rev. ed. 1968 [Ger. 1921]), Martin Dibelius, (*From Tradition to Gospel,* London, 1934 [Ger. 1933]) and the works of Hermann Gunkel. On the latter, see the attractive account by W. Klatt, *Hermann Gunkel,* 1969. On the development of form criticism down to the present cf. the surveys of G. Iber, *ThR* 24 (1956/57), 283-338, and the supplement to the fourth German edition of Bultmann (1971).

[2] This section is based on the model of language constructed by structural linguistics. The fundamental work here was done by Ferdinand de Saussure (*Course in General Linguistics,* New York 1955 [Fr. 1916]). Saussure
a) distinguishes language as a supra-individual (unconscious) system, *langue,* from the individual speech act (*parole*) and
b) unlike historical linguistics, which uses a diachronic approach, analyses *langue* synchronically as a system, which he regards as
c) a network of syntagmatic relations between elements in the sequence of the sentence and paradigmatic (or associative) relations between similarities and contrasts (oppositions).
Transferred to literary data and in modified terminology, the distinctions between *langue* and *parole,* diachrony and synchrony, syntagmatic and paradigmatic, reappear in our discussion as virtual genre-structure and realisation, diachrony and synchrony and compositional and paradigmatic relations. The description of the search for the '*Sitz im Leben*' as functionalist comes from H. Bausinger, *Formen der 'Volkspoesie'*, 1968, 62. Where necessary we distinguish: 'synchronous', 'diachronous', 'structural' and 'functional' describe the datum, 'synchronic', 'diachronic', 'structuralist' and 'functionalist' its treatment.

are classified as parables this operation is independent of their relations in time or in the history of the tradition.[3]

Form *criticism*, on the other hand, adopts a diachronic approach or, more accurately, it opens out the diachronic search for the origin of and changes in a text by giving it a new dimension. Only the *Sitz im Leben*, that is, a recurrent social situation allowing for the transmitting of tradition, such as liturgy, mission, or instruction, offers a basis for the continuing transmission of oral forms which goes beyond their fixing in writing. While such a *Sitz im Leben* cannot guarantee the continuity of the written text, the possibility cannot be ruled out *a priori* that typical transmission tendencies may enable us to reconstruct the oral prehistory of a text. Form criticism thus becomes the 'history of the synoptic tradition' (Bultmann).

The search for the *Sitz im Leben* considers texts from the point of view of their function,[4] that is as elements in a wider complex of conditions, effects and intentions within (social) life. This does not mean that a broadly functionalist analysis can restrict itself to the description of typical narrative situations. It tries to produce a broader definition of the significance of forms within the relevant social groups. This requires in addition an analysis of historical developments, social conditions and general cultural influences, all of which enable us to understand why people adopted a particular literary form and developed it. Synchrony (the analysis of social structures) and diachrony (the description of historical developments) can hardly be separated here, but they can be distinguished.

Our task is to take these interrelated approaches further. We shall examine miracle stories synchronically as structured forms, diachronically as reproduced narratives, and from a functional point of view as symbolic actions.

---

[3] When Bultmann (*HST* 221 ff.) lists parallels to the individual miracle motifs without paying attention to their chronology, he is using a synchronic approach. This procedure is not unhistorical provided that is assembles parallels from a limited historical area. It only becomes unhistorical when it leaves the area of the ancient world and assembles parallels from every possible popular tradition. This is avoided here. It is something quite different when 'structuralists' play off a synchronic approach against a diachronic one and argue for an a-historical or even antihistorical approach. This is probably just a fashion. On the historical background to this anti-historical mood cf. G. Schiwy, *Der französische Strukturalismus*, 1969, 24ff., 86ff.

[4] The sociological term *Sitz im Leben* (life situation) was soon extended to include the historical and existential situation of a tradition. This development has certainly not increased the clarity of the concept (cf. E. Güttgemanns, *Candid Questions Concerning Gospel Form Criticism*, 1979, 259-60), but it is intelligible.

A. The Synchronic Approach

Form-critical analysis of different genres, compositions and motifs can be deepened by the adoption of structuralist techniques. This involves three steps. The first step is to divide all the connected texts of a particular genre into smaller units and to undertake as complete as possible a classification of all the units, whether persons, motifs or themes. If all the units occurred with equal probability in particular positions the text would be totally devoid of structure. However, even the casual reader of miracle stories notices that the positions of persons and motifs in the sequence of a connected text are not purely arbitrary. The listing of all the literary elements of a genre must therefore be followed by an investigation of their compositional connections. But the analysis is still not yet complete. The third step is to examine the intrinsic connections which exist between all elements specific to a genre independently of compositional sequence. Where these three steps appear we can say that structuralist techniques are being used. Structuralist methods are methods which analyse a text as a network of relations. This is the meaning of 'structure', the composite whole formed by the sum of the relations between elements of coherent and distinct complexes.

Each of the three steps outlined throws up its own problems. Even the isolation of narrative elements is a problem. In this study we distinguish three elements: characters, motifs and themes. Before these are defined in detail it must be pointed out that they are not 'building blocks' of narrative technique which exist independently of each other. Characters and themes have no separate life alongside the motifs; they appear only in them, though they can quite easily be separated from them. If we place all the motifs of a narrative side by side in random order, we can abstract from these motifs the characters of the narrative. They recur in different motifs, but are not identical with the motifs. If we then put together all the motifs in their narrative sequence, we can abstract from this sequence the theme which gives unity and shape to a sequence of motifs. The narrative elements which have been distinguished are thus on different levels of abstraction, but do not relate to each other as *genus* and *species*. They are, rather, mutually dependent entities. Particular themes prefer particular motifs and characters, characters particular motifs and themes, etc. The relations between these heterogeneous elements is no less important for the analysis of the specific structure of a genre than the investigation of relations between motifs, characters and themes on the same level of abstraction.

It must also be remembered that the isolation of elements on the same level of abstraction is always partly a matter of judgment. It is always possible to draw the dividing lines differently. Whether one takes two items as two variants of the same motif or as two motifs is a question of utility. The overriding consideration must always be, 'Does the distinction throw any light on the genre?' This will be elucidated in the following paragraphs in relation to three elements: characters, motifs and themes.

What are characters – as literary elements? The answer would be simple if we could just list all the people who appear in miracle stories: Jesus, the disciples, the centurion from Capernaum and so on. For an analysis of the genre, however, it is not the individuals who are important; the important thing is their role in the story. But this too is complex. For example, the centurion from Capernaum is first a 'vicarious petitioner': that is, the sick person does not make his own request, but someone else does it for him. A look at other miracle stories shows that such characters appear frequently; they may be parents or masters of the sick person, friends or bearers. It would be a natural step to abstract from such 'character variants' the character of the 'vicarious petitioner'. Then, however, the bearers of the sick man in Mk 2.3 and Mt 7.32 would not be included on the sole ground that in Mk 2.3ff. they do not petition on behalf of the sick person. It is definitely more useful to include this character variant too, and this gives us a role 'companion of the sick person', a typical character in miracle stories, which we can distinguish from its individual character variants.[5] In all we obtain seven such characters, abstractions from actual variations of behaviour, the level of abstraction chosen being to some extent subjective.

But there are further questions to be asked. Usually the vicarious petitioner recedes behind the figure of the sick person. However, if the sick person is not present at all (as in healings at a distance), the 'companion of the sick person' becomes the 'opposite number' of the miracle-worker. Previously he or she was a 'supporting actor'; now they leave the field of the supporting

---

[5] The distinction between constant persons and variable individuals derives in substance from W. Propp, *Morphology of the Folk Tale,* 1968 (Russian 1928). Propp refers only to persons. Starting from his work, A.J. Greimas, *Strukturale Semantik,* 1971 (French 1966), 157-77, distinguishes between agents and actors, which corresponds to our distinction between characters and character variants: 'an articulation of actors constitutes a single tale, a structure of agents a genre' (159). Greimas subsequently extends these concepts in a way which has only minimal relevance to the analysis of narrative material. His ideas are taken up by E. Güttgemanns, 'Strukturual-generative Analyse des Bildwortes "Die verlorene Drachme" (Lk 15.8-10)', *LB* 6 (1971), 2-17, esp. 12-16.

actor for that of the opposite number. But these two fields belong to every miracle story: there is always an opposite number as well as characters who stand between the principal actor and his opposite number. What we obtain here is not some arbitrary abstraction, but a structure specific to the genre 'miracle story'. If we now go through all the miracle stories we will find that the seven characters abstracted from their character variants are identical with seven possibilities for occupying the field of the opposite number; that is, these seven characters are also part of the specific structure of the genre which is realised in the character variants of actual texts. This introduces the important distinction between the specific structure of the genre and its realisation. Structures of this sort have a virtual existence.[6] They provide rules for the actual story. The specific features of the genre are seven characters and their possible arrangements in the three fields of principal actor, 'opposite number' and supporting actor. In the individual examples of the genre these positions are filled by different character variants. Note, however, that while the basis for our analysis of genre-specific elements and structures (in this case characters and character fields) is all the examples of synoptic miracle stories, this does not mean that all the elements of this structure are realised in every example.[7] When they are realised, however, they are usually realised in a particular order (which is merely a segment of an implicitly presupposed order). Even so, however, they have no more than the status of a norm which is by no means automatically operative in every story, while their infringement, modification and further development are among the narrator's resources: manipulating the rules is a proof of art.

The problems mentioned in relation to the analysis of the characters recur in the case of the *motifs*. By motifs, we mean the smallest non-independent narrative elements. They often appear as simple sentences or can be reproduced as such, even if in other places they consist of several sentences or only a single sentence element. There is no need to point out particularly that here too decisions with a certain latitude are unavoidable, but miracle

---

[6] It is possible to philosophise at length about the 'ontological' status of genre structures. Realists and nominalists will never be able to agree here. There seem to me to be objections against the compromise interpretation of forms as 'ideal types' in Max Weber's sense put forward by L. Honko, 'Genre Analysis in Folkloristics and Religion', *Temenos* 3 (1968), 48-66, esp. 61. The best description, in my view, is that of R. Welleck and A. Warren, *Theory of Literature* (1949), who argue that genres are 'institutions' or 'institutional imperatives' (N.H. Pearson, quoted, p. 226).

[7] Cf. a similar problem in W. Propp, *Morphologie*, 28. Not every tale has to contain all the functions recognised as specific to the genre.

stories in particular offer a favourable basis for practicable demarcations. For, to a much greater extent than other New Testament literary forms, they consist of recurring stereotyped narrative features. If we wish to distinguish motifs from one another in this area, all we have to do is to compare all the miracle stories. A listing together of the narrative features x, y and z with the motif A is then possible when these same features appear linked to each other in other parallel miracle stories, while being preceded or followed by varying narrative features.[8]

Another possible approach would be to find grammatical features which would justify the subdivision of the narrative sequence into motifs (the reference above to a simple sentence was simply a rough indication of the extent of a motif). This linguistic approach certainly offers greater exactness, and it may even be possible. It has not been adopted here because the narrative elements which recur in a number of miracle stories, the typical motifs, differ greatly in their grammatical formulation. Any attempt to distinguish them grammatically would require the specification of transformation rules and the like. It is, however, possible that the grammatical and narrative structure of a text might be closely related without being identical. The approach adopted here, a comparison of all the texts belonging to a form and the abstraction of the recurrent features relevant to the narrative, is at least practicable. It is also the approach of classical form criticism.

Motifs are elements formed by comparison and abstraction which occur in the actual texts only in a series of variants. We therefore distinguish motifs and motif variants,[9] and stress again

---

[8] S. Thompson defines, 'A motif is the smallest element in a tale having a power to persist in a tradition' (quoted by I.M. Greverus, 'Thema, Typus und Motiv', in *Vergleichende Sagenforschung,* 1969, 392). Our concept differs from his in three ways:
a) The motif is not identified by its persistence within the diachronous tradition, but by its stability in a number of examples of the genre which are in synchronous relation.
b) Thompson includes persons and objects in motifs. Our definition is narrower: 'narrative unit' means segments in the process of narration. On the other hand, if the definition of the motif as a unit of action ('plot-element', Wellek and Warren, 217) is compared: descriptions of a state are also narrative units although in these cases no action is present.
c) Motifs are not 'minimal units' absolutely, but the minimal units relevant to the narrative, and an element of judgment is unavoidable in their definition. Cf. the criticism of Thompson's concept of the motif in A. Dundes, 'From Etic to Emic Units in the Structural Study of Folktales',*JAF* 75 (1962), 95-105, esp. 96: 'A minimal unit may thus be defined as the smallest unit useful for a given analysis with the implicit understanding that although a minimal unit could be subdivided, it would serve no useful purpose to do so'.
The concept of the motif used above is, however, close to Propp's concept offunction (*Morphologie,* 25ff.), especially in the requirement that motifs must first be defined independently of the characters engaged in the action. Their attachment to characters must not be investigated until the second stage. Again, both here and in Propp motifs (or functions) are studied as structural factors; e.g. their compositional position is examined.
[9] A. Dundes, 'From Etic to Emic Units', 101ff., distinguishes between motifemes and allomotifs. 'Motifeme' is an analogical formation modelled on 'phoneme', 'lexeme', etc. Just

that the listing together of various motif variants as constituting a particular motif contains an element of individual judgment. For example the approach of the person seeking help can be treated as a motif which includes the motif variants: cries for help, falling on one's knees, pleading and expressions of confidence. Equally 'pleas and expressions of confidence' can be treated as a motif which exists in different variants, ranging from the reproachful demand for help through the sceptical question to the blind expression of confidence. Where various possibilities for making distinctions exist, our study generally chooses the one which stays closest to the text. The motifs obtained in this way are then combined into further motif groups as appropriate. Here again the dominant consideration is the utility of classifications and distinctions for the analysis of the structure of the form, since, like characters and character fields, motifs and motif groups also belong to the virtual structure of the form. The actual text contains only character and motif variants.

A mere sequence of motifs does not produce a narrative. We use the term 'themes' for the basic ideas of narratives which give internal shape and completeness to a sequence of characters and motifs. The healing of a sick person is a different theme from rescue from a dangerous situation or the gift of vital necessities. It is true that such themes are often called motifs, but in our context this would not be a useful terminology to adopt. A theme may have specific motifs, but every theme includes a number of motifs, even some which recur in other themes. Themes, then, are larger elements; they organise the individual motifs into a compositional whole and divide the miracle stories thus given shape into subordinate forms.[10] The distinction between genre-specific structure and its actual realisation reappears here too: the themes abstracted by us from a series of miracle stories exist in reality only in theme variants.

On the basis of these distinctions we can attempt a first, still inadequate, definition of the genre insofar as it can be defined without taking into account diachronic and functionalist

---

as the phoneme is distinguished from the physical sound by its position in the phonological system, the motifeme is distinguished from the allomotif by its structural significance for the genre. This distinction is valid even apart from the esoteric aspects of structuralism, as has been shown by A. Laubscher, 'Betrachtungen zur Inhaltsanalyse von Erzählgut', *Paideuma* 14 (1968), 170-94.

[10] Cf. I.M. Greverus, 'Thema, Typus und Motiv. Zur Determination in der Erzählforschung', in *Vergleichende Sagenforschung*, 390-401: 'By "theme" I mean the underlying idea out of which a narrative grows and which holds the narrative together. This underlying idea is realised in the material. The material is composed of the smallest material units, the motifs, and the so-called "epic additions"' (397).

considerations. Genres are inventories of character, motifs and themes which we abstract from character, motif and theme variants found in various examples of the genre. Our first task is to list the characters, motifs and themes as completely as possible. The unattainable regulative cognitive goal of this activity is to make this list as complete as possible so that every example of the genre can be described as a combination of characters and motifs within a specific theme. Classical form criticism has already taken this process of classification a long way, especially in the case of motifs. It was, however, interested almost exclusively in motifs, for which striking parallels exist in comparative religion. Completeness was not the aim.[11]

The listing of the various literary elements is only a preliminary operation. The really important task is the analysis of their mutual relations. This analysis is carried out in two dimensions. Each text is constituted first as a sequence of characters and motifs, second as a juxtaposition of texts, especially of texts from the same genre. These are always implicitly present, even if we claim to have only a particular text before us. If we talk, for example, about 'typical motifs' in this text, we have already presupposed such a juxtaposition: typical features can only be extracted from parallel texts. We call the first sort of relations compositional, the second paradigmatic. Since complexes of relations are structures, we go on to talk about compositional and paradigmatic structures, of sequences and fields.

The analysis of compositional structures presents no particular problems. Starting from recurrent motifs, we attempt to recognise particular forms of composition. The object of the analysis is to find a specific compositional structure underlying all miracle stories. This specific structure does not have to be fully realised in every miracle story: now and again only sections of it are actualised.

In the analysis of compositional structures we can build on the analyses of classical form criticism. For the analysis of paradigmatic relations, however, it gives us no model. We may indeed assume that every exegete is guided by such relations when he examines and interprets particular elements, but this is largely an unconscious process, not because these relations are so hard to pick out, but rather because they appear all too obvious. The analysis is based on the natural idea that an inventory of literary

---

[11] We shall distinguish 33 motifs. Bultmann, HST, 218-26, lists 22, but they are subsequently grouped as variants of seven motifs.

elements displays intrinsic relations independently of its realisation in compositional sequences. In connection with the analysis of characters and motifs in tales H. Bausinger speaks of 'kinship relations': 'When we say "wicked stepmother", this denotes not just one person, but at least one other person is involved – usually of course the poor abused stepdaughter. But what is here an actual kinship relation holds in a transferred sense for all motifs. They are part of quite specific kinship relations, and there are motifs with connections on almost all sides while others are less rich in their connections and always appear in the same context.'[12] Such kinship relations also exist in miracle stories, for example intrinsically opposed motifs such as 'faith' and 'doubt' (opposed motifs analogous to the oppositions of phonemes and lexemes on the linguistic level). These opposed motifs are inseparable, even when they are not realised in one and the same story. Wherever there is a reference to faith, scepticism and mockery are present in the background as alternative possibilities; we can even say that all the genre-specific motifs are present in every miracle story as excluded or realised possibilities, just as the paradigms of a language (*langue*) are implicit in every sentence, even though only one form of the paradigm is instantiated. To distinguish them from compositional relations within a single text we call these systematic or intrinsic relations which we infer on the basis of a comparison of texts from the same form 'paradigmatic', and define the 'form-critical field' as the composite of all paradigmatic relations of literary elements. Once we recognise that all literary elements are part of such form-critical fields, it becomes impossible to give an adequate description of any item without sketching its diverse relations within the field.

We are here using an idea put forward by A. Jolles. Jolles defined genres as fields of linguistic gestures (motifs): 'What we have called a legend is firstly no more than the particular placing of the gestures in a field'.[13] However, this means a considerable modification of his 'energetic' concept of field; equally Jolles' term 'motif' corresponds rather to our 'theme'. In addition, we also apply the concept of the field to larger units such as genres and sub-genres, so following Jolles' question 'how far the sum of all recognised and distinguished structures forms a single internally coherent and articulated whole with an underlying organisation – a system'.[14] This is not to suggest a search for a timeless

---

[12] *Formen der 'Volkspoesie'*, 155.
[13] A. Jolles, *Einfache Formen*, 1st ed. 1930, 46.
[14] *Einfache Formen*, 7.

system, but for historical structures, 'systemoidal' complexes which do not combine to give closed systems. Linguistic structuralism has stimulated an awareness of such complexes in other disciplines. The form-critical field analysis undertaken here is indebted particularly to the widespread interest in the study of word-fields among German speaking scholars.[15]

A structural synchronic approach therefore investigates literary relations on the compositional and paradigmatic levels, and analyses compositional sequences and fields of literary elements.[16] Since we can distinguish three constitutive elements of the genre (characters, motifs and themes), since all elements have to be examined for both compositional and paradigmatic links, and since motifs are also related to characters and themes (and *vice versa*), we obtain a range of investigative categories, which are set out in the following table:

| List of literary elements | Structures | |
	Compositional sequences	Paradigmatic fields
1. Characters	Sequence of characters	Field of characters
2. Motifs a) Connection with character b) Connection with each other c) Connection with themes	Sequence of motifs Associated motifs Compositional position	Field of motifs Motifs connected with characters Contrasted motifs Thematic setting
3. Themes	Compositional forms	Field of themes

---

[15] I have derived particular stimulation from lectures by L. Weisgerber on the 'four basic forms of language study' (1962/63). Cf. his book, which is in many areas a complete treatment, *Die vier Stufen in der Erforschung der Sprachen,* 1963. There is a short survey of work on word fields in S. Ullmann, *The Principles of Semantics,* 2nd ed. Glasgow and Oxford 1957, 157-70, 309-17. A detailed account of recent work, paying particular attention to the further development of word field study by E. Coseriu, is provided by H. Geckeler, *Strukturelle Semantik und Wortfeldtheorie,* 1971.

[16] The structuralist study of narratives has two roots. The first is W. Propp's work on the 'morphology of the folk tale' (1928), which concentrates on analysis of the compositional structure of narratives. Independent of this is Claude Lévy-Strauss' approach. Lévy-Strauss examined the páradigmatic relations of narrative elements, the hidden logic of myths and

The miracle story genre was not however transmitted to us in isolation; individual examples are always found within the wider set of relationships of a framework genre. Again, the miracle story genre has particular paradigmatic relations with the other genres transmitted in the framework, just as the various examples of the gospel 'framework' genre can be shown to be both historically and intrinsically interrelated. Accordingly we obtain two further investigative categories:

4. *Genres*	Composition within the framework genre	Field of all Synoptic genres
	=	
5. *Framework narrative*	Composition of the framework	Field of the Synoptic Gospels?

We shall now explain and illustrate these various categories by giving an example of each.

1. Characters

a) Sequences of characters. Miracle stories show, for example, a typical sequence of characters at the beginning. The miracle-worker appears first, and then the person seeking help. The frequent variation in the sequence of characters in the introduction to controversies makes this observation seem less banal than it might taken on its own.

b) Field of characters. The field of characters is made up of the typical relations of all the characters who appear in miracle stories. In the Johannine miracle stories, for example, demons are absent. This change in the stock of characters restructures the whole field.

---

sagas. Cf. for example his classic analysis 'La geste d'Asdival' (1958), ET: E.R. Leach, ed. *The Stuctural Study of Myth and Totemism*, London 1967, 1-48. Whereas Propp analysed a whole genre, Lévy-Strauss analyses only various individual narratives; in other words, he does not look for paradigmatic relations within the whole genre, across the whole range of examples of a genre. There is a workable definition of the structuralist study of narrative inaugurated by these two scholars in M. Pop, 'Aspects actuels des recherches sur la structure des contes', *Fab* 9 (1967), 70-77: 'As in any structural system, in popular narratives motifemes, significant elements with particular functions, constitute, through their reciprocal relations, patterns and models with which the genre operates. The decipherment of motifemes, the study of their correlations on the paradigmatic and syntagmatic planes and the isolation of the structured model therefore constitute the object of structuralist research' (71). There is a survey of research in E. Meletinsky, 'Zur strukturelltypologischen Erforschung des Volksmärchens', in W. Propp, *Morphology*, 181-214. There is a detailed bibliography in R. Breymayer, 'Bibliographie zum Werk Vladimir Jakovlevic Propps und zur strukturalen Erzählforschung', *LB* 15/16 (1972), 67-77. See esp. his essay on Propp. ibid., 36-66.

2. Motifs

a) Sequences of motifs. If a motif a constantly appeared in connected texts along with motif b, we would have an ideal case of 'associated' motifs. To the best of my knowledge this ideal case nowhere occurs. However, two motifs frequently associated are healing by touch and demonstration by a proof of power (*cf.* Mk 1.31). In such cases we shall often find that it is not motifs as such which are associated, but specific motif variants. – A factor in the compositional arrangement of motifs is their compositional position. The acclamation always comes at the end, but others appear in the exposition and the conclusion, for example the faith motif (Mk 2.5 and 5.34). Combining all the individual observations about the compositional position of motifs gives us the compositional structure of miracle stories in general.

b) Fields of motifs. In addition to faith and doubt, other examples of motifs in paradigmatic opposition are rejection and acclamation, encouragement and rebuff. The most important motifs (or motif variants) in the miracle stories can be combined into pairs of opposites. However, every motif is also (from a different point of view) in opposition to yet other motifs. The faith which overcomes difficulties is not only in opposition to human distrust, but also to the barriers which the miracle-worker himself sets in the way of the person seeking help. This gives us a multi-dimensional complex of oppositions. One source of this multi-dimensionality is the fact that motifs are associated with various people, with demons, human beings and divine beings. There are motifs which have a fundamental association with the same character, for example, the healing word which always appears in the mouth of the miracle-worker, and others, such as the command to silence, which appears not only in the mouth of the miracle-worker, but also in those of his attendants (Mk 10.48). As well as the association of motifs with characters, their attachment to particular themes is also significant. Healing touch, for example, appears only in healings, never in exorcisms. This motif has a relatively fixed thematic setting;[17] others are much more open.

3. Themes

a) Compositional forms. Alongside the general compositional structure of miracle stories, there are specific compositional forms, realisations of sections of the form structure, which are characteristic of particular themes, even if they do not appear exclusively attached to particular themes. In all gift miracles, for example, the composition has final stress:

---

[17] The concept of the 'setting' of an element comes from W. Kramer, *Christ, Lord, Son of God*, London 1966 (German 1963), where it refers to the occurrence of a christological title in a formula. The idea is applied here to the characteristic features of miracle stories and denotes the occurrence of motifs in particular themes, though it can also refer to the connection of motifs with particular genres. The motif of wonder, for example, has two settings, miracle stories and disputes (cf. Mk 12.17).

concluding motifs, especially the demonstration and its variants, occupy much more space than the miraculous process itself (the multiplication, transformation or gathering of the gift-objects).

b) Field of themes. Various themes can also be treated as sub-genres. The way in which these form a 'systematic' complex can be illustrated by an Old Testament example. According to C. Westermann, *The Praise of God in the Psalms* (1965), (Ger. 1954), the account of the suppliant's distress, the subsequent praise which records his rescue and generalising, descriptive praise form a systematic complex, of which particular elements may be realised in the individual sub-genres. In the psalm of lamentation the praise-report is anticipated, in the psalm of thanksgiving it is expressed, and in the hymn it is presupposed. In this way themes and sub-genres of the 'psalm' constitute a form-critical field.

4. Genres

a) The composition of the Synoptic genres within the gospels. Extending the analyses of classical form criticism, we distinguish four compositional genres: combinatory, ordering, typifying and bridging compositions. Examples of combinatory composition occur wherever a transition from one pericope to another is created by special narrative techniques, while bridging composition occurs where there is a reference across the immediately following or preceding pericope, recalling something past or announcing something to come.

b) Genre field. This is not some sort of timeless systematisation of all popular narrative genres,[18] but the possibility of historically limited form-critical fields can hardly be denied *a priori*: even the synoptic genres could constitute a form-critical field. For example, within the sayings tradition 'parables' are closer to narratives than to Wisdom logia. By examining such relations at close quarters and from a distance, we may be able to uncover a web of relations.

5. Framework genre

We are justified in speaking of a field of the various examples of the gospel framework genre if the possibilities of the gospel genre are realised in the four gospels in a recognisably 'systematic' way. For our purposes, however, this is only a marginal problem.

We can now improve on the definition we gave above of a genre. Genres are collections of characters, motifs and themes structured

---

[18] W. Kosack, 'Der Gattungsbegriff "Volkserzählung"', *Fab* 12 (1971), 18-47, has made an interesting attempt to establish a system of all folk genres merely by describing the mutual relations of the individual genres, their closeness and distance. Such universal schemes should, however, be viewed with scepticism. A simpler two-dimensional scheme is proposed by G. Scott Littleton, 'A Two-Dimensional Scheme for the Classification of Narratives', *JAF* 78 (1965), 21-27. An interesting feature of these schemes is that their procedure resembles that of field analysis, though it seems to me most relevant in a historically limited sphere.

compositionally in sequences and paradigmatically in fields. We discover the elements and structures specific to a particular genre by abstraction from actual character, motif and theme variants. Nevertheless we may assume that they are not just abstractions. In human creations the rule *'universalia ante rem'* ('Universals precede particulars') applies: the structures of the miracle stories were at some point (usually unconsciously) norms of the narrative process, guiding the narrator in the shaping, transformation and reproduction of his stories. This distinction between virtual literary structures and their realisation can link in with ideas of A. Jolles, who attributed a virtual character to 'simple forms', but made a distinction between them and their realisation as the 'actual and present simple form'.[19] H. Bausinger has characterised this relationship very well: the 'field is always present, but it is realised only in linguistic instantiation – just as an electrical field is always present, but can be shown to exist only by a test charge'.[20] A useful analytic approach to the idea of the virtual field and its realisation is provided by the structuralist models which, in their different variants, derive from Ferdinand de Saussure. The New Testament writings have their own *langue* of characters, motifs and themes which are realised in the particular text,[21] and here too it is possible to identify the structures of this *langue* only when one distinguishes synchrony and diachrony and separates syntagmatic ('compositional' in our terms) and paradigmatic relations. The form language of the New Testament writings is thus to be regarded as analogous to linguistic norms, as socially transmitted norms learned and internalised by a narrator, by which not only the narrator but also the listeners are unconsciously guided. The structuralist analysis of the literary form therefore leads on – as in classical form criticism – by its own internal logic to functionalist analyses and investigations in the sociology of literature.

---

[19] *Einfache Formen*, 46-47; quotation from 47.

[20] *Formen der 'Volkspoesie'*, 57.

[21] The *langue-parole* model was first successfully applied to the analysis of oral narrative material by P. Bogatyrev and R. Jakobson, 'Die Folklore als eine besondere Form des Schaffens', in *Donum Natalicium Schrijnen*, 1929, 900-13, where the relation between an orally transmitted work and its various reproductions was seen as analogous to that between *langue* and *parole*. The work itself, according to the authors, is subjected to a preventive censorship by the community, i.e. like language it is a socially based structure of norms which is individually varied. It would be better to treat, not the individual work, but its genre, as the *langue*. Social control acts especially on the specific motifs, themes, stylistic elements and compositional forms of a genre. This would also make it impossible to present a relation between a work and its reproduction analogous to that between *langue* and *parole* as a characteristic of oral literature, since authors who compose in writing are also bound by the norms of the genre. In this respect oral and written literature are comparable. A short

Models from linguistics, such as the distinction between structure and realisation, synchrony and diachrony and so on, will always be illuminating for the study of literature. Nevertheless caution is required in transferring linguistic terminology to literary phenomena. Literary forms exist only in language, but form a particular stratum in language, a formation in a sense over and above linguistic strata, and there are arguments in favour of allowing literary forms a relative autonomy from basic linguistic strata:

i) Literary forms can be translated into other languages. The same tale realised in various linguistic structures possesses form-critical identity. It remains a tale.[22]

ii) A motif identical in terms of form criticism can have various grammatical realisations within the same language; it remains the same motif.

---

time afterwards R. Jakobson (with J. Tynianov) rightly extended the *langue-parole* model to written literature (cf. 'Probleme der Literatur- und Sprachforschung', *Kursbuch* 5 [1966], 74-76) and so abandoned the not very satisfactory (H. Bausinger, *Formen*, 44) contrast between oral and written literature. Recognising the common features of written and oral tradition also shows up the differences more clearly. The 'writing' author can make individual variations in the norms of the genre in each new work to a much greater degree than the oral composer because he is removed from the immediate presence of the public and its expectations. Once composed, however, the work cannot be much altered. In oral transmission the narrator cannot remove himself from the preventive censorship of the community: anything that does not attract listeners has no basis for existence. The author is much more closely tied to the norms of the genre, and so the stereotyped elements in his compositions become much more prominent. On the other hand, any reproduction of an individual tradition is here a creative variation. The traditions do not congeal into 'authentic' versions.

A comparison between oral and written compositions is not quite the same thing as the analysis of the transition from oral composition to written. E. Güttgemanns has applied the *langue-parole* model to this process, but comes to contradictory conclusions. According to p. 262 (*Candid Questions*), the oral state corresponds to *parole* and the written state to *langue*, while according to pp. 279-80 it is precisely the reverse: tradition is equated with *langue* and redaction with *parole*. However there is a correct analogy between supra-individual genre norms and *langue* and examples of the genre and *parole* which I overlooked in Bultmann, *GST*, Supplement, 4th Ger. ed., 14. In the meantime E. Güttgemanns has been using the terms 'competence text' and 'performance text'.

[22] The argument from translatability is used by Wellek and Warren (*Theory*, 145-46) against the idea of a purely linguistic analysis of works of art. A relative independence of important levels of a narrative from language is also emphasised by A. Dundes. Cf. the review by B. Nathhorst, 'Genre, Form and Structure in Oral Tradition', *Temenos* 3 (1968), 128-35. Dundes distinguishes three levels: 'The first is the formal or structural level, which is independent of language. Hence the plot or structure of folktale can theoretically be put into any language of the world. The second level is that of content. It also survives translation but tends to be variable and less constant than form. The third is the linguistic level, which is completely dependent on the particular language in question. The elements on this level, often called stylistic features, cannot ordinarily survive translation' (129). The argument from translatability also appears in C. Lévy-Strauss, 'The Structural Study of Myths' in *Structural Anthropology*, 1963, 206ff.

iii) Linguistic structures determine the possibilities of utterances to the extent that one can make a clear distinction between 'right' and 'wrong'. The normative function of literary forms is different. There are no right and wrong miracle stories, but at most beautiful and less beautiful ones. Literary norms evidently make a further selection from the many possibilities allowed by linguistic norms.[23]

iv) Linguistic structures seek to guarantee communication in general. Literary forms express a common view in particular, more or less typical historical situations. They are forms of expressions belonging to specific human interpretations of the world and to specific social groups to a much higher degree than the different languages. To prevent misunderstandings, let us sum up. Literature exists only as language, and while it is possible to extend the term 'language' to any linguistically transmitted meaning and consign its investigation to linguistics, there is no obvious reason why linguistics should be equally competent to interpret legal, philosophical, religious and literary texts. However, irrespective of whether various levels are assumed to exist in language, or specific literary levels rooted in primary linguistic data, in either case our premise holds: structuralist linguistic methods developed for the analysis of primary linguistic data (in phonology, syntax and semantics) are not directly applicable to literary forms, but serve as models because of structural similarities. Literary studies – inspired by these models – must develop their own structural methods. Methods, even if not indigenous, must nevertheless be judged as if they were.[24]

---

[23] M. Lüthi, 'Urform und Zielform in Sage und Märchen', *Fab* 9 (1967), 41-54 gives a good example of the way generic norms are superimposed on linguistic structures. Although 'the green wood' is linguistically an obvious phrase it almost never appears in folktales 'because the tale is concerned with action and not with the description of moods or states. It says "the great wood" or "the dark wood", the "gloomy wood" because it is possible to get lost in big, dark woods and dangers lurk in them, whereas the phrase "the green wood" has no relation to any action. . . . The aims of the genre's style here defeat the intrinsic movement of language' (51).

Formal poetic genres cannot be used as an argument against the distinction between linguistic and literary norms. While the norms of linguistic structures usually operate more or less automatically, linguistic and literary norms must be reconciled with great art if the verse or rhyme is not to sound clumsy.

[24] B. Allemann, 'Strukturalismus in der Literaturwissenschaft', in *Ansichten einer künftigen Germanistik*, 1969, 143-152, distinguishes four forms of structuralism in literary criticism (148ff.): A. A direct application of linguistics to literary texts. B. The extension of structural linguistic analyses into the domain of literary criticism – in the same way that classical rhetoric used grammar. C. Specifically literary structural analyses. D. Cultural structuralism, which includes extra-literary factors. An alternative distinction might be: textual linguistic, literary critical and cultural structuralism. Textual linguistics (A) investigates linguistic structures. The distinctiveness of literature then appears as an overarching linguistic structure, which leads to a 'stretching' of linguistic concepts: terms such as 'macro-syntax', 'supersign' and 'supra-segmental textemes' appear. Literary critical structuralism (C), on the other hand, accepts the existence of specifically literary units, norms and structures which reshape the primary linguistic material. Consequently it is best able to build on traditional formal analyses and their concepts. Position B stands between textual linguistic and literary critical structuralism. Its main field is stylistics. To linguistics language with strong stylistic features appears as an anomaly, as a deviation from normal

B. The Diachronic Approach

By diachronic methods we mean all approaches which analyse texts as the product and the source of developments, as elements in a process of tradition.[25] The diachrony of texts is frequently presented by analogy with the strata of deposits in archaeology which have to be removed to reveal the original. Simple then would automatically mean older and complicated secondary – an assumption which has drawn justified criticism.[26] The opposite assumption, which tries to see a tendency to simplification and refinement in all processes of tradition, would of course be no less dogmatic. In both cases the inadequacy lies in the one-dimensional approach, which regards literary developments exclusively as a relationship between various individual texts. If a, a' and a'' are texts and the horizontal arrow represents the development between them, we get the following picture.

$$a \longrightarrow a' \longrightarrow a''$$

On the other hand, if we look at texts, not just in their mutual relations, but also as realisations of compositional and field structures, diachronic analysis acquires an additional dimension.

---

usage. For literary analyses the same phenomena are positive signs of a desire to impose literary form, which makes a deliberate selection from the available linguistic possibilities and occasionally creates new possibilities. This is thus a possible meeting-point for the textual and literary approaches. Cultural structuralism (D) takes extra-literary social and anthropological structures into consideration. The danger of a 'panstructuralism' (Allemann, 150) is particularly great here. History is seen as variations of timeless structures, even though such structures and in particular belief in them are themselves elements in history.

All approaches are legitimate, but a specifically literary critical structuralism is probably the most likely at the moment to be productive, whereas 'a theoretical model of literature erected on literary foundations' lies, as Allemann remarks (151) 'at an almost utopian distance', fascinating though these distant peaks may be.

[25] As far as I know the first person to introduce 'the contrasting ideas of "synchrony" and "diachrony"' into exegesis was W. Richter ('Formgeschichte und Sprachwissenschaft', *ZAW* 82, 1970, 216-25; *Exegese als Literaturwissenschaft*, 1971, 35-36, passim). Previously there was no comprehensive term for the common element in all the approaches which distinguish primary, secondary and tertiary and elucidate a text in terms of its earlier states or in terms of previous states of its parts. Diachronic methods include textual criticism, literary criticism, redaction and tradition criticism, and to a large extent also the history of religions. Occasionally the term 'tradition history' is used in such a broad sense that it becomes almost identical with 'diachronic approach'. This extension has certainly not contributed to the clarity of the term.

[26] Cf. e.g. E.P. Sanders, *The Tendencies of the Synoptic Tradition*, 1969, 13-26; H. Bausinger, *Formen*, 62; E. Güttgemanns, *Candid Questions*, 310f. V. Taylor (*The Formation of the Gospel Tradition*, 6th ed., 1957, 122ff., 202ff., passim) regards more complexity as a sign of originality.

Virtual genre structures are realised not just in the simultaneity of a number of examples of the genre, but equally in the succession of different versions of the same narrative.[27] We now modify our diagram accordingly: A is the generic structure of *a* and a vertical line represents the realisation of A in *a*. We assume here that texts *a* and *a'* are realisations of the same structure, but that the development from *a'* to *a''* is associated with an alteration of underlying structures.

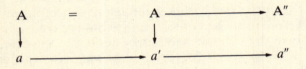

Synchronous realisations of a genre in different examples and diachronous modifications within the tradition history of a single example of the genre are naturally only comparable to a limited extent. The differences are much greater in the first case than in the second. Comparison is, however, possible in one point: diachronous changes in texts usually remain within the framework of existing generic structures and actualise virtual relations within compositional sequences and paradigmatic fields. An individual tradition is comparable to a musical theme, which is exploited by means of various given forms of variations. Abandoning the metaphor: tradition and redaction are reproductions of the same structures; the history of the tradition and the redaction are part of an all-embracing 'history of reproduction'. There are no archaeological strata in a text, only whole units of text freshly reproduced each time from the stock of the genre. The model of archaeological strata does not do justice to the texts, but it would be a gross exaggeration to deny its heuristic value. It still remains useful to distinguish elements incorporated at a particular stage and features freshly realised from the genre's stock (so called redactional additions). We must also allow for the possibility that a

---

[27] This relation between structure and realisation was picked out as long ago as 1929 by P. Bogatyrev and R. Jakobeon (see above, n. 21) as a characteristic of folklore transmission. S. Lo Nigro, 'Tradition et style du conte populaire', *Internat. Kongress der Volkserzähl-ungsforscher* (1961), 152-60, describes it as follows: 'The analogy between popular poetry and linguistic phenomena has proved the best way of explaining the oral transmission of tales. If each language is a living process realised by a dialectical relation between the speaker and a pre-existing institution, the tale which we call popular is no less so' (154). Here, however, the pre-existing institution is not so much the individual story as such but as part of a genre.

narrator may increase the genre's stock of specific motifs and motif variants: there are also 'narrators of genius' who not only reproduce from inherited patterns but also create new patterns. These, however, may be allowed to be exceptions. The first question to be asked is always whether the new element is an actualisation of possibilities specific to the genre. Against the background of such virtual generic structures the one-sided distinction between tradition and redaction must certainly be made more relative.

This new view of diachrony in tradition history presupposes that the virtual structures of the genre are more than theoretical constructions of the analyst, that they prove to be determining factors in the process of tradition. A number of observations from recent work point in this direction. They are worth reporting here.

The search for structural sequences and fields of persons and motifs is in the nature of the case not unknown. We may recall what H. Bausinger called the 'kinship relations' of motifs, which he rightly assumes play a crucial role in 'the variation, reshaping and amalgamation of tales',[28] that is in three different types of diachronous processes of tradition:

i) M. Lüthi[29] has drawn particular attention to a specific form of variation, the development of traditions which reveal previously hidden possibilities. Lüthi thinks that this phenomenon must be explained in terms of goals operating both as forms and as forces. What he interprets as an entelechy immanent in the motifs is perhaps the 'pull' of paradigmatic structures. The 'goals as forces' consist mainly in the fact that each motif is surrounded by associations with related motifs which are realised in the course of the process of transmission. For example, where a prohibition is mentioned, there will sometime also be a report of a breach of the prohibition: 'in tales and sagas an event contained by entelechy in a motif unfolds as a result of its own internal dynamic. The motif follows the law by which it was established.' Put more succinctly, it draws after it other motifs in paradigmatic association with itself.

ii) A second possibility of diachronous transmission processes is reshaping or 'mutation' (Lüthi's term).[30] Lüthi explains this in a similar way: A motif is varied in different versions of a narrative until an (accidental) variation of the motif actualises a whole new motif field and so restructures the narrative.

iii) Amalgamation and contamination is a third possibility of diachronous development. In this context G. Ortutay has drawn attention to the

---

[28] H. Bausinger, *Formen*, 155.

[29] *Urform und Zielform*, 49; cf. also idem, 'Aspekte des Volksmärchens und der Volkssage', *GRM* 16 (1966), 337-50.

[30] 'Urform und Zielform', 49. The biological metaphors 'entelechy' and 'mutation' must naturally be used with caution.

significance of internal 'affinities'.[31] This involves 'a particular form of behaviour of types, motifs and formal elements which can be described as a unique attraction or affinity: related or similar types and constructions exert an attraction on each other and the laws of attraction create new types and new forms by way of the variants.'

The creative development, reshaping and amalgamation of traditions are here seen in each case against the background of virtual relations between motifs, characters and themes (even when these processes are given different names). This means that diachronous transmission processes are seen as actualisations of structurally predetermined possibilities. It is our task to show these processes in operation in the transmission of miracle stories. For this purpose we (usually) restrict ourselves to a limited section of the diachronous transmission process, to the changes which can be identified in the New Testament itself (the pre-Marcan stage, Mark, Luke, Matthew) and examine successively literary elements of different extent: motifs, individual narratives and the framework genre.

i) The diachronic investigation of selected motifs is intended to show that the distinction between tradition and redaction is much less sharp than is usually assumed in literary critical analyses. Even in the case of motifs generally accepted as redactional (e.g. the command to silence), a probability can be established that an existing element has been creatively modified, that, for example, 'redaction' consists in the actualisation of virtual paradigmatic relations, and that changes are thus to be seen against the background of virtual generic structures.

ii) The same applies to the reproduction of whole narratives. Here we have to show that this too takes place in structurally predetermined dimensions – even if it is not possible to identify any tendencies governing the transmission which hold good for all the synoptic traditions.

iii) Finally we have to show that the composition of miracle stories within the framework of the gospels depends on predetermined possibilities, particularly on the narrative resources of individual traditions. Here we need to examine only the contribution of the miracle stories. On practical grounds no distinction is made at this point between a synchronic and diachronic approach.

---

[31] G. Ortutay, 'Begriff und Bedeutung der Affinität in der mündlichen Überlieferung', *Int. Kongress der Volkserzählungsforscher* (1961), 247-52, quotation from pp. 248-49; cf. Ortutay, 'Principles of Oral Transmission in Folk Culture', *Acta Ethnographica* 8 (1959), 175-221, esp. 216-21.

Diachronic analysis of the history of reproduction leads to a deeper understanding of virtual literary structures: any attempt to interpret all modifications simply as combinations of distinct elements is ruled out. Reproduction constantly produces individual, new features; structures themselves change. They should not be treated as if they were static. Their creative and historical character must be maintained. The possibility must be maintained that compositional and paradigmatic structures would make it possible to generate many other miracle stories. In other words, literary structures too are 'generative'. In this respect the ambitious aim of constructing a 'generative poetics' of the New Testament (E. Güttgemanns) is justifiable.[32]

Nevertheless the polemic conducted in the name of 'generative poetics' against tradition history is, in my view, substantially mistaken. My (brief) observations to this effect prompted E. Güttgemanns[33] to make another summary of his position: 'When this critic attributes to me a total rejection of tradition history, this also shows that the main point has still not been grasped. I do not completely reject tradition history. Rather, together with the majority of those working in the field of linguistics, I merely deny that the "sense" function of a "text", for example a gospel, can be explained in historical categories as the diachronic product of a process of addition and aggregation of small units of "meaning" . . . for linguistics it is, rather, the performative manifestation of a "base" which constitutes "sense", a manifestation of, that is, the "grammar".'[34] The passage quoted contains in fact three contrasts, diachrony/synchrony, part/whole and base/performance, which we will discuss in turn.

i) Linguistic phenomena undoubtedly derive their sense from synchronous linguistic structures; equally on the literary level the first rule is that the synchrony of a text is more important to its sense than its diachrony. Agreement on this point is easy.[35] This does not, however, entail a downgrading of diachronic study:

---

[32] A. Dundes ('From Etic to Emic units', 104) calls the structural analysis of folk tales begun by Propp a 'generative grammar', but uses the term metaphorically. In New Testament studies a programme for a 'generative poetics' was drawn up by E. Güttgemanns and others, 'Theologie als sprachbezogene Wissenschaft', *LB* 4/5 (1971), 7-37. There is a more recent and, in my opinion, better description in Güttgemanns, 'Linguistisch-literaturwissenschaftliche Grundlegung einer neutestamentlichen Theologie, *LB* 13/14 (1972), 2-18.

[33] In the supplementary volume to the 4th German edition of Bultmann, *GST*, 13-14, where it was impossible to substantiate my criticism in detail. The present study also implicitly challenges in many places E. Güttgemanns, *Candid Questions*, 1979 (Ger. ed. 1970).

[34] E. Güttgemanns, 'Grundlegung', 12.

[35] I am rather puzzled as to why I am accused of not understanding this point. In the supplementary volume to Bultmann, p. 14, I wrote approvingly, 'that the content, structure and truth of a statement cannot be deduced by the methods of tradition criticism . . .'.

a) The synchronous sense is undoubtedly better understood if it can be compared with the sense of previous versions of the text. The diachrony of a text is of great importance at least as a *ratio cognoscendi*. This does not inevitably mean falling victim to the genetic fallacy of identifying the background and origin of a phenomenon with its sense.

b) It is also undeniable that references back to things from the past are immanent in the texts. This begins with the most explicit form of diachronous backward reference, the quotation, and continues in the use of extracts from sources, revisions of earlier material, thematic models, deliberate archaisms and so on. Reference to something earlier is immanent above all in an oral tradition. Its reproduction is consciously seen as the passing on of tradition. 'The variant is always a modification of something (a type of tale, a motif, a style, for instance) which comes to life in the variant but with which the variant is nevertheless not identical, which it is constantly trying to reproduce – this is, after all, the source of the tradition's energy – but from which it nevertheless constantly deviates, now in unimportant features, now in important ones. Of course the variant is always a creation realised at a given moment, but it always proclaims the existence of a form already historically realised, and so expresses something new or different only in relation to that, and it is by doing this that it acquires the right to be called a variant' (G. Ortutay).[36] Even if we would like to emphasise more strongly that relatively enduring generic structures underly all diachronous variants, it is impossible to ignore the fact that the narrators wanted to pass on something that had come down to them – a sense we do not have when we use linguistic structures. Deliberate backward references are part of the text itself. Here diachrony is not just a *ratio cognoscendi* but also a *ratio essendi* of synchronous sense.

c) Nevertheless a text cannot be limited to what is deliberately expressed in it; that would be a case of the intentional fallacy. The generic structures which unconsciously guided the narrators have also been taken into the historical process. Texts may be able to acquire through historical analysis a sense 'for us' which no-one in the past saw or could have seen. Possibly there is no 'sense in itself', but only a multiplicity of possibilities waiting to be realised – which does not exclude the fact that we can clearly falsify a set of suggested interpretations of the sense of a text. The synchrony of a text therefore certainly constitutes the sense of the text – at least those aspects of the sense which were associated with the texts of those people who lived in them as immediately as we do in our language. However, this synchronous sense has come into being only as a result of a diachronous process, analysis of which reveals new aspects of sense to us.

ii) The relation of part and whole is not in principle identical with the contrast between diachrony and synchrony (as in the gospels). The relation of part and whole is immanent in every text, independently of its

---

[36] 'Affinität', 246.

previous or subsequent history. The requirement that a text should always be interpreted as a whole is generally recognised as the hermeneutical circle of part and whole. However in cases where the parts were in fact once an independent whole (as in the gospels) they can naturally also be interpreted on their own.

Güttgemanns has now drawn on *Gestalt* and holistic psychology to reinforce his exegetical demand that every small unit in the gospel must be interpreted in the context of the whole.[37] Now *Gestalt* and holistic psychology have not only demonstrated experimentally the significance of the whole for perception; they have also discovered in our perception a tendency to 'pregnant form', which, for example, makes an uncompleted circle look like a perfect circle. It is only on a closer look that we discover the particular elements which do not fit. Applying this to the problem discussed by Güttgemanns, we can say that even though a gospel must be considered (synchronically) as a total form, it makes sense to examine the individual elements for gaps, tensions and discrepancies which may give us indications of a history of reproduction preceding the text.

The problem of the possibility of discovering the diachronous dimension of the text must naturally be separated from the question of the intrinsic significance of the whole for the sense of the text. Principles of interpretation of wholes cannot here be applied indiscriminately to all texts: our expectations of homogenous structure are less in the case of a collection than in that of a continuously written letter. In cases where the parts of a particular genre did not come into existence synchronously, they must in each case be interpreted in themselves as a whole. And when a text displays a number of diachronous versions, each version must be expounded as a whole – including, naturally, the final version. Diachrony and synchrony cannot be opposed here.

iii) Arguments from holistic and *Gestalt* psychology have recently given way to a generative approach: 'In my book I had demonstrated that the theory prevailing in form and redaction criticism of the genre "gospel", namely of the addition and aggregation in the history of the tradition of individual units of "meaning" to produce a total christological "sense" for the text type is linguistically untenable. I demonstrated this untenability with the help of the "Ehrenfels criteria" of *"Gestalt"* because I assumed that *"Gestalt"* theory was the easiest to present as a point of contact between traditional exegesis and linguistics. Even then I could naturally have mounted a much more substantial demonstration using Noam Chomsky, the generative approach and modern syntax, though I doubt that this would have contributed to the general understanding of my thesis. As it is, most critics have not even seen where the fundamental crisis for current scholarship arises as a result of the findings of linguistics.'[38] But the transition to a generative approach does not give rise to any argument against tradition history. It is, after all, part of the

---

[37] *Candid Questions*, 287ff.
[38] 'Grundlegung', 10.

definition of 'generative base' or 'competence' that it always 'generates' a number of performance texts, and one example of this is the various versions of a text within a tradition history. Willingness to accept the distinction between a virtual generic structure and its realisation in a number of examples of the genre itself makes it necessary to adopt a tradition-historical approach.

It remains rather unclear what is meant by 'generative base'. Now and again specific generic structures seem to be meant. But it comes as a shock to be told that the path from text to sermon is 'nothing other than a methodically controlled transformation of the Greek performance "text" into our German competence "text":[39] neither does the journey from text to sermon take place within the same genre nor is it the individual sermon which could be described as a "competence" text', but at most the rules specific to the sermon genre. In the first quotation given above a particular example was given: the base which constitutes the sense is the grammar. Are the norms specific to a genre now being described metaphorically as the 'grammar' of a genre? Or are sentences and literary complexes being placed on the same level? The norms of language are however different in status from the norms of genres, even if they are not independent of each other. And, apart from that, the regulative goal of generative grammar must be to make it possible to reconstruct a language exactly by means of formation and transformation rules. In the case of literary forms this seems to me impossible. (In relation to Biblical texts we might well recall here another 'generative method', that of F. Oetinger, who sought by means of an 'organic presentation of scripture' to defend Biblical truths which could not be rigorously proved against a mentality which argued *more geometrico*.)[40]

The valuable elements of 'generative poetics' do not contradict form criticism or tradition criticism. The application of the results of linguistic research is to be welcomed. In my view there can be no doubt that linguistics is becoming an important foundation science of all interpretative disciplines. These new lines of discussion must therefore be taken seriously, even if at first all sorts of interference make a real discussion difficult: the claim to have a universal method, an occasionally heavily exaggerated polemic,[41] a not very communicative terminology. Where, in my view, more fundamental objections are justified is where 'historical categories' are rejected.

C. The Functionalist Approach

We do not understand traditions until we understand them in terms of their historical life-context. Neither can their de-

---

[39] 'Theologie als sirachbezrene jakissenschaft', 30.
[40] See the account in H.G. Gadamer, *Truth and Method* (London, 1975), 26-29.
[41] Cf. 'Theologie als sprachbezogene Wissenschaft', 37, where 'universality of method' is said to be the aim, see also 'Grundlegung', 3, where we are told that 'traditional exegesis must be made to face squarely the bankruptcy of its traditional arguments'.

velopment be derived from structures specific to a genre, nor are these structures taken from the historical life-context. Genres are much more the expressions of historical life-worlds; their variations go back to changes in historical and social life. The synchronic and diachronic approaches thus lead with inner necessity to the functionalist approach. This treats texts as elements in a wider life-context of conditions, intentions and effects; it analyses texts no longer as ἔργον, but as ἐνέργεια.[42]

Although this life-context includes causal and intentional factors, it cannot be treated as exclusively causal or intentional. The causal-genetic approach has its limits in cases where different intellectual movements arise in the same historical situation. An example: there are certainly causal connections between the eschatological expectations of Judaism at the end of the first century BC and the historical and social situation of Palestine. But there were various forms of eschatological expectation. There were would-be Messiahs, the Qumran community, the Baptist movement, primitive Chistianity and in addition non-eschatological outlooks. There were different responses to the same situation. To treat them purely in terms of intention would, however, be very unbalanced. Historical effects can never be explained by intentions alone.

If the primitive Christian message of the imminent end were to be understood only in terms of its intention, it would be impossible to explain why the failure of the end of the world to occur did not produce a deep crisis, why eschatological statements were passed on for so long, why they constantly came to life again. It is a natural assumption that they had a function outside their intention, one which gave them an objective sense even when their self-understanding was refuted by the passage of time. A possible function would be to create inner freedom in the face of ancient society and its norms by destroying the world in mythical images. The function of a tradition always includes both causal and intentional elements. Functionalist analysis thus seeks to combine elements which seem at first to be in irresoluble conflict. The discovery of the historical and social conditions underlying religious texts and the interpretation of their self-understanding

---

[42] The distinction between *ergon* and *energeia* derives, of course, from Humboldt ('Schriften zur Sprachphilosophie', *Werke* III, 1963, 418). His approach to language in terms of energy has been continued particularly by L. Weisgerber (cf. *Stufen*, 16, 92ff.), and also by E. Cassirer (*Philosophy of Symbolic Forms*, 4th ed. 1964). A. Jolles applied it to the study of literary genres: 'What a line of thought, what attitude to life, what intellectual preoccupations gave rise to this world of forms . . .?' (*Einfache Formen*, 34).

leads at first to a 'hermeneutical conflict',[43] however the relation between causal conditions and intellectual intentions is defined. It is necessary to distinguish closed determination models and open action models.

Determination models derive from the wish to define the scope and limits of the various factors *a priori*. It makes no difference whether a causal or teleological determination is assumed and the problems of history are solved 'materialistically' or through 'salvation history'. Equally a double determination of Max Scheler's type may be assumed:[44] cultural intentions which determine the content of a tradition (its 'thusness') and causal factors on which the realisation of this content (its existence) depends. In each case the result is anticipated. Models of this sort are consequently of little value for research.

A preferable starting point is the undeniable fact that traditions are the product of human actions. Various aspects can then be distinguished:
a) Actions are a response to situations. The agent, however, always has only a limited and fragmentary awareness of these situations. He attempts to become conscious of them. This aspect is emphasised by 'reflection models': in our intellectual traditions , on such a view, there takes place a growth of awareness of factors which originally operated unknown to us, a transmutation of determination into intention.[45]
b) Actions always stand in a relationship to other attempts to respond to existing situations. There are always a number of possibilities of response. These are talked through in the different traditions. This aspect is singled out by the 'stage model':[46] our traditions represent competing attempts at a response which are in dialogue and conflict with each other.
c) Among the possible attempts at action, some establish themselves because they best correspond to the situation. This correspondence is relatively independent of the intentions of the agent, though always mediated by intentions. Outside their own intentions, actions can prove to be 'functional'. This 'functional model' includes the aspects mentioned previously: the reason why intention and function can diverge is that the situation is always understood only fragmentarily, and leaves scope for a number of attempts at a response.[47]

Within the functionalist approach texts are analysed in terms of an 'action model'. Texts are specified forms of human action. They

---

[43] P. Ricoeur, *Die Interpretation*, 1969, 70 passim.

[44] M. Scheler, *Die Wissensform und die Gesellschaft*, 2nd ed. 1960, 21.

[45] On this see K.O. Apel, 'Szientistik, Hermeneutik, Ideologiekritik', *Hermeneutik und Ideologiekritik*, 1971, 7-44.

[46] The term comes from H.J. Habermas, *Zur Logik der Sozial-Wissenschaften*, Phil. *Rundschau* Beiheft 5 (1967), 82.

[47] For functionalist analysis in sociology cf. O. Schreuder, 'Die strukturell-funktionale Theorie und die Religionssoziologie', *IJR* 2 (1966), 99-134.

are symbolic actions,[48] use polyvalent signs and so require interpretation.[49] Functionalist analysis of texts investigates both the determinants of their historical and social situation and also their intentions, but above all how well they measure up to an objective task, the formation of human existence in the widest sense. Such an analysis brings together elements which are sharply divided in the 'hermeneutical conflict', partly by looking for an objective sense in the traditions which is not contained in their intentions, partly by showing how the power of conditioning factors is transformed in them into human intentions. Between hermeneutical restoration of a traditional self-understanding and its harsh destruction, it takes a third path, that of understanding. It relativises without creating disillusionment. It interprets without subordinating itself to the self-understanding of the tradition.

The overarching life-contexts in which traditions are functionally active can be analysed only if we one-sidedly isolate certain aspects. In the enquiry that follows we shall distinguish three functional aspects of miracle stories: their social function in primitive Christianity and ancient society, their religio-historical function within the development of ancient religion in general and their existential function within the ancient life-world. The first stage of the analysis will start in each case with the recognisable social, religio-historical and existential conditions, and the second with the social, religio-historical and existential intentions.

---

[48] The term was coined by K. Burke (*The Philosophy of Literary Form. Studies in Symbolic Action*, Baton Rouge, Louisiana, 1941: quoted from the German ed.: *Dichtung als symbolische Handlung*, Frankfurt 1966), whose aphoristic explanations do not lend themselves to systematisation (but see p. 11). Three aspects may be stressed: (1) Symbolic actions are connected with challenging situations, and seek to meet them in a specific way (style, strategy, pp. 7ff.). (2) Symbolic actions derive from unconscious factors. This means on the one hand a recourse to psychoanalytic methods of interpretation, but on the other hand that the symbols are not regarded as the product of unconscious processes, but as acts of the ego trying to assert and transform itself (pp. 42ff.). (3) Symbolic actions have a communicative function (p. 11), are part of a conversation (p. 106). This aspect is studied with the aid of sociological categories.

[49] This connection between symbolism and hermeneutics is made by P. Ricoeur (*Interpretation*, 20f.). His definition of the term 'symbol' is somewhat one-sided: 'Symbol exists where language produces signs on different levels in which meaning is not content to denote something, but denotes another meaning which can be grasped only in and by means of its communication' (p. 29). However in the case of polyvalent signs (polysemy) it is often impossible to decide what is the primary and what the secondary meaning – at least by means of diachronic methods. Here too there is a disagreement about whether all symbols were originally metaphors. Perhaps there is an original connection of a number of elements of meaning, and not just transfers of meaning (Cf. P. Wheelwright, 'The Semantic Approach to Myth', *Myth* 1958, 95-103, who uses the term 'diaphors'). 'Symbols' are thus to be taken as polyvalent signs, but the relations between the various elements of meaning which are visible may be left open.

1. The Social Function of Primitive Christian Miracle Stories: an Analysis through the Sociology of Literature

The sociology of literature examines the relationship between texts and interpersonal behaviour. It examines the behaviour of those who compose, transmit, interpret and receive texts.[50] This definition is somewhat misleading since it makes texts and interpersonal behaviour look like different entities, while texts themselves are forms of interpersonal behaviour, symbolic interactions embedded in other forms of human behaviour. A more precise definition would be that the sociology of literature analyses texts as symbolic interactions. The specifically sociological aspect of this analysis consists in the fact that it examines the interpersonal symbolic action preserved in the texts as (1) typical and (2) conditional behaviour.[51]

The most important typical elements in this behaviour are traditors (active custodians of the tradition), receivers (passive custodians of the tradition),[52] and recurrent intentions underlying their relationship, such as instruction, entertainment or the attempt to win ones listeners to one's point of view. These three elements form the '*Sitz im Leben*'.

The conditions influencing this behaviour can be divided into three groups: (1) socio-ecological factors such as an urban or rural

---

[50] Cf. the definition in H.N. Fügen, *Die Hauptrichtungen der Literatursoziologie*, 4th ed. 1970, 14: 'The sociology of literature deals . . . with the action of the people engaged in literature; its object is the interaction of the persons engaged in literature'. Fügen distinguishes between the method of the sociology of literature and a 'socio-literary' one (esp. 23ff.): 'The socio-literary method is concerned with the recognition of particular aspects of a literary work and their causal origin in a particular social fact' (27). In contrast, he says, the sociology of literature limits itself 'to the discovery of typical sequences and modes of behaviour and functionalist explanations of them' (29). If the approach of the sociology of literature is regarded as a historical approach to the elucidation of transmitted texts, it is, of course, hardly possible to separate the two. More appropriate, in my view, would be a distinction between a general sociology of literature and a specific (which always means historical) literary-sociological analysis. What is quite wrong is an a priori exclusion from the sociology of literature of the study of 'details' and the search for causal connections.

[51] M. Scheler, *Wissensformen*, 17, mentions these two aspects as features of the specifically sociological approach. On the idea of 'symbolic interaction', cf. G.M. Vernon, 'The Symbolic Interactionist Approach to the Sociology of Religion', *IJR* 2 (1966), 135-55.

[52] C.W. von Sydow, 'On the Spread of Tradition', in *Selected Papers on Folklore*, 1948, 11-43, esp. 15-18, and 'Folk-Tale Studies and Philology', ibid. 189-219: 'Most of those who have heard a tale told and are able to remember it, remain passive carriers of tradition, whose importance for the continued life of the tale consists mainly in their interest in hearing it told again, wherefore they point out the active carrier of the tradition, the traditor, as a good narrator and call upon him to narrate'. (204). This distinction was introduced into New Testament exegesis by T. Boman (*Die Jesusüberlieferung im Licht der neueren Volkskunde*, 1967, 11ff.), but it does not justify giving less prominence to the *Sitz im Leben* for the history of the transmission of the synoptic tradition, certainly not if that is argued by an appeal to recent folklore studies. Cf. for example, H. Bausinger, *Formen*, 43ff.

environment, (2) socio-economic factors such as different social strata, (3) socio-cultural factors such as the norms and values of different groups in the population.

Now all that is preserved are the texts. The behaviour which once took place in and with them can now only be recovered by analysis, construction or analogy.[53]

a) An analytic inference moves from the form and content of a tradition to its *Sitz im Leben*. Since the only behaviour of interest is typical behaviour, this procedure is based primarily on typical features of texts, motifs, themes and structures specific to genres.

b) The constructive procedure assembles all direct statements about the presumed *Sitz im Leben*, whether direct references or narrative descriptions of transmission situations, in order to ask how far this *Sitz im Leben* has affected the text.

c) The analogical method makes inferences from related contemporary phenomena (which in turn are also investigated analytically and constructively) to the tradition being studied.

In other words, the sociology of literature studies the conditions and intentions of texts as typical forms of symbolic interaction. Conditions and intentions are in this way examined with regard to the function of the tradition which does not simply follow either from conditions or intentions. For this purpose we make use of two functionalist models from the sociology of religion, the integration model and the conflict model.[54]

According to the integration model the primary purpose of religious acts is the integration of the individual into the community. They give him stability in the face of extreme situations of suffering, hopelessness and injustice. B. Malinowski studied the religious traditions of simple cultures from this point of view.[55] Like classical form criticism, he began by identifying their '*Sitz im Leben*', with the advantage of being able to observe directly through field-work what historical analysis must painfully infer.

The integration model, however, is one-sided.[56] No society is completely integrated; all are permeated by conflicts, which leave

---

[53] See the methodological remarks in Bultmann, *HST*, 5-6.

[54] Cf. for example F. Fürstenberg, *Religionssoziologie*, 1964, 13ff., where a distinction is made between an integration thesis and a compensation thesis. 'Compensation', in fact, is only one possible function of religious texts in social conflicts. Protest is another.

[55] B. Malinowski, *Myth in Primitive Psychology* (1926). I have had direct access only to the chapter 'The Role of Myth in Life' (pp. 11-45), which appears in German in Kerényi, *Die Eröffnung des Zugangs zum Mythos* (Darmstadt 1967), 177-93. Malinowski's book was not obtainable through the German library system.

[56] Cf. the criticism of functionalist analyses of oral tradition in H. Baumann, 'Mythos in ethnologischer Sicht', *Stud. Gen.* 12 (1959), 1-17, 583-97; see esp. the stresss on conflict, p.

traces in their traditions. Often a conflict model is more appropriate. The function of religious traditions is here seen less as relating to the integration of the individual into society than to the conflict of different strata and groups, with claims being made, compensated for or domesticated.

The role of the sociology of literature would then be to interpret miracle stories as symbolic interactions in which processes of integration and conflict take place. Naturally their self-understanding transcends this function within a particular social context, but they can be understood only in terms of this context. Only in it do they acquire the power to convince. They may give a biased reflection of reality, they may contradict all experience; their credibility depends on none of this. No, their power to convince is socially based. Symbolic actions are social groups' ways of interpreting social reality, of transforming it into 'symbolic worlds of meaning'[57] in which they can live. Only when the symbolic constitution of reality is performed by a number of people can the individual feel at home in the 'interpreted world' –[58] this the more so, the less aware he is of its contours. Even if symbolic worlds of meaning approach us with the claim to be objective reality, a claim without which they cannot develop any force, they are nonetheless created by human actions.

2. The Religio-historical Function of Primitive Christian Miracle Stories

Religio-historical study investigates the contribution of primitive Christian miracle stories to processes of development. How far are they dependent on earlier traditions; how far do they provide impulses for further development? It is obvious that it would be too simple to separate sociological and historical enquiry or to set

---

588. Integration models and conflict models are not mutually exclusive. Every integration can be understood as an attempt to neutralise conflicts and every conflict as a failed attempt at integration and a search for new forms of integration. Integration into a particular group also means conflict with others, etc. On the wide-ranging sociological discussion between integration and conflict theorists see the introduction by D. Rüschemeyer in T. Parsons, *Beiträge zur soziologischen Theorie* (1964), 9-29.

[57] Cf. P. Berger and T. Luckmann, *The Social Construction of Reality*, New York 1966, London 1967: 'The symbolic universe is conceived of as the matrix of all socially objectivated and subjectively real meanings; the entire historic society and the entire biography of the individual are seen as events taking place *within* this universe. What is particularly important, the marginal situations of the life of the individual . . . are also encompassed by the symbolic universe' (114). The importance of such marginal situations in the miracle stories needs no further emphasis.

[58] Rilke, *Duino Elegies*, 1: '. . . and the perceptive animals soon see that we are not very reliably at home in the interpreted world'.

one against the other: the contribution of primitive Christian miracle stories to processes of conflict and integration always tells us something about their contribution to broader processes of development and vice versa. They are simply different aspects of the same thing. The particular contribution of religio-historical study lies simply in the closer attention which is given to the temporal sequence of texts and events together with the careful description of the individual, atypical and unique. The historical approach has a tendency to be idiographic and the sociological to formulate laws – in spite of all the objections which are rightly brought against an over-simple contrast between the two.[59]

Belief in miracles has no timeless function. What in one period represents a complete upheaval in the way of seeing the world is in other periods reactionary superstition. The whole of primitive Christianity is a sign of a profound transformation in which ancient culture embraced a 'new' irrationalism, which took hold generally in the great social and political crises of the third century. In this context the function of the miracle stories, which until now has been interpreted with the very general sociological categories of 'conflict' and 'integration', must be specified historically. It must be described within the framework of a change which eludes general categories. Here again we are driven to a double approach, depending on whether we start from the historical self-understanding of the miracle stories or from their historical conditions. The miracle stories have of course a 'historical' awareness of their own: they seek to testify to the unique miracles of Jesus. They are symbolic actions provoked by the historical Jesus. Nevertheless they do not reproduce historical reality, but an intensified form of it. At the same time they are unmistakably part of a general expansion of ancient belief in miracles, that is, are elements in a wider process which becomes established behind the backs of human intentions and is visible only to historical hindsight. The contradiction between the historical intention and the conditioned nature of primitive Christian miracle stories leads

---

[59] Sociological and functionalist approaches are often regarded as 'unhistorical'. This misunderstanding is a result of the origin of the concept of function in biology, where it means the objective suitability of parts of an organism for the survival of the whole. Human acts, however, can never be brought exclusively under the concept of 'survival'. On the contrary, there is probably no culture in which various strivings for survival do not express a desire for more than survival. Indeed, it is one of the insights of functionalism that even the survival of individual and society presupposes the acceptance of values and norms which in turn become necessary to survival. What is 'functional' and 'dysfunctional' in a culture has been very differently defined in history, and changes. T. Parsons, *The System of Modern Societies,* New Jersey 1967, rightly presents under this title a social history of Europe starting with primitive Christianity.

to a second form of the 'hermeneutical conflict'. Here too, of course, functionalist analysis can reveal connections. Where a new understanding of life which is not legitimated by traditions is opened up in symbolic actions, the contradiction with prevailing values, norms and symbols can be justified by an appeal to revelation.

3. The Existential Function of Primitive Christian Miracle Stories

While the structures of a historical life-world certainly pre-exist the individual, equally certainly this life-world only exists when it is appropriated by individual men and women: socially based certainty must be 'internalised', historical change enacted, traditional meaning transformed into motivation. Only what comes within the horizon of the individual life-world is 'existential'.[60] 'Existential' here means simply 'relevant to the problem of how the individual is to cope with his life'. Of course this question is closely connected with the way a society solves its problems of integration and conflict and the course taken by its general development, but it is not exhausted by these. We need only remember that each individual's life-world comes to an end, while society and history continue to exist.

Primitive Christian miracle stories grapple with actual existential problems, with the extremes of human hopelessness. They are not 'enacted parables',[61] which mean something quite different, the overcoming of sin or the like; they are concerned with real poverty, real distress. In this connection it should be remembered that even such 'timeless' existential situations of distress such as illness and despair are always experienced within a historical 'horizon of meaning': illness in the ancient world is something different from illness in an industrialised society. Even the existential analysis of miracle stories is a historical and critical task.[62]

---

[60] The terms 'horizon' and 'life-world' come from phenomenology, but have been adopted by hermeneutics (cf. H.-G. Gadamer, *Truth and Method,* s.v. 'Horizon') and sociology (cf. P. Berger and T. Luckmann, *The Social Construction of Reality*).

[61] A. Richardson, *The Miracle Stories of the Gospels* (1941), 57. To be distinguished from this is the metaphorical use of ideas of healing in biblical language, which has been studied by J. Hempel (*Heilung als Symbol und Wirklichkeit im biblischen Schrifttum,* 2nd ed. 1965, esp. 302-12); Hempel also speaks of healings themselves as symbols (302), though with a strong emphasis on their material character.

[62] H. Bausinger's statement about the genre 'legend' (*Formen,* 56) applies here: The particular intellectual activity is 'provoked by the existing material, by the data of reality. The events of the persecution of Christians do not call for the unravelling of a riddle, naive moralising or humour, but for *imitatio,* and this uses the material to produce the new reality in its linguistic gestures'. What E. and L. Edelstein (*Asclepius* II, 1945, 162) say about miracles applies also to miracle stories: 'Even miracles, one should think, can be accounted for only against the background of the society in which they happen. . . .'

Symbolic actions are the object of existential analysis insofar as they deal with existential situations. To act means to deal with and to change situations. However, changing situations is not just a matter of practical interventions: situations are also changed by the symbolic transformation of experience, by action using (more or less) complex signs, that is by naming, judging, interpreting, by telling stories, speculating and imagining. These symbolic actions are no less important than practical changes. Human beings could not endure the reality which confronts them unless they tried to transcend it by means of symbolic actions in order to transform it into a human world of meaning,[63] into that network of symbols which alone makes communication possible, overcomes traumatic experience, and makes it possible to confer meaning. We are engaged in this symbolic transformation of reality day in day out, and even at night we do not stop. Our dreams prove it: 'The symbol-making function is one of man's primary activities, like eating, looking or moving about. It is the fundamental process of his mind, and goes on all the time'.[64] The existential function of texts consists in the symbolic mastering of reality.[65]

This process can be analysed from two sides, firstly in terms of its existential intentions and of the influences on it. In terms of their intentions, primitive Christian miracle stories seek to come to terms with the extremes of human life by testifying to a revelation: they testify to the action of a divine figure, of 'the Holy One of God' (Mk 1.24), who can transform disease and distress. On the other side, however, they can be seen as an expression of a human desire for a life freed from distress, a desire which comes more and more to the fore the more the religious atmosphere of primitive Christian miracle stories seems to suspend a strict control on what is said and believed to be reality. Sceptical though one may be of psychoanalytical hermeneutics, on general grounds it can hardly be denied that religious symbolic actions are connected with deep-seated wishes, fears and experiences which are detached from the language under our control; not that such wishes, fears

---

[63] On this anthropological insight, cf., in addition to Cassirer's *Philosophy of Symbolic Forms,* the book he wrote in exile, *An Essay on Man. An introduction to a Philosophy of Human Culture,* New Haven, Conn. 1945. See also W.E. Mühlmann, "Umrisse und Probleme einer Kulturanthropologie', *Homo Creator* (1962), 107-29.

[64] S.K. Langer, *Philosophy in a New Key,* Cambridge, Mass 1942, 3rd ed. 1957, 41. The terms 'symbolic transformation' and 'fabric of meaning' come from her.

[65] The beginnings of such an understanding of texts are to be found in existential interpretation and in A. Jolles' (occasionally ridiculed) doctrine of 'simple forms', the imbalances of which can be avoided; cf. the careful discussion in Bausinger, *Formen,* 51-64. Bausinger refers explicitly to Cassirer in 'Strukturen des alltäglichen Erzählens', *Fab* 1 (1958), 239-54, 245-46.

etc. feature as a mysterious background in religious symbolic actions, for which reason these actions have an attractive power which eludes conscious explanation.[66] This is where the conflict between reductionist and restorative exegesis assumes its sharpest form. There is no doubt that the miracle stories are aiming at something quite different: they seek to address human beings as the targets of a kerygma which not only makes a subconscious appeal but also imposes obligations.

The hermeneutical conflict runs through all functionalist analyses. Let me again offer a summary discussion. The basic question is always, 'Are the miracle stories projections of social, historical and psychological factors or evidence of divine revelation?' Reductionist and restorative hermeneutics are here implacably opposed. Both place the centre of meaning of texts outside human subjectivity, either in a historical, social or psychological process operating without its knowledge or in a direct revelation confronting human beings from outside. Both tend to the view that the texts reflect something, either human (all too human) reality or revelation. This hermeneutical conflict is perhaps inescapable today for anyone seriously investigating the meaning and truth of religious tradition. We possess no general hermeneutic which could bridge the gulf, and yet it would in the long run be an intolerable hermeneutical surrender simply to accept it. If it is to be overcome, both restorative and reductionist hermeneutics must make concessions.

Today we can no longer regard miracle stories as evidence of divine intervention in the normal course of things. 'Diseases and their cures have their natural causes, and do not depend on the action of evil spirits or on their casting out. This puts an end to the New Testament miracles as miracles.'[67] Of course there were miraculous phenomena, unlikely cures and wonder-working charismatics, but it was only symbolic intensifications which transformed these miraculous phenomena into the paradoxical action of divine beings. Comparable symbolic intensifications of reality characterise however, the whole of the New Testament.

---

[66] Which is why the psycho-analytical dogma that only what is repressed is symbolised and what is symbolised is only what is repressed is so far from being correct. It is not accurate, for example, in the case of the best known instance of psycho-analytic interpretation of myth, Freud's interpretation of the Oedipus story. The desire to kill and incest are not symbolised at all: the father is really killed and the mother really married. For a discussion of this interpretation and of psycho-analytical hermeneutics in general, see the judicious book by W. Schmidbauer, *Mythos und Psychologie* (1970).

[67] Bultmann, 'New Testament and Mythology', in H.W. Bartsch, ed. *Kerygma and Myth*, London 1953, 1-44.

The historical Jesus becomes the kerygmatic Christ, primitive Christian communities the 'body of Christ', a new religious movement the start of a new world. Everywhere symbolic actions transcend historical, social and existential reality. 'Empirical' reality is always seen as containing more than ordinary events. It becomes transparent, revealing the holy. On this interpretation miracle stories are neither mere projections of non-intentional factors nor reflections of divine intervention. They are symbolic actions of human subjectivity in which a revelation of the holy is given shape and 'empirical' reality transcended.[68] This needs explanation.

The description of the internal structure of the 'holy' is the task of the phenomenology of religion. Like all experience, the experience of the holy is constituted by human acts. We must therefore look for its natural and cultural conditions (which does not mean derive it from these conditions). This experience can be characterised descriptively by five features, pregnancy, competition, dominance, transparency and ambivalence. We shall discuss these in turn.[69]

1. Pregnancy

The holy appears in objects and events with a pregnant structure – the moon at night, a lonely mountain, the thorn bush in the desert or the miraculous phenomena which underlie the miracle stories. It always stands out from its environment. An 'ontological fissure' runs through

---

[68] The related concept of 'symbol' and 'symbolic action' has been shaped by three traditions.
a) Ernst Cassirer's philosophy, which draws its inspiration from Kant, understands 'symbolic forms' as all objectivating acts by which mind gives categorial structure to experience: myth, language and cognition, all of which require the mediation of the senses. In addition to the *Philosophy of Symbolic Forms* (New Haven, Conn. 1953), cf. *Wesen und Wirkung des Symbolbegriffs,* 4th ed. 1969.
b) In Sigmund Freud's psycho-analytic theory (e.g. 'New Introductory Lectures on Psychoanalysis', *Standard Edition,* XXII (1964), 12ff. the symbol is a veil. Its true meaning has been driven into the unconscious and appears in consciousness in a distorted form in symbol, in myth, ritual and dreams. For a critical account see A. Lorenzer, *Kritik des psychoanalytischen Symbolbegriffs* (1970). In C.G. Jung's work the symbol has a much more positive role; it steers the libido towards new goals. Cf. the systematic account in J. Jacobi, *Komplex Archetypus Symbol in der Psychologie C.G. Jungs* (1957).
c) In the classical period of German philosophy and poetry 'symbol' became the antithesis of 'allegory' (cf. the account in Gadamer, *Truth and Method,* 64-73). This contrast between the artificial combination of meaning and surplus meaning in allegory and their fundamental connection in symbol is influenced by neo-Platonic ideas. Paul Tillich's *Symbol und Wirklichkeit* (1962) is also in this tradition.
[69] Since R. Otto, *The Kingdom of God and the Son of Man,* (1938, Ger. 1934), New Testament exegesis and the phenomenology of religion have usually gone their own ways. The dialogue between the phenomenology of religion and theology has been kept alive for the most part by 'philosophical' Christians: P. Tillich and P. Ricoeur, *The Symbolism of Evil,* 1969.

reality.[70] The forms of the holy stand out sharply from everything profane. These forms have the same characteristics as signals which evoke behavioural responses in the animal world, viz. improbability and simplicity.[71] This is why human beings cannot be imposed upon in religion 'like animals', as Marx sharply suggested;[72] for they cannot in fact respond to the pregnant forms of this world like animals. There is a hiatus between the 'triggering' form and the behavioural response as a result of the less differentiated instinctual structure of human beings which leaves scope for very different sorts of behaviour. The only equivalent in human beings to the signal stimuli are therefore general appeals, which are experienced as an indeterminate imperative which leaves open what is to be done. Human beings have to articulate for themselves their answer to the reality which presses in on them. Their first response is in ritual behaviour, which, unlike practical behaviour, submits to the object, accepts its claim, portrays it and so acknowledges its existence. Nevertheless, the response can also occur in other symbolic actions, in myths, speculations and narratives.

2. Competition

Human beings are not (like animals) sensitive only to a few forms with specific relevance to their lives, but to everything which has a pregnant form in their perceptual fields, to the whole world in its obtrusive and exciting power, to the many competing appeals of the world. Consequently, almost everything has been worshipped in the history of religion as the object of the revelation of the holy: the sky, the sun, the moon, the stars, the trees, the earth, mountains, human beings and so on.[73] It is true that every culture has specific hierophanies which are specifically relevant to it but, if one considers the history of religion as a whole, it looks rather as though human beings were feeling their way through the whole world in order to find the hierophany which corresponds to their nature. It is this activity which shows the openness of human beings to the world. They are not tied definitively to any hierophany. They can keep on rejecting appeals which are valid in their culture. They can serve other gods. They are natural heretics. However, in order to stabilise their behaviour, they must 'select' a number of forms from the whole range and symbolically intensify their appeal: in the cultic image the pregnant form becomes extra-pregnant; in the myth the dominant deity becomes extra-dominant – it defeats all others. Gods are intensified appeals of this world. Only as intensified forms can they make

---

[70] S.S. Acquaviva, *Der Untergang des Heiligen in der industriellen Gesellschaft* (1964), esp. 24ff. (on the 'ontological break', cf. 33ff.).

[71] For the anthropological aspects of religious experience I have relied largely on A. Gehlen, *Urmensch und Spätkultur* (1964). While this book does not set out to offer a theory of religion, it contains fundamental elements for one.

[72] K. Marx and F. Engels, *The German Ideology*, London 1964.

[73] Cf. esp. M. Eliade, *Die Religionen und das Heilige*, 1954, 19ff., and any other phenomenology of religion.

human behaviour, which cannot be stabilised by the perceptual world alone, binding (which means primarily socially binding).[74]

3. Dominance

Qualities of appeal have power to impose obligations on human behaviour and this is what gives them their dominance.[75] They are experienced as an Other who speaks to us and commands.[76] They command apodeictically and categorically. On the other hand, there is a tension between their commands and the essential indeterminacy of the appeal. The command is always the transformation of an unspecified obligation into a specific one. Consequently, the specific and 'valid' response behaviour can always be questioned. This uncertainty also leads to symbolic intensifications. In their symbolic actions human beings are looking for a world which will clearly motivate their actions, for that homeland from which they know that their openness to the world has excluded them. Whenever they wish to motivate their actions, therefore, they construct extra-pregnant figures of good and evil, love and hate, the divine and the demonic. Each of these worlds of meaning formed by symbolic intensification is associated with a specific historical life-form, with a specific structure of motivation. A change in the structure of motivation is always connected with a change in the world of symbolic meaning, and is created by new symbolic actions, which are often set up as absolute and turned against the previously valid world of meaning. Primitive Christianity is undoubtedly one of the most radical attempts to bring about a total restructuring of human motivation, to create a 'new man'. This is the source of its fascinating power to create myths, the grandeur of its symbolic intensifications. The image of the historical Jesus alone, impressive though it may be, would never have been able to bring about this profound restructuring of ancient life-forms and structures of motivation. The figure of the historical Jesus had to be raised to that of the mythical Christ, to the dominance of the eschatological Lord of the Worlds and cosmocrator. And even today all attempts to base faith on the 'historical' Jesus are likely to be vain, not because of the difficulties presented by the sources, but because only the crucified Son of God who reigns over all other powers has that motivating force which matches the unconditional character of Christian faith.

4. Transparency

The perceivable and the intensified form are not identical, but the perceived (historical, 'empirical') form nevertheless implicitly includes its

[74] The concept of the 'intensified form' comes from W.E. Mühlmann, *Kulturanthropologie*, 37ff: 'The symbolic world is not simply 'a repeat of reality'; it is an intensification of reality' (37). In his language Muhlmann draws on Goethe: cf. the reference to 'intensified forms' (*gesteigerte Gestalten*) in Schiller's *Reliquien*, stanza 9.

[75] The aspect of power has been examined particularly by G. van der Leeuw, *Phänomenologie der Religion*, 2nd ed. 1956: ET of 1st ed. *Religion in Essence and Manifestation*, London 1938.

[76] This aspect has been described frequently, and particularly well, in my view, by H. and H.A. Frankfort, *Before Philosophy* (1949), 12ff.

intensified form. This is the basis of the unique transparency of hierophanies: what is holy is not the tree which is worshipped, but the commanding deity which appears in it. It is not the man Jesus who is the object of faith, but the revealer of God. The actual form, the manifestation of the holy, is always in tension with the indeterminate character of the appeal which appears in it. The more consciously the indeterminate appeal is heard, the greater becomes the transcendence of the deity over its actual manifestations, the clearer it becomes that the manifestation of the holy not only reveals, but also conceals. The absolute appeal, the holy compulsion, cannot ultimately have their source in any perceivable form, but only in the transcendent source which cannot be perceived. Their appropriate manifestation can then be only that specific form which points totally to what is made manifest, in which revelation takes place only in the paradoxical form of concealment.[77] However, the specific manifestation of the holy becomes transparent for the world too: theophany and ontophany go together.[78] The tree of life becomes transparent to reveal life in general; the 'historical' Jesus reveals the structure of the whole of the history at the centre of which he stands. In this way every revelation of the holy opens up a structured universe, centres on itself a symbolic *world* of meaning. The transparency of hierophanies thus includes a rational element, an element of order, structure, formation. The holy is anything but the 'irrational'.

5. Ambivalence

Rudolf Otto, in his classical analysis of the holy,[79] showed that the ambivalence of *tremendum et fascinosum* is a basic structure of the holy, the ambivalence of being attracted and crushed by a power which makes human beings sink into dust. This does not require shattering, emotional experiences. These are not the essential. What is essential is the stabilised tension between the conflicting impulses of attraction and repulsion which symbolic actions of ritual and language seek to achieve. This tension is another result of the human condition: in an animal any 'quality of appeal' is unequivocal, produces either approach or flight, but in a human being contrary impulses conflict. Human beings have a sense of being both attracted and pushed away by everything which they perceive as qualities of appeal. They even perceive contradiction as an appeal. This ambivalence creates an unstable equilibrium, an area of supreme vigilance. An achieved equilibrium is marked by calm, freedom and clarity and is very different from being overwhelmed by emotions. But this equilibrium is threatened as is shown by the history of religion with its eruptions and revolts. The equilibrium can also be stabilised at different

---

[77] Paul Tillich in particular stressed this transparency in the manifestation of the holy and made the paradoxical transparency of the holy in the symbol of the crucified Christ the centre of his Christology. Cf. his *Systematic Theology* II, 3rd imp. 1964.

[78] The connection between theophany and ontophany is stressed particularly by M. Eliade, e.g. in *Myths, Dreams and Mysteries*, London 1960; id., *The Sacred and the Profane*, New York 1961.

[79] R. Otto, *The Idea of the Holy* (Ger. 1917).

levels. Human beings do not meet the demands of the bottomless riddle of reality until they experience the most extreme contradictions as an appeal and a disturbance, until they combine in their symbols the most radical absurdity and the most radical experience of salvation – the two are combined in the central biblical symbol of the cross.[80]

The experience of the holy can be appreciated only through its history. General anthropological considerations can contribute only aspects. Within our cultural sphere a drastic restructuring of the holy has taken place on three occasions, in Greece, in Israel,[81] and in primitive Christianity. The Greek gods have rightly been interpreted as forms (better, intensified forms) of our reality.[82] So convincing was the vision with which they were seen and represented that they have remained alive in literature into our own time. It is characteristic of them that they make scarcely any demands. They have no authoritative claim to bring revelation. They are simply there. In relation to such figures with no authoritative dominance human beings are completely free. They can turn them into objects, look at them, shape them. No commanding imperative compels men and women to avert their gaze. The restructuring of the holy which took place in Israel was quite different. We need think only of the commandment to make no image of the deity. This commandment rules out any possibility of being overwhelmed by perceivable, pregnant forms of this world. The quality of appeal of the world – everything in heaven, on earth and under the earth – has lost its power. God reveals himself, not in visible form, but in the spiritual event of the word, in the word of the commanding imperative and the promising future, behind which there stands the absolute dominance of Yahweh. In both Greece and Israel a characteristic feature of the holy was in each case given one-sided priority, in the one case form, in the other dominance. In contrast, primitive Christianity brought more than selection and refinement. There now took place a more radical transformation of the experience of the holy. From now on the holy appears neither in the impressive form of Greek gods nor in the dominance of an absolute imperative. Instead revelation takes place in the broken form of the cross, which exposes the commanding imperative as a curse. The cross is folly to the Greeks and a scandal to the Jews (1 Cor 1.23). In my view the form of the holy here defined remains valid even today.[83]

---

[80] The *coincidentia oppositorum* is an essential feature of the structure of the holy and its symbols (cf. M. Eliade, *Die Religionen*, 474ff.).

[81] On this cf. H. and H.A. Frankfort, *Before Philosophy*, 237-63.

[82] Notably W.F. Otto, *Die Gestalt und das Sein* (1955); *Theophania* (1956); *Die Wirklichkeit der Götter* (1963).

[83] The concept of the 'holy' is in the first place a concept from the phenomenology of religion and is neutral because phenomenology suspends judgment as to the reality or validity of a phenomenon. The use of this 'neutral' term is open to criticism, but it seems to me to have a value when one is reluctant to use the term 'God' without a precise definition of the context and also rejects the many theological substitute formulas. Cf. the volume edited by C. Cope, *Die Diskussion um das Heilige*, Darmstadt 1977.

Perhaps it is now possible to reach a compromise in the conflict between reductionist and restorative hermeneutic. The symbolic intensification of reality, which reductionist hermeneutics treats as merely a projection of non-intentional historical, social and mental factors, can now be seen as intentional and a basic feature of human existence. Openness to the world and an undifferentiated instinctual structure force human beings to justify their actions and motivations by means of 'extra-pregnant' figures. Not only natural factors are at work here, but also human creative subjectivity. Of course this does not say everything about religious texts. As *symbolic* actions they remain elements in a functional life-system; as symbolic *actions* they transcend it. They point to a revelation of the holy. And, in my view, there are no adequate reasons to reduce the meaning of such a revelation to its 'functional context of life'.

In conclusion let us emphasise that the approaches outlined here are meant to be judged solely by the texts to be interpreted. Although many ideas have been taken over from other disciplines, the guiding principle all along was the exegesis of quite specific texts. The aim of this exegesis is, in all its approaches, to interpret a tradition in the context of its time. One simple reason for the historical bias of this study is that synchronic, diachronic and functionalist analyses would not have been possible without taking account of parallels from the history of religion. (The distinctive feature of the comparative section is simply that these parallels are examined once more in their context, developmentally.) Thus all general considerations and methodological questions must be measured by their contribution to a historical and critical task, here, the exegesis of primitive Christian miracle stories. They have therefore been developed only to the extent that they are required for our exegesis. Methodological reflection without exegesis would be empty, exegesis without methodological reflection blind.

Part One

Miracle Stories as Structured Forms (Synchronic Approach)

CHAPTER I

CHARACTERS: CATALOGUE, FIELD AND COMPOSITION

The first task is to compile a catalogue of all the characters. In all three Synoptics this comprises the same characters (including the demons), though in individual miracle stories Matthew and Luke omit (Matthew five times, Luke twice)[1] or add (Matthew twice, plus two duplications) characters.[2] The following table provides a summary. The abbreviations are as follows: M=Miracle-Worker, S=Sick Person, D=Demon (in so far as a demon appears in the miracle stories as an active character), C=Companion (father, mother, bearer of the sick person),[3] c=Crowd, O=Opponent, d=Disciples.[4]

MSDCcOd	Mk 9.14ff.	MSc	Mk 1.40ff.
MSCcd	Mk 5.21ff.	MSd	Mk 1.29ff.
MSCcO	Mk 2.1ff.	Mod	Mk 6.34ff.; 8.1ff.
MSDc	Mk 1.21ff.; 5.1ff.	MSC	Mk 7.24ff.
MScO	Mk 3.1ff.; Mt 9.32ff.; 12.22ff.; Lk 13.10ff.	MOd	Mt 17.24-7
		MSO	Lk 14.1ff.
MScd	Mk 5.25-34; 10.46ff.	Md	Mk 4.35ff.; 6.45ff.
MSCc	Mk 7.31ff.; 8.22ff.; Mt 8.5ff.	MS	Lk 17.11ff.

The complete form-critical field of characters is realised only in the Marcan version of the 'epileptic boy'. The structure of characters here may be analysed as an example. Two poles stand out:

---

[1] Mt 8.1ff., 14ff., 20ff.; 17.14ff.; 20.29ff.; Lk 9.37ff.; 18.35ff.
[2] Mt 8.23ff.; 15.21ff. Duplications: Mt 8.28ff.; 20.29ff. In the realisation of the character field Mt is much more independent of Mark than Luke: 9 Matthaean changes contrast with 2 Lucan ones.
[3] 'Companions' includes those sent as vicarious petitioners, all those who take the part of the sick or possessed person.
[4] It might be suggested that this list ought also to include nature, but if nature is regarded as an active character (say in Mk 4.35ff., wind and waves), it is made a demonic force.

miracle-worker and demon. The one belongs to the divine, the other to the anti-divine sphere. They are the real leading actors; all the other characters have only secondary roles, on the side of the sick person the father, on the side of the miracle-worker the disciples, and between them the public, divided into those who reject (scribes) and those who accept (crowd). Diagrammatically we have:

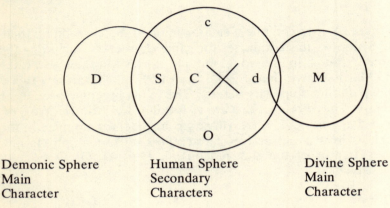

Demonic Sphere
Main
Character

Human Sphere
Secondary
Characters

Divine Sphere
Main
Character

The three-fold division of the field is a characteristic of all miracle stories, even when an intermediate field of characters seems to be missing:

i) In the Stilling of the Storm (Mk 4.35ff.) only Jesus and the disciples are present, but a tendency to a tripartite field can be noticed. Mark talks about 'other boats' (4.36) Matthew introduces marvelling 'men' at the end (Mt 8.27).

ii) At the Walking on the Lake (Mk 6.45ff.) only the disciples are present. However, in the Matthaean version Peter becomes prominent (Mt 14.27ff.). He becomes Jesus' true opposite number, while the other disciples occupy the field of secondary actors and acclaim the miracle (the usual role of the public).

iii) In the Healing of the Ten Lepers (Lk 17.11ff.) one of the lepers is a leading actor, the grateful Samaritan; the others become secondary actors.
   Again in Mk 1.40-44(45) there seems originally to have been a contrast between only two characters. Here the 'priest' (1.44) functions as the public. In addition, all three evangelists introduce the 'crowd' into the story.

We see that the tripartite field can be filled by a variety of characters. The individual characters have no fixed position in the form-critical field: disciples become an applauding public, other leading actors become secondary actors. The structure of the field remains the same, but the characters change. The sections of the field define, not specific characters, but 'roles', which may be assumed by different characters. The only constant is that the field of the miracle-worker is always occupied by the same character, while the realisation of his opposite number is variable. All the characters who form the intermediate field may take on this role, and the intermediate field becomes correspondingly smaller. In the epiphanies the miracle-worker becomes his own 'opposite number': the miraculous action takes place in him. He is the object of the miracle.[5] We can illustrate the variability of the opposite number in a table:

Field of Secondary Characters	Opposite Number	Miracle-Worker	Example
dOcCS	Demon	M	Mk 9.14ff.
dcC	Sick person	M	Mk 5.25ff.
(d)cs	Companion	M	Mk 7.24ff.
cS	Opponents	M	Mk 3.1ff.
d	Crowd	M	Mk 6.34ff.
(c)	Disciples	M	Mk 4.35ff.
d	Miracle-worker		Mk 9.2ff.

Since the catalogue of characters comprises seven characters and each character can occupy the field of the opposite number, we obtain seven themes of miracle stories – a provisional classification which we shall have to justify in detail later. With a demon as the opposite number we talk of exorcisms, with a sick person of healings, with opponents of rule miracles (the issue is always sacred rules). In feeding miracles the crowd is the opposite number, in lake miracles the disciples: we distinguish these into gift and rescue miracles. Epiphanies are a marginal case. Miracle stories in which a companion is prominent (as petitioner: Mk 7.24ff.; Mt 8.5ff.) divide between exorcisms and healings. Bultmann treats them as an appendix to the apophthegms; they belong together, but form a sub-group within exorcisms and healings.[6]

The analysis of the form-critical character field of the Synoptic miracle stories can be used for a comparison with other miracle stories. The Johannine narratives differ in two ways. First, they

---

[5] At the transfiguration the disciples are companions of the person on whom the miracle is worked, while Moses and Elijah take their normal position as companions of the miracle-worker.
[6] HST, 38-39.

have no demons and, second, they polarise the intermediate field much more sharply, for, while the people and the Jewish authorities have quite different reactions, both fail to recognise the revealer and are therefore contrasted with the 'believers'. Since changes in the field are always a restructuring of the whole, both changes could be regarded as going together. Specifically, the 'Jews' in the Gospel of John could be said to have taken over the role of the demons (cf. esp. Jn 5.1ff.; 9.1ff.), who refuse to release the sick person who has been cured, actively oppose revelation, and are judged by the revealer as representatives of the κόσμος (9.39). In the form-critical field of characters the demons are missing, but instead human beings (represented by the 'Jews') have become demonic. Today this development must arouse mixed feelings.

Analysis on the paradigmatic level must be supplemented by an investigation of compositional structures. Here three characteristics of the sequence of characters can be observed:

i) The miracle-worker always appears first. The only exceptions are in Mark (1.40; 5.25; 8.1) and in Q (Mt 12.22ff. parr.). The fact that the oldest layer of the tradition occasionally deviates will provide a basis for a diachronic analysis.

ii) The opposite number does not appear on the scene until there has been a mention of the coming or of the existence of the miracle-worker (and of the crowd which accompanies him or flocks to him). This typical order justifies us in talking about a 'bipartite introduction'.

iii) Whereas the story regularly opens with the miracle-worker, the conclusion varies. In 16 out of 21 cases the conclusion is formed by the characters who at the beginning appeared in second or third position.[7]

---

[7] Significantly, apart from Mk 1.40ff., the exceptions are the four miracle stories from the special Matthaean material.

CHAPTER II

MOTIFS

A. The Catalogue of Motifs

The motif analyses of classical form criticism will be developed in various ways. First, all the motifs will be listed so that (ideally at least) any miracle story can be understood as a combination of motifs. Second, the connections of motifs will be investigated (in other words the compositional position or setting of the motif and so on). Sometimes no relevant connections will be found; often they are trivial, or they do not appear until the catalogue of motifs is complete. Thirdly, comparative parallels from other religions are listed for the individual motifs. Here two considerations are to be taken into account. The first is concerned with formal differences between parallels. Parallels from narrative texts are obviously of greater significance than comparable motifs from other genres, medical treatises, instructions for spells, reflections, sayings and so on. There is a fundamental distinction between imaginative and narrative motifs,[1] but since motifs may 'travel' through different genres, they are listed together. The second point concerns differences in time between the parallels. The synchronic approach can only deal with a definable historical area, in this case the ancient world; internal chronological divisions within this area will be methodologically (and provisionally) ignored in compiling the catalogue of motifs, since all ancient texts do come from the same cultural area and can therefore be studied by synchronic methods.[2] On the other hand, for the analysis of the structures of a specific genre a stricter concept of synchrony will be used and the only miracle stories which will count as synchronous will be those of the Synoptics (including Acts); the Fourth Gospel

---

[1] Cf. F. Harkort, 'Volkserzählungstypen und -motive und Vorstellungsberichte', *Fab* 8 (1966), 208-23.
[2] Unlike Bultmann (*HST,* 220ff.), we do not cite parallels from the popular tradition of other periods. Structural analyses are occasionally criticised for using 'unhistorical' methods. This accusation is unjustified. It could equally be brought against classical form-criticism when it compares, for example, synoptic traditions and motifs with popular traditions from quite different areas. 'Synchrony' is not synonymous with timelessness, but means 'contemporaneous' in various respects.

will be cited only secondarily. For practical reasons diachronic observations will be listed in the case of some motifs: these motifs will not be discussed again in Part 2 (the diachronic part).

1. The Coming of the Miracle-Worker

Variants: Usually the coming of the miracle-worker is described by ἔρχεσθαι εἰς (or similar expressions) and a reference to a place. There may be a distinction between the starting point and the destination ('synagogue' and 'house' Mk 1.29), or the initial place reference may be supplemented by more specific details (Capernaum and Synagogue in Mk 1.21). All three elements: place of origin (Mt 8.1; 9.27; 9.32), destination (Mk 4.35; 6.45 etc.), place specified (Mk 3.1 etc.) also appear independently. The compositional situation is always the introduction. The motif never appears second. Only a subsidiary element, the specifying place reference ('House'), can function as the introduction to the middle section (Mk 5.38; Mt 9.28; 17.25) and come at the end (Mk 9.28; cf. 7.17; 10.10).

The motif has its setting in almost all the themes of New Testament miracle stories, but occurs rarely in disputes, which usually begin with the appearance of the opponent (cf. Mk 2.15, 18; 7.1; 8.11; 10.35; 12.13, 18, 28, 35). As a result the subject of the dispute appears as something presented to Jesus from outside, the miracle in contrast more as Jesus' activity, something to which he is impelled from 'within' (cf. Lk 5.17).

2. The Appearance of the Crowd

Variants: The miracle-worker may come across the crowd (Mk 1.21; 3.1; 9.14; Lk 8.40), bring it with him (Mk 5.24; 10.46; Mt 8.1; 14.13; Lk 7.11) or attract it by his activity (Mk 1.45; 2.1f.; 5.14f.; 5.21; 6.30ff.; 7.32). The introductory scene may be expanded by 'teaching' from Jesus (Mk 2.1f.; 6.34).[3] The compositional position is usually the first element of the introduction; however, in the variant 'attracting the public' the motif may also appear in the second element (Mk 7.32) or after the miracle (Mk 1.45; 5.14f.) and in this position may be expanded into an independent summary (Mk 1.32-34; 3.7-12; 6.53-56).

The setting may be, apart from miracle stories, apophthegms (Mk 2.13; 3.20; 10.1) and set speeches (Mk 4.1ff.; cf. Mt 4.23-25; 9.35-38; Lk 6.17-19). In Mark the recurrent structure of the

---

[3] Cf. E. Schweizer, 'Anmerkungen zur Theologie des Markus', *Neotestamentica* (1963), 93-104, esp. 93ff.

motif (six times) must be stressed. The gathering of the crowd is described with similar verbs (συνάγεσθαι, συνέρχεσθαι, συμπόρευεσθαι), underlined by a ὥστε-clause stressing the consequent restrictions (three times) and ends with the remark that Jesus taught (four times). Mark probably transferred the motif from its original setting (miracle stories) into other genres.

3. The Appearance of the Distressed Person

Variants: The sick person is encountered (Mk 1.23 etc.), in the majority of cases (five times out of nine) in house and synagogue. The sick person comes (Mk 1.40; 5.25f.; (10.49); Mt 9.27), he is carried up (Mk 2.1ff.; 7.32; 8.22; Mt 9.32; 12.22). In raisings of the dead the miracle-worker meets the funeral procession (Lk 7.11ff.; *vita Apoll.* IV, 45; Apul. *Florida* 19). Further details in O. Weinreich, 171-174. Settings are all the themes of miracle stories. In gift miracles the distressed persons are always encountered. Which variant of the motif is used also depends on whether the story is set in the open air – if so, the sick person comes or is carried up (exceptions: Mk 5.1ff.; Lk 17.11ff.) – or in an enclosed space, when he or she is present (exception: Mk 2.1ff.). To this extent there are grounds for talking about 'associated motifs'.

4. The Appearance of Representatives

Among parallels from outside the New Testament the following may be mentioned: Genesis Apocryphon XX, 21f.; *vita Apoll.* III, 38. Strab. (XVII, 801) knows that at the Serapium at Canopos petitioners asked for the healing sleep for others (ὑπὲρ ἑαυτῶν ἢ ἑτέρους). The representative is the paradigm of a request made in faith (Mt 8.5ff.; Mk 5.21ff.; 7.34ff.; 9.14ff.). While the motif of faith is independent of that of the 'representative', the latter in the New Testament is never independent of the motif of faith. The two are associated motifs. Cf. also Strab. XVII, 801: πιστεύειν καὶ ἐγκοιμᾶσθαι . . .

5. The Appearance of Embassies

Variants: Parents or connected persons send to the miracle-worker and ask him to come (Lk 7.1ff.; Acts 9.36; Jn 11.1ff.; b. Ber. 34b; Lucian, *Philops.* 11; *vita Apoll.* IV, 10). Alternatively, the request has already been made to the miracle-worker when embassies bring fresh news about the state of the sick person (Mk 5.35; Jn 4.51). In Lk 7.6 a second embassy conveys a declaration of trust and humility from the suppliant. The compositionial position is usually the introduction or the exposition, though the motif can also be a device for creating tension in the middle of the narrative (Mk 5.35; Lk 7.6) or resolve the tension at the end (Jn 4.51).

The principle setting is healings, here particularly raisings of the dead (Mk 5.35; Jn 11; Acts 9.36ff.) or healings of people close to death (Jn 4.46ff.; Lucian, *Philops.* 11). Since a spatial separation between miracle-worker and the distressed person is presupposed, the embassy motif occurs frequently in healings at a distance: Mk 7.24ff.; Mt 8.5ff.; b. Ber. 34b.

The motif is often 'associated' with a motif of delay, which creates excitement, particularly in the case of those close to death. 'Do not delay,' (Acts 9.38) is the message the disciples in Joppa send to Peter. The official begs Jesus (Jn 4.49) to come 'before my child dies'. Apollonius shows his supernatural abilities by brooking no delay. When the plague-stricken Ephesians send to him, he says: 'it would be wrong to delay the journey, but spoke: "Let us go," and was at once in Ephesus, whereby, I believe, he equalled Pythagoras, when he was at once in Thurioi and Metapontion' (*vita Apoll.* IV, 10). Jesus shows his sovereignty over space and time in the opposite way. In John 11 he deliberately delays his departure: 'Lord, if you had been here, my brother would not have died.' (11.21, 32). The most attractive narrative use of the motif of delay occurs in Mk 5.21-42. In association with 'delays' the embassy motif may be part of the exposition, and in association with 'demonstrations' it may form part of the conclusion. When the messengers return from R. Ḥanina ben Dosa, they find that the sick person was cured precisely at the moment the miracle-working rabbi prayed (b. Ber 34b). In Jn 4.51f. the time proves the miraculous character of the healing at a distance. In Matthew the motif of the hour occurs four times: in 8.14 and 15.28 it is associated with the return of the vicarious petitioner. The fact that in 9.22 and 17.18 it appears independently of this context shows that it has become a formula.[4]

6. The Appearance of Opponents

Variants: The opponents make their appearance in order to spy on Jesus from the start (Mk 3.1ff.; Lk 14.1f.; Mt 17.24), or they reply to Jesus' actions (Mk 2.1ff.; Lk 13.10ff.; Mt 9.32ff.; 12.22ff.) with hostile questions. While disputes usually begin with the arrival of the opponents, in miracle stories the opponents are not usually mentioned until after the coming of the miracle-worker (Mk 3.1; 9.14; Lk 14.1; Mt 17.24), in the middle of the narrative (Mk 2.6) or only after the miracle (Lk 13.14ff.; Mt 9.34; 12.24). Both

---

[4] On this see H.J. Held, 'Matthew as Interpreter of the Miracle Stories', 2nd impression 1973, 165-299; cf. 230-32.

genres can be the setting for the motif, but the compositional position is specific to the genres.

7. Reasons given for the Appearance of 'Opposite Numbers'

In the New Testament the reason for the coming of people seeking help is occasionally stated as having 'heard' of Jesus (Mk 5.27; 7.25; 10.47; Lk 7.3; Jn 4.47; Acts 9.38; cf. Mk 3.8; Lk 6.8). In cultic healing sanctuaries the coming of petitioners is partly explained by divine oracles:[5] ἐχρημάτισεν ὁ θεὸς ἐλθεῖν runs the formula in the Roman Asclepium (SIG ³ III, 1173). Apellas begins his thanksgiving inscription: μετεπέμφθην ὑπὸ τοῦ θεοῦ (IG IV, 955). Aristides mentions that he was called by the God (or. II §83 §103). Competition between different sources of healing is reflected in referrals as a result of divine inspiration. Eratocles comes in this way from Troezen to Epidaurus (Epidaurus 48). Asclepius sends the sick to Apollonius of Tyana (*vita Apoll.* I, 9; IV, 1), Serapis to Vespasian (Tac. *hist.* IV, 81; Suet. *Vesp.* 7; Dio Cass. LXV, 8). The competition between miracle-worker and established sanctuary is also marginally present in the New Testament: Jesus sends the cured leper to the priests, who were the official authority for declaring a cure (Mk 1.40ff.). In Jn 5.1ff. Jesus is in competition with ancient healing sanctuaries. On the other hand, miraculous referrals, or that people are sent to Jesus by oracles do not occur in the New Testament, although these motifs are not in principle alien to it (Mt 2.12 etc.; Acts 8.26ff.; 9.10ff.; 10.4ff.).

8. Description of the Distress

The variants of the motif correspond to various situations of distress and to themes such as disease, possession, distress at sea, want. Disease and possession are often specified by name: Mark and Matthew talk about 'a leper' (Mk 1.40 par.). Luke, on the other hand, often qualifies a generic term (ἀνήρ etc.) with a descriptive phrase or relative clause and talks, for example, about 'a man full of leprosy' (5.2; cf. Lk 5.18; 8.27, 35; 13.11; 14.2; 17.12, also 4.33). The reports of the cures at Epidaurus begin with short descriptions of the sufferer: 'A boy dumb. He came to the sanctuary . . .' (5). In addition to the present state the past or the future may be mentioned. Thus the length of the distress is emphasised, particularly in the case of diseases: Mk 5.25f.; 9.21; Lk 13.11; Acts 3.2; 4.22; 9.33; 14.8; Jn 5.5; 9.1; cf. R. Bultmann,

---

[5] O. Weinreich, *Antike Heilungswunder* (1909), 112 (abbreviation AH).

HST, 221. (Add to his references: *vita Apoll.* VI, 43; Epidaurus 1.)
The experience of despair implied in the length of the illness is
stressed by references to unsuccessful attempts at a cure: Mk 5.26;
9.14ff.; Jn 5.1ff; cf. O. Weinreich, 195-197. Add to the references:
Genesis Apocryphon XX, 20; Lucian, *abdic.* 4; Diog. *Laert.* VIII,
69. In the case of exorcisms unsuccessful attempts to fetter the
demon may be mentioned (Mk 5.4). The motif 'length of the
distress' is also present in gift and rescue miracles: it is not until the
fourth watch of the night that Jesus comes to the disciples who are
being buffeted by the wind and waves (Mk 6.48). The crowd has
already been with Jesus for three days – evidently without food
(Mk 8.2). The 'length of the distress' has a counterpart, when
projected into the future in the 'tendency to an unhappy ending'.
The state of the woman with a flow of blood has got worse (Mk
5.26). The possessed boy is getting thinner (9.18). The demon
wants to kill him (9.28). The man bitten by a viper already looks
decayed (Lucian, *Philops.* 11). The widow of Sarepta expects
death by starvation (1 Kings 17.12). Stories of rescue at sea in
particular may provide vivid illustrations of the tendency to an
unhappy ending: Mk 4.37; Acts 27.20; Homeric Hymn 33.11f.

The compositional position is the exposition. The motif may be
repeated. Thus we find two descriptions of the epileptic boy in the
exposition (Mk 9.17f. and 21f.) or a repetition after the miracle
when recovery is demonstrated by a comparison with the unhappy
state previously: Mk 5.15; 5.34 (contrast of 'peace' and 'scourge'),
Lk 13.16; Jn 9.8; Acts 3.10; Epidaurus 1.

Setting: Whereas the description of the state of distress is
essential to exorcisms, healings and rescue miracles, it may be
absent in the case of gift miracles. Cf. Mk 6.35ff. In Jn 2.1ff. the
term 'distress' hardly applies.

9. Difficulties in the Approach

Variants: The appearance of the suppliant does not in itself mean
that he is in contact with the miracle-worker. There are often
obstacles in the way. They are usually constituted by the crowd
accompanying the miracle-worker (and by his disciples): the
paralytic has to be let down through the roof to Jesus because of
the crowd (Mk 2.4). The woman with the flow of blood also meets
Jesus in a crowd which is pressing round him (5.24). The father of
the epileptic boy must first get past the impotent disciples before
he reaches Jesus (Mk 9.14ff.), and the blind Bartimaeus is driven
away by Jesus' companions before he is noticed by Jesus (Mk
10.48). What a torment it is to have the source of potential healing
before one's eyes but not to be able to reach it is shown in Jn 5.1ff.

The impediment to an approach, however, may lie in Jesus' own words, cf. Mk 7.27, possibly also Mt 8.7 (Bultmann, HST, 39).

The association of the motif with persons has already been mentioned. The source of the impediment may be the crowd, the disciples (9.14ff., probably also 10.48) or Jesus himself. Matthew, in the story of the 'Syrophoenician Woman', has partly transferred the motif from Jesus to the disciples (15.23).

Impediment and faith are 'associated motifs'. Faith in miracles is overcoming obstacles.[6] The word 'believe' is always used by Jesus in these contexts: in the unusual efforts people make to reach him *he* sees faith (Mk 2.5). He uses the word in exhortations to confidence (Mk 5.36 and 9.23). He acknowledges faith when he dismisses suppliants (Mk 5.34; 10.52; Mt 15.28; cf. Mk 7.29), in other words, it is for the suppliant to overcome the obstacle, but for Jesus to acknowledge this as faith. The best illustration of the associated motifs 'impediment – faith', occurs where representatives come to Jesus. It is here that the greatest impediment is found – rejection by Jesus himself (Mk 7.24ff.; Mt 8.5ff.). Here we have a matchless formulation of the ambivalence of this faith made up of insistence and humility: 'I believe; help my unbelief!' (Mk 9.24). The insistence lies in the claim of 'omnipotence' ('All things are possible to him who believes' 9.23), humility in distancing oneself from such omnipotence.

10. Falling to the Knees

Variants: The sick (Mk 1.40), the possessed (5.6) and their representatives (5.22; 7.26) fall on their knees before Jesus to attract attention and to express confidence. The people sent by Serapis to Vespasian kneel in a similar way before him (Tac. *hist.* IV, 81). The reverence may be associated with the request before the miracle (Mk 1.40; 5.6; 5.22; 7.26) or with the confession after the miracle (Mt 14.33; Lk 5.8; 17.16), with declarations of trust (Mk 1.40ff.; 5.2ff.; 7.26ff.) and acclamations of Jesus with a title (as 'Son of God'), Mk 5.6; Mt 14.33, as 'Kyrios' in Lk 5.8 (for each of the various associated motifs there is a different compositional position).

11. Cries for Help

Variants: Suppliants approach Jesus crying out (Mk 10.47; Lk 17.13; Mt 15.22). The cries of the possessed (or of the demons) are

---

[6] J. Roloff, *Das Kerygma und der irdische Jesus* (1970), 160, n. 198, appositely observes 'that Jesus-stories dealing with faith often attract the motif of resistance'.

different. They are resistance to the miracle-worker (Mk 1.23f.; 5.7; Acts 16.17): the demon senses his master.

Associated motifs: Matthew frequently doubles the suppliants (exception: 15.22) simply on the ground that two shout louder than one. At least he doubles only where the motif of the cry of help is also present. Cf. 8.29f: δύο δαιμονιζόμενοι . . . ἔκραξαν, 9.27: δύο τυφλοὶ κράζοντες, 20.30: δύο τυφλοὶ . . . ἔκραξον. The exception (15.22) is to be explained by the fact that here the mother is pleading on behalf of her daughter. Elsewhere 'duplication' and 'cries for help' in Matthew are associated motifs and explain each other. Where two people are cured, there is no need to look for a legally necessary number of witnesses (G. Braumann)[7] or any combination of two miracle stories (E. Haenchen)[8] as an explanation.

12. Pleas and Expressions of Trust

Variants: The pleas capture the ambivalence of the sufferers towards the miracle-worker. The nuances range from the accusing complaint: 'Teacher, do you not care if we perish?' (Mk 4.38), through despairing pleas: 'If you can do anything, . . . help us.' (Mk 9.22), and the cry for help: 'Jesus, son of David, have mercy on me!' (Mk 10.48; Lk 17.13; Mt 9.27; 15.22) to the pure declaration of trust: 'If you will, you can make me clean.' (Mk 1.40; 5.23, 28; Lk 5.5).

Associated motifs: these variants are nevertheless not only set alongside each other paradigmatically, but may also be connected compositionally. In these cases the plea and the expression of trust form two separate elements in the narrative. Between them in every case comes a remark which brings the situation to a climax, an action or an event:

Mk 7.24ff.	Plea (7.26)
	Rejection (7.27)
	Declaration of humility and trust (7.28)
Mk 9.14ff.	Plea (9.22)
	Exhortation (9.23)
	Declaration of trust (9.24)

---

[7] G. Braumann, 'Die Zweizahl und Verdoppelungen im Matthäusevangelium', *ThZ* 24 (1968), 255-66. Similarly J.M. Gibbs, 'Purpose and Pattern in Matthew's Use of the Title "Son of David"', *NTS* 10 (1963/64), 446-64, esp. 457.

[8] E. Haenchen, *Der Weg Jesu* (1966), 197 (on Mt 8.28).

Mk 10.46ff.	Plea (10.47f.)
	Rejection (10.48)
	Renewed plea (10.48)
	Exhortation (10.49)
	Expression of trust (10.51)
Mt 8.5ff.	Plea (8.6)
	Rejection/exhortation? (8.7)
	Expression of trust (8.8ff.)
Mt 9.27ff.	Plea (9.27)
	Entry into the house (9.28)
	Expression of trust (9.28)

The expression of trust here is in each case provoked, is a step beyond the plea: the dismissal must be overcome and the exhortation taken up. The miracle stories constructed in this way are among the most beautiful in the New Testament. If others are less impressive by contrast (Mk 7.31ff.; 8.22ff.), it is not because of miraculous manipulations, but because there is no corresponding internal action.

Settings for pleas and expressions of trust are healings, exorcisms, and rescue miracles. In gift miracles they are largely absent. In the latter the initiative comes from the miracle-worker. Also in Jn 2.3 there is no direct request, but a statement: The wine has run out.

13. Misunderstanding

Variants: The miracle is often not expected. People hope for help within the context of the normal. The disciples think they are to buy a large quantity of bread (Mk 6.37). The sick man at the pool of Bethesda is waiting for someone to bring him down to the water at the right time (Jn 5.7). The lame man at the gate of the Temple thinks that Peter and John mean to give him alms (Acts 3.5). Raisings of the dead in particular happen unexpectedly. Jesus' remark, 'The girl is not dead but sleeping' (Mk 5.39) is misunderstood. Martha connects the promised raising of the dead with the future eschatological life (Jn 11.24). When Apollonius stops a funeral procession the mourners think, 'He is going to make a speech like the funeral speeches which provoke lamentation' (*vita Apoll.* IV, 45). There is an interesting variant of 'misunderstanding' in 2 Kings 5.5-7. Not only miracles which are being announced, but also miracles which have already happened are misunderstood. The disciples think Jesus is a ghost when he walks over the lake (Mk 6.49). The master of the feast thinks that a new and better wine has been served (Jn 2.10).

The setting for misunderstanding is mainly unexpected and unusual miracles: raisings of the dead, rescue and gift miracles. These are the least expected. The compositional position is either the exposition, if the miracle is not announced by an (obscure) remark or action, or the conclusion.

Associated motifs: Misunderstanding and the miracle-worker's initiative are associated motifs. Where people misunderstand imminent miracles or miracles which have already happened, they have not looked for miracles; the initiative has come from the miracle-worker (there is a possible exception in Jn 2.1ff.). These are cases of misunderstood initiatives. The miracle-worker is advancing into an area which goes far beyond the realm of the possible.

14. Scepticism and Mockery

Variants: Even when a person suspects the possibility of a miracle, he remains sceptical. The mourners laugh at Jesus (Mk 5.40). There is an undertone of scepticism in the plea, 'If you can do anything, help us . . .' (9.22). The τί ἔτι σκύλλεις; (5.35) is also resigned and sceptical. The convincing of sceptics by miracles is the theme of a number of healings from Epidaurus (3, 4, 9, 36). Sometimes a miracle is performed on the sceptics themselves (3, 4, 36), though not without a punishment for their unbelief; sometimes the person who believed from the beginning in the face of mockery of others is vindicated (9). Doubt is called ἀπιστεῖν (3), ἀμαθία (4), blind confidence εὐηθία (9). The scepticism here relates to the possibility of a miracle at all, but in other stories the focus of mistrust is the means of healing: 2 Kings 5.11, Epidaurus 37 (in R. Herzog's reconstruction, 23 f.), Lucian, *abdic.* 5: παρῆν δὲ καὶ ἡ μητρυιὰ φοβουμένη καὶ ἀπιστοῦσα (when the disinherited son wishes to cure his father). The main contexts are healings, with some exorcisms (Mk 9.22).

15. Criticism from Opponents

Variants: In the case of opponents, scepticism and resignation express themselves in criticism of the miracle-worker. The criticism is directed either at the forgiveness of sins associated with the healing (Mk 2.5ff.), or the breach of the sabbath (Mk 3.1ff.; Lk 3.10ff.; 14.1ff.; Jn 5.1ff.; 9.1ff.), or at an implied alliance with Satan (Mt 9.34; 12.24). The essence is the assertion that Jesus is a sinner, that he breaks sacred rules, and has even allied himself with the forces of evil.

The compositional position of the criticism is before the miracle (whereby Jesus anticipates rejection; cf. Mk 2.5ff.; 3.1ff.; Lk 14.1ff.) or after its performance (Lk 13.10ff.; Jn 5.1ff.; 9.1ff.; Mt 9.32ff.; 12.22ff.).

The context is the apophthegmatic miracle stories which we call rule miracles because they centre on the breaking of rules.

16. The Resistance and Submission of the Demon

Variants: The demon senses its master. The range of behaviour goes from direct aggression to total capitulation. In Acts 19.16 the demon makes a violent attack on the exorcist. The female demon Agrat uses this possibility as a threat, but is unable to carry it out: 'If there had not been a proclamation about you in heaven that Hanina and his knowledge of the Law should be treated with care, I would have brought you into peril' (b. Pesaḥim 112b/113a). In Mk 1.23 and 5.7 the apotropaeic character of the demon's words can be glimpsed through the capitulation: ὁρκίζω σε and οἶδα σε are standard defensive invocations (O. Bauernfeind).[9] The evangelists will have understood it as capitulation.[10] Cf. Mk 5.6 προσεκύνησεν. Such a capitulation appears in the story of the exorcist God Chonsu, who is addressed by the evil spirit in these terms: 'You come in peace, great God, you who cast down the evil spirits . . .' (AOT, 78f., cf. further Bultmann, HST, 231-32).

Associated motifs: Frequently the tension between resistance and capitulation is relieved by a plea for a concession: the demon is ready to abandon his victim, but asks to be allowed to enter into the pigs (Mk 5.12), that a sacrifice should be offered to him (AOT, 78f.) or that he should continue to be allowed to roam on particular days (b. Pesaḥim 112b/113a).

17. Pneumatic Excitement

The miracle-worker reacts to situations of distress with his emotions, his pneumatic excitement. This is described by the verbs σπλαγχνίζεσθαι (Mk 1.41; 6.34; 8.2), ὀργίζεσθαι (Mk 1.41 v.l.), ἐμβριμᾶσθαι (Mk 1.43; Jn 11.33, 38), συλλυπεῖσθαι (Mk 3.5) and στενάζειν (Mk 7.34). In Mk 9.19 the sigh is interpreted in the exclamation, 'O faithless generation, how long am I to be with you? How long am I to bear with you?' We may assume a similar implication generally: the miracle-worker suffers because of the barrier between human distress, blindness, unbelief, and the realm

---

[9] O. Bauernfeind, *Die Worte des Dämonen im Markusevangelium* (1927), 3ff.
[10] So E. Haenchen, *Weg*, 88, n. 7; G.M. de Tillesse, *Le secret messianique* (1968), 79.

of super-human salvation.[11] Dibelius[12] – and, following him, C. Bonner – have interpreted this sighing as being filled with divine power, and it is indeed an example of a 'state of pneumatic excitement', an intrusion of numinous power, though the nuance of suffering and complaint should not be overlooked. The main context of the motif is healings. In a rule miracle (Mk 3.5) the miracle-worker's 'grief' is caused by human blindness to the sacred. Association with characters: pneumatic excitement in the first place affects only the miracle-worker, though the related motif of the ἔκστασις of the public after the miracle is also relevant: both are ecstatic states.

18. Assurance

Variants: The miracle-worker may provoke faith himself, ask about its presence (Mt 9.28; cf. Jn 9.35ff.), rebuke its absence (Mk 4.40/Mt 8.26; Jn 4.48; Lk 17.17) or – this is the most frequent variant – create it by a word of assurance:

Mk 2.5	My son, your sins are forgiven.[13]
Mk 5.36	Do not fear, only believe.
Mk 6.50	Take heart, it is I; have no fear.
Mk 7.29	For this saying you may go your way; the demon has left your daughter.
Mk 9.23	All things are possible to him who believes.
Mk 10.49	Take heart; rise, he is calling you.

The θάρσει (Mk 6.50; 10.49), which Matthew inserts in Mk 2.5 and 5.36 (cf. Mt 9.2, 22)[14] is fully in character (the motif also appears in Mt 8.13; Lk 7.13; 13.12; Jn 4.50; Acts 3.6; 20.10; 27.22). Lk 8.50 is the transformation of a rebuke into a word of assurance. In Jn 11 the word of consolation alone occurs five times (vv. 4, 11, 15, 23, 25), a baroque intensification. Parallels can also

---

[11] E. Lohmeyer, *Das Evangelium des Markus,* 16th ed. 1963, 69-70: '"Wrath and grief" or "wrath and sympathy" – both are features of the divine figure dwelling for a time on earth, who came for the sake of human beings and is hated by sinners.'

[12] *TG,* 85f.; C. Bonner, 'Traces of Thaumaturgic Technique in the Miracles', *HThR* 20 (1927), 171-81.

[13] A. Dupont-Sommer (*Exorcismes et Guérisons dans les écrits de Quomrân, Suppl. Vetus Testamentum* VII (1960), 246-61) wants to see Nabonid's prayer as a promise of forgiveness of sins by a Jewish exorcist, but the translation is disputed.

[14] Josephus twice inserts a θαρρεῖν in his account of a miracle of Elijah: ἀλλὰ θαρροῦσα ἄπιθι (*ant.* VIII, 322); παρεκελεύετο θαρρεῖν (*ant.* VIII, 326).

be quoted from texts outside the New Testament. Whereas the assurance in the New Testament is always very general and notably appeals for faith, in the other texts there is always a particular promise:

vita Apoll. III, 38	Take heart, said the wiseman, he will not kill him when he reads this . . .
vita Apoll. IV, 10	Take heart, he said, today I will end the illness . . .
vita Apoll. IV, 45	Put down the coffin, he said, for I will end your tears for the girl.
vita Apoll. VII, 38	I have given you a proof of my freedom, so take heart.
Lucian, *Philops.* 11	Take heart, he said, I will immediately bring here a Babylonian, one of the so-called Chaldaeans, who will heal the man.
Hymn of Isyllus (IG IV, 128)	Take heart; at the right time I will come. But wait here.

The compositional position of the motif is either the exposition or the conclusion (if the miracle is merely promised in the narrative, eg. Mk 7.29). There is in addition the word of assurance which recognises faith, after the healing (Mk 5.34; 10.52), though this is merely a modification of the word of assurance as promise transposed to this compositional position, as Mk 5.34 shows: 'Go in peace, and be healed of your disease.' The wording presupposes that the healing does not take place until after the utterance. Matthew therefore changes the text so that the healing comes after the word of assurance (Mt 9.22).

The context is all the New Testament miracle genres. The motif is only absent in feeding miracles.

19. Argument

Variants: The word of encouragement counters the ever-present danger of resignation, while argument counters rejection based on rules. Argument frequently takes the form of an either-or question:

Mk 2.9	Which is easier, to say to the paralytic, 'Your sins are forgiven,' or to say, 'Rise, take up your pallet and walk'?

Mk 3.4	Is it lawful on the sabbath to do good or to do harm, to save life or to kill?
Lk 14.3	Is it lawful to heal on the sabbath, or not?
Mt 17.25	From whom do the kings of the earth take toll or tribute? From their sons or from others?

Another form of argument consists in contrasting the behaviour of the opponents with their own objection: they too rescue animals on the sabbath (Lk 13.15f.; 14.5), their disciples too drive out demons (Mt 12.27). The compositional position of the either/or question is always the exposition. The miracle is an answer to the question raised. It is introduced in this sense in Mk 2.10: 'That you may know that . . .'. Other arguments follow the miracle (Lk 13.14ff.; Mt 12.25ff.). The context of argument is always rule miracles.

20. The Withdrawal of the Miracle-Worker
Variants: The miracle-worker appears indifferent to the distress. He sleeps in the boat (Mk 4.38). He wants to pass on (Mk 6.48) – like a supernatural being who does not belong to the human sphere. When people seek help he may reject them (Mk 7.27; Jn 2.4), rebuke them (Jn 4.48), ignore their request (Jn 11.6). Behind these motifs can be seen the divine miracle-worker who moves across the earth as a stranger, who is on earth only temporarily (Mk 9.19).[15] Jesus' retreat into solitude (Mk 1.35, 45; 6.32), his dismissal of the person cured (Mk 5.19f.) should also be mentioned in this connection.

The compositional position of the motif is the exposition, where it contrasts with the distress and the pleas of the sufferers. In Mark we find it (probably in redactional compositions) at the end of miracle stories (1.35, 45; 5.19).

21. Setting the Scene
Variants: The miracle is preceded by preparations, for the most part changes of place. The sick person must be brought along (Mk 10.49; 9.19). He or she must look up (Acts 3.4), come into the centre (Mk 3.3) or simply come forward (Lk 13.12). The pall-bearers are told to put the coffin down (*vita Apoll.* IV, 45). The disciples are sent across the lake (Mk 4.35; 6.45). All these

---

[15] Cf. M. Dibelius, *TG* 278; E. Lohmeyer, 'Und Jesus ging vorüber' in *Urchristliche Mystik* (1955), 57-79. Vespasian also withdraws at first, but for a different reason – he is sceptical. (Tac. *hist*. IV, 81).

instructions concern the people on whom the miracles are performed. Others are directed to the public. They are excluded: Mk 5.40; 7.33; 8.23; Acts 9.40; 1 Kings 17.19; 2 Kings 4.4, 33. In Mt 9.28 the healing does not begin until after the entry into 'the house'; in Mk 9.25 the miracle has been performed before a crowd gathers. The exclusion of the public has numerous comparative parallels. According to Ov., *met.* VII, 255ff., those present on the occasion of a rejuvenation spell are ordered away: 'Jason and the servants she tells to stand far off, and orders them to turn their worldly eyes from the mystery. They hasten to obey her words.' At an invocation of the dead the dead person complains (Hld. 6.15): 'And you even dared to perform these mysteries which are so appalling that they should be covered in silence and darkness not just for yourself, but to unveil the fate of the dead before such witnesses.' Apuleius (Apul. *apol.* 42) is accused of casting a spell on a boy in a remote place in front of a small altar and a lamp after sending away all strangers and in the presence of a small number of initiated witnesses (*remotis arbitris, secreto loco . . . paucis consciis testibus*); the boy collapsed and subsequently could no longer be brought to his senses. Lucian reports (*Philops.* 16) of an exorcist that he takes people on one side. The magical papyri order that the magic action should be performed 'in a lonely place' (PGM III, 616f.). No-one should be present (PGM XII, 36f.). In the case of cultic healings the banning of the public is taken for granted. The sacred space is taboo, it is the *abaton*, the inaccessible. Epidaurus 11 tells the story of a curious person peering down from a tree, injuring his eyes in falling from the tree, but nevertheless being healed by Asclepius. In the Roman Asclepium the inscriptions make a clear distinction between the healing in the interior and the public thanksgiving and rejoicing (SIG ³ III, 1173). It is beyond doubt that the activity of the deity is supposed to take place in secret.[16]

The compositional position of orders concerning the scene is in two cases the introduction (to miracles of rescue at sea: Mk 4.35; 6.45). Otherwise they normally directly precede the miracle proper.

Associated motifs are a variety of features associated with mystery: an order to keep the matter secret (Mk 5.43; 7.36; 8.26; Mt 9.30), ῥῆσις βαρβαρική (Lucian, *Philops.* 16; Mk 5.41; 7.34), and striking miraculous actions: 1 Kings 17.21; 2 Kings 4.34f.; Acts 9.40.

---

[16] Cf. T. Hopfner, *Griechisch-ägyptischer Offenbarungszauber* II (1924), 17.

22. Touch

Variants: The touching has 'as its primary purpose to strengthen someone suffering from physical or mental weakness' (H. Waagenvoort).[17] It cures fever (Mk 1.31; Acts 28.8), leprosy (1.41), haemorrhage (5.27), dumbness (7.33), blindness (8.23; Mt 9.27ff.; 20.29ff.), crooked limbs (Lk 13.13), dropsy (Lk 14.4), lameness (Acts 3.7) and can rescue a person from death (Mk 5.41; Lk 7.14; Acts 9.40; cf. *vita Apoll.* IV, 45; Ov. *fast.* VI. 753f.). It usually takes place as the laying on of hands, a familiar miraculous gesture, and in this form it is sought after (Mk 5.23; 7.32), probably also where the text has only ἅπτεσθαι (Mk 3.10; 8.22; cf. 10.13 and 16). The touching may be carried out also with other parts of the body: Pyrrhus cures people with diseased spleens with his foot, in which there is said to have been 'divine power' (Plut. *Pyrrh.* 3, 7-9). Raisings of the dead are brought about by touching with the whole body in 1 Kings 17.21; 2 Kings 4.34. In addition contact with clothing (Mk 5.28; 6.56), handkerchiefs (Acts 19.12), even a touch from a shadow (Acts 5.15) can have healing power. The assumption is always that the touch transfers miraculous vital power to the sick person (cf. esp. Mk 5.30; Lk 6.19). The more intense the contact, the more vital force can be transferred: hence the contact with the whole body in the case of the dead. The slighter the healing contact is, the greater does the power which passes seem to be: hence the cases of indirect contact by means of clothes, cloths and so on. For further details cf. Bultmann, HST, 222.

An associated motif is the demonstration of acquired power by activity. Peter's mother-in-law serves, (Mk 1.31), the girl who has returned to life walks about and eats (5.41f.), the dumb man moves his tongue (7.35), the blind man can follow Jesus (Mk 10.52), etc. Everywhere revival and a renewal of strength is assumed.

Contexts are, therefore, always healings (in the New Testament at least). There is no case of an exorcism being carried out by the laying on of hands.[18] In the healings we see the beginnings of an understanding of illness as weakness, as ἀσθένεια, which differs

---

[17] H. Waagenvoort, s.v. 'Contactus', RAC III, 405.
[18] O. Böcher, (*Dämonenfurcht und Dämonenabwehr*, 1970, 171) says: 'The original gesture of the exorcist is the laying on of hands,' but the healings of Asclepius he cites are no more exorcisms than Apollonius' raising of a dead person (*vita Apoll.* IV, 45) or Vespasian's healings (Tac. *hist.* IV, 81). Cf. S. Eitrem ('Some Notes on the Demonology in the New Testament', *SO* Fasc. Suppl. XII, 1950, 37): 'Often it was simply impossible for any exorcist to place his hand on a furious madman.' This applies, of course, only to true possession. In the case of illnesses caused by demonic activity we do find laying on of hands, e.g. in *Genesis Apocryphon* XX, 29.

from the attribution of disease to demons, even if there is a formulaic reference to πνεῦμα ασθένειας (Lk 13.11).

23. Healing Substances

Healing 'force' can radiate from material substances. For example, in Lucian's *Philopseudes* the guests discuss animal skins and such like which may give the sick host health and strength. The underlying idea is that of sympathetic magic. Snake-bite is cured by a stone from a virgin's grave (Lucian, *Philops.* 11). Spittle is regarded as a remedy for eye-disease (Plin. *nat.* 28, 7) and therefore appears in healings of blindness (Mk 8.22ff.; Jn 9.1.ff; Tac. *hist.* IV, 81). In Epidaurus healing substances were rubbed into the eyes of the blind and those with eye-diseases (4, 9). These are not at all primitive manipulations. The idea that real connections exist between whole and part, original and copy, between things which are related and touching, is a general feature of all mythical thought; in this respect there is no difference between the most sublime myths and the most primitive miracle stories.

However, if we want to apply medical criteria, it must be admitted that an archaic form of medicine was practiced in Epidaurus. R. Herzog, in his book on the miracles at Epidaurus, has assembled the parallels from the medicine of the time, which is the only standard by which the practice at Epidaurus may be measured.[19] In general, healing by means of words and commands is much further from medicine than the search for some 'simple remedy'. The thematic context for 'healing substances' is almost always healings. However, in Jos. *ant.* VIII, 2, 5 a root is used to draw a demon out of the nose of a possessed person through a ring.

24. Miracle-Working Word

Variants: The word acts either as a word of power (command, threat, invocation), through its mysterious content, or indirectly, in that an order is carried out and the miracle results.

a) The word of power is particularly appropriate where a hostile demonic power is involved. Demons are banished by the word: ἐξέβαλεν τὰ πνεύματα λόγῳ (Mt 8.16). They are threatened (ἐπιτιμᾶν: Mk 1.25; 9.26 [Lk 4.41]).[20] Cf. the threats in Lucian,

---

[19] R. Herzog, 'Die Wunderheilungen von Epidauros', *Philol. Suppl.* XXII, 3 (1931), 65ff., 139ff.

[20] H.C. Kee, 'The Terminology of Mark's Exorcism Stories', *NTS* 14 (1967/68), 232-46 connects ἐπιτιμᾶν with the tradition of Old Testament Judaism, and claims that the original context of the idea is the cosmic contest between God and the demonic powers. Cf. *Genesis Apocryphon* XX, 29.

Philops. 16 and 31, *vita Apoll.* III, 38. Apollonius banishes an *empusa* with insults (*vita Apoll.* II, 4). He speaks to the demon of the fooling boy as 'a master to his rascally, intriguing and impudent servant' (*vita Apoll.* IV, 20). Words of power occur also in healings: A leper is rebuked (Mk 1.43), the fever is threatened (Lk 4.38f.). Here the healing procedures have a flavour of exorcism. The same applies to the command to be still in the stilling of the storm (Mk 4.39), whose closeness to Mk 1.25 and ancient *katadesmoi* is unmistakeable.[21] The calling up of a storm is implied in PGM III, 226-228, which mentions the god's seal 'before which . . . the most exalted demons (shudder) and before which the sea must be silent when it hears it'.

b) The effect of the word of power is increased by the aura of mystery. It may be spoken in a foreign language: αἰγυπτιάζων (Lucian, *Philops.* 31), as ῥῆσις βαβαρική (*Philops.* 9; cf. *Philops.* 16; *dial. meretr.* 4; Plut. *Quaest. conv.* 706; Mk 5.41; 7.34).[22] What is spoken is mostly powerful names, βαρβαρικὰ ὀνόματα (Lucian, *Menippus*, 9; *Philops.* 12; Plin. *nat.* 28, 4.6; Hld. VI, 14; PGM VIII, 20f. Further material in T. Hopfner, *Offenbarungszauber* I, 181-88). These foreign names are secret, which is why they are also called κρυπτὰ ὀνόματα (PGM IV, 1609-11; cf. PGM I, 216f; XII, 236 f, 240; XXI, 1).

Consequently it is wrong to make them widely known. Magicians and miracle workers always speak softly. Apollonius speaks the crucial words secretly: τι ἀφανῶς ἐπειπών (*vita Apoll.* iv, 45), as do Lucian's magicians (*Menippus* 7; *Lucius* 12). Eucrates, though he says of himself πάντων ἐκοινώνει μοι τῶν ἀπορρήτων (*Philops.* 34), does not learn the magic words for transforming the mortars from his great master Pancrates.

He has to discover them by stealth: 'But one day I secretly heard the magic word as I was standing in a dark place: it had three syllables.' Words with miraculous force are therefore recited πρὸς τὸ οὖς (PGM IV, 2164f., 909f.). Soundless speech arouses suspicion of magic. 'This keeping secret of magical πράξεις is familiar to all nations and periods, for the very simple reason that passing on the magic formula or names could give other people

---

[21] Cf. E. Rohde, *Psyche*, 5/6th ed. 1910, 87-88 (n. 3), 356, 424; also S. Eitrem, 'Notes', 30-31. Cf. PGM VII, 396, 967ff.; IX, 4; XXXVI, 164.

[22] The motif survived in literature. Cf. Lessing, *Der junge Gelehrte* I, 1: 'The doctor finally believes he has you really in his power when, by a legion of barbaric words, he makes the healthy sick and the sick even sicker.'

immeasurable power, which they might even use to the detriment of the person from whom they had obtained the power.'[23]

c) Words are not only the direct cause of a miracle. Often the miracle occurs when words are acted upon: Lk 5.4; 17.14; Jn 9.7; Mk 8.6f.; Jn 2.7.

Settings are all themes. However, nuances are always associated particularly with certain themes: words of power and threats with exorcisms, mysterious words with healings (Mk 5.41; 7.34). On the other hand miraculous words do not appear in gift miracles. The command is quite 'normal': bread and fishes are to be distributed, water fetched, nets let out.

The associated motifs follow from the various preferred contexts: words of power and threats are associated with the demon's resistance, his violent exit and destructive demonstration of his power, mysterious words are accompanied by a touch of the hand (Mk 5.41; 7.33; *vita Apoll.* IV, 45) and protected by commands of secrecy (to be distinguished from commands to be silent): Mk 5.42; 7.36.

25. Prayer
Occasionally prayer-like gestures or prayers are found. In Mk 6.41 and 8.6 we have the usual blessing. There is nowhere any indication that the multiplication of the loaves results from this prayer. Mk 7.34 (ἀναβλέψας εἰς τὸν οὐρανόν) is a prayer-like gesture, Jn 11.41f. a proper prayer: 'Father, I thank thee . . .'. Prayers are frequent in healings by disciples (Acts 9.40; 28.8). Prayer is recommended to the disciples in Mk 9.29 as a means of exorcism. Healings through prayer occur in the Old Testament and Judaism: 1 Kings 17.21; Ḥag. 3a (healing of two dumb men) and b. Berakoth 34b (two healings through prayer performed by Ḥanina ben Dosa). Prayers lead to the stilling of storms (Jn 1.14; j. Berakoth 9.1; b. Baba mezia 59b). It is reported that Pyrrhus cured people with diseased spleens by touch, but also sacrificed a white cockerel (Plut. *Pyrrh.* 3, 7-9).

26. Recognition of the Miracle
The miracle can be recognised without any emphasis on its miraculous character (Mk 1.42; 3.5; 4.39b; 6.51; 7.30; 8.25; Mt

---

[23] T. Hopfner, *Offenbarungszauber*, II, 15. On pp. 14-19 there is a discussion of various secrecy motifs surrounding the magical action. See also O. Herzig, 'Lukian als Quelle für die antike Zauberei' (1933), 10. H.D. Betz, *Lukian von Samosata und das Neue Testament, TU* 76 (1961), 154, n. 4. The *Bonner General-Anzeiger* of 24 Dec. 1971 carried a report of a British exorcist, Canon Pearce-Higgins, who kept a medieval formula of exorcism in reserve for difficult cases, which he kept a strict secret: 'It is so powerful that I wouldn't dare to tell you it,' the canon said.

9.33; 12.22; Lk 14.4; 17.14; Jn 9.7; Acts 9.40; 14.10; 20.12; 28.8). Often, however, the recognition of the miracle is given a particular emphasis by means of the motif of suddenness, the motif of the hour, and the violent departure of the demon.

The miracle takes place suddenly: εὐθύς (Mk 1.42; 2.12; 5.29; 5.42; 7.35; 10.52), εὐθέως (Mt 8.3; 14.31; 20.34; Lk 5.13; Acts 9.34; Jn 5.9). Matthew often omits the suddenness motif, while Luke uses fairly regularly the word παραχρῆμα (4.39; 5.25; 8.44, 47, 55; 13.13; 18.43). A mass of evidence from outside the New Testament has been collected in O. Weinreich, 197f. To this may be added: Lucian, *Philops.* 7; *Lex* 12; *abdic.* 5; *ver. hist.* I, 40; II, 41; *Charon,* 7; *Asin.* 12 (further references to Lucian in H.D. Betz, *Lukian,* 157, n. 3); Antiph., *Metragyrtes Fragm.* 154 (θᾶττον); PSI IV, 435. Rescues from distress at sea also take place suddenly: BGU 423, 8; *Hom. Hymn.,* 32. 23. Compare also the stereotyped magic formula, 'Quickly, quickly. Soon, soon.' (PGM III, 35f., 84f., 123f., IV, 122, 153, 1593, 1924, 2037, 2098, 2911f.; VII, 248, 254, 259, 331, 373, 472f., 993; VIII, 52, 63, 84; XII, 58, 81, 143, 396 etc.). The motif which is in opposition to that of suddenness, healing by degrees, appears only in Mk 8.24f. Another technique used to stress the miraculous nature of the event is the 'motif of the hour', often in association with healing at a distance (Mt 8.13; 15.28; Jn 4.52; b. Berakoth 34b) and sometimes independently of it (Mt 9.22; 17.18; Acts 16.18). In exorcisms the unusual nature of the 'cure' is emphasised by the violent exit of the demon: Mk 1.26; 9.26. This is the demon's last attempt at resistance.

27. Demonstration
Variants: The miracle is usually not simply recognised, but also demonstrated by a new act. The form of the demonstration varies according to the thematic context.
a) In healings the newly acquired physical power is demonstrated by activity: the man who had been sick serves (Mk 1.31), carries his bed (Mk 2.12; Jn 5.9; Lucian, *Philops.* 11), or a stone (Epidaurus, 15), can walk and follow (Mk 5.42; 10.52; Plut. *Cor.* 13: on the variants of this motif in the tradition cf. O. Weinreich, 174). The girl who has come back to life eats (Mk 5.43) and utters sounds (*vita Apoll.* IV, 45).
b) Demonstration by the destructive violence of the departing demon often occurs in exorcisms. The demon confirms his expulsion by leaving visible traces outside the person, driving a herd of swine into a lake (Mk 5.13), knocking over a beaker full of water

(Jos. *Ant.* VIII, 2, 5) or overturning a pillar (*vita Apoll.* IV, 20).[24] In Lucian, *Philops.* 16 he flees as visible black smoke. The plague demon who had been stoned (he had been disguised as a beggar) turns up again under a pile of stones as a slain dog: proof that he was not a human being (*vita Apoll.* IV, 10).

c) In food, wine and fish miracles (which we treat under the general heading of gift miracles) the existence of the miraculously increased, transformed or produced objects is authenticated by counting (Mk 6.43f.; 8.8f.; Jn 21.11). The motif is modified by Porphyrius (*vita Pythag.* 25) where the miracle consists in the prophecy of the correct number of fish caught. The quantity of the objects can also be stressed by noting that they exceed the need and the technical possibilities of storing them: in 2 Kings 4.6f. the jars cannot contain the oil. In 2 Kings 4.44 there is bread left over. At the draught of fishes the nets break (Lk 5.6), the boats begin to sink under the weight (5.7). In the wine miracle the demonstration takes the form of confirmation by the impartial master of the feast that the wine is wine (Jn 2.10). The importance of the number and the abundance shows that the miracle here has a quantitative dimension.

d) Epiphanies include demonstrations of the reality of the apparition. Jesus shows that he is no ghost by getting into the boat (Mk 6.51). The risen Jesus eats (Lk 24.36ff.), lets himself be touched (Jn 20.24ff.). Apollonius appears to his disciples: 'Take hold of me, he said, and if I slip out of your grasp then I am a spirit from Persephone's kingdom, like the gods of the underworld who appear to those who are saddened by mourning; but if I remain under your touch, convince Damis that I am alive and have not left the body' (*vita Apoll.* VIII, 12).

Associated motifs: We may recall again the connection between touch and demonstration of physical power. In the demonstrations of gift miracles it is notable that they are always combined with the great unobtrusiveness of the miracle itself. The demonstration is the first sign that a miracle has taken place. The process itself remains secret.

28. Dismissal

Variants: The dismissal usually consists of two-part utterance of the miracle-worker, ὕπαγε followed by another imperative or a pronouncement that the healing has taken place. Outside the New

---

[24] Cf. *Act. Verc.* 11, discussed in R. Reitzenstein, *Hellenistische Wundererzählungen*, 2nd ed. 1963, 54.

Testament the only evidence for the concluding dismissal is in editorial remarks: the exorcist in Lucian, *Philops.* 16 sends those who have been cured away (ἀποπέμπει). In Diog. *Laert.* viii, 67 Empedocles is described as ἀποστείλας τὴν νεκρὰν ἄνθρωπον. In New Testament miracle stories the presence of saving faith is always emphatically noted (Mk 5.34; [7.29]; 10.52; Mt 8.13; Lk 17.19), those cured are sent away to give thanks and to spread the news (Mk 1.44; 5.19) or handed over to their relatives (Lk 9.42; 7.15; cf. 1 Kings 17.23; 2 Kings 4.36f.; *vita Apoll.* IV, 45: 'And the child uttered a sound and returned to her father's house'). A similar sending back to the family could also underlie Mk 2.11, whereas in Mk 8.26 the motif has been transformed into its direct opposite: the cured man is told not to go back to his village.

Associated motifs. The dismissal is found particularly where the suppliants come to seek help. If the miracle-worker comes to the suppliant, the concluding dismissal is changed into a handing over to the relatives. The compositional location is always the conclusion, though the motif may be combined with other concluding motifs and come before the real conclusion of the miracle story (e.g. Mk 2.11; 5.19). The context is almost always a healing. However, in the feeding miracles there is a hint of a dismissal (Mk 8.9). In the parallel, Mk 6.34ff., the story begins with the disciples' suggestion that the people should be dismissed (6.36), and in 6.45 the people are dismissed.

29. Command to Secrecy

Variants: Commands to secrecy appear within miracle stories (Mk 1.44; 5.42; 7.36; Mt 9.30), independent and linking apophthegms (Mk 8.30; 9.9). Indirect commands to secrecy appear in Mk 8.26 and perhaps Mk 5.19: the cured man is sent back to tell what has happened only at home, but disobeys the command. Commands to secrecy are to be distinguished from commands to be silent. The 'be silent', (Mk 1.23; 4.39) has its compositional position in the miraculous process itself, as a variant of the word of power; the command to secrecy follows the miracle. The closest parallels are the stereotyped commands of secrecy in the magical papyri, which forbid the dissemination and transmission of the powerful magic formulas. Usually the command is a simple κρύβε. The initiate is a mystic bound to silence by an oath: Μύστης με σιγᾶν ὅρκος οὐδ'ἐᾶ φράσαι (Lucian, *trag.* 272). 'But even if you want to bring along a fellow initiate, so that only he and you hear the words (i.e. of the god), he must remain pure with you for (7) days . . .' (PGM IV, 732-35). If the initiate wants to pass on the spell, the rule is: 'But if you wish to reveal it to him (the other initiate)

make sure that there is no doubt about his suitability as a person
. . .' (738ff.). There is a collection of commands to secrecy in
PGM, Part 2, I, C.

Associated motifs are either dismissal conclusions (Mk 1.43f.;
5.19; 8.26) or wonder and acclamation conclusions (Mk 5.42;
7.37). Since dismissals themselves are in the nature of a command
or a charge, there is a close formal fit between them and commands
to secrecy, but the command to secrecy contrasts with wonder and
acclamation conclusions: secrecy and the wonderment of the
crowd are in opposition. These passages reveal another association
of motifs, since the commands to secrecy are only one motif
expressing a general theme of secrecy. Both in Mk 5.21ff. and
7.31ff. the public is first removed and then a healing takes place
which uses ῥῆσις βαρβαρική.

Contexts: Commands to secrecy also occur in Mark outside
miracle stories, in summaries (1.34; 3.12), where the closeness to
the commands to silence is unmistakable, also in one apophthegm
(8.30) and after one epiphany (9.9). The compositional position in
all four cases is the conclusion of the narrative unit.

30. Wonder

Variants: The motif of wonder comprises all the narrative elements which express astonishment, fear, terror, and amazement.
Wonder may be described either by a verb: θαυμάζειν (Mt 8.27
etc.), ἐξίστασθαι (Mk 2.12 etc.), φοβεῖσθαι (Mk 4.41 etc.), θαμβεῖσθαι (Mk 1.27), ἐκπλήττεσθαι (Mk 7.37) or by a noun: ἔκστασις (Mk 5.42), φόβος (Mk 4.41; Lk 7.16), θάμβος (Lk 4.36).
These linguistic nuances reflect two variants of the motif, amazement as a reaction and amazement as a state, reacting with dismay
to something and being astounded. Amazement as a state is frequent in Mark (5.42; 6.51; 10.32; 16.8). Matthew and Luke each
develop the motif in a different direction. Whereas Mark usually
attributes amazement to people who are not further specified
(third person plural), Matthew almost always gives a specific subject:[25] men (8.27), disciples (21.20), the crowds (9.8; 9.33; 12.23;
15.31). This is usually followed by a participle, καὶ λέγοντες (8.27;
9.33; 19.25; 21.20) or βλέποντας (15.31), or a co-ordinate verb
(12.23; 13.54). In other words, Matthew always specifies what it is
that the amazement is about (22.22 is an exception). Luke, on the
other hand, nominalises 'fear' and 'trembling', makes them the
grammatical subject, so that it appears as though numinous states
were taking hold of people: καὶ ἐγένετο θάμβος ἐπὶ πάντας (4.36;

---

[25] K. Tagawa, *Miracles et Évangile* (1966), 96.

cf. καὶ ἐθαμβήθησαν Mk 1.27), καὶ ἔκστασις ἔλαβον ἅπαντας
. . . καὶ ἐπλήσθησαν φόβου (5.26; cf. ὥστε ἐξίστασθαι πάντας Mk 2.12), ὅτι φόβῳ μεγάλῳ συνείχοντό (8.37; cf. ἐφο-
βήθησαν Mk 5.15), φόβος ἐπέπεσεν ἐπ'αὐτόν (1.12), θάμβος γὰρ
περιέσχεν αὐτόν (5.9), ἔλαβεν δὲ φόβος πάντας (7.16). The
Lucan terminology is based on the idea of an enthusiastic state.
Parallels from outside the New Testament are not very common.
Trajan and Hadrian react with amazement to Egyptian miracles.
After the superiority of Serapis to the Jewish God has been shown,
we are told: θεασάμενος δὲ Τραϊανὸς ἀπεθαύμασεν (Pap. Ox. X,
1242). Hadrian gives a magician an increased fee: θαυμάσας τὸν
προφήτην διπλᾶ ὀψωνία αὐτῷ ἐκέλευσε δίδοσθαι (PGM IV,
2454 f).[26] We also find a crowd amazed. After the miraculous
clearing of a field of snakes and pests we are told: ἡμεῖς δὲ
ἐθαυμάζομεν (Lucian, *Philops.* 12), after a healing: οἱ παρόντες
δὲ ἐθαύμαζον (*abdic.* 5), after Lucius has been turned from a
donkey into a man: '*populi mirantur religiosi venerantur tam
evidentim maximi numinis potentiam*' (*Apul. Met.* X, 13). The
account of the first miracle at Epidaurus ends with the repetition of
a dedicatory tablet: Οὐ μέγεθος πίνακος θαυμαστέον, ἀλλὰ τὸ
θεῖον . . . E. Peterson has shown that wonder (in association with
acclamation) became the typical conclusion in the Christian miracle stories of the second to tenth centuries.[27] In the pre-Christian
parallels the motif is not so frequent as to allow us to speak of a
stereotyped concluding motif in ancient miracle stories: 'These are
isolated examples' (K. Tagawa).[28]

Character associations: The motif appears as amazement on the
part of individuals (Mk 6.6; Mt 8.10) and on the part of a crowd of
people. The term 'choral ending' would include only the second
variant of the motif and not distinguish between a wonder
conclusion and an acclamation conclusion (close though the
association of the two motifs is).[29] We therefore depart from the
terminology of classical form criticism.

Contexts: The motif appears not just in miracle stories, but also
in travel narratives and at the fulfilment of prophesies, in short,
connected with a variety of extraordinary phenomena.[30] In the

---

[26] In a different context θαυμάζειν is very frequent in the magical papyri: PGM IV, 161,
775, 791-92, 2445, 3170-71, XIII, 239, 252.
[27] E. Peterson, ΕΙΣ ΘΕΟΣ (1926), 183-222.
[28] *Miracles*, 93.
[29] M. Dibelius, *TG*, 53, 57, 67, 75f.
[30] G. Bertram, *TDNT* III, 27-42. H.D. Betz (*Lukian*, 159) can find only one reference to
amazement after a healing (*abdic.* 5); elsewhere there is 'amazement' in Lucian at the
unusual, the aesthetic, the erotic and the fantastic.

New Testament there is a second context, apophthegms. In this case in Mark the amazement is always a specific reaction, as indicated by a reference to the object (ἐπὶ with dative: 1.22; 10.24; 11.18; 12.17) or by explicit questions (10.26; 6.2). The specific reason for the amazement is more in accord with the rational character of apophthegms (or of teaching, Mk 1.22).

The compositional position is essentially the conclusion of miracle stories, though the motif is the actual conclusion only in Mk 5.20. In two places it has found its way into the introduction to miracle stories: Mk 1.22 and 9.15. Otherwise it may appear in the middle of miracle stories or miraculous narratives (Mk 5.15; 16.5; 9.6).

An associated motif is the acclamative conclusion, though it can also occur independently, which is the justification for differentiating the two motifs (Mk 5.20, 42; 6.51). Conversely, there are also acclamations without wonder (Lk 17.15f.; 13.13, 17).

31. Acclamation

Variants: 'By acclamations are meant the cheers, often rhythmically phrased and uttered in chorus, with which a crowd expresses applause, praise and congratulation or rebuke, execration and demand.'[31] The difference between acclamation and wonder is that in acclamation there is always a verbal comment on the miracle or the miracle-worker, which may vary considerably. The acclamation may be mentioned in general terms, without reference to its content (implicit acclamation), for example δοξάζων τὸν θεόν (Lk 18.43; cf. 8.47; 9.43; 13.13, 17; Acts 3.9). Among 'detailed acclamations' (Mk 1.27; 2.12; 4.41; 7.37; Mt 9.33; Lk 19.37f.) of particular interest are 'titular acclamations', which confer a title on the miracle-worker (Lk 5.8; 7.16; Mt 12.23; 14.33; Jn 1.49; 6.14; 9.35-38; Acts 8.10; 14.12; 28.6). We use the term 'acclamation' for all linguistic comments on miracles, whatever particular nuance may be predominant, joy (e.g. Lk 13.17), praise (e.g. 13.13), thanksgiving (e.g. 17.16), confession (5.8). Analogies from outside the New Testament are discussed in detail in Part 2.

Contexts for acclamations are a great variety of genres and theme complexes. E. Peterson has described acclamations in worship, theatre, law and politics. We are concerned only with 'aretalogical acclamations', (that is, those which appear in miracle stories). Nevertheless other acclamations also occur in the New Testament, in worship (e.g. 1 Cor 14.25), and politics (Acts 12.22; 19.34).

---

[31] T. Klausner, s.v. 'Akklamation', RAC I, 216-33 (the quotation is from 216).

Character associations: In miracle stories the acclamation is usually, though not necessarily, spoken by a crowd. There are also acclamations from individuals (Lk 5.8), often in the presence of a crowd, which sometimes joins in (Lk 5.25f.; 18.43). Associated motifs: see under *Wonder*.

32. Rejection

Variants: The converse of wonder and acclamation is the rejection of the miracle-worker. The motif appears particularly in sayings and apophthegms in which miracles are the object of σκανδαλίζειν (Mt 11.6; 11.20-24; Mk 6.3). This motif, which was reinforced by the experience of Christian missionaries, if not indeed its product, comes into the miracle stories in three ways. Instead of acclamation there may be direct rejection (Mk 3.6; 5.17; Acts 16.19ff.; Jn 5.9ff.). Luke constructed this sort of rejection by analogy with his wonder conclusions (see above): αὐτοι δὲ ἐπλήσθησαν ἀνοίας (6.11) corresponds to ἐπλήσθησαν φόβου (5.26). Or the rejection may appear alongside the acclamation. Such divided reactions appear in Mt 9.33ff.; 12.23f.; Jn 9.8-39; 11.45ff. (without a reference to a miracle, Jn 7.12f.; 7.40f.). The opinions of the people in Mk 6.14f., are also divided reactions to a miracle, but seem not to be a total rejection. A third possibility is to quote the acclamation, but dismiss it as a misunderstanding: Jn 6.14f.; Acts 14.11ff. I know of no analogies from outside the New Testament for any of the three forms of rejection. Formally rejection is very close to acclamation and could also be treated as a paradigmatic variant of this motif.

33. The Spread of The News

The miracle-worker's reputation spreads fast. In the relevant sentence the subject is either the 'fame' ἀκοή (Mk 1.28), λόγος (Lk 7.17), φήμη (Mt 9.26) or the people who spread the news (Mk 1.45; 5.14, 20; 7.37; Mt 9.31). In Luke we occasionally find ἐγένετο γνωστόν (Acts 9.42; 9.17).[32] There is a parallel in Pausanias, II, 26, 5.

B. The Compositional Structure of the Motifs

After listing and describing all the motifs, we can set about the task of analysing their mutual relations on the compositional and paradigmatic level in context. Since we have already specified the

---

[32] G. Schille ('Die Topographie des Markusevangeliums', *ZDPV* 73 (1957), 133-66) regards such remarks as 'reports of findings', i.e. as giving the names of the districts the miracle stories have been taken from.

positions of the motifs in the composition, a summary account is all that is needed here. Four possible positions may be distinguished: the introduction (consisting of two elements), the exposition, the middle and the conclusion. Motifs 1-7 belong to the introduction and describe the appearance of characters, motifs 8-20 belong to the exposition. They are not a direct preparation for the miraculous action, but build up an internal tension which is released by the following narrative. Technically they may be sub-divided into motifs of approach, motifs of retreat and motifs which describe an aspect of the miracle-worker's behaviour. Motifs 21-26 form the middle, the miraculous event proper, which begins with a scene-setting and ends with the pronouncement of miracle. The remaining motifs (27-33) belong to the conclusion, where all the characters involved may appear: the distressed person (demonstration), the miracle-worker (dismissal and command to secrecy), secondary characters (wonder and acclamation). According to their most usual position we distinguish introductory, expositional, central and final motifs.

Of all these motifs the narrator of a miracle story realises only a limited number at any one time. Potentially he has all the motifs at his disposal. In each narrative unit he makes an (unconscious) choice. In the following table the combination of motifs into groups outlines the possibilities of choice: these groups also function as paradigms. At the various positions in the composition, the narrator can choose between them – or he can realise them in compositional sequence. In the choice of a motif (or of its paradigmatic variants) he is not absolutely free. The position in the composition is largely pre-determined. However, one indication of the freedom the narrator does possess is the number of motifs which appear at different positions.

	The Compositional Structure of the Motifs	
Introduction (Introductory Motifs)	1. The coming of the miracle-worker	
	2. The appearance of the crowd.	
	The appearance of	3. Distressed persons.
		4. Representatives.
		5. Embassies.
		6. Opponents.
	7. Reason for the appearance of opposite numbers.	

Exposition (Expositional Motifs)	8. Description of the distress. Approach of the miracle-worker.	
		9. Difficulties.
		10. Falling to the knees.
		11. Cries for help.
		12. Pleas and expressions of trust.
	Drawing back.	13 Misunderstanding.
		14. Scepticism and mockery.
		15. Criticism.
		16. Resistance of the demon.
	Behaviour of the miracle-worker.	17. Pneumatic excitement.
		18. Encouragement.
		19. Argument.
		20. Withdrawal.
Middle (Central Motifs)	21. Setting the scene. Miraculous action.	
		22. Touch.
		23. Healing substances.
		24. Miracle-working words.
		25. Prayer.
	26. Recognition of the miracle.	
Conclusion (Final Motifs)	Opposite numbers: Miracle-worker:	27. Demonstration.
		28. Dismissal.
		29. Commands to secrecy.
	Supporting actors.	30. Wonder.
		31. Acclamation.
		32. Rejection.
		33. The spread of the news.

C. The Motif Field

The next step is to examine the mutual relations of the motifs in the paradigmatic field independently of the compositional structure. The initial recognition of the existence of such connections leads to the division of expositional motifs into motifs of approach and motifs of drawing back. Between these two groups of motifs there is an intrinsic opposition. In this section we shall make a systematic search for 'opposed motifs', each of which defines the content of the other. A field analysis of this sort proceeds by classifying in various ways the units discovered by breaking down the structure of the composition.

The character field gives us the basis for a first classification: we distinguish motifs 'associated' with demons, human beings and divine beings (the miracle-worker). This gives us three sub-fields. We shall first take the 'human' motifs in which we have already observed the contrast between difficulty and faith. The motif of difficulty articulates awareness of a boundary: the human will to overcome suffering is faced by apparently unsurmountable obstacles. 'Opposed' to this motif is the boundary-crossing motif of faith, that is, those cries for help, pleas and expressions of confidence by which the suppliants ignore the difficulty. Jesus calls this attitude, whose volitional character is clear, 'faith' – θέλειν is synonymous with πιστεύειν.[33] While the motif of difficulty stresses the boundary, the motif of faith breaks down boundaries. Both have in common the reference to the will.

Misunderstanding, scepticism and mockery and criticism are also 'boundary-stressing' motifs, but the boundary does not appear as an obstacle to a will which comes up against it, but as a perceived obstacle which prevents the very emergence of an effort of the will to overcome it. These motifs stress the cognitive aspect of the boundary. Within the certainty of the ordinary, everyday world of meaning 'misunderstanding' is the only sensible attitude. It deals with the possible and wastes no time on the boundary with the impossible, but takes it as unquestionably obvious, not noticing the gaps and breaches in it. 'Misunderstanding' shows us this ordinary world in which the limits of our action and expectation are clearly marked, a world in which we live, breathe and exist, in which unquestioning activity leaves the boundary unmentioned and thereby makes it all the more powerfully present as an implicit assumption.

'Scepticism and mockery' presents this self-assured world on the defensive: it is defending itself against any claims to cross the boundary. The cracks in the ordinary world are seen, but treated as non-existent – most effectively by collective ridicule. However damaged this world may be, even though death, blindness and deformity be its signs, liberation from evil is still rejected as a rational possibility.

---

[33] H.J. Held, 'Matthew as Interpreter', 278ff. Cf. 'According to your faith be it done to you' (Mt 9.29) and 'Be it done for you as you desire' (Mt 15.28). Compare similarly Mk 10.51-52 and Mt 15.28.

'Criticism' moves from defence to attack. Possible boundary-crossings are seen as not only meaningless, but as even illegitimate, as breaches of sacred rules. The sacred, the great disturber of the normal world of meaning, is claimed as its strongest prop, in the name of which the boundary is fiercely defended – even if crossing the boundary should mean saving life and preserving it.

The emphasis on the cognitive aspect of the boundary reveals a normal world, not yet broken open by an intervention from outside; it reveals that world in action, on the defensive, attacking. Possible crossings of the boundary are regarded as non-existent, meaningless or illegitimate. Potentially opposed motifs are those which denote a deliberate crossing of the boundary. Cries, requests and expressions of trust show that people will deliberately take the risk of crossing the boundary. They address the miracle-worker as a supernatural being (for example as the son of David), that is, they know that his help would be the intervention of super-human power. The centurion from Capernaum is aware of the (legitimacy) barrier between himself as a gentile and Jesus. He knows that he is not worthy but asks nonetheless. The Syro-Phoenician woman admits that she is one of the dogs who get the leavings, but she does not give up. The father of the epileptic boy realises that he is going to have to cross the boundary separating him from omnipotence if he wants to win Jesus' assurance of the faith to which all things are possible – and still says 'I believe', even while recognising the boundary in ἀπιστία. In this way cries for help, requests, and expressions of trust show not only a willingness to cross the boundary, but also a realisation that the boundary being crossed is that of the possible and the legitimate. They depict crossings of the boundary in cognitive terms and are thus to be contrasted with a cognitive emphasis on the boundary; they are 'boundary-crossing' motifs. In the miracle the boundary is 'really' crossed. However, even after the miracle the normal world of meaning fights against the intrusion into its order. Rage fills its representatives (Lk 6.11), fear overcomes people and they send the miracle-worker away (Mk 5.15). The obstacles may have been really overcome, the arguments refuted; there nevertheless remains an affective rejection of any transcending of the familiar world of meaning. There remains the σκανδαλίζειν (Mk 6.3; Mt 11.6). This 'reaction of rejection' stresses the boundary in affective terms. The contrasted 'boundary-crossing' motif is 'wonder' and 'acclamation' (usually the result of 'wonder'). The disturbing effect of this invasion of the familiar, legitimated and interpreted world leaves an unmistakable echo: φοβεῖσθαι, θαμβεῖσθαι and ἐκπλήττεσθαι are ambivalent terms, but the pull of fascination is stronger than the pressure to shrink back from the boundary, ecstatic crossing is stronger than repulsion. Wonder and acclamation show crossings of the boundary in affective terms. It is not will, but an affective state reacting to the prospect of crossing the boundary which drives people beyond the bounds of the familiar world of meaning.

The motif field has thus turned out to be structured in two further ways. The main feature is the opposition between stressing and crossing the boundary. Boundary-stressing and boundary-crossing motifs also have a volitional, cognitive or affective aspect, though none of these can be sharply distinguished from the others: every boundary-stressing motif is in opposition to every boundary-crossing motif. The intersection of the two perspectives produces six sub-fields in the form-critical field of motifs.

The Motif Field (Human Perspective)

	Boundary-stressing Motifs	Boundary-crossing Motifs
Volitional aspect	Difficulty	Overcoming of the difficulty (faith)
Cognitive aspect	Misunderstanding Scepticism and Mockery criticism	Cries for help Requests and expressions of trust
Affective aspect	Reaction of rejection	Wonder Acclamation

However, the two aspects mentioned are not sufficient to describe the structure of the motif field. So far we have looked at the boundary only from the human viewpoint, but in the miracle stories it is also considered from the point of view of the miracle-worker and, not least, from that of the demons. We shall see that the classifications of the 'human' motifs apply here too.

'Difficulty' means that the human being cannot approach the miracle-worker who brings salvation. Corresponding to this on the side of the miracle-worker is his 'withdrawal'. He avoids the human being, deliberately goes past him: καὶ ἤθελεν παρελθεῖν αὐτούς (Mk 6.48). He may refuse the plea (Mk 7.27) or even reject it as in contradiction to his mission (Mt 15.24). The leper's plea clearly formulates what is important also for the miracle-worker: ἐὰν θέλῃς δύνασαί με καθαρίσαι (Mk 1.40). There is a stress on the volitional character of the boundary from the miracle-worker's point of view as well, of course not as opposition to this boundary, but as a conscious establishment of it.

The contrasting attitude on the part of the miracle-worker is the initiative for the miraculous action and the action itself. Here too the intention is stressed: θέλω καθαρίσθητι (Mk 1.41). The unintentional transfer of power is seen as a great exception (Mk 5.25ff.). Usually most of the 'central' motifs (the calling forward of the sufferer in the scene-setting, touch, the healing substance, the miraculous word) are intentional crossings of the boundary on the part of the miracle-worker. In other words, in relation to him as well we can isolate the volitional aspect of the stressing and crossing of the boundary. The same applies to the cognitive aspect. The miracle-worker stresses the boundary by his dismissal of the public and his command to secrecy. He wants to withdraw the miraculous action from perception and knowledge, wants to remain incognito himself. Conversely, he allows the human beings who encounter him a cognitive participation in the possibilities which lie beyond the normal world of meaning. By his assurance he opens new perspectives: 'The child is not dead but sleeping' (Mk 5.39). Here a world of certainties, the death of the girl and the irrevocability of that death, begins to totter. The assurance is a crossing of the boundary which anticipates the real transcendence of the boundary in the miracle. And the arguments with which Jesus confronts his critics also have a cognitive structure: they challenge the fundamental legitimacy of the customary world of meaning and establish a new concept of the sacred.

The affective stressing of the boundary on the part of the miracle-worker consists in 'pneumatic excitement', where the element of complaint, grief and suffering at human distress predominates. Characteristic of this is the cry, 'O faithless generation, how long must I be with you?' (Mk 9.19), in which the barrier between human beings and miracle-worker becomes explicit. The contrasting boundary-crossing motif is rare, but certainly occurs: in Mt 8.10 Jesus 'marvels' at the faith of the centurion. Jesus' compassion (Mk 6.34; 8.2) is another such crossing of the boundary. These 'emotions' of Jesus are part of the logic of the form-critical field of miracle motifs, which we can now fill out in a second diagram.

The Field of Motifs (Miracle-Worker's Perspective)

	Boundary-stressing Motifs	Boundary-crossing Motifs
Volitional aspect	Withdrawal	Initiative Miraculous action

Cognitive aspect	Dismissal of the public Command to secrecy	Word of assurance Arguments
Affective aspect	Pneumatic excitement (negatively tinged)	Compassion Amazement

We have examined the boundary illustrated in the miracle stories from the human and the divine perspective. One more perspective is left, the demonic. Here too a distinction can be made between the stressing of the boundary and its crossing. Boundary-stressing motifs are those which denote the occupation of a human being by a demon, boundary-crossing motifs those which portray the departure of the demon. Three aspects can be distinguished here too. The volitional aspect appears in the descriptions of the possessed as a victim of the demon (Mk 9.18, 22) and also in the demon's resistance (Acts 19.16). The cognitive aspect appears in the demon's use of miraculous knowledge in self-defence: οἶδα σε (Mk 1.24), ὁρκίζω σε (Mk 5.7), τὸν Ἰησοῦν γινώσκω καὶ τὸν Παῦλον ἐπίσταμαι (Acts 19.15), the affective aspect in the demon's excitement when near to the miracle-worker: it cries out (Mk 1.23) and throws the sick person into a convulsion (9.20). It scents its master. Corresponding to these boundary-stressing motifs is the crossing of the boundary when the spirit actually leaves the possessed: volitionally in the demonstration of the departure in destructive violence, cognitively in the plea for a concession which anticipates the departure, and affectively in the demon's last violent outburst (Mk 1.26; 9.26). This gives us a third table.

The Field of Motifs (Demonic Perspective)

	Boundary-stressing Motifs	Boundary-crossing Motifs
Volitional aspect	Occupation of the human being	Demonstration of the departure
Cognitive aspect	The demon's miraculous knowledge	Plea for a concession, capitulation
Affective aspect	The demon's excitement	Final outburst

Fundamental to the field structure of the motifs is the distinction between boundary-stressing and boundary-crossing motifs. All other sub-classifications are related to this fundamental division. The motifs illustrate the boundary from various points of view which cannot be sharply differentiated; the purpose of the threefold division into will, knowledge and feeling is rather to indicate that human existence as a whole is engaged. The boundary provokes the human being in his or her totality.

The three perspectives are also complementary. Within the human perspective the boundary is seen as fore-ordained, in the divine perspective as established, in the demonic perspective as a defended boundary. The whole mythical world, divine, human and demonic, is involved in the miracle.

In conclusion we offer some general considerations on field analysis in form criticism. The fields sketched out here suggest an excessively systematic, symmetrical and static order. The limitations of any 'systematics' are clear. One obvious reason is that not all the motifs have been built in: the introductory ones, for example, have been omitted. In addition, the distinction between cognitive, volitional and affective aspects is much less clear than the distinction between boundary-stressing and boundary-crossing motifs or their grouping into demonic, human and divine. It should also be remembered that all abstractions, classifications or oppositions, in a word all analytic operations, imply an element of subjectivity, a constructive intuition. Alternative analyses are quite conceivable. Nevertheless I regard the analysis proposed here as useful. It does not claim to have discovered a system, but merely to indicate some systematic connections which may be identified by means of the concept of the 'form-critical field' in preference to a 'form-critical system' which, in my view, does not exist.

The impression of a perfectly symmetrical paradigmatic structure also needs to be corrected. It is well known that the main emphasis in the miracle stories is on the miracle-worker and his opposite number. Consequently in each case the motifs associated with these characters have greater narrative importance. Nevertheless this does not alter their mutual connections.

Finally, it must be emphasised that the aim of this exposition is not to capture the outline of some 'structures', but to follow the movement of the 'symbolic action'. The analysis of structures is a preliminary. It is as little an end in itself as the analysis of forms in classical form criticism was. It is of course possible – as K. Burke remarks sarcastically – [34] to treat a text 'by structuralist methods, i.e. to consider it as though it had not been written by a living individual, but owed its origin to the circumstance that someone threw a few alphabets into the air and that these alphabets fell to the ground in a meaningful order.' Even the structure of a text becomes more intelligible 'when we look for the function of the structure'.[35] And in Burke's terms that means analysing it as a symbolic action. (In our context 'alphabets' of course becomes catalogues of motifs.)

---

[34] *Dichtung als symbolische Handlung*, 74.
[35] *Dichtung als symbolische Handlung*, 75.

CHAPTER III

THEMES

Miracle stories do not effect a general crossing of the boundary; in them the narrative imagination is concerned with quite specific situations of distress. These situations appear within the genre 'miracle story' as different themes and the mutual relations between these themes produce a logically structured field of themes. Field analysis provides a posteriori confirmation of the value of the classification. Other divisions are however possible. If we use the criteria employed by classical form criticism to differentiate genres, we obtain three groups, according as the distinction is made mainly on a functional, a compositional or a paradigmatic level, i.e. is based on the 'life situation' (*Sitz im Leben*), the 'structure' or particular typical motifs. Occasionally criteria from different levels are combined, though it has not so far been possible to produce classifications which coincide on all three levels. However, if we hold to the definition of a genre in terms of the coincidence of features on all three levels, it is then useful when dividing miracle stories into different groups not to use the terms 'genre' or 'sub-genre'. This is another reason for the use of 'theme' in this section.

1. Classifications on the functional level
A classification in functional terms was proposed by G. Schille.[1] According to him all miracle stories belong fundamentally to 'missionary discourse genres', but have different purposes. 'Pure exorcisms and miracles stories' seek to draw attention to Jesus; 'mission legends' in addition give an aetiological account of existing communities. Legends fall into two groups. 'Community foundation legends' deal with the origin of individual communities, while 'area legends' are concerned with missionary activity in districts as a whole. The healing of Bartimaeus, for example, is on this view a foundation legend of the Jericho community and the story of the 'Syrophoenician' woman an area legend of Syria and Phoenicia. This classification combines almost opposed functions,

---

[1] G. Schille, *Die urchristliche Wundertradition*, 1967, 24-27.

the aetiology of existing groups of Christians and the winning of new Christians. The first function points back to the past, the second towards the future. The first is internal, the second is external. What is being proposed here is not a single 'life situation', but two. However, if two 'life situations' belong to a genre, the 'life situation' cannot define the genre, and the latter must already exist independently of the former. Schille's proposal must be discussed later as a contribution to the functional analysis of miracle stories, but for a classification of the genre it offers nothing.

A functional criterion is also implicit in M. Dibelius' distinction between paradigms and novellas. Essentially, both are part of mission, but differ in that paradigms, as model sermons, are all along integrated into a wider genre (sermon), while the novellas stand on their own. Paradigms are transmitted by preachers and novellas by narrators. But one may fairly ask whether novellas do not also preach and paradigms tell a story.[2]

2. Classifications on the compositional level

Dibelius' distinction between paradigms and novellas is based primarily on observations at the compositional level. Four of the five characteristics of the paradigm he lists belong here,[3] rounding off, brevity, emphasis on a saying of Jesus and the sermon conclusion. The first feature is common to novellas and paradigms. Brevity can hardly be considered a distinguishing mark between the two genres. L.J. McGinley has rightly pointed out that many paradigms and novellas are the same length.[4] The paradigm Mk 2.1-12 is greater in length than the average novella, while the novella Mk 8.22-26 is shorter than, say, Mk 14.3ff. The third criterion, the emphasis on a saying of Jesus, is not applied consistently by Dibelius: what difference is there between the command to silence and the saying about faith in the paradigms Mk 1.23ff. and 10.46ff. and the corresponding sayings in the novellas Mk 4.39 and 5.34? In the story of the healing of Peter's mother-in-law there is (in Mark) no saying of Jesus, and yet Dibelius discusses this story among the paradigms.

In contrast, Bultmann uses this criterion so strictly that he

---

[2] E. Schick, *Formgeschichte und Synoptikerexegese*, 1940, 107: 'Both forms, the "paradigm" and the "novella", are suitable, in content, form and style, for use in preaching.' The paradigm-novella distinction is also criticised by E. Fascher, *Die formgeschichtliche Methode*, 1924, 57-78; L.J. McGinley, 'Form-Criticism of the Synoptic Healing Narratives', *ThSt* 3 (1942), 47-68, 203-230, esp. 54-57, 212-16.

[3] *TG*, 37ff.

[4] *ThS* 3 (1942), 214.

removes all miracle stories which contain teaching by Jesus from the genre 'miracle story' and includes them among 'apophthegms'. Here they form a sub-group: healings of Jesus, along with other events, 'occasion' sayings;[5] the miracle has been 'completely subordinated to the point of the apophthegm'.[6] The description of miracles as the 'occasion' of sayings, however is not always appropriate. From the point of view of the composition the 'occasion' would be expected to precede the saying of Jesus. In three out of five examples, however, this is not the case (Mk 3.1-6; Lk 14.1-6; Mk 2.1-12), and here in each cases the either-or question is decided only by the subsequent miracle. Here the miracle and the saying together constitute the point. On the other hand, in Lk 13.10ff. and Mt 12.22ff. the miracle is the occasion for a debate, as it is in Mk 5.25ff. and Lk 17.11ff. for a dialogue, but this does not force us to include these narratives among the apophthegms. What it does do is confront us for the first time fully with the question whether there are particular types of composition in which the basic compositional structure of the miracle story is varied or partially realised.

3. Classifications on the paradigmatic level

It is tempting to subdivide miracle stories by specifying different motifs or combinations of motifs, but this criterion is also not sufficient to enable us to differentiate sub-groups. Miracle stories as a whole can certainly be distinguished from all other genres by an inventory of their motifs, but for sub-groups this is possible, if at all, only in the case of exorcisms. In his list of miracle motifs Bultmann rightly listed motifs of exorcism separately, but without making a fundamental distinction between healings and exorcisms.[7] Exorcisms are not a special case. As we shall see, while specific motifs or motif variants can be listed for all themes, to define themes requires a further investigation going beyond individual motifs. Not all theme-specific motifs are present in every realisation of the theme; some motifs run through various themes, and themes may appear in specific motifs without being identical with them. Most form critical classifications try essentially to define such themes, but differ in taking different elements of the content as the basis for their classification.

It is tempting to distinguish miracle stories by their objects.

---

[5] HST, 12.
[6] HST, 220.
[7] HST, 209.

Bultmann follows this principle of classification when he distinguishes miracles in the natural sphere and miracles in the human sphere. In the theme field, this means an 'opposition' between nature and human beings. Objects can be further differentiated by physical objects (bread, fish, lake, etc.) or characters (the blind, lepers, the lame etc.). H. van der Loos has carried out such classifications.[8]

Another possible basis for classification is the 'subjects' of miracles, since miracles can spring from a variety of motives. O. Perels accordingly distinguishes miracles of assistance and power miracles.[9] The second group includes the walking on the lake and the finding of the ass's colt (Mk 11.1ff.). The 'display miracles' of the Fourth Gospel could probably be taken as a variant of the power miracle, and the self-help miracles in apopryphal infancy gospels as a variant of the help miracles. T.A. Burkill's typology also starts from the 'subject' of the miracle: he distinguishes miracles performed through human agency.[10]

A third criterion for classification within the genre is the interaction between subject and object. Burkill distinguishes the types of miracles performed through human agency into firstly, an 'exorcism' and a 'non-exorcism' class and secondly, miracles in the natural world and miracles in the human world. Both classifications overlap; there are exorcisms in the natural world (the stilling of the storm) as well as in the human world. The overlapping classifications produce a four-member form critical field. From a consideration of the whole of the ancient miracle tradition, G. Delling has proposed a typology which deserves serious consideration.[11] He distinguishes cures, prodigies, epiphanies of gods, proof miracles (in which the supernatural character of an individual is demonstrated), rescue and punishment miracles. Here too the dynamic of the action is primary, the rescuing, the punishing, the healing, etc.

This variety of classifications by theme makes it natural to ask which principle of classification is most appropriate to the miracle stories. The field analysis of the motifs has already answered this question: if 'crossing the boundary' is a basic feature of all miracle

---

[8] H.v.d. Loos, *The Miracles of Jesus*, 1965.

[9] O. Perels, Die *Wunderüberlieferung der Synoptiker in ihrem Verhältnis zur Wortüberlieferung*, 1934, 70.

[10] T.A. Burkill, 'The Notion of Miracle with Special Reference to St Mark's Gospel', *ZNW* 50 (1959), 33-48, esp. 43-44.

[11] G. Delling, 'Zur Beurteilung des Wunders durch die Antike', in *Studien zum Neuen Testament und zum hellenistischen Judentum*, 1970, 53-71, esp. 55-56.

stories, the stories must be further subdivided according to the way this boundary crossing is seen, where it takes place and which characters it brings into prominence. All three approaches, in other words, must be combined, that based on the object, that based on the subject and that based on the interaction between subject and object. Now a field analysis of themes of course depends in advance on the possibility of classifying miracle stories by various aspects, if they are not merely to be set out in an unrelated way, but linked and contrasted through a multiplicity of connections. The best classification must therefore be the one which combines the most aspects.

A necessary preliminary to a field analysis of themes is a catalogue of themes. The methodological problems of the classification of motifs recur here. Here again it is often a matter of taste whether we list two theme variants or two independent themes. This does not mean that the distinctions which follow are purely arbitrary. The use of comparative parallels can strengthen the basis for individual classifications. In addition, a stricter criterion of synchrony is applied in field analysis. The analysis deals only with New Testament, and especially synoptic, miracle stories; it is possible, and indeed likely, that a field analysis will turn out differently if it is based, for example, entirely on the miracle stories of Philostratus' life of Apollonius.

A. The Catalogue of Themes

1. Exorcisms

Only a few exegetes regard exorcisms as an independent theme.[12] It is held to be difficult to separate them from healings, since here too demons are regarded as the cause of disease.[13] Nevertheless a distinction is necessary. Firstly, some New Testament summaries show that a distinction was recognised between exorcisms and healings (Mk 1.32-33; 3.10-11; 6.13; Lk 6.18-19; 7.21; 13.32). In the secondary ending of Mark exorcisms are not merely listed

---

[12] E.g. T.A. Burkill, 'Notion', 43-44.

[13] Cf. F. Fenner, *Die Krankheit im Neuen Testament,* 1930, 21-26; O. Böcher (*Dämonenfurcht und Dämonenabwehr*) interprets as demonic almost anything which has any analogy with something which can obviously be regarded as demonic. The result is that exorcisms and healings can no longer be distinguished. But Böcher's whole approach is quite different too; he wants to analyse ideas of faith. We, on the other hand, are interested solely in form-critically relevant motifs and themes. In this study, therefore, the question whether a healing motif comes diachronically from an exorcism motif is not considered. The only important thing is its present position within the New Testament genre 'miracle stories'.

separately, but also separated from healings by other charisms (Mk 16.17-18). The exorcism motifs in healings also tell in favour of rather than against a distinction between the two themes. The motifs may be divided into two groups: demonological aetiologies of illness and techniques of healing which use exorcism. Demonological aetiologies can be clearly distinguished from the possession which requires exorcism: in the latter the demon inhabits the victim, in the former it causes the disease. The healer deals with the effects of the demon's action, the exorcist with its presence. The symptoms which may be explained as demonological in healings consist in anomalies which can be attributed to the actions of a demon and interpreted as its 'scourge' (μάστιξ), 'blow' (πληγή) or 'binding' (δεσμός). In the case of 'demonic scourges' the demonic background is so weak that in Mk 3.10 and Lk 7.21 μαστίγες can be mentioned alongside 'unclean spirits' but without being attributed to them. On the other hand the idea of 'demon's fetters' does not imply the presence of the demon: Satan, who has bound the woman, does not live in her.[14]

A second point of contact between exorcisms and healings lies in the use of exorcism in many techniques of healing. ἐμβριμησάμενος (Mk 1.43), however, should not be cited as an example.[15] It also appears in the raising of Lazarus in Jn 11.33, which is clearly distinct from an exorcism. On the other hand, there is no mistaking the features of an exorcism in the healing of Peter's mother-in-law in Luke. The reworking of the Marcan story is probably determined by the context:

Whereas Mark stresses the 'teaching' of Jesus and the astonishment it produces (1.22, 27), Luke in both places refers to 'the word' (4.32, 36). This removes the tension which can be felt in Mark between the teaching and the miracle, and the authoritative Logos can be identified with the command of exorcism. Luke also reworks the subsequent story of the healing of the mother-in-law in terms of this motif. Whereas in Mark she is healed by touch, in Luke the fever is threatened as though it were a demon which had to be driven out by a word of exorcism. Fever is often regarded as a demon.[16]

---

[14] S. Eitrem, *Notes,* 37, wants to delete this motif as secondary. In general he often tends to regard demonological features as accretions. F. Fenner (*Krankheit,* 25), on the other hand, regards the distinction between possession and illness as a sign of an earlier stratum of the tradition.

[15] As it is by J.M. Robinson, *The Problem of History in Mark,* London 1957, 40.

[16] On the tension between teaching and miracle, cf. Bultmann, *HST,* 209. On the demonological aetiology of fever, cf. R. and M. Hengel, 'Die Heilungen Jesu und medizinisches Denken', *Festschrift R. Siebeck,* 1959, 331-61, esp. 340-41.

By inserting features of exorcism Luke has composed two testimonies to the power of the exorcising Logos. However, the healing of Peter's mother-in-law merely has the superficial features of an exorcism; it is not an exorcism. A vital feature is missing, the departure of the demon. An exorcism can take place only when a person is not simply impeded in one function by a demon, but has lost his autonomy to the demon. Where such 'possession' occurs, the demon must leave. In form-critical terms, the demon must be an opposite number, not just a subsidiary character hidden in the background.[17] We can now positively list the characteristics specific to the genre exorcism:

a) The person must be in the power of the demon
This is illustrated in two motifs, in the description of the distress and in the departure of the demon. The distress is portrayed – especially in Hellenistic Greek texts – as the suppression of human identity:

'. . . and the boy no longer had his own voice; he spoke in a low, gruff man's voice, and his eyes looked more like a stranger's than his own' (*vita Apoll.* III, 38). 'You are not the instigator of this evil, but the demon which controls you without your knowledge. And indeed the youth was possessed, but no-one knew' (*vita Apoll.* IV, 20). 'The victim himself says nothing, but the demon replies in Greek or in a foreign language . . .' (Lucian, *Philopseudes.* 16).

But the demon does not just suppress the human personality; it also tries to destroy it: 'It makes threats about precipices and gorges and talks of killing my son' (*vita Apoll.* III, 38). 'And it has often cast him into the fire and into the water, to destroy him' (Mk 9.22). 'The spirits of evil men which enter into the living and kill them unless help comes in time' (Jos. *bell.* VII, 6, 3).

This demonic violence is also displayed in exorcisms. The demon puts up a final resistance and takes revenge on the innocent victim for the loss of its dwelling place: '. . . and the boy was like a corpse; so that most of them said, "He is dead."' (Mk 9.26). 'But the youth rubbed his eyes as though he were waking from sleep' (*vita Apoll.* IV, 20). 'The possessed man immediately collapsed' (Jos, *ant.* VIII, 2, 5).

The departure of the demon is a final danger for the possessed person; his or her life is at risk. In Jos, *ant.* VIII, 2, 5 there is no report that the person recovered from unconsciousness. In Mk

---

[17] For example, it is unimportant whether the letting down of the sick person through the roof once had exorcistical significance, as H. Jahnow ('Das Abdecken des Daches Mc 2,4 Lk 5,19', *ZNW* 24 [1925], 155-58) supposes. Against this assumption: S. Krauss, 'Das Abdecken des Daches Mc 2,4 Lc 5.19', *ZNW* 25 (1926), 307-10.

9.26f. it is not clear whether death was real or apparent. We can understand why Luke, in describing the exorcism at the synagogue at Capernaum, adds, unlike Mark, 'he came out of him, having done him no harm' (4.35): he knows that the demon can still harm the victim when leaving him. Exorcism is all too often the opposite of a healing; it is an injury which makes a subsequent healing necessary (Mk 9.27).

b) The battle between the demon and the exorcist

It is illustrated by the association of the central motifs of conflict with both main characters. Attack and resistance use the same means. This interchangeability of motifs has no analogy in healings. It can be demonstrated in four places:

aa) Possession is not just a characteristic of the sick person. The exorcist too must be filled with divine powers. He is God's holy one (Mk 1.24) and is regarded as possessed (3.20ff.).[18]

bb) Both opposed characters possess miraculous knowledge. The demon scents its conqueror (cf. the confessions of the demons), and the exorcist tracks down the demon. Apollonius of Tyana recognises an *empousa* in the bride of one of his followers (*vita Apoll.* IV, 25), discerns in a young man's laughter at his 'weighty' discourses a demonic conspiracy (ibid. IV, 20), unmasks a dirty beggar as the plague demon (IV, 10), and knows exactly where a rabid dog is to be found (VI, 43). This is Philostratus' attempt to show that all his miracles are due to his miraculous knowledge, that he is wise by God's gift, but not God.

cc) The two antagonists use the same techniques of adjuration. The οἶδα formula (Mk 1.24) appears in the New Testament on the lips of the demons, and in ancient magical papyri on the lips of exorcists.[19] The ῥῆσις βαρβαρική is initially an exorcist's or healer's technique (Mk 5.41; 7.34). The original idea that the unintelligible or archaic has greater power is soon rationalised, and we have the exorcist talking to the demon in its own foreign language. It follows that the demon should also speak in a foreign language, as in Lucian, *Philops.* 16: '. . . the demon replies in Greek or in a foreign language (βαρβαρίζων), or in the language of whatever country he comes from.'[20] The same interchangeability of

---

[18] Cf. PGM, 3205-06: 'I conjure you . . . because I wish you to enter into me . . .'; PGM XIII, 795-96: 'For you are I and I you. Whatever I command must happen. For your name is the only defence in my heart. . . .' Cf. K. Thraede, 'Exorcismus', RAC VII, 44-117, esp. 54.

[19] O. Bauernfeind, *Worte der Dämonen*, 13-18. The transformation of this motif in the synoptic exorcisms was noticed by Bultmann, HST, 209, n. 1. He describes the situation as 'unusual', but in fact it is part of the internal 'logic' of exorcisms.

[20] The demon must speak. Cf. PGM IV, 3041ff.: 'You too speak, whatever sort of demon you are, a demon of the heaven, of the air or of the earth, or from under the earth or from the underworld, or an Eabusaeic or a hersaeic or a Pharisaic, say which you are.' PGM XIII, 242-44: 'To a person possessed by a demon say its name and hold sulphur and bitumen

motifs occurs in the case of names. The demons use the name Jesus as 'son of the most high' (Mk 5.7) and 'holy one of God' (Mk 1.24), while the exorcist frequently uses the name of a god in the exorcism of a demon (Mt 7.22; Acts 19.13ff.).

dd) Violence too is a feature of both sides. The demon is violent against human beings, the exorcist against the demon. This is the only explanation for the plea to be spared. μή με βασανίσῃς (Mk 5.7) and ἐδεῖτο μὴ βασανίζειν αὐτό (vita Apoll. IV, 25). The demon for its part exploits the weakness of its opponents: it falls upon the sons of Sceva and overpowers them so that they are forced to flee naked (Acts 19.13-18).[21]

The characteristic features of exorcisms, therefore, are constituted, not by particular motifs, but by their association with specific characters: the most important motifs are associated both with the exorcist and with the demon. In the struggle both sides employ the same strategies for attack and defence.[22] The possessed person appears as the battlefield, the 'boundary' as the front.

c) The destructive activity of the demon in nature

This is the final aspect which ought to be highlighted. This appears partly in the demonstrations which belong to exorcisms and partly in the object-related exorcisms in which places and times are freed from demonic activity.[23] These features make it clear that the exorcisms have to be seen in the context of a cosmic conflict. The possessed person is the theatre of a conflict between supernatural, extra-human forces. Particularly in view of this situation it should however be emphasised that in the New Testament the only exorcisms are from people; there are no exorcisms of places. There is certainly no lack of references to the extra-human activity of

---

against his nose. Immediately (εὐθέως) it will speak and depart.' On this cf. C. Bonner, 'The Technique of Exorcism', HThR 36 (1943), 39-49, esp, 41-47. The parallels tell against the view of O. Herzig, Lukian, 32, n. 68, who regards the passage of Lucian's Philopseudes quoted above as a sarcastic additon by Lucian.

[21] On violent resistance by demons, cf. T. Hopfner Griechisch-ägyptischer Offenbarungszauber I, 1921, 56, 82ff. The spirits of the dead which for various reasons have not found rest and exist as demons prove to be particularly vindictive. Spirits of the dead seem to come into Mk 5.1ff. (cf. their staying near the graves, 5.3,5); perhaps it was once known that they had scores to settle with the Gerasenes – certainly the destruction of a herd of pigs is no mean revenge. On the power struggle between the exorcist and the demon, cf. also H.D. Betz, Lukian, 153: 'The demons will submit, but unwillingly, and try to destroy the magician to escape the pressure. In this power struggle . . .'.

[22] The transformation of the motifs is also recognised by O. Böcher (Dämonenfurcht, 169): The logic of exorcism is to a great extent the same as that of sympathetic magic: the exorcist uses his knowledge about the demons to defeat them, as it were, with their own weapons.'

[23] Lucian, Philops. 31; vita Apoll. II, 4; b. Pesaḥim 112b/113a. Cf. also the stories of demons in the school and the baths in Bill. IV, 535 and IV, 516.

demons, as the destruction of the heard of swine (Mk 5.13) and the saying about the wandering demon (Mt 12.43-45) show, but the purpose of the struggle between Jesus and the demonic forces is exclusively the liberation of the enslaved personality. The threat from demonic forces is seen as present exclusively in human beings.[24]

2. Healings[25]

The mere absence of demonological motifs is not a distinctive feature of healings as opposed to exorcisms; what is distinctive is that the motifs of conflict are replaced by images of the transmission of a healing power, images which doubtless bring us closer to the dawn of medicine than do the powerful words of exorcism. Nevertheless, we should be applying foreign categories to the miracle stories if we attempted to distinguish them by their closeness to or distance from medical action. Both sorts of miraculous act, exorcisms and healings, are the exercise of a numinous power. The distinction is a matter of emphasis: In exorcisms this power triumphs aggressively; the *mysterium tremendum* predominates. In healings the dominant aspect is the *mysterium fascinosum*, of course revealing its other side, refusal and rejection, but on the whole inviting and radiant. The one is no more rational than the other.[26]

This very general distinction can be illustrated from the logia source. This discusses miracles explicitly on three main occasions (if we ignore Mt 8.5ff.), and on each of the three has a different category of miracle in view. The miracles refused in the story of the temptation are confirmatory signs (as in Mt 12.38ff.), in the Beelzebub conversation exorcisms are the subject (Mt 12.22ff.), and in the reply to the Baptist's questions (Mt 11.2ff.) only healings are mentioned. Exorcisms are seen in the context of

---

[24] H.D. Betz, *Lukian*, 146, remarks, in a comparison of the New Testament and Lucian, 'The summaries (in the New Testament) and the miracle stories told concentrate on human beings.'

[25] Raisings of the dead are a category of healings. Not only can almost all ancient raisings of the dead by miracle-workers be regarded as the resuscitation of people only apparently dead (R. Herzog, *Epidauros*, 142f.), but the typical motifs are also the same. In both cases the transmission of power takes place by touch.

[26] The ancients were well able to distinguish between doctors and exorcists. Cf. Ulpian. *dig.* L. XIII, 1,3: 'Si incantavit, si inprecatus est, ut vulgari verbo impostorum utar, si exorcizavit, non sunt ista medicinae genera.' Even within the context of belief in miracles, distinctions are possible here. The miraculous healings at Epidaurus, for example, are closer to medical practice than the New Testament healings. It is characteristic that exorcisms do not occur there. At Epidaurus religion and archaic medicine are linked (cf. Edelstein II, 139-80). The god 'acted as a physician; his healings were miracles – for his success was beyond all human reach – but they were strictly medical miracles. On the other hand, this rationality of Asclepius' treatment seems strangely interwoven with the fantastic and the unreal' (Edelstein II, 154). What Edelstein calls 'medical miracles' we call 'healings'.

the universal struggle between the rule of God and the rule of Satan. The exorcist himself can be suspected of being Satanic, destructive. Here we see the frightening side of the power at work in Jesus. On the other hand, the answer to the Baptist's questions, by associating healings with the preaching of the gospel, stresses the helping, light side of Jesus' activity.

It is difficult to name particular motifs specific to the theme of healing because every individual motif can be part both of the struggle of exorcism and of the transmission of beneficent power. The ambivalence of miracle-working as an activity can be observed everywhere; even where a motif in the New Testament seems to belong almost exclusively to healings (as in the case of the laying on of hands), a quick look at the history of religion corrects the New Testament findings.

This ambivalence of the motifs can be shown in the attitude to the miracle-worker expressed in wonder and acclamation. In Mk 5.1ff. the destructive conflict between exorcist and demon makes so strong an impression that the usual positive attitude to the miracle-worker changes into a negative one, and he is asked to leave the district. His presence is uncomfortable. In the acclamations after the expulsion of the demon in Capernaum, too (Mk 1.23ff.), perplexity and bewilderment are the main feelings. The situation at the healings 2.1ff. and 7.32ff. is different. Here the crowd reacts by praising God (2.12). 'He has done all things well,' they exclaim (7.37). The same motif receives a slightly different nuance in the different themes, in one place more as terror, in another more as fascination. In the rest of this section this is illustrated by reference to the three motifs which are associated in the New Testament primarily with healings:

a) Healing power

The term δύναμις and its associations are not in themselves a mark of healing action (cf. Lk 4.36), though the militant and threatening 'power' is clearly distinct from the mana-like fluid which goes out from Jesus to the woman with the issue of blood and stops her bleeding. Here no alien personality is driven out, no magical compulsion is exercised; instead we are told that the woman was cured by a beneficent influence.[27] Some may object to accepting

---

[27] K. Thraede, 'Exorzismus', RAC VII, 62, asks, 'Does the sequence healing-trembling-falling down in Mk 5.33f. indicate an original exorcism, distorted here?' The term μάστιξ would be a better clue. Cf. PGM V, 169f. In this connection cf. too; 'Make all spirits subject to me, that every demon may be obedient to me, in heaven and in the air and on earth and under the earth and on solid earth and in the water, and any visitation or scourge of God' (164ff.). In the New Testament, however, the demonological sense has been weakened. So also S. Eitrem, Notes, 29f.

this idea as therapeutic, but the story itself regards it as such. It stresses at the beginning that the woman had suffered much at the hands of many doctors and had come to Jesus – come, as it were, to the true doctor, who would satisfy her longing for a medical cure. At the end, the statement of faith, 'Your faith has made you well,' is followed by καὶ ἴσθι ὑγιὴς ἀπὸ τῆς μαστιγός σου, the only case in the New Testament where this occurs. This promise of health, together with the mention of the doctors, gives the idea of δύναμις a therapeutic slant.[28]

b) Healing touch

In Mk 5.25ff. the transmission of healing power is carried out by touch. This transmission of power is probably tacitly implied wherever there is a report of touching or the imposition of hands. Nowhere in the New Testament has the laying on of hands a threatening character; it is always a gesture of help, radiating power.[29] This is confirmed by the analogy of the laying on of hands to bless and ordain. The laying on of hands is thus a healing motif. Only in two summary notices in Luke does it appear in connection with the departure of demons (Lk 4.40f.; Acts 19.11f.), and here the connection of the laying on of hands in Lk 4.40 or the touch in Acts 19.11f. with the departure of the demons is not totally unambiguous.[30] Outside the New Testament, in contrast, we find clearer references to the laying on of hands in exorcism.[31] The early Church, too, was familiar with a laying on of hands in exorcism from as early as the 2nd century,[32] and this later became a standard part of the catechumenate. Cyprian[33] describes its effect as the exercise of coercive force: 'videbis sub manu nostra stare vinctos (i.e. the demons) et tremere captivos quos tu suspicis et veneraris ut dominos'. Not the helping, but the iron hand, is the mark of exorcism.

Nevertheless even in the non-Christian world of antiquity the laying on of hands was regarded as a specific gesture of healing.

---

[28] E. Stemplinger, Antike und moderne Volksmedizin, 1925, distinguishes between demonological explanations of disease and popular medical ideas based on concepts of force or power. (40).

[29] J. Behm, Die Handauflegung im Christentum, 1911, regards the laying on of hands as 'the imparting of sacred life-force, as a transmission of power in a real, physical sense' (156).

[30] A. von Harnack, Lukas der Arzt, 1906, 136, believes that Luke, unlike the other evangelists (though this is certainly wrong as regards Mark), 'mentions only the healings [in the summaries] and makes a sharp distinction between natural and demonic diseases (because the latter required a quite different medical treatment)'.

[31] Evidence in J. Behm, Handauflegung, 106. See also Genesis Apocryphon XX, 22, 29.

[32] J. Behm, Handauflegung, 65-69.

[33] Demetr. 15 (CSEL 3,1, 361f.).

Solon says of the doctor: τὸν δὲ κακαῖς νούσοισι κυκώμενον ἀργαλέαις τε ἀψάμενος χειροῖν αἶψα τίθησ'ὑγιῆ (frag. 12, 61f.)[34] Seneca also writes: 'medico, si nihil amplius quam manum tangit' (*benef.* VI, 16.2), where *manum tangere* has probably become a technical term for 'take the pulse',[35] a secondary rationalisation of a magical healing gesture.

The preferred setting of the motif and its presentation as a gesture of help and of the imparting of power are not the only signs that touch in the New Testament is predominantly a gesture of healing; another is its association with other motifs. Where touch occurs, healing is proved by the demonstration of activity. The problem was mainly weakness, ἀσθένεια, a lack of vivifying power. We have here signs of a more neutral understanding of disease than the demonological one.

c) Healing agents

Power may be transmitted, not merely by touch, but also by healing substances. The two belong together: medicaments are δύναμεις and the 'hands of God' (Plut. *quaest. conv.* IV, 1, 3).[36] In the New Testament spittle is 'the only "remedy" in the medical sense';[37] its association with the laying on of hands (Mk 8.22ff.; 7.32ff.) shows how closely related the two motifs are. In Mk 8.22f. there is a background image of medical treatment; after a first application of the substance the doctor enquires about the effect,[38] and then repeats the treatment. A parallel from outside the New Testament may perhaps confirm this medical slant. When Vespasian was about to cure a blind man in Alexandria on the instructions of the god Serapis, he first obtained a medical opinion that a cure was not impossible (Tac. *hist.* IV, 8.1-3). Again, however, we must qualify: spittle can also be used in exorcisms, though there it seems to belong more to the 'gesture of spitting as a sign of contempt',[39] which continues to have an aggressive significance in

---

[34] Cf. O. Weinreich, *AH*, 35; J. Behm, *Handauflegung*, 115 n. 4.

[35] So H. Waagenvoort, 'Contactus', 412, contra J. Behm, *Handauflegung*, 113, n. 4.

[36] Additional texts in O. Weinreich, *AH*, 37 and H. Waagenvoort, 'Contactus', 412.

[37] R. and M. Hengel, 'Heilungen', 348. Cf. also E. Stemplinger, *Volksmedizin*, 55.

[38] E. Lohmeyer, *Markus*, 159: 'Jesus' words sound like the question of a doctor asking if the remedies already used have worked'. R. Otto, *The Kingdom of God and the Son of Man*, 1937: Jesus' healing 'went beyond the exercise of mere skill in healing; he was a miraculous physician. But at the same time he really was a physician, and on occasion he used the remedies of folk medicine' (356). The 'miraculous physician was really a therapeutes, i.e. a physician, and therefore gave advice natural in a doctor.' (308). Even R. and M. Hengel, who as a rule try to show the total difference between Jesus' miraculous activity and medical practice, here admit: 'Here it might be possible in some circumstances to compare Jesus' actions with those of an ancient doctor' (346).

[39] K. Thraede, 'Exorzismus', 52; O. Böcher, *Dämonenfurcht*, 218-20.

our own day. Perhaps such a gesture of spitting in exorcism was reworked in Jn 9.6. Now its purpose is to form a healing paste out of spittle and earth.[40]

Though exorcisms and healings are closely related, the specific characteristics of exorcism and healing are quite distinct. Attack and the communication of power to help are different things. The first idea leads to an interpretation of illness as occupation by outside forces, the second to an interpretation of it as weakness. The miracle-worker's assistance is accordingly different in each case. In the former his action is aggressive; he shows the dark, repelling side of his numinous power. In the latter, in contrast, he radiates beneficent power, so revealing the light, 'fascinating' side of his gifts. To identify form critically the specific characteristics of healings is not a matter of specifying particular motifs; what is specific is rather the compositional relationship of the motifs, the association of healing touch and healing substances with the demonstration of vivifying power.

3. Epiphanies

Any miracle can be regarded as an epiphany. Epiphanies in the narrower sense, however, occur when the divinity of a person becomes apparent not merely in the effects of his actions or in attendant phenomena, but in the person himself. Other miracles should be called epiphanies or 'epiphany stories' only in a second-ary sense.[41] On the other hand, the walking on the lake can be treated as an epiphany,[42] though here it is part of a rescue miracle, that is, has no formal independence, like most 'soteriological epiphanies',[43] which take place in the context of sea rescues or freeings of prisoners. The 'partial epiphany' can be regarded as a special case.[44] In this there are only the typical signs which accom-pany an epiphany: doors open on their own, the earth shakes, terror spreads – the appearance of the person being manifested is merely assumed, not described. Both special cases, soteriological and partial epiphanies, can be subjected to thematic analysis.

---

[40] Oil is another healing substance. Its medical use can be seen in Lk 10.34, but it was also used in exorcisms. Cf. PGM IV, 3008; K. Thraede, 'Exorzismus', 52. On other healing substances used in popular medicine, cf. E. Stemplinger, *Antike und moderne Volksmedizin*, 40-44, 56ff.

[41] M. Dibelius, *TG*, 94.

[42] T.A. Burkill, 'Notion', 42.

[43] E. Pax, 'Epiphanie', RAC V, 832-909.

[44] O. Weinreich, 'Türöffnung im Wunder-, Prodigien- und Zauberglauben der Antike, des Judentums und des Christentums', in *Genethliakon W. Schmidt*, 1929, 200-464; cf. 252.

Epiphanies can be divided (on the paradigmatic level) into theophanies, christophanies, angelophanies and pneumatophanies.[45] C.H. Dodd classifies appearance narratives by 'summary' and 'descriptive' narrative style,[46] i.e. by a compositional criterion: for example, Mt 28.8-10 belongs to the first class and Lk 24.13-25 to the second. However, if, in the Emmaus story, we remove the long conversation in whole or in part, the narrative which remains is no less 'summary' in style than the other appearance narratives.[47] Functional classifications are also an obvious possibility: narratives which encourage the worship of the being made manifest frequently have features of cult aetiology. The commissioning of particular people serves to legitimate them or to justify their activity.[48] The best course, however, is to refrain from making too precise distinctions and do no more than emphasise a number of important motifs.

Characteristic motifs of an epiphany are extraordinary visual and auditory phenomena, the terrified reaction of human beings, the word of revelation and the miraculous ἀφανισμός or disappearance.[49] We did not discuss these motifs in our field analysis of miracle motifs, though they can easily be classified into boundary-stressing motifs (fear, ἀφανισμός) and boundary-crossing motifs (the appearance, the word of revelation). These general motifs are supplemented by specific ones, the association of the epiphany with the cult, specific commissions and acts of rescue.

The existence of elements of cult aetiology in the New Testament epiphanies is undeniable, even if this is not a reason for regarding the particular narratives as cult aetiologies. Who can read, say, the Emmaus story without thinking of the unrecognised presence of Christ in the Eucharist?[50] And while listening to the baptism narrative a Christian will think of his or her own baptism: he or she has also gone down into the water and received the

---

[45] E. Pax, ΕΠΙΦΑΝΕΙΑ. *Ein religionsgeschichtlicher Beitrag*, 1955, 171ff.

[46] C.H. Dodd, 'The Appearances of the Risen Christ. An Essay in Form-Criticism in the Gospels', in *Studies in the Gospels. Essays in Memory of R.H. Lightfoot*, 1955, 9-35.

[47] P. Schubert, 'The Structure and Significance of Luke 24', in *Festschrift R. Bultmann, BZNW* 21 (1954), 165-86; F. Hahn, The Titles of Jesus in Christology, 1969, 376-78; J. Roloff, *Kerygma*, 256-58.

[48] Reasons for the mission: H. Kasting, *Die Anfänge urchristlicher Mission*, 1969, 34-45; legitimation of individual leaders in primitive Christianity: W.O. Walker, 'Postcrucifixion Appearances and Christian Origins', *JBL* 88 (1969), 157-65. Similar views in U. Wilckens, *Auferstehung*, 1970, 29 passim.

[49] 'It is I,' (Mk 6.50; Lk 24.39; cf. Acts 9.5), 'Do not be afraid' (Mt 28.5; Lk 2.10; 1.13; 1.30), the pax (Jn 20.19,26), a voice from heaven (Mk 1.11; 9.7).

[50] Cf. H.D. Betz, 'Ursprung und Wesen christlichen Glaubens nach der Emmäuslegende (Lk 24.13-32)', *ZThK* 66 (1969), 7-21.

pneuma and adoption to be fortified against the onslaughts of Satan.[51]

Aetiological motifs attached to places can also be looked for in the New Testament epiphanies. Some exegetes want to treat the legend of the empty tomb as a local cult aetiology. They claim that the appearance at the tomb justifies an annual Easter commemoration at the empty tomb – an interesting hypothesis, but not without difficulties.[52] In any discussion of local aetiological motifs the story of the transfiguration must be mentioned,[53] not because in it sacredness is conferred on a particular site, but because that idea is rejected. Peter's suggestion that they build huts is rejected as an inadequate response to the manifestation (Mk 9.6), but is it not the 'normal' reaction to the appearance of a god, the wish to provide at the site of the appearance a place where worship is possible? 'Is the suggestion of building huts perhaps to be connected with the provision of a place (a tent) for the appearance of the god?'[54] Within primitive Christianity it is a remarkable fact that no one thought of marking the sites of the Easter appearances by making them cult sites. Could this rejection of local veneration of the sites of epiphanies have left a trace in the story of the transfiguration?

If the questions raised are legitimate, the transfiguration story must be a former Easter appearance.[55] The end is rather curious: 'And suddenly looking around they no longer saw anyone.' This implies a miraculous ἀφανισμός of all the figures. The qualification, 'but Jesus alone with them' could be a subsequent addition, particularly since in the immediate context of the gospel the narrative has to continue with Jesus, who therefore cannot be allowed to remain absent. The whole story can be

---

[51] Dibelius argues against regarding the account of the baptism as an epiphany. He says (TG, 271ff.) that an epiphany presupposes that the god already is what it appears as in the epiphany. For this reason an epiphany cannot contain an adoption. Another possible view is given in Pax, ΕΠΙΦΑΝΕΙΑ, 172f., who claims that the baptism is a vision, and that there would only be an epiphany if Jesus appeared temporarily in his glory. But, despite all the arguments, it is undeniable that we have here a divine being appearing in his majesty. We may follow E. Lohmeyer, Markus, 21ff. in calling Mk 1.9-11 an epiphany. According to Bultmann, HST, 253, the aetiological interest can already be detected in Luke.

[52] G. Schille, 'Das Leiden des Herrn', ZThK 52 (1953), 161-205; L. Schenke, Auferstehungsverkündigung und leeres Grab, Stuttgart 1968. The main problem is why the site of the tomb was so soon forgotten.

[53] H. Schürmann, Das Lukasevangelium, 1969, 564, rejects the description of the transfiguration story as an 'epiphany narrative' on the grounds that here Jesus is made 'transparent', not manifest. I do not understand this. Contra, correctly, Dibelius, TG, 276; E. Lohmeyer, Markus, 179; Bultmann, HST, 259-61. H.P. Müller, 'Die Verklärung Jesu', ZNW 51 (1960), 56-65, distinguishes between an enthronement narrative and an epiphany.

[54] W. Bousset, Kyrios Christos, 1970, 102.

[55] See Bultmann, HST, 259 and the works listed in the Supplement (p. 432).

regarded as an expanded ἀφανισμός portraying Jesus' translation into heavenly glory. First, the transformation says that Jesus is entering the heavenly world. White is the heavenly colour, and there is explicit stress on the fact that such a whiteness does not exist on earth. Second, there is no mention of a reverse transformation. The heavenly *doxa* seems originally to have been envisaged as permanent. Third, this would give a better reason for the appearance of Elijah and Moses, since both are said to have been translated into the heavenly world (2 Kings 2; Ass Mos). Originally the story may have described how Jesus, after his resurrection in human form – which is how the synoptic Easter appearances envisage him – went with his disciples on to a mountain, where he was transfigured and taken up into heavenly glory. The story would then be a sort of ascension story.[56]

On the whole, the New Testament epiphanies show fewer traces of cult aetiology than of commission aetiology. In the case of angelophanies that is natural: angels are messengers. It is not their appearance, but their message which is the important thing. The main feature of the christophanies is the missionary command (Mt 26.16-20; Lk 24.36-49; Acts 26.12-18 parr. Acts 1.2ff.).[57]

An example of a *soteriological* epiphany is the miraculous walking on the lake. The typical motifs are the extraordinary visual phenomenon, the φάντασμα, the withdrawal of the god (παρελθεῖν), the word of revelation, 'It is I,' the numinous amazement of the disciples. In the Johannine version there is a hint of a miraculous ἀφανισμός: at the sudden landfall Jesus seems to have disappeared.

The inclusion of all appearance narratives with the baptism narrative and the transfiguration under the heading 'epiphanies' is not very common. M. Dibelius describes the transfiguration and baptism as 'myth',[58] and it is true that these epiphanies are based on a mythical event, an act of God in relation to a divine being distinct from himself. Jesus is exalted to become son of God; he enters into heavenly glory. However, unlike myths, epiphanies

---

[56] The transformation is usually explained by saying that in order to talk to Moses and Elijah Jesus had to become like them: Dibelius *TG,* 276; W. Gerber, 'Die Metamorphose Jesu', *ThZ* 23 (1967), 385-95. However, neither in the baptism nor the ascension stories is Jesus transformed in this way in order to enter into contact with the heavenly world. The absence of any change back is noted by Lohmeyer, 'Die Verklärung Jesu nach dem Markus-Evangelium', *ZNW* 21 (1922), 185-215, cf. 187. Dibelius, *TG,* 276, regards it as hinted at in v. 8b. If we take the story as originally an ascension story or a resurrection appearance, the assumption is, as in Mk 16.12, that Jesus appeared to his disciples after his death in 'another form'. If the idea of a special μορφή for the post-Easter period is accepted, a μεταμορφοῦσθαι is no longer so strange.
[57] Cf. H. Kasting, *Anfänge,* 34-45.
[58] *TG,* 266ff., 271ff., 275ff.

deal only with episodes taken from the mythical event. The term 'myth' applies really to the whole context, the unknown god walking over the earth. Epiphany is to myth as anecdote is to biography: it can be part of a myth, but is complete in itself. There is also another distinction. An epiphany starts from the human position: divine revelation breaks into this domain and remains a mysterious other. In contrast, when we hear a real myth (e.g. the hymn in Philippians), we are already among the μυστήρια τοῦ θεοῦ. This myth takes place in the divine realm and at the same time touches the earth: it presents as abasement what fascinates us in an epiphany as the brilliance of divine glory.

In passing we may consider the miracles which occur in legends, historical narratives (and to some extent in apocalypses too). These are always 'signs' announcing the closeness in space or time of significant events or persons. They always have this referential character, that is, their significance lies outside the miracle. They therefore do not form independent form critical genres, but occur within genres to which miracles are not essential. With the exception of apocalyptic signs, which are still to come,[59] their setting is in biographical legend or legendary historical narrative, that is, narratives which 'gain their point only when set into their context'.[60] Characteristics of such signs are:

1. Signs occur spontaneously
There is no visible miracle-worker, nor any invocations, miraculous practices etc. They come ἀπὸ τοῦ οὐρανοῦ (Mk 8.11). Where the divine origin of signs is no longer totally clear, they may remind a modern reader of ghostly activity. Cf. for example the miraculous opening of the gate before the destruction of the Temple. (Jos. *bell.* VI, 5, 3).

2. Signs are not necessarily miraculous
That is, if 'miracle' is restricted to normally impossible events. The star over Bethlehem could be understood, even in the ancient world, only by someone with special knowledge. Signs are based not on miracles, but on the striking. It must be striking for a person to notice something which remains hidden. Interpretation requires 'expert knowledge'.

3. Between the sign and what is signified there is frequently an analogy
The signs at the deaths of rabbis 'are related to the style and importance of the particular rabbi, his principal activity and achievement. In the case

---

[59] S.V. McCasland, 'Portents in Josephus and the Gospels', *JBL* 51 (1932), 323-35, put forward the interesting view that the signs of the fall of Jerusalem were originally treated as apocalyptic signs and only secondarily, *ex eventu*, applied to the historical events (see esp. 330ff.) In the process, Josephus transferred the signs of the Messiah to Vespasian.
[60] Bultmann, *HST*, 245.

of rabbis who fought against paganism, there would be an event which signified victory over idols: statues or images or the temple of the idols would be destroyed, etc.'[61] The destruction of Jerusalem was preceded by symbolic intimations of the disaster: a star like a sword stood over the city, chariots and armed hosts appeared in the sky and a deranged man shouted all year, 'Woe upon Jerusalem!' (Jos. bell. VI, 5, 3).

Signs occur in the New Testament too, especially in biographical relation to the birth and death of Jesus. The star over Bethlehem and the darkness at the crucifixion frame the life of Jesus. These signs are not independent events, but have their significance only in connection with the birth and death of Jesus. They occur spontaneously, are striking and yet ambiguous (only the centurion recognises the signs at the crucifixion as evidence of the executed man's divine status). In the tearing of the Temple curtain there is an analogy between the miraculous event and the event signified: the dead man ended the old religion, or the mystery enshrouding the life of Jesus has been stripped away.

4. Rescue Miracles

Among rescue miracles we include, not only stories of rescue at sea, but also the freeing of prisoners (Acts 12.1ff.; 16.16ff.). Both groups of miracle stories are concerned with the overcoming of hostile forces, defeating the power of nature or the state. The fact that the two groups present similar images and themes shows how little justification there is for a division of miracles into a natural and a human domain. Rescue miracles include both object domains. They differ from exorcisms in that the miracles are performed on material objects, wind, waves, ships, chains, prison doors. The closeness of the two genres is shown by the command to be silent – typical of exorcisms – given to the raging sea (Mk 4.39), though this does not justify assuming that hostile demonic forces are at work everywhere. What appeals to us in rescue miracles is in fact that they give us some notion of the victory over dull, 'mindless', purely physical violence. In this section we shall discuss three motifs. The first is common to all rescue miracles, and the second and third appear alternatively, irrespective of whether the miracle is a sea rescue or a release miracle.

1. The situation of distress and the petition

Descriptions of distress at sea occur in other genres,[62] especially in the ancient novel. Typical features include the following: the storm makes it impossible to see the sky, water crashes into the ship, the

---

[61] P. Fiebig, *Jüdische Wundergeschichten des neutestamentlichen Zeitalters*, 1911, 60.
[62] Cf. the texts collected in H. Conzelmann, *Die Apostelgeschichte*, 1963, 151ff.

crew tries to jettison the cargo. The situation appears hopeless (Acts 27.20; Aristid., *Serapis hymn* 33); there are cries for help (*Homeric Hymns* 33.8ff.): from the bows the crew invoke the Dioscuri and promise to sacrifice white lambs. Aelius Aristides prays to Asclepius (*Or.* 3); the disciples turn to the sleeping Jesus: 'Teacher, do you not care if we perish?' (Mk 4.38). In Jewish rescue miracles in particular, prayer in distress at sea was given significant theological form. The pleas of the Jews to the true God are more powerful than the prayers of the Gentiles, even the prayer of a Jewish child overlooked at the beginning (j. Berakoth IX, 1). In the story of Jonah the storm is a sign of judgment. Jonah, the prophet who is fleeing from God, is discovered by lot and sacrificed to the waves. This connection of guilt and punishment also appears in another Jewish rescue miracle.

> Rabban Gamaliel too was a passenger in a ship when the raging sea rose against him to drown him. And he said, I think this can only be on account of Rabbi Eliezer ben Hyrcanus (that is, because I helped to have him banished). So he got to his feet and said, Lord of the world, it is revealed and known before you that I did not do this for my glory or for the glory of my father's house, but for your glory, so that disputes in Israel should not increase. And the sea abated from its violence (b. Baba mezia 59b).[63]

The story in its present form implies an error on God's part, as though he had brought an innocent person into danger. Perhaps the guilt of the man endangered at sea was originally much clearer, and his prayer would then have been a confession of guilt to appease God.[64]

In a similar way to the rescues from distress at sea, release miracles include a vivid description of the prisoners' plight.[65] They are bound; it is night;[66] guards make any thought of release seem absurd. In this situation the prisoners pray: προσευχόμενοι ὕμνουν (Acts 16.25), and the prayers may be magical in character – we need think only of the magical papyri with their numerous door spells.[67] Even Origen (*contra Cels.* II, 34) knows of magicians (*goētai*) 'who undo bonds and open doors with spells'. Apollonius

---

[63] P. Fiebig, *Jüdische Wundergeschichten*, 33.

[64] A. Schlatter, *Das Wunder in der Synagoge*, 1912, 71, also thinks that a confession of guilt might have been expected.

[65] On the release miracles, cf. O. Weinreich, 'Türöffnung'.

[66] Acts 5.7ff.; 12.3ff.; 16.9ff.; Artapanus 52ff.

[67] Cf. O. Weinreich, 'Türöffnung', 342ff; R. Reitzenstein, *Hellenistische Wundererzählungen*, 120-22.

of Tyana, suspected of being a magician, can use that very suspicion as an argument against tying him up: 'If you think I am a magician, why are you tying me up? Or if you are tying me up, why do you say I am a magician?' (*vita Apoll.* VII, 34).

2. The epiphany which brings rescue

Rescue from distress at sea may take place (especially in Greek and Hellenistic accounts) through an epiphany of the god. The Dioscuri appear when the situation is desperate: οἱ δ' ἐξαπίνης ἐφάνησαν (*Hom. Hymns* 33.12). The visual basis for this idea is probably the sudden appearance of the stars when the clouds and storm have cleared: their light is taken as the appearance of the gods, the Dioscuri, Asclepius or Serapis.[68] For Serapis, see the description of a rescue by Aelius Aristides:[69]

'O ruler of the most beautiful of all cities, on which you look down as it yearly celebrates the festival in your honour, O light shared by all which lately shone so brightly upon us: then, as the sea began to roar and towered on all sides, and nothing could be seen but the threat of doom and our destruction seemed certain, at that moment you lifted your hands to prevent it, you lightened the veiled sky and let us see land and enabled us to land, so against our expectation (παρ' ἐλπίδα) that ourselves refused to believe it (πίστις) as we set foot on dry land' (*Hymn to Serapis*, 33).

Rescue from the sea and epiphany are also associated in the New Testament in Mk 6.45ff.: Jesus appears, walking across the sea, in a form which creates consternation. In my view attempts to separate rescue at sea and epiphany are mistaken, as is shown by the comparative parallels which link the two.

As with rescue at sea, so in the release of prisoners epiphanies occur. A supernatural being appears to release the captives. In the release miracles from the circle of Dionysus we have λύσει μ' ὁ δαίμων αὐτός, ὅταν ἐγὼ θέλω (Euripides, *Bacchae* 498). In Acts there are two instances of the release of prisoners with angelophanies (5.17-25; 12.3-19).

3. The passenger or prisoner who rescues his companions

Rescue through an epiphany of a god comes from outside. In many rescue miracles, however, there is no such intervention: in these cases the rescue depends on the numinous power of a person

---

[68] On the appearance of stars as appearances of gods, cf. E. Pax, ΕΠΙΦΑΝΕΙΑ, 15f.
[69] Translation from A. Höfler, *Der Sarapishymnus des Aelios Aristeides*, 1935, 20. See the detailed commentary, 111-13.

present in the ship or prison. The two variants of the motif are combined when the passenger who performs the rescue is also a prisoner (like Paul in Acts 27). Generally, however, his status is more easily recognisable. We may think of Caesar and his remark on a dangerous voyage: 'Fear nothing. You carry Caesar, and Caesar's luck goes with you' (Plutarch, *Caes.* 38; similarly Dio Cassius, XLI, 46). Apollonius also possesses this power of protection, and people struggle to sail on his ship: 'They all believed that this man was more powerful than storm or fire or the most dangerous things, and wanted to come and asked to be allowed to join the ship' (*vita Apoll.* IV, 13). Occasionally the saving passenger is at first unrecognised and obscure. No-one believes that this person could have that power. In j. Berakoth IX, 1 it is a child overlooked at the beginning, in Acts 27.14ff. none other than Paul, a prisoner in chains. In a parallel tradition to *vita Apoll.* IV, 13 Apollonius leaves the ship with the words, 'Let us leave this ship, for it would not be good to sail in it to Achaea' (*vita Apoll.* V, 18). Hardly anyone heeds his words and the ship sinks. Inattention to the θεῖος ἀνήρ is revenged. Lucian parodies the motif of the passenger who saves: Peregrinus, ὁ θαυμαστὸς καὶ θανάτου κρείττων εἶναι δοκῶν, howls with the women during the storm (*Peregr.* 43; cf. also *Demon.* 35).[70] Just as the walking on the lake in the New Testament was one of the miracles in which rescue took place through an epiphany, the stilling of the storm belongs to the motif of the passenger who saves and protects. Jesus is asleep. The disciples fight without him against wind and waves. The threatening situation may once have been portrayed by the sinking of the 'other boats' (4.36), which now have no function in the narrative.[71] Be that as it may, the message of the story is that the mere presence of Jesus is reason enough to feel safe from danger.

The release of prisoners may also be brought about by the super-human power of the prisoners themselves. When Pentheus throws Dionysus into the dungeon (Eurip. *Bacchae* 519ff.), Dionysus shakes the palace in which he is a prisoner and makes it collapse (585ff.). A god can release himself, and the ability to

---

[70] H.J. Ebeling, *Das Messiasgeheimnis und die Botschaft des Marcus-Evangelisten*, 1939, 152, has correctly identified the meaning of the motif of the passenger who protects. H.D. Betz, *Lukian*, 172, has the two theme variants in mind when he writes that the rescue is brought about 'by a "divine being", if not by the gods themselves. . . .'

[71] G. Schille, 'Die Seesturmerzählung Markus 4,35-41', *ZNW* 56 (1965), 30-40, regards the other boats as evidence of an originally larger group of witnesses and claims that Mark has transformed the miracle into one for the disciples. On the other hand, it is hard to imagine seeing another boat's distress in a storm from one's own boat without being in danger oneself.

release oneself may even become proof of divinity (*vita Apoll.* VII, 38). A case comparable with this sort of release of prisoners is the freeing of Silas and Paul in Philippi. Luke undoubtedly believes that God saved the pair by his intervention but, probably deliberately, he seeks an ambiguity. The gaoler falls down before the pair and addresses them as κύριοι, who have power to save (Acts 16.30) – a welcome cue for Paul to tell the Gentiles about the true κύριος who alone can save. Even without the assumption of direct literary connections between Acts and Euripides' *Bacchae* (such as O. Weinreich believed he had discovered),[72] the relation in content between the two cases of release of captives is undeniable: in both stories the liberation is due ultimately to the numinous power of the prisoners.

To summarise, rescues from distress at sea and cases of the release of prisoners show comparable motifs and features. In both the rescue is a striking and visible event. Pleas for help beg for it and epiphanies introduce the change of fortune. The rescue is brought about by manifestations of numinous power. Consequently both groups of miracle stories, sea rescue miracles and liberation miracles can be combined as rescue miracles.

5. Gift Miracles

Whereas in rescue miracles threatening dangers are averted and a person is plucked from disaster, the characteristic feature of gift miracles is that they make material goods available in surprising ways; they provide larger-than-life and extraordinary gifts, food transformed, increased, richly available. They could also be called material culture miracles, since they always illustrate problems of human labour, the problem of how to get food to live and wine to feast.[73] Among the features of this material are the spontaneity of the miraculous action, the unobtrusiveness of the miracle itself and the emphasis on the final demonstration.

1. The spontaneity of the miraculous action
This is shown by the fact that gift miracles are never initiated by requests, but always by an act of the miracle-worker. In form

---

[72] 'Türöffnung', 335ff.: the traditions of Acts were 'lightly revised for its editing in book form under the literary influence of Euripides' *Bacchae*' (340).

[73] A. Smitmans, *Das Weinwunder von Kana*, 1966, 31, uses the term 'luxury miracle', as does A. Oepke, *TDNT* III, 207, (Eng. trl.: 'miracles of an extravagant kind'), who evinces a strongly pejorative attitude to the term.

critical terms, the motif 'initiative of the miracle-worker' has particularly strong ties with gift miracles. Although the feeding stories about Elijah and Elisha presuppose 'crying' distress, the victims of hunger do not approach the prophets with pleas: there is only a resigned complaint (1 Kings 17.12). No help is expected from the wonder-workers. In Mk 8.3 the bread miracle is indeed motivated by the idea that without food the crowd would grow weak on their return journey – but Jesus himself expresses this idea; it is not suggested to him in a request. Where a request is made to him, as in Mk 6.35ff., the content is not related to the miracle. On the contrary, because there is no food, Jesus is asked to send the crowd away. The subsequent misunderstanding emphasises the fact that no-one expects a miracle from Jesus. In the miracle of the fishes, too, the initiative comes from Jesus. No-one has asked him to alter the situation resulting from the unsuccessful fishing trip. The unexpected character of gift miracles is illustrated by a bread miracle from the rabbinic tradition:

His [Ḥanina ben Dosa's] wife used to heat the oven every sabbath eve and used to throw fuel in to make smoke because of the shame (that is, because she was ashamed before her neighbours). She had this spiteful neighbour. She (the neighbour) said, 'This is odd, when I know they have nothing, nothing at all. What does all this mean?' She (the neighbour) went and knocked on the door [of Ḥanina's house]. She [Ḥanina's wife] was ashamed and went into the room. Then a miracle took place for her [Ḥanina's wife]: she saw the oven full of bread and the trough full of dough. Then she [the neighbour] said to her, 'Bring a shovel. Your loaves are beginning to burn.' And she [Ḥanina's wife] said to her, 'That's why I went in' (b. Taanit. 24bf.).

Only in one place is there perhaps a request. In Jn 2.3-4 Mary says to Jesus, 'They have no wine.' It would, however, be a mistake to presume that this is a request simply because requests appear as an integral part of other miracle stories;[74] they are absent in comparable gift miracles, which are the closest parallels. It could be that Mary is thinking of a perfectly natural way of dealing with the embarrassment – like the disciples at the feeding miracle – though the reader is naturally intended to hear more in her words.[75]

---

[74] As does Bultmann, *The Gospel of John*, 1971, 116.
[75] For the history of the interpretation of the remark see Smitmans, *Weinwunder*, 15ff.

2. The unobtrusiveness of the miraculous event

This is all the more remarkable because gift miracles are much less likely than exorcisms and healings and yet are described in less 'miraculous' terms. How the miracle takes place is left unclear. The multiplication of the bread and the transformation of the wine have to be inferred. The cause of the miracle remains obscure. There is no reference of any sort to miraculous technique, to any manipulation, to any miraculous words. True, Jesus gives thanks over the loaves, but so does every Jewish father at a meal. The instruction to distribute the bread or to fill the jars with water or to put out to sea is not a miraculous formula any more than Elijah's prophecy, 'The jar of meal shall not be spent . . .' (1 Kings 17.14), a prophecy which could be understood in completely natural terms. Compositionally, this unobtrusiveness of the miraculous event is due to the absence of almost all central motifs. The scene-setting touches are supplemented by other preparatory details (thanksgiving, distribution) and followed immediately by the announcement of the miracle. The motifs connected with the miraculous action are missing.[76]

3. The absence of the central motifs

This also explains the stress on the demonstration. Because the miraculous event is unobtrusive, the reader has to infer it from its consequences, the abundance of bread, fish and oil and the quality of the wine (The explanation of the famous 'wine rule' probably lies in the context: it is an answer to the accusation that the hosts have watered the wine, relying on the fact that the guests, who had already been drinking, would not notice). The lack of vividness and obviousness of the miraculous event can be explained. In my opinion, the reason for them is that in the case of rule miracles, exorcisms, healings and rescue miracles there are analogies in experience, procedures relating to divine rulings, exorcists, doctors in whose activity significant gestures and techniques could be studied; in the case of gift miracles this visual basis must have been lacking. We know of no individuals who offered to multiply loaves or turn water into wine. We know of no magical techniques for producing such miracles.[77] Had they existed, traces of them would

---

[76] This 'reticence' with regard to the miraculous event will be misinterpreted if it is treated as an indication of a historical tradition, as does V. Taylor, *The Gospel According to St Mark*, 1952, 321.

[77] But cf. PGM I, 103f. The 'assistant', at the magician's command, brings 'fire, he brings water, he brings wine, bread and any other food you want.'

certainly have been preserved in the gift miracles. Had there been miracle-workers who promised such feats, there would certainly have been descriptions of requests for their help. Exorcists could be sent for, doctors appealed to, but miracle-workers able to multiply or transform natural products had to appear of their own. Gift miracles lack the background of ordinary activities which gives vividness to other miracles. No type of miracle story derives more from imagination than these: none has so much lightness, so much of the quality of a wish or an unaffected fairy-tale.

Since gift miracles do not arise out of any ordinary activity, they are also not transmitted to provide a narrative background to such an activity (as may be presumed to have happened with exorcisms and healings). Since in the case of gift miracles there is no such activity to give them a meaning, deeper meanings are very soon found in them: they are allegorised. The miraculous draught of fishes is treated as an allegory of mission, the feeding is related to the eucharist, and so on. Despite such early allegorisation, these miracles can be understood only if the longing they express is taken seriously, the longing for unlimited quantities of bread, fish and wine, in short for food for a multitude; they can be understood only if we do not feel ourselves above the longing for the goods of this world to be available without toil and in sufficient quantity. The gift miracles also particularise the experience of a boundary: situations of material want are transcended and a particular negativity is overcome.

6. Rule Miracles

Rule miracles seek to reinforce sacred prescriptions. They may be classified according as they justify rules, reward behaviour in accordance with the rules or punish behaviour contrary to the rules.

Justificatory rule miracles are exemplified by the disputes about the sabbath. In these the absolute obligation to help others prevails over ritual commandments, authority to forgive sins is confirmed (Mk 2.1ff.), inner freedom from the Temple tax demonstrated (Mt 17.24ff.). A classic example of miracles which confirm rules is provided by various miracles of Rabbi Eliezer. Eliezer – by contrast with other rabbis – had pronounced an oven clean, but his more liberal attitude was not accepted and he was banished.

They wanted to tell R. Eliezer of the ban pronounced against him. They said, 'Who will go and tell him?' R. Akiba said, 'I will go and tell him.' He went to him and said, 'Teacher, your fellows excommunicate you.' He [R. Eliezer] took him outside and said, 'Carob tree, carob tree, if the halakah is as they say, be uprooted.' And it was not uprooted. [Then] he said, 'If the halakah is as I say, be uprooted.' And it was uprooted. [He said,] 'If the halakah is as they say, may the tree return into the ground.' It did not return. [Then he said,] 'If the halakah is as I say, may it return.' And it returned. (J. Moed III, 1; parallel version: b. Baba Mezia 59b).[78]

The version quoted shows the same structure as the New Testament rule miracles. A question of law is presented for discussion in the form of an alternative. The miracle decides. It seems to me obvious that the underlying situation is that of a divine ruling. In the miracle the god supports a decision on a rule or law – at least in the view of Rabbi Eliezer, though this was not accepted. Rule-justifying miracles are in fact in sharp contradiction to Judaism, which (particularly after AD 70) sought to organise its life round interpretations of the traditional law. Miracles and revelations, in this view, were a charismatic *revelatio continua*, which could in theory have challenged the legitimacy of tradition itself, and they were accordingly excluded from the establishment of halakah rules by the rabbinic principle, 'Miracles are not to be mentioned.' A. Guttmann traces the origin of this principle, which is not found until after Rabbi Eliezer, to his banning, and makes a good case for the existence in the backround of a more serious problem than the case of the oven – the struggle with Christianity, which used miracles to establish its legitimacy. Rabbi Eliezer may even have been suspected of being a Christian himself; at least he was imprisoned for a time by the Romans as an alleged Christian (b. AbZarah 16b). In my view there is much to support Guttmann's thesis: 'The decline of miracle as regards influencing law and practice goes parallel with the growth of Christianity.'[79]

A rule-confirming miracle from Hellenistic sources is Pythagoras' fish miracle. Pythagoras is said to have predicted the exact number of fish caught in a net:[80]

'And an amazing thing happened: not a single fish which remained out of the water while the counting took place died as long as he was there. Many of the bystanders remembered the previous lives their souls had lived before being bound to their present bodies' (Porphyry, *vita Pyth.* 25).

The theme, which is also found in the New Testament, is used to emphasise an anecdotal point: the fish had to remain alive because

---

[78] There is a detailed comparison of the two versions in A. Guttmann, 'The Significance of Miracles for Talmudic Judaism', *HUCA* 20 (1947), 363-406.

[79] A. Guttmann, 'Significance', 405, followed by M. Hengel, *The Charismatic Leader and his Followers*, 1981, 41, n. 14.

[80] On the miracle cf. L. Bieler, Θεῖος Ἀνήρ, 1967, 105-08.

souls of dead people could have been living in them. The function of the miracle is to confirm Pythagorean vegetarian rules and to demonstrate the doctrine of the transmigration of souls. In this case, admittedly, the rule is contained only indirectly in the doctrine.

In *rule miracles of reward* the validity of the rule has already been established. Anyone who observes it is miraculously saved and protected. A New Testament example is Acts 28.1-6. Paul, after being saved from shipwreck, is bitten by a viper. Everyone expects him to die, and thinks that an evil-doer has finally been overtaken by his punishment: πάντως φονεύς ἐστιν ὁ ἄνθρωπος (28.4). When Paul, to the amazement of all, remains alive, the conclusion is that he is innocent, indeed, a god. Here too the underlying situation is the divine ruling. The question for debate was 'Guilty or innocent?' The miracle decides. Superimposed on this alternative, however, is the idea that immunity to snake-bites is a sign of the θεῖος ἀνήρ and charismatic (cf. Mk 16.18; Lk 10.19).

Immunity to snake-bites also occurs in the Talmud rule miracles of reward.[81] The principle, 'Righteousness delivers from death' (Prov 10.2), is demonstrated in b. Shab. 156b by two examples of preservation from the effects of snake-bite. We quote one of the examples. The Gentile scholar Avlet believes in astrology; stars determine human fate. Schmuel, his Jewish friend, denies this:

> From Schmuel too we learn that no constellation has any importance for Israel. Schmuel and Avlet were sitting there as some people were going to a marsh. Avlet said to Schmuel, 'That man will go and not return; a snake will bite him and he will die.' Schmuel said to him, 'If he i a son of Israel, he will go and return.' As they sat there he went and returned. Then Avlet stood up, threw his burden from his shoulders and found a snake in it, lying divided, in two pieces. Schmuel said to him, 'What have you done?' He said to him, 'Every day we used to collect the bread into a basket and eat it. Today there was one of us who had no bread and was ashamed. I said to them, "I will go and collect the bread." When I reached him I pretended to take bread from him so that he would not have to be ashamed.' He said to him, 'You have done a good deed.' Then Schmuel went out

---

[81] On the rabbinic miracles cf. P. Fiebig, *Jüdische Wundergeschichten,* passim and the criticisms of him in the studies of A. Schlatter, *Das Wunder in der Synagoge*; M. Smith, *Tannaitic Parallels to the Gospel,* 1951, 81-84. See also I. Heinemann, 'Die Kontroverse über das Wunder im Judentum der hellenistischen Zeit.' *Jubilee Volume in Honor of Prof. B. Heller,* 1941, 170-91. On snake-bite miracles in particular, cf. Dibelius, *TG* 135f.

and taught: Righteousness delivers from death. And not just from unnatural death, but from death itself.

Here again an alternative is clearly presented, belief in astrology or a belief in moral retribution. The miracle decides. It is a divine ruling. Righteousness frustrates a prophecy of woe. In b. Ber. 33a we find the principle, 'Observance of the law decides life and death,' raised to the level of a general theory:

> The rabbis used to teach as follows. It happened that a water-snake lived in a certain place which used to injure people. They came and told Rabbi Ḥanina ben Dosa. He said to them, 'Show me its nest.' They showed him its nest. He placed his heel over the opening of the nest and the snake came out and bit him; the water-snake died. He put it on his shoulder, brought it into the school and addressed them, 'See, my children, it is not the water-snake which kills; sin kills.' From that time they used to say, 'Woe to the man who meets a water-snake and woe to the water-snake that meets Rabbi Ḥanina ben Dosa.'

Here it is not a particularly good deed which gives immunity, but sinlessness in general; it is a sort of charism. One more particularly attractive rule miracle of reward is worth telling from the Talmud. After the Roman government had banned phylacteries, a pious Jew was discovered with them. He took them into his hand to hide them. When asked what he had in his hand, he replied, 'Dove's wings.' When he opened his hand, the phylacteries had indeed turned into dove's wings, for 'As the wings on a dove protect it, so do the commandments laid on Israel protect her.' (Shab. 49a).

More numerous than rule miracles of reward are *rule miracles of punishment*. In enforcing rules both ancients and moderns rely more on fear of punishment than on encouragement through praise. It is therefore all the more noticeable that punishment miracles are almost entirely absent from the New Testament. The only example is the story of Ananias and Saphira (Acts 5.1-11), in which a condemnation is confirmed by a miracle. The proximity to the divine ruling is again unmistakable. The story of the withered fig tree (Mk 11.12-14, 20-21) may also be treated as a punishment miracle, even if it remains a mystery what rule the fig tree is supposed to have broken.

A series of punishment miracles is recorded from Epidaurus (and some in Lucian).[82] In Epidaurus their function is to enforce the rules of the temple area. Among the actions forbidden are looking into the sanctuary, expressing doubt, refusing to perform a

---

[82] Cf. H.D. Betz, *Lukian*, 177-79.

vow, keeping thank-offerings. The inscriptions in which punishment miracles reiterate these rules take the place of prohibitory signs: Aeschines, who looked into the sanctuary without permission, loses his sight on pointed stakes (11). An unbeliever, who mocked the healings certified by the inscriptions, is called 'Apistos' (Unbeliever) after being healed himself (3). Amphimnestus failed to carry out his vow to give a tenth of his catch of fish to Asclepius and was attacked by fishes as a punishment (47). Pandarus did not deliver Echedorus' thank-offering for his cure and as a punishment received Echedorus' disease in addition to his own (7). Every case is an example of the *ius talonis*;[83] the punishment matches the offence; for example looking at forbidden things brings loss of the eyes. This correspondence gives the punishment miracles an automatic quality. While Asclepius may in the last resort be behind them, he is notably less prominent than in the case of the healing miracles. Often the punishment is lifted, and here we may perhaps speak of 'educative miracles'.[84]

Rule miracles involving punishment are frequent in the Talmud.[85] A judge who breaks the rules of procedure dies unexpectedly (Mek. Mishp. 20), as does a pupil who ventures to decide a halakah in the presence of his teacher (Erub. 63a), or a Roman who pushes a rabbi out of the way in a lavatory (Ber. 62b). Sudden death is the punishment for a rabbi who contradicts an older rabbi (Sifre Num 28, 26) or relaxes the rule of the seventh year without authority (j. Sheb. 38d). The daughter of the emperor Hadrian became a leper because she quoted a biblical text in a mocking challenge to God (Ḥul 60a).

Whereas in the Epidaurus punishment miracles we found a 'moderate' *ius talonis* (mitigated by the lifting of penalties, which reduces what seems to us the unjust severity of any *ius talionis*), in the Jewish rule miracles the issue is almost always one of life or death. Breaches of the law lead to death; observance of the law preserves from death. The law does not chastise; it kills. This seems to us archaic and inhuman, especially in the case of unimportant transgressions, but is a sign of great seriousness about the observance of the divine will: in the presence of God the issue is one of life or death. The Greek punishment miracles are more humane, more educative, and that is certainly no accident.

It has already been mentioned that in the Jesus tradition pun-

[83] O. Weinreich, *AH*, 56, n. 1.
[84] R. Herzog, *Epidauros*, 123ff.
[85] M. Dibelius, *TG*, 144ff.

ishment miracles in the strict sense do not occur. However, the rule-confirming miracles are comparable to the extent that in them too a rule is broken. After the accusation, 'He is blaspheming,' we expect, on the basis of the rabbinic parallels, that the evil-doer should be punished. The opposite occurs: in the miracle God places himself on the side of the rule-breaker. This is also related to the absoluteness of the divine will: healing or not healing on the sabbath means life or death. The difference is that this absoluteness appears, not as a punishing and threatening power, but as help and liberation, as the authority to break away from rules. Here, from within a mythical world, the 'call to freedom' begins to make itself heard.

The New Testament rule miracles are usually included among the apophthegms. This classification could be justified on the ground that the breaking of the sabbath also takes place without a miracle (Mk 2.23ff.). Does this make it an accident when it is associated with a miracle? Is it an accident that miracles have the power to enforce rules? Of course not. Even today we always feel a deep uncertainty about rules, their legitimacy and our efforts to keep them. For the people of the ancient world the problem was even more disturbing. Every mistake, every failure, involved sacred power, produced ominous consequences. Uncertainty in the area of rules took the form of danger from numinous power. In miracles this power indicates what is pleasing to it and what behaviour it abhors. Take the healing of the paralytic. The scribes' anger stems from anything but petty meanness: where God's sovereignty is attacked, the basis of the world order, the connection between guilt and punishment, is challenged. Only the realisation that in miracles God himself takes the side of rule-breaking actions removes the uncertainty and leads to praise of God (Mk 2.12). There is no external narrative arrangement when miracles form the climax of these stories, but an internal link between rule and miracle, word and deed (even if Mk 2.5-10 should happen to be a secondary interpolation).

But if the rule demands a legitimating miracle, the miracle also demands legitimation. The normative force of fact, of the ordinary world of meaning and its expectations, must be transcended. Approaching the miracle-worker often appears in the New Testament as something illegitimate. Gentiles come; outcasts come to the fore. And there is a genuine question. By what right may a person approach the sacred, that alone can neutralise the boundary? Are we not too deeply attached to and involved with the attitudes of the ordinary world: 'Depart from me, for I am a sinful man, O Lord' (Lk 5.8; cf. 7.6). Not just the rule, but also the crossing of the boundary, demands legitimation. On the other hand, the illegitimate is an essential part of it, if legitimacy is measured by the attitudes of the ordinary world; one can even ask whether the breaking of a rule may not be a psychological prerequisite for healings. Breaking taboos produces a psychological tension which may favour physical healing. This is why healings in Epidaurus take place in a tabooed sanctuary and in the New Testament on the tabooed sabbath. In my opinion it is very likely that Jesus and the primitive community performed healings on the sabbath.

The recognition of rule miracles as a genre owes much to M. Dibelius, who called the rabbinic miracle stories centred on rules 'theodicy legends', but in fact meant what is meant by the term 'rule miracles': 'The miracle is not told for its own sake, but for the benefit of the matter for which the Talmud stands, viz. *proclaiming a divine law* by which men must live.'[86] The theodicy problem, however, is only one aspect of rule miracles. The question of theodicy starts from life as it is and asks whether it conforms to the rule. Many of the miracles, on the other hand, begin directly with the rule and then consider the relevant human behaviour. Others take the rule itself as their subject and ask, 'What is sacred?' 'What is forbidden?' The term 'rule miracle' covers all these aspects and, in particular, has the advantage that it can be applied to non-Jewish miracle stories. It is correct to say that the Jewish rule miracles in particular are prompted by the question of theodicy. The pressing and disturbing character of this problem, innocent suffering, the fact that history, both on the grand scale and in detail, does not move in accordance with the norms of justice, forms the boundary that is transcended in these miracle stories. They, however, are already on the other side of the boundary. They attempt to reinforce the conviction that righteousness delivers from death, that the rule is a strong protective force. They present a 'whole world', which will admit only indirectly the full depths of the world's ethical irrationality: where the miraculous is the source of the harmony between law and history, normality must be in a sorry state.

B. The Composition of the Themes

All the miracle stories have the same compositional structure. Nevertheless this structure can be varied. Our question is, do such variations coincide with different themes? For our purposes it is

---

[86] M. Dibelius, *TG*, 146. Most rabbinic miracles are about a rule, as is shown by the typology discussed in P. Fiebig, 'Neues zu den rabbinischen Wundergeschichten', *ZNW* 35 (1936), 308-09. What Dibelius (*TG*, 148ff.) called 'personal legends' also celebrate the pious person who keeps the rule. Instead of 'rule miracles' L. Delekat suggests the term 'authority miracles'. He would include both the person and the rule, and in this respect the suggestion is well worth pondering.

not absolutely necessary that it should be possible to assign a different compositional form to every theme. The question should be thought of instead as whether different compositional forms occur more or less at random across all the themes, or whether some have a greater probability of occurring in particular themes but not in others. Different compositional forms, that is, deviations from the normal composition, are the result of a marked stress on one of the main sections, that is to say of an accentuated realisation of expositional, central or final motifs which is frequently associated with a reduction of other compositional motif groups. Corresponding to the three main sections, we distinguish central-stressed, exposition-stressed and final-stressed compositional forms.

Centrally-stressed compositions are instanced in the narratives Mk 7.31ff.; 8.22ff. which are frequently described as miraculous. They lack an exposition. After the introduction the miraculous action follows on immediately with an indication of the scene. The action itself is stressed by the accumulation of central motifs (touching, therapeutic substances, gestures as in prayer, therapeutic words, or alternatively repeated gestures of healing). Nearly all the miracles from Epidaurus are centrally-stressed in this way: the emphasis is on the therapeutic process.

Exposition-stressed compositions can be divided according to two motifs prominent in the exposition:
i) Motifs of hindrance and faith predominate in the healings at a distance in Mk 7.24ff. and Mt 8.5ff. Here the exposition has become an independent narrative. The centre (the central motifs) are completely absent. The conclusion is no more than a brief reference to the successful healing (or exorcism).
ii) In rule miracles (Mk 2.1-12; 3.1-6; Lk 14.1-6) the expositional argument dominates the whole miracle story. A centre and conclusion are present, but the central and final motifs are subordinate to the expositional motif of 'argumentation'.

Final-stressed compositions may also be of different kinds according to the particular motifs stressed:
i) In gift miracles there is no real centre. Central motifs are barely realised, if we ignore the scene-setting. The miracle itself has to be inferred from the demonstration, and this must therefore be heavily emphasised in the narrative.
ii) In Mk 5.25ff. and Lk 17.11ff. the final stress is produced by the fact that expositional motifs of approach (hindrance and faith) appear only after the miracle. Here the first outward approach is

followed by a second, and it is only in this that the healed man breaks through the real barrier between himself and the miracle-worker.

iii) In some rule miracles the argument follows the miracle. In Lk 13.10-17 it is integrated into the miracle story, and the concluding acclamation formally rounds off the miracle and the debate. In Mt 12.22ff., on the other hand, the appended sayings destroy the framework of the miracle story: the wonder and acclamation separate the argument from the miracle. Here the miracle story is really (also) the introduction to an apophthegm.

Our conclusions can be summarised as follows: different compositional forms do not coincide with different themes, but they do have an affinity with particular themes. Gift miracles are always final-stressed, rule miracles either exposition-stressed or final-stressed. We can now also explain why miracles in which a companion of the miracle-worker becomes his opposite number have not been treated as a separate theme: these are exposition-stressed healings and exorcisms.

C. The Theme Field

A field analysis is based on various classifications of the miracle stories which have to be carried out independently of each other: by characters involved, by object fields, by the perspective within which the boundary is viewed and by the particular ways in which the boundary is crossed.

a) Characters

In our previous analysis of characters we found that any of the seven characters (or groups of characters) which appear may be the target of the miracle. In exorcisms this is the demon, in healings the sick person, in epiphanies the miracle-worker, in (sea) rescue miracles the disciples, in gift miracles the crowd, in rule miracles the opponents. Only the miracle stories in which sick or possessed people are represented by a companion (Mt 8.5ff.; Mk 7.24ff.) do not form an independent theme, but belong partly to healings and partly to exorcisms. Their particularity is their exposition-stressed arrangement, which gives prominence to precisely those motifs which are unaffected by the distinction between exorcisms and healings. This gives us six themes (and a sub-group located in two themes). On the basis of the organisation of the characters in the form-critical field they can be subdivided again: the demon, the sick person and the miracle-worker are 'normally' principal actors, that is, when they appear they are opposite numbers, whereas the disciples, the crowd and the opponents are usually subsidiary characters but do have leading roles in some miracle stories. We can thus identify two sets, exorcisms, healings and epiphanies on the one hand and rescue, gift and rule miracles on the other.

b) Object fields

In this classification we use Bultmann's division of miracles into the natural and the human field, but are forced to modify it considerably. For good reasons the concept of the nature miracle in particular has often been regarded as unsatisfactory. Two considerations are relevant here:

i) The contrast between exorcisms and nature miracles fails because there are both motifs of exorcism in nature miracles and small nature miracles in exorcisms:[87] the demonstrations of the demon's departure into non-human objects and animals. There are also exorcisms which take place entirely in nature, as when a demon is expelled from a house (Lucian, *Philops.* 31) or banned from certain times (b. Pesaḥim 112b; 113a). Exorcisms, in other words, fall between the natural and the human sphere. We cannot, as Bultmann does, contrast them with nature miracles as a sub-group of healings.

ii) There are also difficulties with the term 'nature' miracle. Behind this category may lie the distinction between possible and impossible miracles, as K. Tagawa believes[88] – an inappropriate criterion. A more important fact is that bread, wine and oil are not simply nature, but the results of human processing of natural products. The same is true of the fish miracle. This is not a miracle performed on fish, but a miracle of fishing; human labour has a greater than usual success. 'Culture miracles' would therefore be a much more appropriate term.

A modification is necessary if the division of miracles into a human and a natural sphere is to be made fruitful. The real contrast is not between nature and human beings, but between things and persons: the demons are persons and cultural products are things. We thus obtain two object-fields according as a thing or a person is miraculously changed. Rule miracles belong to the miracles concerned with things. It is always a person who is healed (except in Mt 17.24ff.), but, as Bultmann rightly saw,[89] these miracles are totally subordinated to the theological point. The real miracle is the breaking down of an old sacred rule and the establishment of a new one. Once more, this gives us two sets, exorcisms, healings and epiphanies on the one hand and rescue, gift and rule miracles on the other. In person-oriented miracles principal actors always

[87] T.A. Burkill, 'Notion', 42.
[88] K. Tagawa, *Miracles*, 14.
[89] *HST*, 12, 209.

appear. The object-field and the target person coincide. There is an indirect movement towards the minor characters. In thing-oriented miracles, on the other hand, the object-field and the target persons are distinct: action cannot 'address themselves' to things, but only to persons. The persons indirectly addressed in the person-oriented miracles now come to the fore as a matter of internal necessity: a miracle which takes place in the material field – as opposed to a miracle in the personal field – addresses itself directly to them.

c) Perspectives

In the form-critical field of motifs we were able to distinguish three perspectives, the demonic, the human and the divine. In exorcisms the demonic perspective is paramount, in epiphanies the divine perspective, while healings take place in the sphere of human suffering. This division applies also to miracle stories concerned with things. It is clear that the stormy lake is imagined as dominated by demonic forces. A command to silence as in an exorcism can silence it (Mk 4.39). However, in rescue miracles the forces of the underworld do not appear, even indirectly, as personally active opposite numbers. Epiphanies have their counterpart in rule miracles: the former manifest the divine being, the latter the divine will. In both cases there is a revelation from the divine sphere. In contrast, gift miracles operate to a particular degree in the human world: eating, drinking, work and celebration define the problems they are concerned with. Their counterpart is healings. This gives us groups containing two miracle-stories: exorcisms and rescue miracles, healings and gift miracles, epiphanies and rule miracles. The structure of the mythical world, its division into demonic, human and divine, can be discovered in the form-critical field of themes.

d) Boundary crossings

A central theme of miracle stories is the crossing of the boundary of actual distress. The individual genres highlight different aspects of this boundary. In exorcisms a boundary is imposed on the possibilities of human life by hostile powers, demons and the raging sea. Human beings experience active opposition, are seen driven hither and thither by waves and demons; an outside force restricts the possibilities of their lives, robs them of their personalities and control of their activities, and threatens finally to destroy them physically. Healings and gift miracles illustrate the boundary or limit under another aspect. Here it is not opposition, but want, which restricts the possibilities of human life. Human beings lack the 'power' which gives health and life: they have no nourishment. Their labour seems vain. Here want constitutes the boundary. Human beings are not crushed but devoured. Finally, in epiphanies and rule miracles the central experience of the boundary is the hiddenness of the divine nature and will. Even in the world of miracle stories there is an awareness that human beings do not live by bread alone, that human blindness and rigidity destroy life from within. Even the person who has been healed is lost if he does not participate in the sacred. That is why he or she is told, 'Sin no more' (Jn 5.14).

The various different emphases on the boundary are matched by different ways of crossing the boundary. Demonic and natural forces must be subdued and brought to submission (cf. ὑπακούειν, Mk 1.27; 4.41). The transcending of the boundary or limit is a battle with an active opposing force. Want, on the other hand, can be overcome only by participation in power and resources, by the radiating of δύναμις and the giving of gifts. Here there is a positive communication of something. Human self-absorption and blindness is met by revelation: the divine being which was hidden becomes visible and recognisable. The important thing here is not that the Son of Man should have authority in heaven (which is concealed), but that this authority should become visible on earth (Mk 2.10). Revelation, participation and subjugation are the three fundamental ways in which the boundary can be crossed; illumination, wealth and liberation their goal, imprisonment, danger and want the boundary. In the crossing of the boundary the divine is always made manifest, but different aspects predominate, in epiphanies particularly the *majestatum*, in healings and gift miracles the *fascinosum*, in exorcisms and rescue miracles the *tremendum*, although a clear division of aspects in this context is impossible. We can now represent the theme field as follows:

	person-oriented	thing-oriented	
demonic perspective	exorcisms demon	rescue miracles disciples	threats/ subjugation
human perspective	healings sick person	gift miracles crowd	want/giving of power and gifts
divine perspective	epiphanies miracle-worker	rule miracles opponents	Being closed/ revelation
	principal actors	minor actors	

The form-critical field of miracle themes and motifs shows us sections of the structure of a bygone, mythical world of meaning, which reveals an amazing logic. Its literary forms are solidified actions in which reality is organised and interpreted. Miracle stories contain an interpretation of actual negativity as danger, want and self-absorption, and they are symbolic actions in which this negativity is transcended.

In conclusion we may briefly discuss the problem of definitely assigning genres to form-critical fields. Two of the genres discussed above are often not included among miracle stories. M. Dibelius discusses epiphanies under 'myth' and R. Bultmann treats rule miracles under 'apophthegms'. Although in my opinion it is useful to distinguish between myth and epiphany and apophthegms and rule miracles, it is also possible to describe the position as being one in which the two genres belong simultaneously to two form-critical fields, miracle stories and the genre of myths or apophthegms.

CHAPTER IV

GENRES

Within a synchronic analysis of the genre 'miracle story' the place of this genre in the field of related genres cannot be ignored. This is not to propose an atemporal tabulation of all the genres of popular tradition; we are dealing only with genres which have a historical connection with the primitive Christian miracle stories and therefore permit a synchronic analysis, that is, all the synoptic genres. Even if we cannot describe these genres in detail here,[1] it is nevertheless possible to indicate briefly the position of the miracle stories in the form-critical field of all synoptic genres – this is all the more necessary the more convinced one becomes that no literary unit can be described until its paradigmatic relations within its field have been specified. The synoptic genres can be divided first into didactic and narrative genres, the tradition of sayings and the narrative tradition. Teaching sets out to regulate and ponder human actions; narrative seeks to depict them. Teaching aims at universal validity; narrative portrays a series of more or less unique events. We thus get a polarity, 'normative universal validity v. successive particularity', which makes it possible, not only to distinguish two groups of genres from one another, but also to place them in order according to their nearness to or distance from these two poles. Between the purely narrative and purely didactic genres there are genres which in different ways partake of both, for example parables and apophthegms. Parables are teaching in narrative form, teaching through a story; apophthegms teaching narrated, a narrative which has as its subject the process of teaching. Parables are teaching in narrative form, apophthegms narratives with a didactic point. We accordingly obtain four basic genres

---

[1] Obviously, no attempt to 'catalogue' the synoptic genres is possible here. On the whole, Bultmann, *HST,* can be followed for this. In my view the distinctive features of parables and apophthegms need to be given more prominence. There are problems about the inclusion of apophthegms among the sayings of Jesus on the basis of the diachronic thesis that they largely derived from them. The basis of study must be the existing data. Synchrony and diachrony must be distinguished. Historical narrative and legend are included above in the single class of 'legendary accounts'.

of the synoptic tradition: sayings, parables, apophthegms and narratives, that is, pure teaching, narrative teaching, narrative with a didactic point and pure narrative.

However, each of these basic genres appears in two variants, which can in turn be contrasted. Both teaching and narrative can be concerned with the typical or the particular. Among sayings we can distinguish normative and kerygmatic. Normative sayings are all those which formulate what is universally valid in experience or action: wisdom sayings, legal sayings and community rules. These sayings are always concerned with rules of experience or action, with what is normal and typical, whether it is the rule which can be observed or the rule which should apply to action. In opposition to the normative sayings we can place all the kerygmatic sayings, that is, sayings which announce or proclaim a particular event, an event which has already taken place (I-sayings, Son of Man sayings) or is in the process of taking place or an event which is to take place in the future (prophetic and apocalyptic sayings). Kerygmatic sayings always contain a message about a particular. They interpret the present and unveil the future.

A parallel distinction exists among parables. Parables which are similes in the strict sense portray typical events. They appeal to general experience. Other synoptic parables, in contrast, portray a relevant particular case, which may even contain improbable, unique features. Apophthegms can be divided similarly. Most are attempts to present the teaching of Jesus, that is, not just what he said at a particular place, but his general teaching on the problems raised. In contrast to these discourses and disputes are the biographical apophthegms, which set out to portray a singular event in the life of Jesus – for example Peter's messianic confession.

In the same way we find two forms of purely narrative genres, miracle stories and legendary reports. Here the miracle stories recount typical elements of the life of Jesus. They can consequently be listed in summaries. They are interchangeable episodes and have no fixed position in the sequence of Jesus' life. Their order is fairly arbitrary. Not so the legendary reports. They deal with the birth, early life, temptation, the journey to Jerusalem and the Passion. They report events which have an unchangeable position in the temporal sequence of Jesus' life.

Accordingly, the form-critical field of the synoptic genres is dominated by two intersecting polarities, 'teaching – narrative' and 'typical – particular'. Of course, the two are not totally independent of one another: narrative genres are closer to the particular and didactic to the typical.

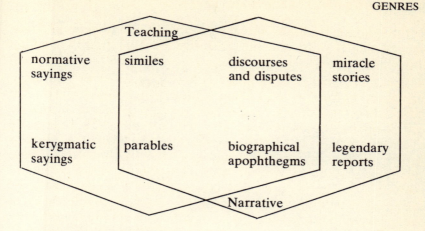

The form-critical field of synoptic genres

To this sketch of the paradigmatic structure of synoptic genres we may append a few remarks about their compositional structure. The synoptic tradition is contained in two major genres, collections of sayings (the sayings source, the Gospel of Thomas) and gospels (the synoptic gospels, the Fourth Gospel). These two major genres correspond to the two intersecting fields of synoptic genres. The didactic genres provide the basis for a compositional arrangement of the sort we find in the collections of sayings; the narrative genres form the basis for the composition we have in the gospels. In a study of a narrative genre only the second development is of interest. Accordingly, the thesis that the composition of the gospels is based on the narrative genres will be discussed in more detail in the second (diachronic) part of the book – though only the contribution of the miracle stories will be examined. Since in this case the origin of the major genre and its form – that is, the diachrony and synchrony of the gospel – are closely connected, the two approaches will also be used together.

Part Two

Miracle Stories as Reproduced Narratives (Diachronic Approach)

CHAPTER I

THE VARIATION OF THE MOTIFS

In the diachronic section of this study we shall consider diachronous modifications of various literary elements, motifs, individual narratives and their composition. In the case of the motifs we must select. We shall analyse two types of motifs, those which come at the beginning and end of miracle stories, i.e. are of major importance on the compositional level, and those which clearly display boundary marking and boundary crossing, the motifs of faith and silence. The principal importance of the second group is on a paradigmatic level.

A. An Introductory Motif:
the Coming of the Miracle-Worker

Synchronic description came to the conclusion that the introductions to the miracle stories typically display a two-part structure: first the miracle-worker appears and then the suppliants arrive. Diachronic investigation asks whether this situation is original. May the coming of the miracle-worker have been moved to its initial position for compositional reasons, to stress the linking function of the character who remains constant in all the pericopes? In the oldest stratum (Mk 1.40; 8.1; Mt 12.22=Q?)[1] there are introductions consisting of a single element. It is also generally assumed that Mark is responsible for the form of the beginnings of the pericopes. Let us summarise the arguments for and against the thesis that the first element in the introduction in Mark is the work of the redaction.

i) All references to the coming of Jesus may be assigned to the work of the Marcan redaction in so far as they presuppose the preceding pericope. Isolated pericopes are unlikely to have begun with the statement that Jesus came from somewhere (1.29; 5.21; 6.34, 45; 7.24, 31). On the other hand we could simply delete the reference

---

[1] Mt 12.22 could in this respect be more primitive than Mt 9.32 and Lk 11.14, since it is hard to imagine that the linking words would have been removed. Apart from this, C. Burger, *Jesus als Davidssohn*, 1970, 77-79, is right in regarding Mt 9.32ff. as the earlier version.

to the starting-point; this is not the same as recognising the whole motif as redactional.

ii) There is disagreement about place names. Bultmann regards them, with the exception of Mk 5.2 and 10.46, as 'links added by the redaction',[2] whereas H.R. Preuss regards them as mainly traditional.[3] In his view, only the Galilean setting derives from Mark: Mark used pericopes which originally had no setting to develop his biographical idea that Jesus had a period of activity in Galilee. K. Tagawa assumes that in his references to places Mark is always thinking of the places where he found his material,[4] and G. Schille even tries to postulate aetiological local traditions of the Christian communities on the basis of the place names.[5] The only point that interests us here is whether the texts contain specific indications of a redactional origin for the place names. This is the case in three miracle stories:

Mk 7.24-30 is about a woman who is 'a Syrophoenician by birth' (7.26). It could be argued that no-one would be described in this way in Syrophoenicia itself, but only abroad, and therefore that the story was not originally set in Syrophoenicia (T.A. Burkill).[6] However the group for whom the description 'Syrophoenician' is intended is not the people who appear in the miracle stories but the listeners to whom the miracle stories are addressed. Now the woman is first described as 'a Greek'. A Christian listener or a Jew could have taken this to mean a Hellenistic Jew. The addition, 'a Syrophoenician by birth', makes things clear: the woman is a pagan from the area. The place reference may therefore also be traditional. Another possibility is that 'a Greek' means here a member of the Hellenistic upper class of Syria, which consisted mainly of Greeks but also included many Hellenised natives. 'Greek' would then be a socio-cultural and 'Syrophoenician' an ethnic description.[7] In this case too there is no argument against a traditional place reference.

Mk 7.31 gives the impression of being a redactional transition. Places are mentioned which have already been mentioned (cf. 7.24; 3.8; 5.20). H.R. Preuss seems to me to have recognised the evangelist's intention

---

[2] *HST*, 241-42.

[3] H.R. Preuss, *Galiläa im Markus-Evangelium*, 1966.

[4] *Miracles*, 15-36. In contrast, G. Schille, *Topographie*, 133ff. sees 'references to places of origin' in Mt 9.26, 31, etc. In order to give the miracle stories an aetiological interpretation, he naturally has to regard the place names as traditional.

[5] G. Schille, *Anfänge der Kirche*, 1966.

[6] T.A. Burkill, 'The Syrophoenician Woman', *ZNW* 57 (1966), 23-37, cf. 35; 'The Historical Development of the Story of the Syrophoenician Woman' *NovTest* 9 (1967), 161-77. The authenticity of the place reference is defended by K.L. Schmidt, *Der Rahmen der Geschichte Jesu*, 2nd ed. 1919, 199.

[7] H. Bengtson, 'Syrien in der hellenistischen Zeit', in P. Grimal, *Der Hellenismus und der Aufstieg Roms*, 1965, 224-54, esp. 252.

correctly. He says that in order to support his Galilee idea Mark wanted to establish a link with Galilee for place references which did not fit into his overall idea. That he should then have gone outside Galilee again by placing the story in the Decapolis is unlikely.[8]

In Mk 8.22 a tension is frequently noted. Bethsaida was a city but in the subsequent story a village is mentioned. Therefore, it is said, the place reference must be secondary.[9] However, apart from the fact that this does not prove redactional origin, ἐξήνεγκεν . . . ἔξω τῆς κώμης implies the previous mention of a place.[10] The assumption of the argument is also false. Bethsaida, also known as Julias, was not a *polis* in the legal sense but the capital of a toparchy.[11] It is therefore not absolutely necessary to postulate a village called Bethsaida as well as the 'city' of that name[12] in order to maintain the originality of the place reference. At all events the miracle story itself as it is told implies a small place: although Jesus goes out of the village the crowd is still so close that the first thing the blind man sees is people. Narrative considerations alone would make ἔξω τῆς πόλεως inappropriate here.

This particular analysis leads to no clear conclusion. There are no compelling grounds for deleting. Since it is hardly possible to explain Jesus' complicated travels as the result of a coherent process of editing, in my view the arguments for a traditional origin prevail.

iii) In five miracle stories the narrative can hardly have begun with the appearance of the suppliants because Jesus is referred to by a pronoun which refers back to a previous mention of him by name: φέροντες πρὸς αὐτόν (Mk 2.3), ἰδὼν αὐτόν (5.23), ἀκούσασα . . . περὶ αὐτοῦ (7.25), φέρουσιν αὐτῷ (7.32), φέρουσιν αὐτῷ (8.22).

iv) In favour of the work of the Marcan redaction in the introductions, however, are motifs typical of Mark. The idea of secrecy is in

---

[8] H.R. Preuss, *Galiläa*, 41. Cf. also K.L. Schmidt, *Rahmen* 200: 'Anyone constructing a framework for a story would not do it in such a roundabout and complicated way.'

[9] Bultmann, *HST*, 213; E. Lohmeyer, *Markus*, 158-59. G. Schille, *Topographie*, 142 disputes this.

[10] K.L. Schmidt, *Rahmen*, 206. The point that 'secondary' does not automatically mean 'redactional' has rightly been emphasised by J. Roloff, *Kerygma*, 129. He believes he has found a reason for a secondary, pre-Marcan, setting of the story in Bethsaida: because of its hostility to Jesus, the unknown place was subsequently identified with the unrepentant city of Bethsaida (Mt 11.21f.). There is, however, no trace of any hostility from the place.

[11] Cf. A.H.M. Jones, *The Cities of the Eastern Roman Provinces*, 1937, 283: 'One, Julias, on the site of Bethsaida at the north end of the sea of Galilee, was not a city: it was merely the capital of the toparchy of Gaulanitis, which remained a "clima" down to the sixth century A.D.' See also A.N. Sherwin-White, *Roman Society and Roman Law in the New Testament*, 1963, 131.

[12] As does Schille, *Topographie*, 142.

the background in 2.1 and 7.24, and the motif of 'the crowd flocking' may also be Marcan.[13]

v) If the first element in each introduction is deleted, the result is beginnings of pericopae which have the same form as that preserved in 1.40 (cf. 1.23; 2.3; 5.25; 7.32; 8.22b). The apophthegms also usually begin with the appearance of the other main characters, though against the use of this as an analogy[14] it may be objected that if apophthegms and miracle stories once had the same type of introduction why have they been treated so differently by the Marcan redaction?

Our conclusion is not unequivocal. Mark seems to have been responsible for the form of the introductions, but to explain them as totally his creations is impossible. On the other hand, there does not have to be a sharp distinction between tradition and redaction. The miracle stories may have been introduced in the oral tradition by a 'title' which included the name of Jesus and (now and again) a reference to a place, something like τοῦτο ἐποίησεν ὁ Ἰησοῦς ἐν Καφαρναούμ. This traditional 'oral framework' would then have been integrated by Mark into the narrative to produce a coherent composition: within his gospel he would have 'reproduced' a traditional element afresh. Suggestions about the form of oral tradition are, of course, always somewhat hypothetical. We come closer to it where the written tradition itself describes the process of transmission, where we do not just have narratives reproduced, but also descriptions of scenes in which they are reproduced. This occurs in the case of parables.[15]

In the case of rabbinic parables the oral framework is unmistakable. The introductory formula *mashal* is an abbreviation for 'I am going to tell you a parable . . .', and addresses the listener directly. Such introductions from the 'oral framework' which address the listener directly also occur in the gospels: 'Listen!' (Mk 4.3; cf. 4.24), 'With what can we compare the kingdom of God?' (Mk 4.30), 'Which of you?' (Mt 6.27; 7.9; 12.11; Lk 11.5; 14.28; 15.4; 17.7).[16]

In narrative traditions such introductions had to disappear if the traditions were to form a connected narrative. They were preserved where story was simply followed by story, as in the Talmud: 'The rabbis taught . . .' (b. Berakoth 33a; 33b); 'A story about . . .' (Tos. Ḥullin II.21). The miracles from Epidaurus also have a

---

[13] Bultmann, *HST*, 343.
[14] Bultmann, *HST*, 242, rightly criticised by Schille, *Topograhpie*, 137.
[15] Cf. J. Jeremias, *The Parables of Jesus*, rev. ed., London 1963, 100-03.
[16] Cf. H. Greeven, 'Wer unter euch . . .?', in *Wort und Dienst*, 1952, 86ff.

title, consisting of the name and place of origin or disease: 'Alcetas from Halies' (18), 'Ambrosia from Athens, lacking an eye' (4). Sometimes the story is anticipated: 'Echedorus got Pandarus' fate in addition to the one he had' (7). Even in the connected *vita* of Apollonius such introductions to miracle stories occur: 'The following deed is also told in Tarsus: A rabid . . .' (*vita Apoll.* IV, 43); 'This is also a miraculous feat by Apollonius: A Virgin . . .' (IV, 45). In Lucian's *Philopseudes,* whose dialogue form brings it close to oral tradition, the healing of Midas is introduced with the words: 'I am going to tell you something amazing . . .' (*Philops.* 11). P. Oxy. XI, No 1382 begins with the title: Διὸς Ἡλίου μεγάλου Σαράπιδος ἀρετὴ ἡ περὶ Συρίωνα τὸν κυβερνήτην. Titles of this sort do not occur in Mark, but in the notices about the spreading of reports of miracles (i.e. about their reproduction in narrative form) there is a hint of such an introduction. The man who has been cured proclaims 'in the Decapolis how much Jesus had done for him' (5.20). Did the introductory oral framework of the story once run, 'Jesus did this in the Decapolis' or, 'Was this proclaimed in the Decapolis?'? The Johannine enumeration of the miracles may also be a remnant of such an oral framework. The relevant notices occur after the miracle, it is true (Jn 2.11; 4.54), but the possibility that they once preceded them cannot be ruled out.

The constant two-element structure of the miracle stories can thus be explained as the result of a consistent transformation of the oral introduction into narrative. Those exegetes who delete the first element of Marcan introductions to miracles are right to the extent that the story proper did not begin until the appearance of the suppliants; they are wrong to the extent that the oral framework antedated Mark. His work (or that of his possible predecessors) consisted in integrating this framework into the narrative. Subsequently Matthew and Luke gave it a formulaic structure, as will be described in Chapter 3 of this Part.

An analysis of the introductory motif shows that a sharp distinction between 'tradition' and 'redaction' is incorrect. The change is structural. The motif was moved from the level of commentary in the oral framework to the compositional level in the connected narrative; it no longer announces the narrative but has become part of it.

B. A Boundary-crossing Motif: Faith

'Let the man who hopes for miracles strengthen his faith.[17] Goethe

---

[17] Goethe, *Faust* II, 1: the throne room.

probably meant that ironically, but it can also be said seriously, and the interaction of faith and miracle can even be regarded as the distinctive feature of the New Testament belief in miracles which places it far above all ancient magic and miracle-seeking.[18] Nevertheless the situation proves to be less clear-cut when we look at the ancient texts. Miracles and faith belong together in ancient thought and appear as related in accounts of miracles. Lucian's *Philopseudes* introduces us to the ancient ideas: Lucian is surprised at the irrational faith of his contemporaries, who vie with each other to believe in miracles. The primary meaning of πιστεῖν here is simply 'to believe something to be possible'. Cleomedes says, 'I used to be even more sceptical than you about such things because I regarded it as totally impossible that they should happen' (*Philopseudes* 13). A person comes to 'faith' by seeing and experiencing something miraculous. As Cleomedes continues, 'But the first time I saw the stranger fly . . . I believed and after long resistance was overcome.' The connection between πιστεῖν and ἰδεῖν occurs frequently. It is the criticism made of the sceptical Tychiades: εἰ ταῦτα εἶδες . . . οὐκ ἂν ἔτι ἠπίστησας, which he skilfully picks up: εὖ λέγεις . . . ἐπίστευσαν γὰρ ἂν εἴ γε εἶδον αὐτά (*Philops.* 15) and repeats again later. Sceptical ideas of this sort seem to be presupposed by the Fourth Gospel when it criticises the connection between believing and seeing (4.49; 21.29). Before we dismiss 'faith' in the *Philopseudes* as a superficial attitude, however, we must remember that this is Lucian the sceptic speaking. For the believers in miracles more is involved. One of their arguments runs: 'If you say such things, you presumably do not believe (πιστεύειν) in the gods either, if you really think that healings cannot be brought about through sacred names' (*Philops.* 13), to which Tychiades replies that he reveres the gods and does not doubt Asclepius' healings, but they were brought about by doctors and medicine. In his reply he replaces the term πιστεύειν by σέβειν. His critics really thought they were doing honour to the gods by attributing all manner of things to them.[19] Iamblichus even defines ἡ περὶ τῶν θεῶν πίστις as μηδὲν θαυμαστὸν ἀπιστεῖν (*vita Pyth.* 148).

Plutarch's attitude to belief in miracles is interesting. It is a combination of enlightened reflection and irrational faith. In *Cor* 38 he offers four different explanations for talking statues. First he

---

[18] W. Grundmann, *TDNT* II, 302f.

[19] R. Bultmann, *TDNT* VI, 174-228 shows how in late antiquity πιστεύειν increasingly acquires a religious sense and becomes a slogan of propagandist religions.

gives a causal explanation for the phenomenon: cracks in the wood may be the cause. Then he mentions his teleological interpretation: the god may give such events a significance for the future. Thirdly he suggests a psychological explanation: it may be a case of perceptions such as those in dreams. For the person who is passionately devoted to the God, he says, what has been 'brought about by the god's superhuman power may do much to strengthen faith'. Finally, he switches to a theological or metaphysical acceptance of miracles. God's action is beyond our understanding: 'when he does something which is impossible for us and brings about something which is unattainable for us, that is not contrary to reason; rather, since he differs from us in every way, he is most unlike us and different from us in his works. But, according to Heraclitus, most divine matters cannot be discerned by unbelief' (*Cor* 38).[20] Before we make an unqualified contrast between the ancient hunger for miracles and the New Testament belief in miracles, we should read this text by Plutarch, that congenial priest of Apollo; we will then find many judgments impossible to maintain.

The connection between faith and miracles also occurs in narratives. Strabo gives brief descriptions of cultic healing sanctuaries: In Epidaurus Asclepius is believed to cure diseases: Ἀσκληπιοῦ . . . πεπιστευομένου (V, 374); in Canopus respected men 'believe' (πιστεύειν) and seek healing sleep for themselves and others (XVII, 1, 17). Here we have left the realm of discussion about miracles: πιστεύειν, used absolutely, is connected with the sleep or incubation necessary for a cure. Faith is not just the business of those who hear of miracles and adopt an attitude to them, but of those directly affected. It is therefore no accident that the issue of faith appears in individual accounts of healing:

> A man who could move only one finger of his hand came to the god as a suppliant. When he saw the votive tablets in the sanctuary he did not believe in the cures and made fun of the inscriptions. In his sleep (in the sanctuary) he had a vision. It seemed to him that as he was playing dice in the room under the temple and was about to throw the god appeared, jumped on his hand and stretched out his fingers. When he had stepped off, he saw himself bend his hand and stretch out each finger on its own; when he had stretched them all out straight, the god asked him whether he still did not believe the votive tablets, and he said no. 'Because before you had no faith in them. though they were worthy of belief, your name in future shall

---

[20] Cf. the interpretation of the Plutarch passage by G. Delling, 'Beurteilung', 70.

be Apistos,' said the god. When day came he emerged from the sanctuary cured (Epidaurus 3).

We see here that an element of discussion and scepticism has even become part of the miracle stories. In contrast to the New Testament, faith is not a condition for the miracle but its consequence. It is the unbeliever who is converted. It is therefore quite untrue to say that psychologically there is no difference between this faith and that in the New Testament.[21] Equally it would be impossible in the New Testament for faith to be called ἀμαθία (Epidaurus 4).[22]

There are, however, also accounts of cures in which faith precedes the miracle. An interesting feature is that this motif, which is comparable to the faith in New Testament miracles, is never associated with the term πίστις or πιστεῖν. Instead we find εὐηθία, τολμέω, ἐλπίς, βούλομαι. A one-eyed man with an empty eyesocket comes to Epidaurus: ἔψεγον (ἐγέλων?) τινες τῶν, ἐν τῶι ἰαρῶι τὰν εὐηθίαν αὐτοῦ (9).[23] His trust is called εὐηθία, simplicity, stupidity. Probably the Epidaurus priests are here turning back on its authors a charge made against visitors to the sanctuary. They are showing that such simplicity leads to success. τολμέω and ἐλπίζω, on the other hand, probably reflect the attitudes of the devotees of Asclepius: τολμῶν is preserved in Miracle 35 as the antithesis of δειλός: a lame man is hesitant about carrying out the instruction to climb up the temple on a ladder. Asclepius is at first reluctant, but then laughs at him for his cowardice: ἀποτολμ [ῶν] δὲ ἁμ[έρας γενομένας ἐπιτέλεσαι ἀσκηθὴς ἐ]ξῆλθε. In a similar situation, when a lame man was reluctant to go into cold water, the inscription may have said that Asclepius cures only the ἐόντ[ες εὐελπίδες] (37). The relevant section is a reconstruction,[24] but solidly based: ἐλπίς is part of the technical vocabulary of miraculous cures, as can be seen from the epigram of the orator Aeschines (AP VI, 330): Θνητῶν μὲν τέχναις ἀπορούμενος εἰς δὲ τὸ θεῖον ἐλπίδα πᾶσαν ἔχων.[25] In my view this ἐλπίς is fully comparable with the faith involved in New Testament miracles.

---

[21] Pace W. Grundmann, *TDNT* II, 303, n. 69: 'Psychologically the utterances of faith on the part of those who come to Jesus for healing have some affinities with the confidence betrayed by those who come to Asclepius.' Cf. R.M. Grant, 'Miracle and Mythology', *ZRGG* 3 (1951), 123-33, esp. 127, who agrees with Grundmann on this point but otherwise attacks his distinction between Christian and non-Christian miracles.

[22] R. Herzog, *Epidauros*, 125f., suggests that the pig which the unbelieving Ambrosia has to provide as a victim 'as punishment' is a joke against the Athenians, who mocked the ἀπαιδευσία of their neighbours in the expression 'Boeotian pig'.

[23] On the conjecture cf. O. Weinreich, *AH*, 87.

[24] R. Herzog, *Epidauros*, 24.

[25] Cf. O. Weinreich, *AH*, 195; R. Herzog, *Epidauros*, 39.

It is a possible argument against all the cases cited that ἐλπίς and πίστις are never the condition or the reason for a cure. There is, however, a text which is comparable in this respect. Philostratus describes how a man who was not cured by Asclepius comes to Apollonius, who enlightens him about the reason for his failure: τοῖς γὰρ βουλομένοις δίδοσι (sc. God), *vita Apoll.* I, 9. Of course the New Testament's 'All things are possible to him who believes,' is bolder, more comprehensive (Philostratus only wants the sick man to draw the conclusions for his own life), but there is an undeniable degree of similarity. The faith associated with New Testament miracles is based on traditional motifs, but articulates them in a new way. How it does so we shall now examine.

Within the synoptic gospels the motif of faith is varied in characteristic ways by a change in its motif associations on the compositional level. We shall begin our analysis with the only miracle story (apart from the Stilling of the Storm) in which all three gospels talk about faith, that of the woman with 'the issue of blood' (Mk 5.24b-34; Mt 9.20-22; Lk 8.42b-48). Observations we make here will serve as working hypotheses for the rest of the study.

In Mark the story is told in a 'commenting-repeating' narrative style. Parallel statements describe events and their evaluation.

Event	*Repetition with Comment*
The woman's distress and the failure of the doctors	Uselessness of consulting doctors
The woman approaches Jesus and touches him.	Inward thought: confidence of being cured
Cure	Realisation of cure or of flow of power
Jesus asks who touched him.	Disciples' comment: a pointless question
Jesus looks round for the person; the woman comes forward.	The woman 'knows' what has happened to her.
The woman falls on her knees and confesses.	Assurance: your faith has saved you.

As the reader can easily check, the 'text' set out in the left-hand column gives a complete narrative sequence. Evaluations, thoughts and sayings, form its inner perspective, which the narrator deliberately stresses as the important part. Faith is connected with this inner drama. It is first hope of a cure despite all her previous frustration, but also a breakthrough to an admission of the truth which must have been difficult for the woman. What difficulties did she have to get over?

The fact that she was breaking the Jewish purity regulations,[26] shame at her disease,[27] a feeling that she had stolen power without authority,[28] all these are only partial explanations of her fear. She probably realised that her action was open to misinterpretation. Touching Jesus could have been understood as an attempt to get rid of her disease by passing it on (cf. Epidaurus 7, where the disease is to be transmitted to a cloth). The touch of a menstruating woman was in any case regarded as harmful (Plin. *nat.* VII, 64).[29] When a beautiful woman – in an eventually successful attempt to approach Sulla – secretly pulls a thread out of his clothing, she assures him: οὐδὲν, ἔφη, δεινόν, αὐτοκράτορ, ἀλλὰ βούλομαι τῆς σῆς κἀγὼ μικρὸν εὐτυχίας μεταλαβεῖν (Plut. *Sulla* 35). She knows that her touch could be regarded as δεινόν. The haemorrhagic woman probably had similar fears. For this reason the narrator stresses her good intentions. Now the ancient reader can have no fear of either a love charm or an attempt to pass on the disease, since, in an unspoken expression of confidence she insists that Jesus can absorb her disease without being endangered himself. It is a faith which incorporates and transcends even the ambivalent and illegitimate. It would be a mistake to see it as an attempt to correct magical faith,[30] but it is the realisation of faith as a crossing of the boundary created by the barriers of legitimacy. Faith is faith tested by difficulties.

The striking omissions in the Matthaean version are well known. The encounter is between Jesus and the woman alone. There are no subordinate roles. The sequence of description and 'commentary' and the tension between cure and subsequent confession are missing; all the features are missing which in Mark present faith as faith which has been tested. In Matthew faith is petitionary faith:
i) The assurance comes before the miracle, the answer to the prayer before the cure. H.J. Held[31] has rightly seen this as a reflection of the community's faith in prayer, as two further features confirm:
ii) In Mark Jesus is well aware that he has been touched, but has to ask who it was that touched him and learns of her confidence only from her admission. Matthew stresses (ἔλεγεν ἐν ἑαυτῇ, 9.21) that the woman's declaration of confidence was an inner event. Jesus

---

[26] W. Grundmann, *Das Evangelium nach Markus*, 3rd ed. 1963, 115.
[27] E. Klostermann, *Das Markusevangelium*, 4th ed., 1950, 51.
[28] H.J. Holtzmann, *Die Synoptiker*, 5th ed. 1901, 135.
[29] Cf. H. Waagenvoort, *Roman Dynamism*, 1947, 173-75. Further examples in T. Canaan, *Aberglaube und Volksmedizin im Lande der Bibel*, 1914, 36-38; G. Buschan, *Über Medizinzauber und Heilkunst im Leben der Völker*, 1941, s.v. 'Menstruation'.
[30] Other views: E. Lohmeyer, *Markus*, 103f.; W. Grundmann, *Markus*, 115; J. Roloff, *Kerygma*, 153f.; K. Kertelge, *Die Wunder Jesu im Markusevangelium*, 1970, 115.
[31] 'Matthew as Interpreter', 240, 284ff.; cf. the fine analysis, 178f.; 215-217.

has direct knowledge of the woman's secret thoughts.[32] The belief expressed in prayer is confident that God knows his children's requests before they express them (Mt 6.8).

iii) The new motif of the 'hour' (9.22: Greek 'from that hour') has its original context in healings at a distance. Has Matthew unthinkingly imported this idea into other stories? That is most unlikely, and this story also shows a distance, that between the community and the exalted Lord. Faith in prayer too only knows that the prayer has been answered through the temporal link between petition and relief of the distress.

Luke has not cut the story as drastically as Matthew, but, like him, he has abandoned an important structural element of the Marcan version, the juxtaposition of event and 'commentary'. One significant change is that when Jesus asks his question everyone disclaims knowledge, including the woman, as v. 47 shows. Instead of (εἰδυῖα) ὅ γέγονεν Luke writes ὅτι οὐκ ἔλαθεν, thereby implying that the woman originally wanted to remain hidden. Since all deny, Peter's reference to the crowd can no longer mean that since so many people have touched Jesus trying to find one is hopeless, and καὶ λέγεις· τίς μου ἥψατο; (Mk 5.31) is therefore omitted by Luke. Since all the people say they have not touched him, Jesus has to insist on the fact of his having been touched. The statement ἥψατό μού τις replaces the question τίς μου ἥψατο;. By this statement Jesus displays his miraculous knowledge before all the people, so that the woman has to recognise that she cannot remain hidden in the face of such penetrating knowledge; she comes and 'proclaims' why she touched Jesus. In Luke the main stress is on this confession by the woman, and he has inserted a completely new sentence here: 'and she proclaimed why she had touched him, before the whole people, and how she had suddenly been cured' (8.47, author's translation). In this sentence the elevated and solemn terms ἀπαγγέλλειν and λαός stand out. One almost has the impression of entering a cultic domain in which God's saving act is being proclaimed before the whole community. Luke's two main changes, the initial denial and the stress on the public confession, show that for him the point is the woman's progress from lying to giving thanks. Faith for Luke is grateful faith. In contrast to Matthew, where the behaviour described as faith comes before the healing in the structure of the story, in the petition, here faith goes to the end, as thanks for the good deed experienced.

---

[32] Unlike H.J. Held (see previous note), I can find no restriction of the miraculous; the miraculous knowledge is, if anything, increased. Narrative compression in Matthew does not mean a deliberate attempt to relativise the miraculous.

The various emphases on faith as tested, petitionary and grateful faith found in one pericope recur in the other miracle stories of the different gospels. In all the Marcan miracle stories the motifs of faith and difficulty are associated. The difficulty may be the invalid's unusual route through the roof (2.1ff.), Jesus' dismissive remark (7.24ff.), the command to silence from his companions (10.46ff.),[33] the daughter's death (5.21ff.). The classic expression of faith which is being tested (and challenged) is the paradoxical confession, 'I believe; help my unbelief!', in which the experience of frustration and a radical transcending of human possibilities fight with each other.

Despite the arguments of R. Bultmann, J. Sundwall, and K. Kertelge,[34] the middle section of the story of the epileptic boy (Mk 9.20ff.) should be regarded, not as an independent narrative, but as a secondary accretion, as the (possibly independent) variants of the tradition in Luke and Matthew show.[35] The most important arguments for the hypothesis that two stories have been combined or an original idea expanded from 9.21-27, the repeated description of possession, the disappearance of the disciples in vv. 21ff. and the repetition of the ὄχλος motif, are inadequate. (a) The repetition of the description of the symptoms makes sense as an intensification. In v. 18 the possessed boy is being slowly consumed, in v. 20 violently attacked. A reason is given for the attack: the demon scents its conqueror: καὶ ἰδὼν αὐτὸν τὸ πνεῦμα . . . (v. 20). Since it is dumb it cannot defend itself with protective words, but only by its destructive activity. (b) The doubting plea, 'If you can do anything, . . . help' (9.22) presupposes the disappointment with the disciples. Whoever composed vv. 22-24 had vv. 14ff. in front of him. The motif of faith in 9.23 picks up v. 19. (c) The repetition of the ὄχλος motif is directly connected with the threat. At this point the parallels begin again. The crowd's rush may previously have been prompted by something more unusual than the father's confession, perhaps the boy's fit. V. 25 then followed either v. 20 or v. 22. The interpolation would then be vv. 21-24[36] or vv. 23-24. Since all attempts to divide the passage are uncertain, our interpretation must be independent of them, while bearing in mind the possibility that the passage which interests us (vv. 22-24) may be an addition – perhaps by the evangelist.

---

[33] K. Tagawa (*Miracles*, 120) also regards the command to silence in Mk 7.24ff. as a test of faith. On Mk 10.46ff. cf. E. Haenchen, *Weg*, 372, n. 4: 'Or are not the crowd's shouts to him to be silent the obstacle which the beggar's faith has to overcome?'

[34] R. Bultmann, *HST*, 211; J. Sundwall, *Die Zusammensetzung des Markusevangeliums*, 1934, 58-60; K. Kertelge, *Wunder*, 174-79. On the analysis cf. also W. Schenk, 'Tradition und Redaktion in der Epileptiker-Perikope Mk 9,14-29', *ZNW* 63 (1972), 76-94.

[35] T. Schramm, *Der Markus-Stoff bei Lukas*, 1966, 129.

[36] J. Roloff, *Kerygma*, 149ff.

The brief dialogue expresses the nature and ambivalence of faith in miracles. The petitioner is credited with faith which goes beyond all human possibilities. It is his faith that is meant. First, the father understands Jesus' words in this sense when he echoes them in 'I believe . . .' and, second, on form-critical criteria Jesus' words are an assurance formula which is always addressed to petitioners and refers to their faith and trust. Only when the faith in question is related to the petitioner does the radical nature of the statement become clear.[37] 'If you can do anything, . . . help us' expects the miracle-worker to go beyond what is humanly possible, the limits of which the disciples have demonstrated. But the miracle-worker turns the question back: if a human being has faith, all things are possible to him. Πάντα δυνατά is a divine attribute in the strict sense.[38] A human being shrinks back from this reaching for divine omnipotence, from this most radical crossing of the boundary of what is legitimate, human and possible. Incited to take this step by Jesus, he does. He cries, 'I believe,' but immediately has to take it back: 'Help me in my unbelief!' It becomes clear here that the miracle stories are actions in which a human being transcends his world's legitimacy barriers in the face of actual suffering. He utters an impotent protest against the suffering, a protest which must reach for divine omnipotence to become effective and which knows that it is only the revealer's assurance which gives it the power to take this step into illegitimacy and also pushes it over the boundary.

Matthew removes the idea of πίστις from three Marcan miracle stories (cf. Mt 9.18ff.; 17.14ff.; 20.29ff.), which tells against H.J. Held's view that the motif of faith is Matthew's critical principle of selection for including Marcan miracle stories.[39] Matthew's interest in the faith motif is illustrated in the three passages he includes which are not in Mark: Mt 8.5ff.; 15.21ff.; 9.27ff., where the motif is always in the form of the faith formula as altered by Matthew to express the faith of prayer: 'Be it done to you according to your faith.'[40] In the first two pericopes the motif of faith is already part of the tradition (cf. Lk 7.1ff.=Q), or at least its beginnings are present in the tradition (cf. Mk 7.24ff.), which leaves as the only

---

[37] J. Roloff, *Kerygma*, 149ff.

[38] R.M. Grant, *Miracles and Natural Law in Graeco-Roman and Early Christian Thought*, 1952, 127-34, has investigated the history of the phrase πάντα δυνατά and collected a wealth of material. Cf., for example, Philo, *opif.* 46: πάντα γὰρ θεῷ δυνατά.

[39] 'Matthew as Interpreter', 298: the connection between faith and miracles is, he says, 'a critical principle in the handing on of the healing stories'. Cf. 209f.

[40] Cf. H.J. Held, 'Matthew as Interpreter', 239ff.

genuinely Matthaean passage 9.27ff.[41] Here the content of faith is specified almost in a definition: 'Do you believe that I am able to do this?' Faith thus consists simply in crediting Jesus with miraculous powers. There is no sign that faith in miracles needs to be qualified.

The stories of the centurion from Capernaum and the Syrophoenician woman also confirm our conclusions so far. Both stories include the motif of faith which has been tested which is prominent in Mark (or alternatively the association of the motifs of faith and difficulty), but it is always petitionary faith which is tested; in Mt 15.21ff. the petition is even duplicated and turned into a solemn appeal. In addition, Matthew has in both cases interpreted the difficulty motif by inserting logia: the barrier to be broken down is the division between Jews and Gentiles. The obstacle of faith has become the obstacle which has been overcome in the course of salvation history, on which Matthew can already look back.[42] Faith in miracles has an important function in salvation history; it does have the power to break through barriers and open a path for salvation into the whole world. This idea certainly contains a historically accurate observation: all nations are susceptible to belief in miracles.

Faith, then, appears in all Matthew's miracle stories (with the exception of 9.2ff.) as petitionary faith. This is shown in the form given to the petition: Jesus is recognised as 'son of David' (15.22; 9.27) and Kyrios (8.6; 15.22). The petition gives expression to a cognitive element of the conviction of Jesus' power. To match the petition, the acknowledgment of faith is given the form of an answer to the petition.

In the Lucan special material the faith formula appears twice, in Lk 7.50 and 17.19. That faith is in both cases presented as grateful faith is clear at first sight.

In Lk 7.36ff. the faith motif has changed its context and appears in an apophthegm. This transfer of motif may derive from Luke.[43] The story of

---

[41] Though according to G. Strecker, *Weg*, 199f., n. 4, this could also be traditional material.

[42] On this interpretation of the pericope in terms of salvation history, cf. G. Strecker, *Weg*, 99-101; W. Trilling, *Das wahre Israel*, 3rd ed., 1964, 88-90. However, to take 'faith' here as meaning acquiring a share in the kingdom of God (Held, 'Matthew as Interpreter', 196) is a piece of illegitimate spiritualisation. What is true is that belief *in miracles* wins a share in the kingdom of God.

[43] Lk 7.50 is regarded as secondary by scholars with very different analyses: G. Braumann, 'Die Schuldner und die Sünderin in Luk VII 36-50', *NTS* 10 (1963/64), 487-93, esp. 490; H. Schürmann, *Lukas*, 529-42; J. Roloff, *Kerygma*, 161-63; R. Bultmann, *HST*, 21. V. 50 is explicitly described as Lucan by A. Jülicher, *Die Gleichnisreden Jesu*, II, 2nd ed., 1910, 299ff., and T. Schramm, *Markus-Stoff*, 31f.

the woman with the issue of blood may have been his inspiration and explain the expanded formula with its addition: 'Go in peace.' In other instances, too, the use of motifs from miracle stories is noticeable at the end: 'Who is this?' probably comes from Lk 5.21. The parable of the two debtors shows how Luke understood the story, as a model of grateful faith.

However, the connection between faith and gratitude is also made clear in the reworking of Marcan miracle stories. In the healing of the paralytic Luke has stressed the jubilation as well as the faith of the man by adding δοξάζων τὸν θεόν (5.25). The cure of the blind man of Jericho is similarly reworked. Luke has an editorial addition: 'and œheæ followed him, glorifying God; and all the people, when they saw it, gave praise to God.' (18.43). And in 8.47 he makes the cured woman proclaim her cure before the whole people. In all places in Lucan miracle stories where faith is mentioned, the author also stresses the gratitude of the cured person, frequently by editorial alterations to the Marcan text. Just as in Matthew there was a constant association of the motifs faith and petition, and in Mark of faith and difficulty, equally consistently in Luke this becomes an association between faith and gratitude.

These redactional reworkings of a motif are not just archaeological strata to be distinguished; they must be understood as a restructuring of compositional relations. Variations of a motif are variations in its motif associations and are realised by the possibilities contained in the paradigmatic field of motifs in various ways. In Mark faith is the crossing of a boundary seen from a voluntaristic point of view. In Matthew a cognitive element is added: the conviction expressed in the petition; in Luke the affective aspect is dominant: acclamation and gratitude are regarded as the essence of faith. In other words, faith is simply the crossing of the boundaries of the human, and is associated in turn with different aspects of that crossing. 'Faith' is therefore not just one motif among other motifs of boundary-crossing associated with human characters, but the essence of all motifs of boundary crossing. This faith is, however, always recognised by the divine miracle-worker. The word occurs almost only on his lips: it is only the revelation of the sacred which provokes crossings of the boundary and legitimates them. In the reproduction of the miracle stories this revelation is realised in the three synoptics from different points of view. The diachronous actualisation of the possibilities immanent in the motif field shows at the compositional level in varying motif associations.

Finally we may compare the New Testament data with those from other sources. The change in the content of πιστεῖν, πιστεύειν, etc. in the context of miracles can be provisionally defined as follows:

i) 'Faith' in the ancient world is primarily an attitude to the miraculous event, whereas in the New Testament it is an attitude on the part of the people involved which is internal to the miraculous event. In both cases it is associated with different characters: outside the New Testament with the listeners to the miracle stories, in the New Testament with the principal actors in the miracle stories. If πίστις occurs in ancient miracle stories themselves, the second character is also a listener to the miracle stories: he reads the inscriptions and makes fun of them (Epidaurus 3, 4). This faith in miracles has a strong cognitive component.

ii) 'Confidence' in the miracle stories on the part of one of the principal actors is not described as 'faith' but given other names: 'hope', 'courage', 'simplicity' and so on. The object of this confidence is usually the healing process (and only occasionally the miracle worker in general). It is primarily volitional in character, being contrasted with the failure of human doctors or the mockery of other people.

The New Testament has combined both aspects and describes the confidence of the main figure in miracle stories by the term which expresses an attitude to miracles as such. This attitude, πίστις, thereby acquires a primarily volitional aspect. The receptivity of the attitude to hearing of the miracle becomes a human act which is constitutive of the miracle: 'Faith saves.' However, the cognitive element is not absent, and is particularly prominent in Matthew ('Be it done unto you according to your faith.'), but there too as an element of the miracle. Thus in the New Testament a motif from the repertoire of ancient miracle motifs is given a new articulation; it acquires a new position in the field of motifs. Individual analogies are therefore inadequate to produce a 'derivation'; we have to look at the restructuring of the whole field, and then we shall be better able to judge both the roots of New Testament miracle stories in the repertoire of ancient miracle stories and their uniqueness. What seems to me unique is that here faith means an act by which a human being crosses a boundary in the face of actual suffering as an answer to a revelation which challenges a human being in his totality.

C. A Boundary-Stressing Motif: the Command to Silence

Commands to silence in many variants occur in ancient magic. The magical process may be designed to bring someone to silence, the process itself may be surrounded with silence, or a command to secrecy may protect miracle-working formulae from transmission to unauthorised persons. Accordingly we distinguish commands to fall silent, actions performed in silence and commands to secrecy.

i) Commands to fall silent are directed at nature, demons and human beings: 'Keep your voices silent in your mouths, all you circling birds, observe silence' (PGM III, 199f.). 'In silence let the earth rest, and let the air rest in silence and let the sea rest in silence. In silence let the wind rest, and in this questioning of the oracle let me not be disturbed by any voice, any cry, any bird-call' (PGM VII, 320-23). Demons are ordered to be silent in the same way, 'Demons in the realm of shadows, tremble and keep silent (σιγὴν τρομέοντες ἔ[χοιτ]ε)' (PGM III, 204). The magician wills that human beings should be incapable of speech: 'I bind X as follows: he shall not speak, shall not resist, shall not speak against me; he shall be unable to look me in the face or speak against me; he shall be subject to me as long as this ring lies buried. I bind his mind and his thought and his reason and his actions, so that he shall be incapable of action against anyone' (PGM V, 321-29). Frustration of speech may play an important role in love charms: 'If she sits she shall not sit; if she speaks to someone she shall not speak; if she looks at someone, she shall not look at them . . .' (PGM IV, 1510f.). In the New Testament there are two commands to fall silent, Mk 1.24 and 4.39.

ii) *Actions performed in silence* as part of magical practices or the receiving of revelations are intended to protect the magician or increase his power. In one case he is ordered, when the god appears, to place his right index finger on his mouth and say, 'Silence, silence, silence, symbol of the imperishable, living God; protect me, silence . . .' (PGM IV, 558-60; repeated: IV, 573, 578, 582, 623). During the receiving of a revelation he must not interrupt with questions: 'But you are to keep silent; you will understand it all on your own . . .' (PGM IV, 728f.). Silence is frequently an ascetic element of the miraculous process. After preparing the miraculous substance or reciting the formula, the magician is to go to sleep, without answering anyone: καὶ κοιμῶ μετὰ τὸ εἰπεῖν, μηδενὶ δοὺς ἀπόκρισιν (PGM V, 397-99). Such instructions are standard: PGM V, 457f.; VII, 748f.; VII, 1011; VIII, 67, here always associated with subsequent sleep. Independently of that context we find at the end of a formula the command: λάλει μηδενί (PGM VII, 1025). To remove a spell the tablet with the spell on must be taken out of the water, and while this is done there must be silence: πορεύου δὲ ἀνεπιστρέπτι μηδενὶ δοὺς ἀπόκρισιν (PGM VII, 439f.). The last command to silence resembles Mk 1.44.[44]

iii) *Commands to secrecy* come immediately before or after magic formulae. Frequently there is a κρύβε. In some places the command is strengthened by an oath. The following examples all come from *Papyri Graecae Magicae*.

---

[44] T. Hopfner, *Offenbarungszauber* II, 83f. connects the formulaic expression κοιμῶ μηδενὶ δοὺς ἀπόκρισιν with the time of sleep: one should not address the dream figures because, according to the superstition and ghost lore of all periods, ghosts disappear when spoken to. However, the last of the examples quoted above shows that the action performed in silence is independent of sleep. O. Böcher, *Dämonenfurcht*, 306-11, groups actions carried out in silence with the passive acts of exorcistical ascesis and offers a different interpretation. According to him, the demons try to enter a speaker's mouth and the surest defence against them is therefore to avoid speaking.

I, 40	At the end of a spell: 'Keep it secret, keep the spell secret and for seven days abstain from intercourse with women' (κρύβε, κρύβε τὴν πρᾶξιν).
I, 130	Immediately after unintelligible magic sounds: 'Tell this to no-one else, but, as you have been honoured by God, the Lord, by Helios, keep this high mystery concealed.'
I, 146f.	Before the speaking of a name engraved on a stone there is a 'Keep this secret.' Then follow meaningless magic sounds.
I, 193ff.	'But pass this on to no-one but the son of your own body, when he demands from you the (magical) powers we have imparted.'
IV, 75ff.	'So say the prayer (to the moon) seven times, and you must also say it again on your return after being cast out. Keep it secret: (there follows a magic formula in Coptic and in Coptic script).
IV, 84f.	After a magic word in Coptic: 'Guard it carefully' (φύλαττε τάδε σφόδρα).
IV, 254ff.	'This magic formula, most great king, is for you alone, for you to guard, personally.'
IV, 851ff.	'I adjure you by the holy gods and the gods of heaven not to tell anyone Solomon's spell and certainly not to use it for a trivial purpose.'
IV, 922	'Now you have received full knowledge of these things. Keep it secret.'
IV, 1251	After a formula: 'Keep it secret. It has already proved its worth.'
IV, 2518f.	After a magic formula: 'Son, keep it secret.'
XII, 29ff.	'I am the one to whom you came under the holy mountain and gave the knowledge of your most great name. I shall guard it, pure, tellig no-one of it except your other initiates for your holy initiations.'
XII, 321f.	'But keep it secret like a great mystery. Conceal it secretly, secretly.'
XII, 334f.	'Keep it secret, secret, the true Uphor, the summary of truth.'
XIII, 740ff.	'I have presented you with the oath which is prescribed for the book; once you have learnt the magic power of the book you must keep it secret, child, for the name of the Lord is hidden in it.'
XII, 1038ff.	'Do not prattle the counter-spell idly about unless you want to make yourself unlucky; keep it to yourself.'

The analogy between these commands to secrecy and the majority of the Marcan commands to silence should be clear without further analysis. Surprisingly, they have not hitherto been used in exegesis of the Marcan material.[45]

We shall examine the commands to silence in three stages. First we shall look at their position in the composition, then at their motif associations, and finally at the linguistic structure of the motifs.

i) The *compositional position* of commands to silence in miracle stories may be the exposition (Mk 10.48), the conclusion (1.44; 5.43; 7.36; 8.26) or the middle (1.25; 4.39); outside miracle stories it is always the conclusion (1.34; 3.12; 8.30). In the story of the transfiguration the command to silence introduces the discussion during the descent (9.9-13), but relates to the preceding pericope. The position of the command to silence in the exposition in Mk 10.48 is an exception, and we shall discuss that first.

C. Burger wants to remove both the command to silence (10.48) and 10.47b-49a as additions by the redaction.[46] He offers the following arguments: (a) The titles 'son of David' (10.48) and 'Master' (10.51) conflict. However that may be, to delete 'Son of David' (which is Burger's main concern) does not require the deletion of the whole section. (b) The crowd, a subsequent addition in 10.46, does not appear in the miracle story proper, but dominates in 47b-49a. If it was part of the original miracle story, we would expect a choral ending. But the absence of a choral end implies nothing, since v. 52 is in the normal style of a dismissal conclusion. There is no motif association between the 'appearance of the crowd' and 'acclamation by a crowd'. The absence of an acclamation is therefore no argument for the existence or non-existence of a crowd in the preceding miracle story. (c) The crowd first bullies the blind man and then shouts to him, 'Take heart!', as though he had lacked courage. The shout, however, is in the normal style of an assurance formula, and in any case the contradiction between discouragement and assurance is only apparent: in Mk 7.24ff. one immediately follows the other. (d) The

---

[45] On the commands to silence in the magical papyri, cf. T. Hopfner, *Offenbarungszauber* II, 16. A possible objection to the use of the papyri in exegesis is that the genres are different: in the papyri instructions for magicians, in the synoptics stories about a charismatic miracle-worker. It is true that this must be taken into account, but it cannot be a decisive objection because points of contact between magical texts and miracle stories are by no means limited to commands to secrecy, as was shown in the cataloguing of motifs in Part I of this book. Moreover, in ancient times Jesus was accused of having been a magician (Origen, *contra Celsum*, 1.28; Sanhedrin 107b), i.e. parallels were seen between him and other magical actions.

[46] *Jesus als Davidssohn*, 42-46, 59-63. Roloff, *Kerygma*, 121-26, interprets slightly differently, regarding the whole dialogue, including the command to silence, as secondary but pre-Marcan.

miracle story contains two petitions, so one must be secondary. A compositional differentiation between petition and expression of confidence, however, is normal style. (e) The command to silence presupposes the Marcan theory of secrecy. However, it is not Jesus who orders silence; he opposes the order.[47]

To sum up: the only command to silence in an exposition is in its usual, traditional position within Mk 10.46ff. If it is removed the story becomes colourless, and the difficulty in the way of faith disappears.

The tradition is also the source of the commands to be silent in the middle of miracle stories. In Mk 1.25 the intention is not to keep secret the supernatural status betrayed by the demon; the whole scene is public.[48] The command to be silent is aimed at the apotropaeic power of miraculous knowledge, not against its manifestation. Mk 4.39 is an unobjectionable parallel without any connection with keeping a secret. On the other hand, all final commands to silence are real commands to secrecy. Within miracle stories they are associated with either dismissal or acclamation motifs. A dismissal is in any case a command, and the formal incorporation of commands to secrecy (or similar commands) is straightforward. Wonder and acclamation, however, inevitably form a contrast.

In editorial summaries, too, commands to silence appear in final position; it is clear that Mark understands these commands as a generalisation of the word of power in 1.25, the normal position of which is the middle of the miracle story. In formal terms this change of position can be described as a motif displacement, and in the content it makes itself felt in a small shift of position. Whereas in 1.25 we have, 'Be silent, and come out of him!', in 1.34 the order is reversed: 'and [he] cast out many demons and would not permit them to speak' (similarly in 3.10-12). Motif displacement is therefore also a modification of content: words of power have become commands to secrecy. Mark emphasises this by giving at one point the reason for the command to secrecy ('because they knew him', 1.34) and at another its purpose ('not to make him

---

[47] Cf. W. Wrede, *The Messianic Secret*, 1971, 279f.

[48] G.M. de Tillesse, *Le secret*, 77-83, regards Mk 1.23-24 as redactional. The crucial argument for him is the agreement with the summaries, though in fact these differ in a characteristic way, as will be shown below. A. Fridrichsen, *Le problème du miracle dans le christianisme primitif*, 1925, 77-79, deletes the demon's confession on the ground that it presupposes disputes about Jesus' status. The demon himself, he says, is defending Jesus against the charge of being a magician. Such selfless help on the part of the demon could, however, have been given a quite different interpretation, namely that Jesus was in alliance with the demon.

known', 3.12). He wants Jesus' dignity to remain concealed and understands 1.25 as well in that sense – in contradiction to its original sense.[49]

Since the two commands to silence we have not yet discussed, 8.30 and 9.9, also come at the end, and in pericopae whose theme is the dignity of Jesus, we may assume in advance that the redaction has influenced them.

ii) The *motif associations* of the commands to silence have to be investigated because in Mark there are six miracle stories with commands to silence and six without. Are there motifs in these miracle stories which explain this presence and absence? In other words, we are investigating the roots of the commands to silence in the content of the stories, and for this purpose will limit ourselves to the final commands to silence since those in the exposition and the middle section have already proved to depend on the content.

(a) In the case of *dismissal conclusions* with commands to silence we must ask whether characteristic associations of motifs or motif variants are present here (and only here). If we look at the three miracle stories under discussion here, we find that one characteristic in all three cases is that the public forum to which the person cured is sent or not sent is absent: the priests (1.43f.), home (5.19), the village (8.26). Dismissal thus becomes a sending to announce the healing. Are these (usually implicit) commands to silence the work of the redaction?

The story of the leper (Mk 1.40ff.) has been a constant invitation to critical surgery; the healing is mentioned twice and the dismissal of the cured man is told twice. Attempts are made either to disentangle two stories[50] or to demonstrate a secondary revision.[51] Neither of these literary critical operations is necessary. The story, like 5.25ff., is told in the repetitive-commenting style.

Event	*Repetition with Commentary*
Coming of the leper and his kneeling	'If you will, you can make me *clean*.'
Touch	'I will; be *clean*.'
Disappearance of the leprosy	'and he was made *clean*'
Dismissal	Command to make the offering for *cleansing*

---

[49] Thus the agreement between Mk 1.23-24 and the summaries, by which G.M. de Tillesse (*Le secret*, 80) justifies the removal of 1.23-24 as redactional, is non-existent.

[50] E. Lohmeyer, *Markus*, 44; W. Grundmann, *Markus*, 50.

[51] R. Bultmann, *HST*, 212, and G.M. de Tillesse, *Le secret*, 41-51, exclude vv 43-44a. E. Klostermann, *Markus*, 14f., calls v. 42 secondary. K. Kertelge, *Wunder*, 68, regards v. 43 as a secondary doublet of v. 41.

The command to silence, which is all that interests us here, was defended as original by M. Dibelius:[52] 'The sick man is healed of a disease which forbade any intercourse with others. The healing therefore only holds good when the legal verdict has been pronounced, when the sick man is described clean by the priestly supervisor and by sacrifices of purification.' But does the doubled μηδενὶ μηδέν not sound definite and unqualified, with no suggestion of a time limit? Must we not draw the conclusion that the command to silence can be regarded as traditional only if it can be understood as absolute? Our segmentation of the pericope shows that 'clean' is the key concept. In my view there can be no doubt that Jesus validly declares the leper clean. He does not say, 'I will; be cured,' but 'I will; be clean.'[53] A sending to the priest would be meaningless if the cured man appeared claiming that he had already been pronounced clean. He has to keep this fact a secret and outwardly conform to the Jewish custom which is really superfluous for him. That is why in the story he is referred not to God, but to Moses, as the authority. A comparable story is that of the Temple tax (Mt 17.24ff.). Both stories fit the context of a Jewish Christianity which respects Temple, sacrifices and Law but, as a result of its new faith is no longer inwardly bound by these authorities. The conflict which has been overlaid with this loyalty can emerge at any time. In later times those who wanted to take part in Jewish worship were wise to keep their Christianity a secret. According to John 9.1ff., even healings by Jesus had to be kept secret if the people healed were not to risk excommunication; and healings in the name of Jesus were forbidden (Tos. Ḥullin II, 21-23). Mk 1.40ff. shows an early stage of this conflict, in which an open break could be avoided by conformity. In this case the command to silence is traditional, because for Mark these problems are far in the past.

The second passage to be discussed, 5.19f., does not contain a command to silence, though Mark will have taken it as doing so.[54] The cured man is sent 'home' – for Mark often a place of secrecy (7.17; 7.24; 9.28; 10.10) – but proclaims the news in the

---

[52] *TG*, 74. Pap. Egerton is no evidence against the originality of the command to silence if J. Jeremias (in E. Hennecke & W. Schneemelcher, *Neutestamentliche Apokryphen* I, 1959, 58f.) is right in saying that the fragment presupposes all four gospels, pace U. Luz, 'Das Geheimnismotiv und die markinische Christologie', ZNW 56 (1965), 9-30, cf. 16.

[53] A. Meyer, *Entstehung*, 41, and E. Hirsch, *Frühgeschichte des Evangeliums* I, 1941, 8, hold the opposite view, viz. that Jesus is annoyed because the leper has asked to be declared clean without going through the proper channels.

[54] W. Wrede, *Messianic Secret*, 140f.

Decapolis. The order and its breach are paralleled in 1.44f. How far Mark himself had a hand in the composition of the end of Mk 5.1-20 is disputed. There seem to be a number of formally correct conclusion formulae.

i) In 5.15 the man previously possessed is seen in his right mind, freed from a demon. Such a demonstration of the miracle could once have formed the conclusion.[55] However, only K. Tagawa suggests that this is a reason for attributing the remainder to Mark.[56]

ii) Equally interesting is the view that the pericope ended with the negative attitude of the people of the area to Jesus (5.17).[57] M. Dibelius and G.M. de Tillesse,[58] see here the line separating tradition and redaction. But can one imagine the miracle story ending on such a negative note?

iii) For these reasons many scholars assume that Mark found the pericope essentially in its present form (though it may have been expanded earlier).[59]

In my view 5.19 is in the style of a dismissal conclusion.[60] It is at this point that we find the break which introduces Mark's theory of the secret into the pericope. The cured man is sent home, but instead tells his story throughout the region; the instruction uses the word ἀπαγγέλλειν, but v. 20 has Mark's typical word κηρύσσειν.[61] The man is told to testify to the mercy of the Lord (God?), i.e. to give thanks for his cure, but the picture in v. 20 is of a missionary who proclaims what 'Jesus' has done for him.[62] If we assume that the work of the Marcan redaction begins with v. 20, it becomes clear why the secrecy motif is so weakly drawn: it was originally not present at all in v. 19, since for the pre-Marcan tradition there was probably no association between 'home' and 'secrecy'. Mark is first to regard 'home' as a place of secrecy and emphasises it by adding the failure to obey the instruction or transforming an existing reference to proclamation into one. He

---

[55] O. Bauernfeind, *Worte,* 34f.; K. Kertelge, *Wunder,* 102f.

[56] *Miracles,* 168-71.

[57] F. Hahn, *Titles,* 291f.; E. Schweizer, *Mark,* 113. Both assume the existence of further pre-Marcan additions.

[58] M. Dibelius, *TG,* 74; G.M. de Tillesse, *Le secret,* 83-88.

[59] R. Bultmann, *HST,* 210; K. Kertelge, *Wunder,* 101f.; E. Haenchen, *Weg,* 195, believes 5.19f. is a stylistic echo of the miracle story. H. Schürmann, *Lukas,* 485, thinks the miracle story was originally aetiological and that the reference to the Decapolis is therefore original.

[60] J. Roloff, 'Das Markusevangelium als Geschichtsdarstellung', *EvTh* 27 (1969), 73-93, esp. 86, n. 56 (gives no reason). E. Schweizer, *Mark,* 113, does not regard 5.19 as the original conclusion, but says the work of the redactor begins at 5.20.

[61] E. Schweizer, *Anmerkungen,* 93ff.

[62] H.J. Ebeling, *Messiasgeheimnis,* 124f., denies a tension between 5.19 and 5.20; in his gratitude, he says, the cured man did more than he was asked.

probably used Mk 1.44f. as a model. In my view we may conclude that the indirect command to silence in 5.19f. does not come from the tradition but was first introduced or reinterpreted by Mark, though it does not follow that Mark reoriented the whole story.

Similarly, Mk 8.22ff. does not contain an explicit command to silence, but Mark has taken the conclusion as such. Attempts to attribute a different interpretation to it are not very convincing. There is no trace of any hostility from demons (S. Eitrem)[63] or human beings (J. Roloff)[64] to explain the move out of the village. E. Klostermann[65] has in my view found the right answer when he suggests that the curious prohibition is 'a redactional expansion of an original word of dismissal'. Since the blind man has been led out of the village, the natural conclusion would be his being sent away back into the village: 'and he sent him home' is in this direction, but the subsequent instruction not to enter the village is in direct contradiction with it. Delete the negative and everything makes good sense: the cured man is to return to his family and friends in the village, that is to say, the man who was previously handicapped will be able to take a full part in social life. By inserting μηδέ Mark has turned this into the opposite because he opposes 'home' as the place of secrecy to public life and interprets the sending home as ruling out publicity.[66] As in 5.19f. he has projected his theory of secrecy on to the motif of 'home'. In both cases Mark's redactional activity consists in turning two variants of the dismissal conclusion, viz. the sending back to the family (home) and publicity, into contrasting motifs and extending the opposition already present in the form-critical field of motifs between secrecy and publicity to these variants. In so doing he actualises possibilities present in potential form in the stock of motifs. He is not introducing anything radically new, but reproducing some miracle stories in a new form within the framework of the possibilities of the genre.

(b) In *acclamation* and *wonder* conclusions commands to silence necessarily appear as foreign bodies.[67] They are regarded as certainly the work of the redaction.[68] And yet there are grounds for

---

[63] *Notes*, 47.

[64] *Kerygma*, 127-31; 'Geschichtsdarstellung', 87, n. 56.

[65] *Markus*, 78.

[66] K. Tagawa (*Miracles*, 168) regards Mk 8.26 as traditional: the prohibition 'contribue à établir le caractère secret du miracle.'

[67] Given the competition between the two motifs, it would naturally also be possible to delete the motif of wonder in 5.42 (K. Tagawa, *Miracles*, 167) or the acclamation in 7.36f. (M. Dibelius, *TG*, 76; V. Taylor, *Mark*, 352; J. Roloff, 'Geschichtsdarstellung', 86f., n. 55).

[68] K. Kertelge, *Wunder*, 110ff., 157ff. – to mention only one example – no longer even refers to the possibility that they may be traditional.

challenging this certainty. In these cases particularly there is a striking motif association between commands to silence and motifs of mystery, ῥῆσις βαρβαρική and the removal of the public. Since there is a large number of examples from outside the New Testament showing that miraculous and magic words were protected by secrecy, it is plausible to suppose that the commands to secrecy in Mark's gospel are also prompted by ῥῆσις βαρβαρική. This would also give us an explanation for the fact that commands to secrecy appear in these miracle stories and not others: the miraculous mysterious-sounding magic word is not to be passed on. Since this function of the command to secrecy is no longer immediately obvious in Mark, it must be pre-Marcan, a suggestion which would gain plausibility if it could be shown that Mark has considerably altered the endings of the relevant miracle stories in other ways. In doing this he may have separated the commands to secrecy from their original context. The following attempts at reconstruction seek to show that Mark did reproduce the stories in this way. It should be borne in mind, however, that the assumption that the commands to secrecy come from the tradition is based primarily on the synchronous motif association, and is only secondly to be confirmed by a diachronic analysis.

A first sign of redactional influence on Mk 5.42f. is the fact that this section, unlike the main body of the story, is in the imperfect. The order of the motifs in the composition is striking:

1. Demonstration	42:	And immediately the girl got up and walked (she was twelve years of age).
2. Wonder		and they were immediately overcome with amazement.
3. Command to secrecy	43:	And he strictly charged them that no-one should know this,
4. Demonstration		and told them to give her something to eat.

The duplication of the demonstration is not in itself striking. A raising from the dead is such an unusual event as to make repeated confirmation understandable. What is striking is the order, the separation of the two demonstrations and the position of the wonder, which one would expect right at the end. But we need only transpose vv. 42 and 43 to avoid all these difficulties: the two demonstrations now come one after the other. For the girl first to eat and then to walk seems logical; she has taken nourishment and can now walk again. The amazement comes in its usual place at the end. The command to secrecy, however, now immediately follows the miraculous phrase, 'Talitha cumi' or rather its translation and explanation.

Such reconstructions are of course always somewhat hypothetical, but two points seem to me certain: that Mark has had a hand in 5.42f. and also that the presence of a magic word and a command to secrecy in the same passage is no accident. If we do not attribute the second feature to Mark (who interprets the secrecy motifs differently; see below), we shall postulate a traditional motif which has been put to a new use by Mark (so E. Lohmeyer, H.J. Ebeling, K. Tagawa).[69]

In 7.36f. the command to silence is usually deleted as intrusive. But what is even more intrusive is the disregard of the command in v. 36b: 'but the more he charged them, the more zealously they proclaimed it,' which comes before the acclamation but seems to anticipate events which can only come after it. In my view this is a certain example of the work of the Marcan redaction. Even after deleting v. 36b, however, we have still not exposed the pre-Marcan form. There remains the curious feature that the sick person is first taken apart from the people, the healing words are spoken specifically to him (λέγει αὐτῷ), which probably means to him alone, but then the crowd is suddenly there. Should not the man be first sent away (cf. 8.26)? A simple alteration could remove the difficulty. The command to silence might once have been in the singular and addressed only to the man, who was the only one to have heard the mysterious word. He is dismissed with his knowledge and is not to tell the miraculous word to anyone else. The crowd's amazement then follows without any difficulty.

To sum up our conclusion: probably all the commands to silence in miracle stories are from the tradition. Where Mark himself introduces a secrecy motif, he does so, not by means of a command to silence, but by reinterpreting traditional motifs (the motif of home) or using motifs already present (the mysterious miraculous word in a foreign language).

iii) The *motif structure* of the commands to silence enables us to check our assumptions so far. Our provisional conclusion is that all commands to silence inside miracle stories are from the tradition (if we ignore the command to secrecy in 9.9 which follows an epiphany; this forms a transition between a miracle story and an apophthegm), and all those outside miracle stories from the redaction. Is it possible to specify a feature which distinguishes the two

---

[69] E. Lohmeyer, *Markus,* 108, believes that only the girl's death is to be kept secret, in order not to show up Jesus' diagnosis of apparent death as false. H.J. Ebeling, *Messiasgeheimnis,* 131-35, regards the command to silence as an example of the humility of the man filled with divine grace, who despises all seeking after glory. The only useful view is that of K. Tagawa, *Miracles,* 167, who draws attention to the motif association with the exclusion of the public.

groups and correlates with the two contexts? Yes: in all three commands to secrecy outside miracle stories – and only in them – we have the singular of the personal pronoun αὐτός: καὶ ἐπετίμησεν αὐτοῖς ἵνα μηδενὶ λέγωσι περὶ αὐτοῦ (Mk 8.30); καὶ πολλὰ ἐπετίμα αὐτοῖς ἵνα μὴ αὐτὸν φανερὸν ποιήσωσιν (3.12); καὶ οὐκ ἤφιεν λαλεῖν τὰ δαιμόνια, ὅτι ᾔδεισαν αὐτόν (1.34). We may therefore conclude that all commands to secrecy outside miracle stories refer strictly to the mystery of the identity of Jesus, which is never the case inside miracle stories. In these there are on the one hand commands to silence in absolute form, with no object (1.25; 4.39; 10.48; 7.36), especially commands to fall silent and the rebuke in 10.48, and on the other a neuter object is mentioned, μηδέν and τοῦτο (1.44 and 5.43). The object of the secrecy is thus a state of affairs not the identity of Jesus. Mk 9.9 is a special case. The grammatical formulation there refers to a state of affairs: the disciples are to keep silent about 'what they have seen' – but what they have seen is the transfigured Jesus revealed as the Son of God, that is, Jesus' true status. From all this we conclude that the traditional commands to silence and secrecy originally appeared in the miracle stories, where they were a standard device, but Mark transferred them to other genres and made them refer to the status of Jesus. In so doing he combined two traditional features. The order to be silent at an exorcism was directed against the apotropaeic use of the knowledge of Jesus' status, but had no implication of secrecy. The command to silence after ῥῆσις βαρβαρική did aim at secrecy, but was not concerned with the identity and status of Jesus. The combination of the two produces a situation in which the identity and status of Jesus becomes the object of the secrecy.[70] Mark will have taken the traditional commands to silence as also having this purpose.

Once again we have found that the model of archaeological strata is not totally adequate (though not without value) for the separation of tradition and redaction. A more appropriate description of the Marcan use of commands to silence results when they are regarded as creative realisations of an existing stock of motifs which constitutes the genre 'miracle story'. Even this new and creative feature did not come into existence *ex nihilo*. When Mark connects the identity and status of Jesus and secrecy, the motif of

---

[70] U. Luz, *Geheimnismotiv*, 9ff., has rightly noted this concentration on the person. I think it unlikely that Mark did not think of the 'secret of the miracle' (i.e. the traditional motifs of secrecy, which have their setting in the miracle stories) in the same way.

acclamation, which represents the recognition of the status of the miracle-worker, and the motif of secrecy are brought into heightened contrast. He is thus actualising a potential opposition present in the field of motifs by modifying the usual contrast between the secret of the miracle and publicity or between the demon's miraculous knowledge and the miracle-worker's counter-measure, to produce a new opposition. He is not introducing an alien feature into miracle stories, but drawing on unrealised potentialities of the form-critical field of motifs, within which a multiplicity of oppositions is possible.[71]

It is interesting to note that the other synoptic evangelists do not follow Mark in his treatment of the secrecy motifs. Where they do not simply delete the command to silence (Mt 8.16f.; 9.26; Lk 6.19), they connect it with more traditional objects. In Mt 12.16 a place is to be kept secret, and Mt 9.30 (if it is an independent tradition) may have the same Jewish Christian background as Mk 1.40ff. Lk 8.56 is concerned with the miraculous event, and makes the prospect of keeping it secret more realistic since Luke has only the disciples and the parents present in the house with the dead girl.

D. A Final Motif: the Acclamation

The history of aretalogical acclamations has been subjected to careful study by E. Peterson in the course of his investigation of εἷς θεός acclamations. 'These acclamations within miracle stories . . . are a feature of Christian literature which can be found in the East from the 2nd to the 10th centuries' (188). Starting from these (post-New Testament) examples, Peterson attempts to discover their previous history. We shall give detailed references to his views, particularly since they are scattered in various places through his book.[72]

1. Functional Aspects

(a) Profane acclamations throw light on the origin of aretalogical acclamations: 'The religious acclamation is linked in its origin with the secular ἐκκλησία. To understand this we must think of an analogy, the ancient view that *mirabilia* of any sort concerned the whole city and therefore had to be discussed by the population as a whole in the ἐκκλησία, i.e. usually in the theatre' (190). Evidence for this claim is provided from Phlegon's

---

[71] For a different view cf. G. Klein, 'Wunderglaube und Neues Testament', *Ärgernisse*, 1970, 13-57, esp. 55: 'Although Mark thus intervenes almost violently in the text of the miracle stories . . .'. For a more accurate view of Mark. See H.J. Held, *Matthew as Interpreter*, p. 284.

[72] The quotations which follow are all from E. Peterson, ΕΙΣ ΘΕΟΣ, and the numbers in brackets refer to the pages. See also T. Klausner, 'Akklamation', *RAC* I, 216-33.

Mirabilia, but it is immediately qualified: 'I do not in any sense . . . claim that the style of paradoxigraphical literature explains the appearance of popular acclamations in (Christian and pagan) miracle stories . . . . I am merely saying that the paradoxigraphical literature provides a certain analogy and a sort of precedent for the appearance of the people in the Hellenistic miracle story' (190).

(b) The aretalogical acclamation in connection with miracles has a missionary function: 'While the need for entertainment may have had no small part to play in the rise of this kind of literature, it must not be forgotten that its main purpose was to meet the needs of propaganda, that is, it was given a missionary role' (213). Peterson also thinks he can detect a juridical function attached specifically to the acclamation; he believes that the presence of the people guarantees the credibility of the miracle (pp 191, 216).

(c) The aretalogical acclamation does not occur in literary works, in Philostr. *vita Apoll.*, Athan. *vita Antonii*, Aug. *civ.* XXII, 8. 'We should probably distinguish between the literary miracle story in the strict sense and popular writings. It certainly seems to me that the acclamation is generally a device of popular literature' (221).

2. Diachronic Aspects

(a) The aretalogical acclamation comes from Egypt. Two pieces of evidence are offered for this claim. The first is a papyrus fragment (P. Oxy. XI. No 1382), in which a miracle story, probably the provision of drinking water on a sea-voyage, ends with an acclamation, εἷς Ζεὺς Σάραπις. The papyrus itself is from the second century A.D., but Peterson suggests 'that the acclamation εἷς Ζεὺς Σάραπις may have originated before Domitian (81-96), at the time of Vespasian's stay in Egypt and that it may have some connection with the healing miracles performed by Vespasian by the power of Sarapis' (217, n. 4). What is certain is – and this is the second support for the suggestion of an Egyptian origin for aretalogical acclamations – that political acclamations were common in Egypt at an early date. Suetonius (*Nero* 20, 3) says that acclamations had been imported from Alexandria. It was in all probability to the Alexandrians that Germanicus' decree on acclamations of the year A.D. 18 was addressed (text in Peterson, 172; cf. also T. Klausner, *RAC* I, 227). The underlying assumption is that Germanicus has been acclaimed as a god. A further piece of evidence for the Alexandrian origin of acclamations is *vita Apoll.* V, 24: the Alexandrians were celebrating the prophetic gifts of Apollonius, but there was no acclamation (222).

(b) The Romans' importation of the acclamation from Alexandria encouraged the entry of the acclamation into miracle stories: 'It seems that the acclamation in miracle stories is typical of Egypt and that it was the adoption of acclamations by the Romans which first encouraged the spread of acclamation formulae in later miracle stories' (195). The thesis that the Romans adopted acclamations comes from Suetonius (see above). Evidently Peterson does not mean that the presence of accla-mations in the miracle stories comes directly from the Romans, but that the use of political acclamations in Rome 'encouraged' the spread of aretalogical acclamations.

(c) Judaism rather than Rome was the immediate model for the accla-mation in Christian miracle stories. Peterson refers to the 'mediating role . . . played by the Jewish miracle story of the Hellenistic period between the pagan and the Christian miracle story' (216). He is mainly thinking here of the Jewish propaganda formula εἷς θεός: 'It is this Jewish propaganda formula which the Christians adopted and which they used, among other things, as an acclamation in their miracle stories. We may assume that they found it already in use for such purposes among the Jews' (216). Peterson can provide no evidence: 'The remains of the Jewish miracle stories which have come down to us and which show Hellenistic influence are few' (216). In another context, however, he does quote an aretalogical μέγας-acclamation from a Jewish apocryphal work (*Bel and the Dragon*, v. 18 and 41).

3. Application to the New Testament

Peterson sees a problem in the fact 'that in the New Testament the acclamation as such does not occur in miracle stories'. He offers three different explanations for this:

(a) 'The reason for this seems to me to be that the miracle story, separated from other contexts, has not yet become a piece of literary propaganda in competition with other religions' (195).

(b) 'It seems that the acclamation in miracle stories is typical of Egypt and it may have been the adoption of acclamations by the Romans which encouraged the spread of acclamation formulae in the later miracle stories' (195). Bultmann (HST 226) has accepted this view.

(c) In his appendices Peterson adds a third explanation: 'The absence of the acclamation from the miracle stories of the gospels may also have a more fundamental reason. Jesus' life lacked the public character ex-pressed in the public announcement constituted by an acclamation' (319).

We shall discuss Peterson's views in order, but we do not intend to embark on a complete survey or exhaustive analysis of the texts he discusses.

1. Functional Aspects

(a) The presence of a crowd in miracle stories has its closest analogy, not in the secular, but in the cultic community: believers are always present in the sanctuary to celebrate God's deeds. Those who have been healed or saved tell their stories here and the community joins in their praise. The same intention can be seen in the thanksgiving inscriptions. In one such inscription Cleo calls on the visitors to the sanctuary to be amazed at the god's feat of healing (Epidaurus 1). Because of the closeness to our motifs of 'wonder' and 'acclamation' we reproduce the inscription

οὐ μέγεθος πίνακος θαυμαστέον, ἀλλὰ τὸ θεῖον
πένθ' ἔθη ὡς ἐκύησε ἐν γαστρὶ κλεὼ βάρος
ἔστε ἐγκατεκοιμάθη καὶ μιν ἔθηκε ὑγιῆ.

In Aristophanes' comedy *Pluto* the chorus in the theatre has replaced the cultic choir.[73] Carion describes the miracle and exults:

ὁ δεσπότης πέπραγεν εὐτυχέστατα,
μᾶλλον δ'ὁ πλοῦτος αὐτός · ἀντὶ γὰρ τυφλοῦ
ἐξωμμάτωται καὶ λελάμπρυνται κόρας,
'Ασκληπιοῦ παιῶνος εὐμενοῦς τυχών (*Pluto*, 633ff.)

The chorus agrees and continues, alternating with Carion:

λέγεις μοι χαράν, λέγεις μοι βοάν.
πάρεστι χαίρειν, ἤντε βούλησθ' ἤν τε μή.
ἀναβοάσομαι τὸν εὔπαιδα καὶ
μέγα βροτοῖσι φέγγος 'Ασκληπιόν.

It could be objected that the chorus here is part of the comedy, but nevertheless it is probably replacing the cultic community. A similar transformation can be seen in P. Oxy. XI. No 1381 (col. IIff.) of the 2nd century A.D., in which a healing by Imhotep is described.[74] The thank offering of the person cured is to be to translate the god's feats into Greek: 'Every Greek tongue will tell your story and every Greek will honour Imuthes, the God of Ptha.' The intended object for this missionary action is the Greek world, which can be reached by writing. The writer appeals to it:

'Draw near, all good and right-minded people, away, you fault-finders and godless.
Draw near, you who have been freed from illness by prayer to the god,
you who practise the doctor's art,
you who seek to live a holy life,
you on whom fortune has smiled,
who have been saved from the dangers of the sea.
Everywhere the saving power of the god has revealed itself.
Now I shall tell of his marvellous manifestations,
of the gifts of his goodness'.

---

[73] For a discussion of the passage see O. Weinreich, *AH*, 108. There is a second acclamation a little later (line 745). With reference to the healing of Pluto in Aristophanes, G. Delling, *Beurteilung*, 66, comments: 'Those who had been cured must have described their experiences in a similar way. . . . In particular, the expressions of praise of the god after a miracle are genuine' (745, 748).

[74] J. Leipoldt, 'Von Übersetzungen und Übersetzern', *Antike und Orient*, 1950, 54-63, esp. 56ff., gives an interpretation of the text.

The order 'Draw near,' seems out of place in a written text. In form-critical terms it is an exclusion formula, as can be seen from the mystery religions.[75] The process of writing has separated this form from its original situation. Addressed to an anonymous literary public, it would be meaningless. The author pretends – thereby reflecting actual practice – that he is standing in the temple and calling on the worshippers to come forward and wonder at the god's miracles.

If Aristophanes and P. Oxy. XI, 1381 give us grounds for inferring thanksgiving before a public and by a public, in the inscriptions of the Roman Asclepium we have direct evidence of it. Here the acclamation conclusion has become standard (SIG³, III 1173):

5ff.   καὶ ὀρθὸν ἀνέβλεψε τοῦ δήμου παρεστῶτος συγ-
χαιρομένου, ὅτι ζῶσαι ἀρεταὶ ἐγένοντο ἐπὶ τοῦ Σεβαστοῦ
ἡμῶν 'Αντονίου.

9ff.   καὶ ἐσώθη καὶ δημοσίᾳ ηὐχαρίστησεν τῷ θεῷ καὶ ὁ δῆμος
συνεχάρη αὐτῷ

13f.   καὶ ἐσώθη καὶ ἐλθὼν δημοσίᾳ ηὐχαρίστησεν ἔμπροσθεν
τοῦ δήμου.

17f.   καὶ ἀνέβλεψεν καὶ ἐλήλυθεν καὶ ηὐχαρίστησεν δημοσίᾳ
τῷ θεῷ.

The first account could be interpreted as meaning that the people were present at the miraculous occurrence, as Peterson believes,[76] regarding the text as evidence for his view that the presence of the people acted as a confirmation of the miracle. However, this is unlikely. As at the sanctuary at Epidaurus, the healings probably took place in the *abaton*. The person who has been cured then 'comes out' and gives thanks 'publicly'. The explicit reference to the coming out in lines 12 and 17, and the emphasis on the public nature of the thanksgiving (δημοσίᾳ), rule out the presence of a crowd at the healing itself. The crowd's jubilation is prompted by the cured person's report, and his expression of gratitude has to be mentioned explicitly three times before the joy of the people.

P. Oxy. XI, 1382, to which we have already referred, must also be discussed here.[77] A helmsman, Syrion, seems to have been saved by the miraculous provision of drinking water at sea. He gives the water to the people of Pharos and then sails off again.

---

[75] So, rightly, Leipoldt, 'Übersetzungen', 62. Mt 11.25-30, however, is not a parallel, though there is one in the πρόρρησις of the mysteries: Isocrates, *Panegyricus*, 157; Lucian, *Alex.* 38; Rev. 22.15; Philo, *Spec.* I, 324-45; *mut.* 204.

[76] ΕΙΣ ΘΕΟΣ, 191.

[77] On this see O. Weinreich, 'Neue Urkunden zur Sarapis-Religion', SGV 86. 1919; ΕΙΣ ΘΕΟΣ, 217-21.

According to this account of the miracle, which has survived only in fragmentary form, 'those present' were called upon to acclaim the god:[78] . . . καὶ καταχωρίζεται. ἡ ἀρετὴ ἐν ταῖς Μερκυρίου βιβλιοθήκαις. οἱ παρόντες εἴπατε εἷς Ζευς Σάραπις [. . .] This text is all the more interesting because it makes the acclamation clearly distinct from the account of the miracle proper. The two are separated by the reference to the library of Mercury. In other words, it is not the Pharians who are called on to make the acclamation (if so, the previous reference to them in the third person would be hardly conceivable), but the listeners to the miracle story. In the light of the parallels already discussed, we may assume that this text presupposes a cultic situation.[79] The acclamations could also take the form of a short attribution of a title. After Aelius Aristeides has bathed in the freezing river and been cured, the watching crowd responds to the 'miracle' with a μέγας-acclamation; καὶ βοὴ πολλὴ τῶν τε παρόντων καὶ ἐπιόντων τὸ πολυύμνητον δὴ τοῦτο βοώντων, μέγας ὁ Ἀσκληπιός (Aristid. or. XLVIII, 21). Gratitude for and acknowledgment of miraculous rescue, however, also often took the form of longer hymns of praise. Many of these hymns have survived.[80] They were so typical of the cult of Asclepius that *paian,* originally a technical term for hymns to Apollo, became the standard name for these hymns to Asclepius.[81] This is further confirmation of our assumption that the acclaiming, marvelling and exultant crowd in the miracle stories derives its precedent from the liturgical community – rather than the secular assembly.

(b) On the other hand, the assumption that miracle stores and acclamations have a missionary intention is probably correct. The missionary intention is explicit in the description of the Imhotep healing in P. Oxy. XI, 1381. In my view, however, the legal function of 'making a public announcement' is secondary to the dependence of praise on a celebrating community and of individual acclamation on the acclamation of the group.

(c) The absence of aretalogical acclamations in many miracle stories cannot be explained by the difference between popular and elevated literature. The healings from Epidaurus, which belong to

---

[78] ΕΙΣ ΘΕΟΣ, 221; M. Dibelius, *Die Formgeschichte des Evangeliums*, 72, n. 1 (no Eng. trl.) leaves open the question whether it is an imperative or an indicative.

[79] So, rightly, R. Reitzenstein, *Hellenistic Mystery-Religions*, 1978, p. 96, n. 41: 'Pap. Oxyrh. 1382 offers a confessional formula as an acclamation of the community at the conclusion of the worship service.' For a contrary view, see E. Peterson, ΕΙΣ ΘΕΟΣ, 221, n. 3: 'I do not need to stress that nothing in the papyrus fragment indicates a liturgy.'

[80] See the collection of texts in Edelstein, *Asklepios* I, 325-36.

[81] Cf. Edelstein II, 199-208.

popular literature, contain no acclamations but Aristophanes, who belongs to world literature, has two. There is also an implicit acclamation in the miracle stories told by Augustine (*civ.* XXII, 8). Augustine got a woman to report her healing 'in the presence of the other women, who marvelled greatly at it and praised God'. In my view a different explanation for the frequent absence of acclamations is to be preferred. In the examples given the acclamation always followed the *account* of the miracle, not immediately on the miraculous *event* as such; in other words, all the miracle stories were intended to provoke wonder (and acclamation), but did not necessarily anticipate them. Under particular form-critical conditions, in addition to the miracle itself, the process of reporting the miracle is also retained, for example when miracle stories become part of another genre, comedy (Aristophanes) or missionary texts (P. Oxy. XI, 1381). The accounts of healings from the Roman Asclepium, with their stereotyped acclamations, also distinguish between the miraculous event and the report of the miracle and place the people's joy after the report. In one sense all miracle stories aim at amazement and approval, but they do not for that reason all contain acclamations. The acclamations may rather be part of the 'oral framework', which was not necessarily integrated into the story so as to become gradually a fixed element, as in the following cases: A man gets up from his bed after being cured: καὶ τὸν θεὸν ἀναβοήσας ἀπήει τοῖς ἑαυτοῦ ποσὶ διὰ τῆς πόλεως οἴκαδε ὑγιής (Dion. Hal. *ant.* VII), though here there is no acclamation from a crowd. The Apollonius aretalogy from Delos is different (IG XI, 1299). Sarapis came to the aid of his servant in court: ἅπας δ'ἄρα λαὸς ἐκείνων σὴν ἀρετὴν θάμβησεν ἐν ἤματι καὶ μέγα κῦδος σῶι τεύξας θεράποντι θεόδμητεν κατὰ Δῆλον.

2. Diachronic Aspects

(a) One response to the claim that aretalogical acclamations originated in Egypt is to ask whether acclamations of the god manifested in a miracle are not fairly widespread phenomena which, while they lend themselves to typological classification, are difficult to trace to a historical origin. A very old example (not quoted by Peterson) does point to Egypt (Pap. Anastasi V, 9f., 13th cent. B.C.):[82]

'Come to me and care for me; for I am a servant of your house. Let me speak of your strong deeds, in whatever country I may be. So will

---

[82] Text from E. Erman, *Die Literatur der Ägypter*, 1923, 377.

the multitude say, "What Toth does is great"; they will come with their children to stamp them.'

Nevertheless the Old Testament and the Septuagint also contain responses to miracles which resemble acclamations. They occur in three contexts: in connection with signs showing Yahweh to be God, in healings by charismatic miracle-workers and (a minority) in miraculous punishments. It is characteristic that the situations in which the Israelite religion shows itself in these texts in acclamations usually involve competition with another religion.

On Mount Carmel the people are faced with a choice between Yahweh or Baal. After Elijah's fire miracle they fall on their faces and cry, 'Yahweh is God, Yahweh is God' (1 Kings 18.39). In the Septuagint the assertion formula ἀληθῶς is added: 'Αληθῶς κύριός ἐστιν ὁ θεός, αὐτὸς ὁ θεός.[83]

Motifs from the miracle on Carmel appear in 2 Macc 1.18ff. The miracle is followed, not by an acclamation, but by a prayer which begins with an acclamation: κύριε κύριε ὁ θεός, ὁ πάντων κτίστης (1.24). There are also two comparable examples from *Bel and the Dragon*. In both cases there is a choice between Yahweh and Baal. After a miracle resulting from a trick by the priests the king confesses, Μέγας εἶ, Βηλ, καὶ οὐκ ἔστιν παρὰ σοὶ δόλος οὐδὲ εἷς [cf. var. lect.] (v. 18), but after a second miracle realises the truth: Μέγας εἶ κύριε ὁ θεός τοῦ Δανιηλ καὶ οὐκ ἔστιν πλὴν οὗ ἄλλος [cf. var. lect.] (v. 41).[84] Similarly the doxologies in the book of Daniel are connected with miracles demonstrating the majesty of the one God (2.47; 4.34; 3.28; 6.25ff.). But stories of healings and raisings from the dead also include acclamations. After being freed from leprosy, the Syrian Naaman confesses, 'Behold, I know that there is no God in all the earth but in Israel' (2 Kings 5.15), and the widow of Sarepta, after the raising of her son, says, 'Now I know that you are a man of God, and that the word of the LORD in your mouth is truth' (1 Kings 17.24). In the first case there is again a situation of competition. For the Syrian Naaman the competent God, strictly speaking, would have been Rimmon (2 Kings 5.18). In both cases there is no crowd, and the miracles involved also have no cultic associations (which would presuppose the presence of a congregation), but are accounts of charismatic miracle-workers.

---

[83] On the ἀληθῶς formula cf. E. Peterson, ΕΙΣ ΘΕΟΣ, 313.
[84] Peterson (ΕΙΣ ΘΕΟΣ, 207) ascribes the μέγας acclamation at this point to Hellenistic influence.

Aretalogical acclamations also appear in a third context. In 2 Macc 6.37 Antiochus Epiphanes is threatened that he will be brought by torments to confess μόνος αὐτὸς ὁ θεός ἐστιν (i.e. Yahweh). Here the acclamation follows an anticipated punishment miracle. Comparable are the expiatory inscriptions of the 2nd and 3rd century A.D. from Asia Minor published by F. Steinleiter in which the god against which the person has sinned is praised in an acclamation.[85] The inscriptions are indications of gratitude testifying that the punishment was rescinded. Here too the subject is the god's marvellous deeds: εὐλογῶν σου τὰς δυνάμεις (no. 9).

In the miracle stories of Old Testament Judaism we do not find the contrast between miracle and acclamation, thanksgiving by the individual and agreement of the crowd, which we found to be a feature of the cultic situation in pagan sanctuaries. Here the miracles themselves – and not just the reports of the miracles – culminate in acclamations of Yahweh. The acknowledgment of Yahweh is the point, and it is emphasised by the situation of competition with other gods. The evidence as a whole does not really support the view that aretalogical acclamations originated exclusively in Egypt, and in particular the examples Peterson cites in support of this view are all later than the Old Testament and the Septuagint.

For example, Peterson denies such an Egyptian origin for the expiatory inscriptions from Asia Minor: 'It seems to me impossible to substantiate even a general assumption that the expiatory inscriptions from Asia Minor which begin with acclamations only derived these acclamations from contact with Egyptian sources. These acclamations from Asia Minor are much more likely to be of Iranian origin.' However, he immediately continues: 'The acclamation in the aretalogy, however, raises a different problem, and here I regard the influence of the literary Egyptian aretalogies on the other aretalogies as very probable' (ΕΙΣ ΘΕΟΣ, 142).

(b) But what about Peterson's claim that aretalogical acclamations were encouraged by the political acclamations imported by the Romans from Egypt? It is certain that acclamations were not introduced into miracle stories in this way, but it is possible that the aretalogical type of acclamation may have undergone change because of the influence of the political acclamation. A person who is acclaimed has a claim to power and authority. This fact was

---

[85] F. Steinleitner, *Die Beichte im Zusammenhang mit der sakralen Rechtspflege in der Antike*, 1913. On these acclamations, cf. also Peterson, 200ff.

constantly emphasised by the significance of acclamations in the political life of the empire (cf. Germanicus' decree). This claim to power may have rubbed off on to the later Christian miracle stories. Here it is often unmistakable. When Thecla (Act. Paul. 26ff.) has been sentenced to fight the beasts by an unjust judgment of the governor of Antioch and is saved by a miracle, the governor himself is forced to capitulate: 'And the governor immediately issued an edict in these terms: "I release to you Thecla, the holy servant of God." But the women all cried out with loud voices and praised God with one voice, saying, "There is one God and he has saved Thecla," so that the whole city shook with their shouting' (*Act. Paul.* 38). Here the Christian community is proclaiming its claim over the city and the governor; the acclamation takes place in the theatre, the city's forum. The history of aretalogical acclamations begins with liturgical thanksgiving and leads to religio-political claims to power. The New Testament acclamations, of course, fall into neither category.

(c) The claim that Jewish aretalogical acclamations played a mediating role between Egyptian and Christian acclamations can no longer be maintained if the Egyptian origin of acclamations in general is questionable. The Jewish acclamations must be understood in terms of Old Testament tradition. The Qumran texts include a prayer by a man named Nabonid who has been cured by a Jewish miracle-worker. His healing is written down 'to give honour and great glory to the most high God' (*Prayer of Nabonid* 5). The Christian New Testament acclamations may represent a continuation of Jewish tradition.

3. Application to the New Testament

E. Peterson found no 'true acclamations' in the New Testament, that is, titular acclamations after miracles. We must correct this view. Dibelius has already drawn attention to Lk 7.16,[86] to which may be added Lk 5.8; Mt 12.23; 14.33; Jn 1.49 (4.42); 6.14 (9.37). In Acts Simon Magus (8.10) and Paul and his companions (14.11f.; 16.30; 28.6) are acclaimed. It is true that the individual passages show formal differences, but common to all is the giving of honorific titles to miracle-workers after a miracle, whether in the form of a question or the declaration of a conviction, whether the acknowledgment is referred to indirectly or quoted in full.

Lk 7.16   Fear seized them all; and they glorified God, saying, 'A great prophet has arisen amongst us!' and 'God has visited his people!'

---

[86] *TG*, 75.

Lk 5.8	But when Simon Peter saw it, he fell down at Jesus' knees, saying, 'Depart from me, for I am a sinful man, O Lord.' [9]For he was astonished, and all ...
Mt 12.23	And all the people were amazed, and said, 'Can this be the Son of David?'
Mt 14.33	And those in the boat worshipped him, saying, 'Truly you are the Son of God.'
Jn 1.49	Nathanael answered him, 'Rabbi, you are the Son of God! You are the King of Israel!'
Jn 6.14	When the people saw the sign which he had done, they said, 'This is indeed the prophet who is to come into the world!'
Acts 8.10	They all gave heed to him, from the least to the greatest, saying, 'This man is that power of God which is called Great.'
Acts 14.11f.	And when the crowds saw what Paul had done, they lifted up their voices, saying in Lycaonian, 'The gods have come down to us in the likeness of men!' [12]Barnabas they called Zeus, and Paul, because he was the chief speaker, they called Hermes.
Acts 16.30	[Silas] brought them out and said, 'Lords, what must I do to be saved?'
Acts 28.6	But when they had waited a long time and saw no misfortune come to him, they changed their minds and said that he was a god.

The striking feature is not the absence of titular acclamations in general, but their total absence in the Marcan miracle stories, where only acclamations without titles occur (1.27; 2.12; 4.41; 7.37). Acclamations (15.39) and cries resembling acclamations (Mk 6.14f.) occur only outside miracle stories. How is this absence of aretalogical acclamations in the oldest gospel to be explained?

The absence of acclamations in many ancient miracle stories was partly explained earlier as resulting from the fact that acclamations and expressions of wonder may have belonged to the oral framework. Is this explanation applicable to the New Testament evidence? There are the fact signs in all three gospels – of various kinds – that acclamations may have been part of the oral framework, that they were regarded as a reaction to the *account* of the miracle and not to the *event* of the miracle. In Mk 7.36f. the order is command to silence, breach of the command, proclamation of the miracle and only then the acclamation: 'He has done all things well.' (7.37). In the Marcan redaction (v. 36b is probably editorial) the acclamation refers to the account of the miracle, as does the expression of wonder in 5.20: 'And he went away and began to proclaim in the Decapolis how much Jesus had done for him; and all men marvelled' (another example of Marcan redaction). In 6.14ff. Herod comments on miracles (δυνάμεις) without having seen them. They have been reported to him: καὶ ἤκουσεν ὁ βασιλεύς (6.14). Reports provoke comments including a title, inadequate though they may be. Cries similar to acclamations in 6.2 refer to miracles (δυνάμεις),[87] though no miracles have occurred. Mark may have been thinking of previous miracles,[88] though he does not say that news of them had reached Jesus' home town. Was he able to dispense with such a note because for him διδάσκειν (6.2) included accounts of miracles? In other words, did he superimpose on the meeting in the synagogue a Christian missionary meeting at which teaching about Jesus' miraculous feats provoked wonder (and rejection)?

Once we have admitted in the case of Mk 7.36f.; 5.19f.; 6.14f. that in Mark's view acclamations (and wonder) could be part of the oral framework, we inevitably notice that there is a tension between all the acclamations in Mark and the preceding miracles.

Once it has been admitted in the case of Mk 7.36f.; 5.19f.; 6.14f. that in the Marcan scheme acclamations (and wonder) could be part of the oral framework, it is impossible not to be struck further by the narrative tension between all the acclamations in Mark and the miracles which precede them. They have not been completely integrated into the narrative of the miracle stories. Mk 7.37 refers not just to the healing of the deaf and dumb man, but to all Jesus' miracles: καλῶς πάντα πεποίηκεν, καὶ . . . In the case of 1.27, the question has often been asked why the witnesses of the exorcism in the synagogue at Capernaum exclaim, 'What is this? A new *teaching*?' when there is no trace of any 'didactic features' in the exorcism itself and the brief reference to Jesus' teaching in 1.22 betrays the hand of Mark? Is this a reason for deleting the motif of teaching in v. 27 too?[89] Has the question about the 'new teaching' pushed out a more obvious question about Jesus' identity, 'Who is this?'[90] 'New teaching', however, is a missionary term (Acts 17.19; cf. 13.12). The stories of missionaries are new teaching. The term can

---

[87] Σοφία can also refer to the miracle-worker's knowledge. Lucian calls a Syrian exorcist σοφιστής (*Philopseudes*, 16), and the magician may be a σοφός (cf. L. Bieler, *Theios Aner*, 76ff.; R. Reitzenstein, *Mystery Religions*, 297). In my view, however, it is more likely that 'wisdom' here means teaching; cf. Mk 1.27.

[88] Cf. E. Grässer, 'Jesus in Nazareth', *NTS* 16 (1969), 1-23, on the problems of this pericope.

[89] *HST*, 209.

[90] R. Pesch, 'Ein Tag vollmächtigen Wirkens Jesu in Kapernaum (Mk 1,29-34.35-39)', *BL* 9 (1968), 114-28, 177-95, 261-77, esp. 118.

be explained without difficulty if we refer the acclamation, not to the exorcism itself, but to the description of it, that is, if it was originally not Jesus, but a Christian bearing witness to and teaching about his powers of exorcism, who prompted the acclamations. Mark runs the synagogue service and the missionary service into one. He is conscious of the demonstration of the new teaching at Christian meetings through descriptions of exorcisms. The acclamation, which belongs to the oral framework, has been incorporated into the description and blended with it.

2.12 should perhaps be explained similarly. A tension exists between the acclamation and the preceding narrative insofar as it is unclear who is meant by 'all': certainly the scribes would have little reason to rejoice at their defeat.[91] Nor is the critical deletion of vv. 6-10 of much help here; the lack of integration of the acclamation into the narrative remains a problem at least for the Marcan version of the miracle story. Is not the simplest explanation here too that behind the anonymous acclaiming crowd we see the hearers of the miracle story, visible behind the attendant ὄχλος.

This poses the literary critical problem of Mk 2.1-10 in a new way.[92] The contradiction between the acclamation from all the bystanders and the presence of opponents of Jesus was one of the weightiest arguments for the excision of vv. 5b-10. (If we ignore the possibility that this is an example of an oral framework which has been integrated into the narrative, Mk 12.17 might be compared; here Jesus' opponents are 'amazed'.) We do not wish to settle the issue, but the following points raise difficulties: a) It is hard to maintain that v. 5b is not part of the original story; it is in the normal form for an assurance. It has been rightly argued[93] that the key words 'to forgive sins' must have been part of the traditional miracle story if the introduction of the discussion about the forgiveness of sins is to make sense. If 5b is accepted as traditional, however, there are difficulties about deleting 6-10 on grounds of both form and content: for formal reasons because an assurance is an anticipated healing but almost never immediately introduces the healing, and for reasons of content because it is scarcely conceivable that the provocative reference to the forgiveness of sins could have remained without an effect on the narrative. b) With

---

[91] Cf. Bultmann, *HST,* 15.

[92] The analysis first advanced by W. Wrede ('Zur Heilung des Gelähmten [Mc 2,1ff.]', *ZNW* 5 [1904], 354-58') has been most recently argued out in detail by I. Maisch, *Die Heilung des Gelähmten. Eine exegetisch-traditionsgeschichtliche Untersuchung zu Mk 2,1-12,* 1970. The counter arguments of R.T. Mead ('The Healing of the Paralytic – a Unit?', *JBL* 80 [1961], 348-54), who argues for an independent unit, are inadequate. W.G. Kümmel, *Die Theologie des Neuen Testaments,* 1969, 40, pronounces it (without giving reasons) an independent unit.

[93] F. Hahn, *Titles,* 226, n. 11 (note given in full in *Hoheitstitel,* 228, n. 2); W. Grundmann, *Markus,* 54f.; Schürmann, *Lukas,* 286.

regard to the change in the persons spoken to between vv. 10 and 11, we shall discuss later the possibility that v. 10 is an element of 'commentary' within the narrative which to a certain extent emerges from the narrative and addresses the reader directly. However, if we do decide that 5b-10 (or 6-10) is an addition, there is every reason to admire the narrative technique of the second author, who has turned the two distinct levels of composition 'assurance' (5b) and 'word of healing' (11) into an either-or question and so actualised a new 'opposition' in the paradigmatic field of motifs. For the form he could take as a model the structure of a number of rule miracles, which settle alternative questions by miracles and prefer compositions with the stress on the exposition.

There is a third acclamation conclusion in 4.41. The contrast between it and the narrative are clear here again. The disciples who have just been rebuked for their lack of faith are now able to recognise Jesus' status: someone who can command the wind and the waves must be a divine being. In Matthew the lack of narrative integration of the acclamation is even clearer. Matthew must also have seen that the acclamation was (possibly) part of the oral framework of the miracle stories. This is the only explanation for his sudden introduction, at the end of the quelling of the storm, of 'the men'. They cannot conceivably have been present on the crossing, and yet they share in the danger to the boat, the despair of the disciples and the defeat of the storm – as listeners to the primitive Christian miracle story. 'The ἄνθρωποι in our passage are obviously intended to represent the men who are encountered by the story through preaching.'[94]

How independent of the preceding pericope Matthew can make an acclamation conclusion is also shown by Mt 14.33: 'And those in the boat worshipped him, saying, "Truly you are the Son of God."' A boat is not a good place for prostration. Through it we can catch a glimpse of a different situation: listeners moved by the proclamation recognise Jesus as the Son of God, a situation referred to by 1 Cor 14.24f.: unbelievers take part in a community meeting, hear the preaching of the community, 'and so, falling on his face, he (sc. the unbeliever) will worship God and declare that God is really among you'.[95] Here too it may be noticed that acclamations may belong to the oral framework of preaching.

The development in Luke goes in a quite different direction.

---

[94] G. Bornkamm, 'The Stilling of the Storm in Matthew', in *Tradition and Interpretation*, 56.

[95] G. Bornkamm, 'Stilling of the Storm', 56, has already cited 1 Cor 14.24f. to explain Mt 8.27.

Here the integration of the acclamation conclusion is well advanced.[96]

A good example is the reworking of the exorcism in the synagogue at Capernaum. The contrast which is noticeable in Mark between teaching and exorcism has been reduced because the 'teaching' is called 'word' and the exorcism takes place by means of the 'word' (4.36). The unevenness at the end of the account of the stilling of the storm is also removed. In place of the charge of unbelief, πῶς οὐκ ἔχετε πίστιν; (Mk 4.40) there is the question about faith, 'Where is your faith?' (Lk 8.25), which is answered by the acclamation.

Luke, however, has not only smoothed out the tensions evident in Mark, but also given the conclusion a new shape of his own. Only in his version is the acclamation, usually praise of God, spoken by individuals. In several places he has altered the Marcan text in this way. At the healing of the paralytic he adds to the statement that the man went away cured δοξάζων τὸν θεόν (5.25). Only then comes the crowd's acclamation. The same contrast between the individual and the people has been introduced into the story of the healing of the blind man in Jericho. Luke's addition is: '(and he followed him) glorifying God; and all the people, when they saw it, gave praise to God' (18.43). In the pericope of the woman with the issue of blood Luke stresses that she 'declared' her healing before the people (8.47). Luke adds to Mark's text: '(and told him) in the presence of all the people why she had touched him, and how she had been immediately healed' (8.47). The woman with the bent back praises God after her healing (13.13) and the people join in after the debate about the sabbath: 'and all the people rejoiced at all the glorious things that were done by him' (13.17).

The distinction between the individual and the people appears only in Luke; it must come from his editorial work. The model for this Lucan treatment of the acclamation conclusion is cultic thanksgiving, which was performed by an individual before the community, which then joins in: in Acts 3.1-10 the man who has been cured hurries to the Temple and praises God before the amazed people. This treatment ties the acclamation, which is part of the oral framework where it is self-explanatory, more firmly into the development of the narrative, and at the same time makes its original position clear. The people's praise refers not

---

[96] K. Tagawa, *Miracles*, 98, has the same phenomenon in mind when he says of the Lucan redaction of the wonder and acclamation motifs (which he does not distinguish): 'Il explique l'étonnement et la crainte en psychologue et les motives logiquement et quasi historiquement, y voyant des attitudes possibles des témoins de chaque scène.'

only directly to the miracle, but also to the individual's praise, is an answer to and extension of his praise, to his account of the miraculous healing.

We thus find indications in all the synoptic gospels that acclamations may have belonged to the oral framework of the miracle stories and, even when fully incorporated into the narrative, still reveal that oral framework. For our interpretation of the miracle stories this implies that even where no acclamation is described we may assume that one is intended. And vice versa, where acclamations have become an integral part of miracle stories, they still indicate an intended oral framework of acclamation. The people in their praise and the disciples in their confession are waiting for the reader to take his place beside them and join in their praise. All miracle stories seek to provoke a response to the miracle-worker: it is with this purpose that they address listeners and readers.[97] Their missionary function (which will be discussed in Part III) arises out of their structure.

Our diachronic investigation has found that the acclamations may originally have been part of the oral framework of the miracle stories. In the course of time, however, the answer to the miracle stories increasingly became a part of the story. In the New Testament this process reaches a climax in Luke, while in this respect Matthew seems sometimes more primitive than Mark. The 'absence' of acclamations in the New Testament, insofar as such an expression has any justification, can now be explained by this connection with the oral framework. This does not make E. Peterson's ideas on this subject invalid. Only the second explanation for the absence of acclamations with titles in the New Testament is invalid; the idea that acclamations originated in Egypt and were transmitted by the Romans is a problematic assumption. The first and third explanations, however, may well contain an element of truth – though not an adequate interpretation of all the New Testament evidence, since the view that acclamations as such are not present cannot be maintained. Nevertheless we are left with the fact that acclamations with titles are completely absent from Mark but appear increasingly in later writings.

(a) The absence of acclamations with titles in Mark may be connected with the fact that miracle stories 'had not yet become pieces

---

[97] Cf. W. Schmithals, *Wunder und Glaube,* 1970, 13: 'By reporting the reactions of the audience at the time the narrator also seeks to provoke the hearer or reader of the story in the present to react.'

of literary propaganda in the competition with other religions'.[98] We saw (from an examination of Old Testament acclamations) that situations of competition gave rise to confessions as an integral element of miracle stories; they embodied a choice against other forms of confession. Is there evidence for similar phenomena in the New Testament? We can answer this question affirmatively. All the acclamations in Acts reveal a situation of competition; acclamations are rejected as un-Christian. In the cases of pagan miracle-workers (Acts 8.10),[99] hybrid politicians (12.22) or alien gods (19.34), the reasons for the rejection are obvious. But Christian miracle-workers are also acclaimed as though they were pagan gods or gods in human form (14.11f.; 16.30; 28.6) – and it is probably not purely accidental that Luke is forced to combat such a misunderstanding. For Luke acclamations by title of earthly miracle-workers or rulers belong to the sphere of paganism. In making the acclamations in his gospel in the main praise God (and not the miracle-worker Jesus), he may be making a deliberate effort to stress the distinction between Christian thanksgiving and the pagan apotheosis of human miracle-workers.[100] Certainly he increases the number of acclamations. The possibility cannot be excluded that this is connected with the evident sharpening of the situation of competition. The rise of acclamations, however, still does not explain their absence in Mark.

(b) As an explanation for the absence of titular acclamations in Mark's gospel Peterson's third hypothesis seems to me questionable, not for historical reasons but in terms of redaction criticism. It was not the secret character of Jesus' life which excluded titular acclamations, but Mark's theory of secrecy, though it does presuppose the existence of acclamations on the paradigmatic level as motifs in opposition to the commands to secrecy. Did he deliberately not actualise them in his composition? Did he not take them over from the oral framework of the miracle stories? A number of observations support this assumption.

i) It is no accident that within the synoptic tradition titular acclamations occur only in the Lucan and Matthaean miracle stories which have not been influenced by Mark; the special material existing

---

[98] E. Peterson, ΕΙΣ ΘΕΟΣ, 195. M. Dibelius, *Formgeschichte*, 72, n. 2, concedes that this argument has relative validity.

[99] On this see H.G. Kippenberg, *Garizim und Synagoge*, 1970, 332ff. He rejects the use of the acclamations collected by Peterson to interpret Acts 8.10, but sees the parallel. He points instead to doxologies in which the Samaritan community praises God's saving action.

[100] On the subordinationist character of Lucan acclamations, cf. K. Tagawa, *Miracles*, 98f. On Lucan subordinationism in general, cf. H. Conzelmann, *Die Mitte der Zeit*, 5th ed. 1964, 158ff.

independently of Mark contained them. In addition, two parallel traditions of Marcan miracle stories which may be independent of Mark contain titular acclamations, the feeding miracle (Jn 6.14)[101] and the walking on the lake (Mt 14.33). The possibility therefore cannot be ruled out that versions of miracle stories already existed in Mark's time which included acknowledgments of Jesus' status. The problem is, did Mark know of such miracle stories?

ii) Mark implies a connection between miracles and titular acclamations because in a number of places he criticises the disciples' failure to make such acclamations. In 6.52 he stresses, 'for they did not understand about the loaves, but their hearts were hardened.' The idea is repeated at 8.17, 21.[102] What Mark is criticising here is the lack of christological insight. He is implying that an acknowledgment of Jesus' Messiahship might already have been expected after the miracle of the loaves. Has Mark omitted it here (or failed to take it over from the oral framework) in order to present the disciples as slow to understand?[103] The parallel Jn 6.14 makes this hypothesis seem possible, but even apart from that we can say that Mark knows that the miracle of the loaves could have been followed by a christological confession. There is no confession, in terms of content because of the disciples' failure to understand and formally because a motif present in the paradigm was not realised in composition.

iii) Aretalogical titular acclamations do occur outside the form-critical context of individual miracle stories. Mark was able to include them despite his secrecy theory because they are uttered by demons, express inadequate views or, because at the end of the gospel they are no longer any threat to its constant theme of secrecy. We have already drawn attention to the displacement of motifs in the confessions of demons in the Marcan summaries (1.34; 3.11): in individual exorcisms they appear in the exposition (1.24; 5.7), in summaries at the end. This final position corresponds to the compositional position of titular acclamations in

---

[101] F. Hahn, *Hoheitstitel*, 391f., regards Jn 6.14 as original. Cf. H. Clavier, 'La multiplication des pains dans le ministère de Jésus', *TU* 73 (1959), 441-57. R. Bultmann, *The Gospel of John*, 210, on the other hand, takes it to be a secondary addition. The only statement one can make with any probability, in my view, is that 6.14 is not a Johannine addition: ἀληθῶς does not go very well with John's view of the acclamation as a misunderstanding.

[102] It is redactional. Cf. E. Schweizer, *Mark*, 160f.; K. Tagawa, *Miracles*, 77: J. Roloff, *Kerygma*, 246-51.

[103] The absence of a choral acclamation has been noticed by many writers: H.J. Held, 'Matthew as Interpreter', 182, n. 4; B. van Iersel, 'Die wunderbare Speisung und das Abendmahl in der synoptischen Tradition', *NovTest* 7 (1964/5), 167-94, esp. 183.; H. Schürmann, *Lukas*, 524, and J. Roloff, *Kerygma*, 244, conclude from this that it is not a typical miracle story.

miracle stories. That is Mark's model. He is placing the motifs command to silence and (titular) acclamation in opposition and treating the demons' confessions as final titular acclamations.

In Mk 6.14-16 we have, not confessions of demons but human, though inadequate, responses. Within Mark's composition they illustrate Herod's bad conscience, but in the original anonymous speakers were probably commenting on Jesus' miraculous feats. This association of titular acclamations with miracles probably belongs to the tradition. The parallel passage 8.28 (where there is no direct association with a miracle, though an indirect one is established through the echo of 6.14f.) is secondary to 6.14f.,[104] as a detailed comparison shows:

i) In 8.28 the switch from accusative to nominative is striking: Ἰωάννην/ Ἠλίαν/εἷς τῶν προφητῶν. Only the first two clauses give a syntactically correct answer to τίνα με λέγουσιν οἱ ἄνθρωποι εἶναι; Matthew corrects the last clause and puts it in the accusative, as do a number of manuscripts. A second peculiarity is the absence of ὅτι in the last clause; it would be normal with a dependent statement, and can only be left out in direct speech.[105] Originally the whole reply may have been in the nominative and been direct speech. The question in 27b demands an answer with an accusative and infinitive of indirect speech. The evangelist puts the first two clauses in the accusative and only leaves the previous nominative unchanged at the end since the influence of the question is less strong here. This implies that Mark has turned direct speech into indirect. The original grammatical construction is now visible only at the end of v. 28.

ii) Who is meant by οἱ δὲ/καὶ ἄλλοι/ἄλλοι δὲ? At the beginning it is the disciples, but then the problems start. If οἱ δὲ/καὶ ἄλλοι/ἄλλοι δὲ are coordinate, the translation has to be: 'and other (disciples said that some thought him) to be Elijah'. Then, however, the last clause no longer makes sense: 'Other (disciples), however, said that he (was) one of the prophets,' contradicts the obvious meaning, since in the following question Jesus turns to the disciples in a deliberate antithesis: 'But you, who do you say that I am?' By ἄλλοι δὲ Mark can only have meant anonymous persons, but if that is so οἱ δὲ and καὶ ἄλλοι must also refer to unnamed persons. Mark seems to have introduced a break into his list of popular opinions by making οἱ δὲ refer to the disciples, and this is further confir-

---

[104] O. Cullmann, *The Christology of the New Testament*, London 1959, 2nd ed. 1963, 31-36, takes 6.14ff. as historical. E. Percy, *Die Botschaft Jesu*, 1953, 230, and G.M. de Tillesse, *Le secret*, 311f. argue for its originality over against 8.28, F. Hahn, *Titles*, 221, n. 435, assumes interdependence, Bultmann, *HST*, 302 the originality of 8.28; so also R. Meyer, *Der Prophet aus Galiläa*, 1940, 10, 31f., 38ff.

[105] J.H. Moulton, *A Grammar of New Testament Greek*, 1963, III, 306: '. . . it looks as if προφήτης is direct speech, with ὅτι introducing a mere exclamation of the people, in 6.15, and in the same way there is no need for ἐστιν in 8.28 if ὅτι is thought of as introducing the direct speech εἰς τῶν προφητῶν.'

mation of the hypothesis that he has attributed what were originally utterances of the people to the disciples.

iii) The first ὅτι is strange because an accusative and infinitive is not introduced by ὅτι. The great majority of manuscripts have corrected here, either by reading οἱ μὲν as in Mt 16.14 or by deleting ὅτι with Lk 9.19. The fact that ὅτι reappears in the third clause is probably a further sign that originally all the answers were constructed like the third, i.e. not as accusative and infinitives but as declarative sentences introduced by a ὅτι of indirect speech.

All three observations lead to the same conclusion: Mark has transformed the utterances of an unknown crowd in direct speech into reports about the crowd and its views given by the disciples. The original text which can be seen underneath Mk 8.28, however, corresponds exactly to Mk 6.14f.; there the people (or Herod) are the speakers and all the clauses have nominatives and are introduced by ὅτι. It is therefore very probable that Mark has used the tradition contained in 6.14f. a second time as the exposition of a Messianic confession. By transforming what were originally acclamations of the miracle-worker Jesus by anonymous persons into indirect reports he has transferred the whole debate about Jesus' status into the esoteric circle of the disciples, who are 'on the way' by themselves. Mark was prompted to make the change by his theory of the secret. In 6.14f., in public, he can allow only a few inadequate views attempting to understand Jesus the miracle-worker. The titular acclamation provoked by miracles can take place only within the narrow confines of the disciples' conversation.

Jesus' hidden majesty is publicly proclaimed by only one person, the centurion at the cross. The relationship between his confession and the immediately preceding miraculous events is unmistakable. His confession 'thus corresponds to the acclamatory conclusions of miracle stories or even martyrdoms'.[106] Has Mark perhaps avoided realising titular acclamations anywhere else in order to highlight this one confession? I regard it as very likely.

To sum up: Mark is aware of the connection between miracles and titular acclamations. In the few miracle stories independent of Mark titular acclamations occur, as they also do in two (possibly) independent parallel traditions to the Marcan miracles. When

---

[106] P. Vielhauer, 'Erwägungen zur Christologie des Markusevangeliums'. *Aufsätze zum Neuen Testament*, 1965, 199-214.

171

Mark was using the synoptic tradition to produce his gospel, miracle stories with titular acclamations were probably in existence. Moreover Mark's theory of secrecy gives him a redactional interest in omitting such acclamations, though on the other hand as a result of his theory of secrecy he presupposes implied confessions as an opposed motif to commands to silence by concentrating the secret on the status of Jesus. The most probable interpretation of this situation is, in my view, that Mark deliberately did not include titular acclamations in his gospel at the end of miracle stories. That is not to say that in the case of any miracle story we can postulate an omitted acclamation (though that is possible);[107] it means that the titular acclamation is part of the repertoire of Marcan miracle stories which Mark consciously chooses not to realise at this point.

Diachronic analysis of selected motifs has shown that tradition and redaction cannot always be separated like archaeological strata, but must be understood as variations of prior compositional and paradigmatic possibilities. We have examined two motifs which have a distinct position in the composition and also two motifs of crucial importance to the paradigm.

At the level of composition we found that an introductory motif which is often deleted as an editorial addition, the place reference, contained a 'core' of tradition, which could never be reached by stripping away editorial elements. Any attempt to remove the 'shell' to get to the original material is totally inadequate here. What has happened is that the same elements have taken up a different position within the compositional structure: an introductory oral framework has become the first element of an intricately woven narrative. We can see a comparable process in some places at the end of miracle stories: the acclamation from the oral framework has been incorporated into the narrative.

On the paradigmatic level changes between tradition and redaction showed themselves to be actualisations of potential relationships in the form-critical field of motifs, changes of position within the field. 'Faith', for example, occupies a different position according as it has to prove itself against opposition, expresses itself in confident petition or grateful emotion. It appears in turn as a boundary-crossing motif in volitional, cognitive and affective aspects and in each case is in opposition to a different boundary-

---

[107] F. Hahn, *Hoheitstitel*, 391f., indirectly suggests that a choral conclusion has been lost in the feeding of the 5000, and K.G. Reploh, *Markus – Lehrer der Gemeinde*, 1969, 212f., makes the same suggestion for Mk 9.28.

stressing motif, difficulty, doubt, rejection. The diachronous process of transmission is here drawing on possibilities of the genre which already exist paradigmatically. The same process can be seen in Mark's use of traditional commands to be silent or keep something secret. Here the opposition between secrecy and revelation is realised in a new way which is latent in the structure of the form-critical field of motifs. In the case of titular acclamations in Mark's gospel we have an example of a decision not to realise a motif or motif variant.

The stock of motifs remains relatively constant, but within the tradition history of the genre new oppositions of motifs, motif variants and motif groups are constantly actualised. Motif variants become opposed motifs, new groups of motifs are formed, etc. The list of oppositions produced by the field analysis of the motifs offers only a general framework which potentially includes a great many more potential oppositions.

CHAPTER II

THE NARRATIVE REPRODUCTION OF THE INDIVIDUAL STORIES

The importance of potential genre structures for the diachronous transmission process has to be demonstrated not only for the variation of individual motifs, but also for the transmission of connected, originally independent narratives. This task is particularly necessary if one regards the assumption of general transmission tendencies in the synoptic tradition, that is in oral and written transmission, in literary and textual history – irrespective of any particular genre – as having been disproved by E.P. Sanders' investigations.[1] This is not a reason for exegesis to limit itself to a description of modifications of no more than individual significance; it must also look for middle-range transmission tendencies. Even Sanders' studies leave plenty of room for this; the fact that, despite ignoring all distinctions within the history of the synoptic tradition, they still found some general transmission tendencies (for example the tendency to direct speech) is certainly no discouragement to look for particular forms of development of the transmission process under particular conditions – for example, within the genre 'miracle story'. Of course even here it would be a mistake to expect unvarying regularities.[2] We shall consider there to be grounds for employing the term 'typical transmission tendencies' when:

a) we find a limited range of possible modifications which draws on the structural possibilities of the genre, or

b) there is evidence for typical processes which appear in their realisation, independently of the authors in whose work they are realised.

---

[1] E.P. Sanders, *Tendencies,* 272: 'There are no hard and fast laws of the development of the Synoptic tradition. . . .' – 'Some particular writers would have an editorial custom contrary to the general course of development.'

[2] Bultmann, *HST,* 6, referred to 'regularities' independent of the different genres. In carrying out his programme, however, he generally matches tendencies to modification to the different genres separately, and even quite general tendencies are not studied across the whole synoptic tradition, but (pp. 307ff.) only in the narrative genres. In other words, Bultmann in practice makes many more distinctions than at first appears from his introductory statement of principle, with the result that much criticism of him is exaggerated.

The investigation here will show that each author has a preference for particular transmission tendencies, but that these are nonetheless typical possibilities. It can usually be shown, not only that the various evangelists had other possibilities at their disposal, but also that what are thought of as 'individual' tendencies to modification also occur elsewhere. For the present we shall ignore the distinction between written and oral transmission. The significance of the medium of transmission for the history of transmission will be examined separately in the next section of this chapter.

A. Transmission Tendencies: Compression, Expansion, Affinity

G. Ortutay distinguishes 'degressive', progressive and affinity processes, the disintegration of a tradition, its creative expansion and its combination with similar motifs.[3] The terms 'degressive' and 'progressive' will not be used here because they could imply a value judgment. An abridgement of a tradition can in fact mean the selection of the essentials, even if the narrative technique seems poorer (cf. Mt 9.2ff.). Conversely the development of a tradition can lead to baroque overloading (for example in Jn 11). We shall therefore distinguish between compression, expansion and affinity. Our thesis is that in these different transmission tendencies the specific structures of the genre are important. They may not necessarily have controlled the process of transmission (non-literary factors play an important role here), but they do form a sort of framework for various possibilities of change.

i) Compression. By 'compression' is meant all shortened reproductions of whole narratives. Matthew in particular has shortened the miracle stories. It is unnecessary to list these abridgements in detail;[4] we shall concentrate here on one aspect, the importance of previously existing structures of the genre for the Matthaean abridgements. One indication of this is that Matthew frequently has a simpler compositional structure than Mark. The basic compositional structure of the genre 'miracle story' acts as a sort of sieve; the elements and motifs unnecessary to a realisation of the basic structure are omitted.

---

[3] G. Ortutay, 'Begriff und Bedeutung der Affinität in der mündlichen Überlieferung', 248; 'Principles of oral transmission in Folk Culture', *Acta Ethnographica* 8 (1959), 175-221.

[4] H.J. Held, 'Matthew as Interpreter', passim, has subjected it to a more detailed investigation. Since this is a basic study of Matthew, there is no need to give constant references in this section.

This can be seen very clearly in the story of the woman with 'the issue of blood'. Here the Marcan version has a somewhat unusual composition which stresses the purpose of the miracle. The healing takes place and is then followed by a dramatic process in which – as usually in the exposition – an obstacle is overcome, giving us two passages with expositional motifs. This departure from the usual structure indicates a skilled narrator. There is only one point at which he has been unable to integrate completely a motif in his composition. In the dismissal conclusion we have: 'Go in peace, and be healed of your disease' (Mk 5.34) – as though the woman had not already been healed.

The usual order, expositional motifs followed by healing, has prevailed here and this gives Matthew a basis for his version. He starts from the normal compositional structure, introduces the healing only after the assurance of faith and links this assurance, in normal style, with the woman's expression of confidence. Naturally, the whole dialogue, which presupposes a prior transmission of power, must then disappear. Whatever the theological reasons for this compression, technically it consists in a simplification of the composition which takes the Marcan version as a basis and follows the basic structure specific to the genre. It would be slightly unfair to say that Matthew has 'cut' here; what he has done is to reproduce the story afresh on a simpler basic pattern.

A comparable process can be observed in the story of the exorcism at the Gadarene sea (Mt 8.28-34). In Mark Jesus twice orders the demons to leave (5.8, 13); the second time the order is transformed into permission to go into the swine. The demons' request for mercy also appears twice, first in negative form (the demons do not want to leave the country, 5.10), and then in positive form: they ask to go into the swine. This dramatisation of the story disappears in Matthew. To realise a simple basic compositional structure all that is required is one plea for mercy and one exorcistic command. It is also sufficient for the variety of concluding motifs in Mark (amazement, rejection, dismissal, reference to the spread of the story, amazement) to be reduced to one, the rejection of the miracle-worker.

The compression in Mt 9.2-8 can also be understood as a reduction to a simpler compositional structure. In Mark the healing of the paralytic has a double exposition. Matthew reduces this to one. As the source of tension he chooses, not the overcoming of external obstacles, but the rejection of the hostile arguments of Jesus' opponents. He is mainly interested in the ἐξουσία – a key word which he specifically repeats in the acclamatory conclusion (9.8).

Finally we may mention the 'epileptic boy' (Mt 17.14-21). Irrespective of the question whether Matthew and Luke are following an independent variant of the tradition, we may assume that they had Mark's text before them, and that their deviations can therefore be treated as modifications. In both, the double exposition disappears. Only the overcoming of the disciples' ineffectualness remains as a 'difficulty' motif in the exposition; the overcoming of doubt in the suppliant disappears. We shall discuss the Lucan version in somewhat more detail – if only to show that 'compression' is a general transmission tendency and not just a peculiarity of Matthew's.

The disappearance of the dialogue about 'unbelieving faith' is made possible by a switch of motif variants in the exposition. In place of a resigned account of the disciples' unsuccessful attempt at healing there is the trusting request: note the specifically Lucan words, 'I beg you . . . for he is my only child' (9.38). The Lucan ἐβόησεν is along similar lines. Since, despite his discouraging experience with the disciples, the father still believes in Jesus' miraculous power, there is no need for a discussion about his faith. This makes the exposition simpler. Another sign that the normal basic compositional structure is being followed is Luke's removal of the wonder motif, which in Mark appears in the exposition (Mk 9.15), to its usual place in the conclusion and his rounding-off of the conclusion by a preceding dismissal motif. He deletes the subsequent discussion with the disciples. It is not necessary to complete the basic compositional structure, but Luke provides a substitute. By means of the linking clause, 'But while they were all still marvelling . . .' (9.43b) – the only time that a final wonder motif is used both as an introduction and as a link – he connects the prophecy of the passion closely with the exorcism. This picks up again the complaint about the faithless and perverse generation (9.44), and the disciples' inability to understand this (even more heavily stressed in Luke than in Mark) corresponds to their inability to perform the exorcism.

Compression of compositional structures is always at the same time a reduction of the possibilities present in the paradigmatic fields. In Matthew, for example, the character field is much more thinly populated than in Mark and Luke. While there is a general tendency to fill out a tripartite field of principal characters, subsidiary characters and miracle-worker, in Matthew the field of subsidiary characters is occasionally empty. In 'Peter's Mother-in-Law' both Jesus' companions and the representatives of the sick woman are absent. There are only two characters, Jesus and the woman (Mt 8.14f.). The same applies to 'The Woman with an Issue of Blood' (Mt 9.20ff.): here the crowd and the disciples have disappeared. The main effect of this reduction of subordinate roles is a reduction in dialogues; in 'Peter's Mother-in-Law' (8.14f.) the hint of a dialogue between Jesus and the other people in the house has gone. The exorcism at the sea at Gadara (8.28ff.) has had two dialogues cut. In 'Jairus' Daughter' (9.18ff.) the dialogue between the messengers, the father and Jesus, leading to the assurance of faith, has been dropped. The elements of dialogue in 'The Woman with the Issue of Blood' (9.20ff.) have been reduced to plea and answer. In 'The Epileptic Boy' the discussion about faith (17.14ff.) is missing, and in 'The Blind Man of Jericho' the conversation between the blind man, the crowd and Jesus (20.20ff.). These cuts are certainly not accidental; a Jesus who engages in conversation does not fit the picture of the miracle-worker who acts with divine authority. Jesus does not ask questions, does not discuss, does not issue orders through intermediaries; he makes summary, firm decisions.

The cuts made on the basis of a simplified basic compositional structure go hand in hand not only with a changed realisation of the character field but also with different emphases in the form-critical field of motifs, though this takes the form less of the introduction of new motifs than of a switch of motif variants.

Matthew has stylised the petition motif into a solemn appeal. Jesus appears as a divine miracle worker regarded in advance as having complete power. In 8.25 a critical complaint has been replaced by the appeal, 'Save, Lord; we are perishing.' In 15.22; 15.25; 17.15 and 20.30 a simple request has been replaced by κύριε ἐλέησον or variants. In 9.18 the father's trust appears from the start to be boundless, since the girl has already died. Κύριε often appears in the request: in 8.2, 25; 15.22, 25; 17.15 and 10.30, 31 the title is demonstrably redactional, and in 8.6; 9.28; 14.28 this is likely. A common feature of all these alterations is that a criticism or simple request is replaced by a solemn appeal showing limitless confidence.

Jesus' majesty is made more prominent by an added stress on his commands. In 9.24 Matthew places ἀναχωρεῖτε before the assurance: Jesus orders the public to be removed right at the start. In 14.18 Matthew introduces a command into the narrative. In 20.32 Jesus gives a command directly to the blind man without using the accompanying crowd as his intermediary. The change of 'he asked' to 'he said' (15.34) also shows this tendency to the commanding saying.

Jesus' majesty is also stressed by wonder and acclamation. After the walking on the water Matthew does not have the Marcan motif of incomprehensibility, but of prostration and acclamation (14.33). The rejection is given a characteristic twist in 8.34: 'And behold, all the city came out εἰς ὑπάντησιν τῷ Ἰησοῦ.' Jesus is greeted like a king,[5] a conqueror

---

[5] Cf. E. Peterson, 'Die Einholung des Kyrios', ZSTh 7 (1930), 682-702.

begged to spare the country. In the acclamation in 8.27 'the men' have replaced the disciples, making Jesus' universal rule more prominent. There are other changes in this direction. 8.14 has 'he saw'. Here the subsidiary characters are eliminated, and Jesus spontaneously acts as miracle-worker. Again in 8.28 it is no longer the possessed themselves who are chiefly in danger from the demons, but passers-by; only Jesus has the power to remain in the place without risk. In 15.27 the Canaanite woman talks about 'the masters' table' instead of 'the children's crumbs'. A total of seventeen changes can be found in Matthew in which individual motifs are stylised to produce a picture of a majestic Jesus (together with another six changes to produce different effects: 9.14, 19; 14.24, 28; 17.15, 16). As well as these changes there are a number of additions which increase the miraculous element or stress the occurrence of the miracle: 9.22; 15.37, 38; 17.18b; 20.34).

All these changes show that the Matthaean reproduction of the miracle stories is dominated by an altered picture of the miracle-worker. His majesty is stressed and the miraculous element highlighted. In the earthly miracle-worker there can already be seen something of the exalted Lord to whom all power has been given in heaven and on earth and to whom the community addresses its solemn prayer. This compression of content is achieved partly by a reduction of the composition to simpler basic patterns and partly through a modified actualisation of the character and motif fields of the primitive Christian miracle stories. Matthew 'reduces the broad canvas of the Marcan miracle stories to the bare essentials in order to highlight more strongly the mysterious dignity of Jesus' (E. Käsemann).[6]

Nevertheless it should be stressed that compression is not a feature peculiar to Matthew. Luke too has reproduced a Marcan miracle story in extremely compressed form (Lk 9.37-43). There must also be examples of compression in Mark, though they can only be postulated by analogy: in extremely compressed narratives elements of the traditional story may occasionally be retained even though in the revised version they make little sense or have no

---

[6] 'The Canon of the New Testament and the Unity of the Church', in *Essays on New Testament Themes*, 1964, 95ff. esp. 96f. In addition to this christological concentration H.J. Held lists three further features of Matthaean editorial work:

a) Abridgements designed to emphasise the element of dialogue in the action and restrict the narrative element. ('Matthew as Interpreter', 168-92.) On the other hand, one finds dialogues are sometimes the elements cut.

b) The motif of faith is more heavily emphasised and counts as a principle of selection (cf. op. cit. 168-92). However, this very motif is often sacrificed in abridgement, as we saw in our study of the faith motif (Part II, IIB above).

c) The theme of discipleship is stressed. Even the disciples, however, are a subordinate theme. With the disappearance of subsidiary characters they lose importance in some stories, and in 8.14ff. and 9.20ff. they are even absent.

function. Matthew, for example, mentions the faith of the bearers in the story of the paralysed man, but does not describe the overcoming of the obstacle which previously gave expression to that faith (Mt 9.2). There are similar echoes in Mark's gospel. At the stilling of the storm other boats are mentioned although they play no part in the story (Mk 4.36). In 'Peter's Mother-in-Law' there is an indication of a conversation with representatives of the sick woman – but Jesus has already entered the house and hardly needs to be told about the sick woman now. Such features are indications that Mark too has occasionally heavily abridged stories from the tradition.

ii) Expansion. In addition to compression there are also contrasting tendencies to enrich an existing tradition. This can take various forms. One way of developing the tradition may consist in making the structure more coherent, making the sequence of motifs more intelligible and arranging them more skilfully. An existing structure can also be given more tension and drama – often at the cost of a smooth, clear narrative thread.

Two changes in particular are used to improve the existing composition, transposition and the addition of explanatory links.[7]

It is no accident that Matthew makes only infrequent use of these possibilities. He has only three transpositions, and here always rearranges the order of immediately consecutive narrative elements (cf. 14.23; 14.26; 15.34). In Luke there are five comparable transpositions (5.12; 8.22; 8.35; 8.41f.; 9.12). Frequently, however, Luke brings motifs forward: 4.31 ('Galilee' from Mk 1.28); 4.33 ('loud voice' from Mk 1.26); 5.12 ('city' from Mk 1.45); 5.17 (opponents of Jesus from Mk 2.6); 8.23 (Jesus' sleeping from Mk 4.38); 8.27 ('city' from Mk 5.14); 8.27 (nakedness from Mk 5.15); 8.42 (the girl's age from Mk 5.42); 9.14 (the number of people present from Mk 6.44). Occasionally there are instances of elements being moved back: 6.11 (ἄνοια = 'hardness of heart' from Mk 3.5); 8.29 (unsuccessful attempts to bind the demoniac after the plea for mercy);[8] 8.46 (the 'power' which has 'gone forth' is now mentioned after the conversation with Peter); 9.43 (The 'amazement' of Mk 9.15 now

---

[7] External criteria make possible a distinction between four types of change: transpositions, additions, modifications and abridgements. The analysis of transmission tendencies has been based on the principle of bringing all changes under these four categories. It shows that Luke prefers the first two (slightly 'more conservative') types of change and Matthew the last two.

[8] The aim of the transposition is to explain why the demon begs to be spared torment. Matthew gives a mythical explanation: he is afraid of the punishments of hell. Luke finds his explanation in the story itself: the demon is afraid that Jesus will try to bind him in other ways.

comes in the usual position at the end). As compared with the three transpositions in Matthew, Luke has nineteen which are of relevance to the narrative, most of them much more important than Matthew's. Luke clearly attaches importance to an orderly narrative sequence.

This is also the purpose of Luke's changes. They often make sense as attempts at assimilation to the context: λόγος replaces διδαχή (4.32), to secure the reference to the exorcism formula. 'And they came out' (4.36) is closer to what is happening than 'obey', and 'beseech' (4.38) is more appropriate to the situation than 'say'. 'Rebuke' (4.39) is certainly also an assimilation to the context of exorcism. The gathering of the crowd is given more plausibility by the desire 'to hear and be healed' (5.15). Διὰ τῶν κεράμων (5.19) eliminates the tension in Mark's double action of removing the tiles and making a hole. Mark's 'We never saw anything like this,' (2.12) seems an inadequate response to the miracle which has just taken place; Luke alters it (5.26). In 8.47 Luke makes the woman describe her reason for touching Jesus secretly (not just to tell 'the truth'), which has more relevance to the context than Mark's general phrase. 'I beg you to look upon my son' (9.38) corresponds to the situation: the boy has still to be brought. In addition to these changes made primarily to improve the composition there are two others (6.11 and 8.24).

Finally we should list the Lucan additions. Their effect is almost always to produce a clearer and more plausible narrative sequence: in 4.39; 5.18; 5.25; 6.6; 6.8 (two additions); 8.31; 8.35; 8.37; 8.42; 8.50; 8.53; 8.55; 8.45; 8.47; 9.38; 9.43; 18.35; 18.36. Note particularly the added acclamation conclusions which round off the narrative: 5.25; 8.47; 9.43; 18.43. A comparison of Matthew with Luke shows that Matthew has fifteen additions which affect the narrative. Of these, however, only seven are improvements: in 8.15; 8.28; 9.8; 14.18; 14.26; 20.34; 8.29 (here the demons' fear of being tormented is explained as fear of the fires of hell), whereas Luke has nineteen additions affecting the narrative.

Once more we find that Luke wants stories that flow better, are smoother, more logical. He is interested in the correct combination, order and linking of the narrative elements. He wants to produce 'an orderly account, καθεξῆς' (Lk 1.3).[9]

Expanding an existing composition, however, is not an exclusively Lucan technique. Matthew too often improves the structure of the story and occasionally even makes it more dramatic. This is clearest in his version of 'The Syrophoenician Woman' (Mt 15.24-28). In Mark the order of motifs is: petition, difficulty, overcoming of the difficulty, assurance. Matthew has reproduced this structural pattern four times:

---

[9] H.J. Held, 'Matthew as Interpreter', 219, rightly says that one of Luke's aims in telling the miracle stories is 'concern for a simple and easy-flowing account of what happened.'

1. Petition:
   'Have mercy on me, O Lord,
   Son of David; my daughter
   is possessed by a demon.'

   1. Rejection:
      'But he did not answer.'
   2. Rejection (by the
      disciples: 'Send
      her away.'

2. Continued petitions:
   '. . . for she is crying
   after us'

   3. Rejection: 'I am
      sent only to the lost
      sheep of the house of
      Israel.'

3. Petition: 'Lord,
   help me.'

   4. Rejection: 'It is not
      fair to take the chil-
      dren's bread and throw
      it to the dogs.'

4. Petition: 'Yes, Lord,
   but even the dogs . . .'

To some extent this heightening of the drama involves a loss of clarity. In Mt 15.16, for example, it is not clear to whom the answer is directed: ἀποκριθεὶς strictly refers to the woman's plea, but in the story it is a reply to the disciples' intervention. Increasing the dramatic element of a story can thus be quite different from making it flow better, but it is something that Luke does too, for example in the story of the centurion from Capernaum, where Luke has repeated the motif of sending messengers. We shall examine this miracle story in a little more detail:[10]

(a) Finding the slave cured on the return to the house,[11] as Luke describes it, is an original feature. Matthew only notes that the slave was healed from that time on, but he has introduced this motif in Mt 15.28b (for Mk 7.30, where the mother finds the daughter recovered on her return), and probably did the same in Mt 8.13.
(b) Originally the centurion spoke himself in Lk 7.6ff., as the wording in the first person shows. Luke has introduced the motif of sending messen-

---

[10] H. Schürmann, *Lukas*, 395-97, regards the Matthaean version as an abridgement of the Q tradition which is better preserved in Luke, but F. Schnider and W. Stenger, *Johannes und die Synoptiker*, 1971, 54-88 explain the features peculiar to Luke as the work of the Lucan redaction. E. Haenchen, 'Johanneische Probleme', *ZThK* 56 (1959), 19-54, esp. 23-31, regards it on the other hand as a Jewish Christian variant of Mt 8.5ff. taken over in essence by Luke. T. Schramm, *Markus-Stoff*, 30f., regards the Lucan text as a combination of Q (vv. 6c-9=Mt) and Lucan special material (vv. 1-6b, 10). He treats μὴ σκύλλου (v. 6c) and 'therefore I did not presume to come to you' (v. 7a) as redactional connections.
[11] F. Schnider/W. Stenger, *Johannes und die Synoptiker*, 60f., makes the interesting suggestion that the description of the παῖς as 'servant' is intended to increase the exemplary quality of the centurion in Luke: he takes care not just of his child, but also of his servant.

gers here. This was, however, part of the original tradition: Jesus was sent for by a first group of messengers (in Luke by the Jewish elders, which may not be original). This is still clear in Matthew too, though he leaves out these first messengers, as he generally eliminates minor characters; the result, however is a certain clumsiness: first the centurion asks Jesus to come and immediately afterwards the centurion declares himself unworthy to receive Jesus in his house. It is more likely that the two contrasting statements were originally divided between two different characters.

(c) The centurion's words were spoken not far from his house: 'I am not worthy to have you come under my roof,' makes most sense in this situation. Lk 7.6a: 'when he was not far from the house' thus contains an element of the old story. In this Jesus was brought from a distant place by messengers and met very close to the house by the centurion.

Luke probably repeated the motif of messengers to produce an effective contrast. The first message stresses that the centurion is 'worthy', but the second announces that he has not felt himself 'worthy' to meet Jesus himself.[12] Nevertheless, the increase in drama is obtained only at the cost of some awkwardnesses in the narrative. It remains only too clear that the centurion previously spoke where there is now the second group of messengers.

In Mark's gospel too, though the diachronous process of transmission can be detected only with great difficulty, there can be no doubt that there are more examples than in the other gospels of the structure which, in the Matthaean version of 'The Syrophoenician Woman', we were able to show to be the result of a process of transmission, namely a repetition of motifs to introduce greater dramatic tension into the story – often at the expense of clarity. In Mk 1.40ff. the leper is spoken to sternly twice (1.41 var. and 1.43), in 5.1ff. almost all the motifs appear in repeated variations, in Mk 5.21ff. the public is excluded twice (5.37 and 5.40); the father of the epileptic boy must twice overcome a difficulty (9.14ff.) and the blind Bartimaeus make his request twice (10.48, 49). Since we know from our observations in Matthew and Luke that such duplications and heightenings are by no means necessarily original, it is tempting to argue by analogy that similar patterns of composition in Mark are also not necessarily original. At least in one case an internal analysis of Mark's text shows that it was Mark who first reproduced the story with the inclusion of such devices for heightening the dramatic tension. This is the story of Jairus' daughter.

(a) The encapsulation of one miracle story inside the other is most

---

[12] This contrast has been developed in detail by F. Schnider and W. Stenger, *Johannes und die Synoptiker*, 61f.

probably the work of Mark.[13] Encapsulations are frequent in Mark:[14] Mk 11.12ff.; 14.1ff.; 14.53ff. Other examples are 3.21, 31-35 and 9.1, 11ff., where there may have been no interruption of a traditional narrative by insertions but there is definitely an insertion in the Marcan composition. Mark has also used 6.7-13 and 6.30-32 to put an editorial bracket round 'The Death of the Baptist'. In other words he is familiar with the technique of encapsulation.

(b) The hypothesis of a secondary encapsulation is reinforced by the observation that 'Jairus' Daughter' is largely in the historic present while 'The Woman with the Issue of Blood' is in the past tense. In the process of encapsulation, however, the past seems also to have got into 'Jairus' Daughter', in four places: 5.21, 24, 37, 42f. The interesting thing about these passages is that they are the beginning and end and a join between the encapsulated narratives (plus 5.37) – that is, points in the story where redactional influence is very probable. It is fairly safe to assume that the conclusion with its command to silence has been reworked by the editors.

(c) But the four verses in the past tense do not stand out on formal grounds only. If the conclusion is ignored, in each case, motifs from the content of the encapsulated story have got into the encapsulating narrative. 5.21 is an anticipatory redactional introduction to 5.25ff.: the crowd introduced here has no function in 'Jairus' daughter', but is used for the unnoticed approach of the woman in v. 27. The crowd appears again in v. 24. Here the key word συνθλίβειν is taken over literally from v. 31 (cf. the redactional summary in 3.9). In v. 37 this crowd has to be removed again so that the healing can take place at a mysterious distance from the public. Since the crowd was only introduced into 'Jairus' Daughter' with the encapsulation, its exclusion is also only made necessary by the encapsulation. If it is accepted that the encapsulation is the work of the editor, then it follows that v. 37 is also, i.e., all the dramatic touches in this story are redactional.

(d) The insertion is not arbitrary. The motif of delay is a feature of the genre. In the case of serious illnesses it increases the tension. The intervening report of the girl's death presupposes that Jesus arrived too late, and so the insertion is simply actualising a possibility present in the genre and in the particular tradition.

The possibility cannot be ruled out that Mark has added dramatic touches in a similar way to other passages. Though it is almost impossible to show this in detail, it is possible to de-

---

[13] E.g. A. Meyer, 'Die Entstehung des Markusevangeliums', *Festgabe für A. Jülicher* (1927), 35-60, esp. 40; E. Von Dobschütz, 'Zur Erzählkunst des Markus', *ZNW* 27 (1928), 193ff.; J. Sundwall, 'Zusammensetzung', 35; G.M. de Tillesse, *Le secret*, 52-57. Original interlocking is argued for by K.L. Schmidt, *Rahmen*, 147f.; H. van der Loos, *Miracles*, 509ff. Bultmann, *HST*, 214, M. Dibelius, *TG*, 72, suggest that the linking occurred before the redactional stage. Cf. now the detailed discussion of the problem in H.W. Kuhn, *Ältere Sammlungen im Markusevangelium* (1971), 200-202.

[14] Not so E. Haenchen, *Weg*, 205.

scribe his narrative style independently since it is not only previous versions which provide a background against which to judge its distinctive features, but also the in-built structural possibilities of the genre. Mark has not merely altered stories from the tradition; he has drawn on the inherent possibilities of the genre to tell them in a new form. This makes it impossible to say that the mode of reproduction we find in his gospel is an individual characteristic. It is much more a typical transmission tendency inherent in the genre and used by other narrators as well. Mark exhibits it particularly frequently, and it is only in that sense that 'his' dramatic style can be distinguished from Matthew's tendency to compress and Luke's to improve the structure of the narrative.

iii) Affinity. If changes are considered against the background of existing genre structures (and not only in relation to previous realisations of these structures), it becomes possible to understand those processes in which earlier versions are neither compressed nor expanded, but have added to them new elements which seem to come from different contexts. In such cases those who want to attribute everything to previous stages of the tradition are usually too quick to infer a variety of sources or a blending of different stories or versions of a story. In no case, however, can this hypothesis be strictly proved. It is sufficient to suppose that paradigmatically related motifs have entered a story, even when they have not been realised in any previous version. Every motif is of course associated with a field of related, similar or contrasted, motifs. Each can operate various associations. Such a paradigmatic affinity of motifs can substantially change a story, particularly when the new motifs do not just attach themselves but act on the story as a whole and bring about the expulsion or modification of motifs from the tradition.

We shall begin with an example which can be monitored. In the Lucan version of 'Peter's Mother-in-Law' the story has attracted an exorcism motif. Jesus 'rebukes' the fever. The context of exorcism is not the only explanation for this. There is a motif present in the story itself which has an inherent affinity with demonological ideas, the pronouncement of the healing: καὶ ἀφῆκεν αὐτήν, 'and it left her,' – as though the disease were a demonic being leaving the person (cf. Mt 4.11).

Jesus' stern words to the leper in Mk 1.40ff. may also represent a motif attracted by inner affinity, since the command to silence activates the whole field of exorcism motifs. This possibility is preferable to attempts to distinguish on literary grounds between stories involving exorcism and stories less associated with it.

Affinity may also result in the coming together of different themes such as exorcisms and healings. This applies also to epiphanies and rescue miracles. In Mk 6.45-52 an epiphany on the water may have attracted motifs from a rescue story.[15]

The curious phrase 'he meant to pass them by' (Mk 6.48), points to the possibility that Jesus does in fact pass them by. This possibility is realised in Jn 6.16ff.; there Jesus remains outside the boat, though the disciples 'want' to take him into the boat. Then, however, he has suddenly disappeared; this has all the features of an ἀφανισμός.[16] The sudden landing is reminiscent of waking from a dream and being surprised at being released from its strangeness into the familiar surroundings of ordinary life.[17] Another similarity with a dream is the contrast between wish and what is seen to happen. This feature is associated on one occasion with Jesus (in Mark) and on another with the disciples (in John). In both cases the connection is the search for real (physical) contact between Jesus and the disciples. This divergence between wanting and doing is reminiscent of Mk 9.5ff.: Peter responds to the manifestation but does not know what to say. Another parallel is Jn 21.12: no-one dares to address the apparition, although they know it is the Kyrios. The epiphany motifs certainly belong to the original substance of this tradition.

It is further a plausible hypothesis that this was originally an appearance in which Jesus did actually 'pass by'. This idea is also implicit in the Matthaean version. The fact that Peter has to go out on to the water to reach Jesus would make much more sense if Jesus did not enter the boat at all. It is also merely a variation of the divergence between wish and event which is implicit in the traditional story. Another piece of evidence pointing in this direction is that the concluding acclamation, 'And those *in the boat* worshipped him . . .' (Mt 14.33) seems to presuppose that the person being worshipped here is not in the boat. The expansion of the story (probably before Matthew)[18] may presuppose a version which was fairly close to John's.

Finally it should be observed that Mark voices the suspicion which a pure epiphany arouses: φάντασμά ἐστιν. Detail by detail, Mark takes

---

[15] So too Bultmann, *HST,* 216; E. Lohmeyer, *Markus,* 131ff.; D. Esser, *Formgeschichtliche Studien,* 125f. Nevertheless it is hardly possible to base what amounts to a literary critical distinction on this assumption. M. Dibelius, *TG,* 100 and 277, takes the opposite view and regards the rescue motifs as original and the epiphany features as accretions.

[16] E. Haenchen, *Johanneische Probleme,* 92, does not recognise this example of a typical ἀφανισμός. Instead he supposes the secondary accretion of a miracle motif and denies that the miraculous landing on the shore is original.

[17] For the categories 'dream', 'vision' and 'hallucination' see the discussion in J. Lindblom, *Geschichte und Offenbarung* (1968), 78-113, who claims in consequence that the term 'hallucination' would be appropriate to a description of the phenomenon (cf. pp 32ff., 113).

[18] Mt 14.28-31 must be regarded as a pre-Matthaean tradition (G. Strecker, *Der Weg der Gerechtigkeit,* 2nd ed. 1966, 199): Jn 21.7f. proves the existence of such Peter traditions. For a different view, G. Braumann, 'Der sinkende Petrus', *ThZ* 22 (1966), 403-414.

pains to prove the reality of the appearance. He stresses that all the disciples saw him (6.50), he makes Jesus get into the boat and notes that at the same time the wind dropped. In other words, what happened was something quite tangible.[19] It is possible that an apologetic tendency has led to the storm and its quelling being painted in more vividly, but the motif was virtually present all along. Where there was a reference to a sea voyage, a boat and a supernatural figure, it would have been surprising if this was not soon realised in the versions of the story. The parallels from accounts in other religions of rescue from distress at sea show how close is the connection between rescue and epiphany. Even if it is no longer possible to decide whether the storm motif was already realised in the earliest versions, we may certainly say that it was present from the beginning in the virtual motif field of 'walking on the sea'.

It is therefore possible that an epiphany at sea has been expanded by the addition of paradigmatically related motifs, though its character has remained largely unchanged. One theoretical possibility is of course that the rescue motifs should gradually push the epiphany motifs into the background. In this way affinity processes can lead to the transformation of traditions. A number of examples show this.

The healing of the ten lepers (Lk 17.11-19) is a transformation of Mk 1.40ff.[20] By variation one leper becomes several; the element of thanksgiving was already present in the sending to the priest. Several lepers brings the possibility of an opposition of thanksgiving and ingratitude and an opposition of authorities: the priest and Jesus (even the 'ungrateful' ex-lepers certainly go to the priest and will have thanked God in his presence). Naturally the detailed reshaping of the story is by no means an accident, but the consequences of historical processes, the switch to a mission to the Gentiles and inner dissociation from the Temple. If one wishes to thank God, one no longer uses the mediation of the Temple, but the mediation of Jesus.

The healing of the two blind men in Mt 9.27-31 is a transformation of Mk 10.46-52.[21] The command to silence is retained but changed into a command to secrecy, and placed at the end in accordance with the normal pattern of composition. Where there is a secret, there is no longer any place for the crowd. Instead the

---

[19] E. Lohmeyer, *Mk*, 134, considers but dismisses the apologetic interpretation of Jesus' boarding of the boat. In my view Dibelius, *TG*, 90, is right.

[20] So Bultmann, *HST*, 33. This is disputed by J. Roloff, *Kerygma* 157f.

[21] The story can hardly be seen as a Matthaean composition (so C. Burger, *Jesus als Davidssohn*, 74-77). For an alternative, cf. J. Roloff, *Kerygma*, 131-33, and G. Strecker, *Weg*, 199f., n. 4.

command to secrecy has attracted the 'house' motif (or, more accurately, a motif variant from the scene setting). The event is now removed from the sight of the public.

Finally we come to the Johannine version of the centurion of Capernaum (Jn 4.46-54). The order visible behind the two synoptic versions, messengers who persuade Jesus to come and centurion preventing Jesus from entering his house, is reversed. The officer (= *basilikos*) himself tries to persuade Jesus to come. The faith motif continues to be associated with him: he believes on the basis of Jesus' word. The messengers, who have been placed later, can now no longer be used for the exposition but acquire a new function as part of the demonstration, that of testifying to the healing in conjunction with the motif of the hour (cf. already Mt 8.13). Here the affinity process has acted less on individual motifs than on the composition as a whole. In the synoptics the normal compositional structure was realised only in part. The accent was entirely on the expositional motifs. In John the story has attracted the missing parts of the composition and distributed the sequence 'officer – messengers' between the exposition and the conclusion. As a result the exposition has been considerably reduced (cf. the officer's expression of trust), while the conclusion has been filled out by the motif of the hour, which is closely associated in the paradigm.

Transformations as a result of affinity processes can be most easily detected where there are several independent variants of the tradition and it can be assumed that their variations also go back to oral tradition. Affinity processes seem to have had greater scope in oral tradition, although this is not true in every respect. One characteristic of written transmission is that it can combine different genres in larger compositions. Correspondingly (on the paradigmatic level) affinity processes can take place on a larger scale between genres, i.e. that motifs can find their way by a process of transfer into other genres. One example is the motif 'the gathering of a crowd', which has firm thematic roots in a number of miracle stories (cf. Mk 2.1ff.; 5.21, 25ff.; 6.35ff.) and in Mark's gospel reappears in the introductions of other genres (2.13; 3.20; 10.1; 4.1ff.). It makes sense wherever the presence of a gathering of any size can be presumed. Conversely, Matthew has occasionally introduced logia into the miracle stories. A real affinity may exist, as for example when he turns the genre-specific motif of overcoming an obstacle into the theological idea that faith overcomes the limitation of salvation to Israel (cf. Mt 8.11ff.; 15.24ff.). These remarks, however, bring us to a new group of problems, the relation of writing and oral tradition.

B. Transmission Media:
Oral Tradition and Writing

Rudolf Bultmann has specifically denied the significance of the distinction between oral and written composition for the history of the transmission of the synoptic gospels, 'because on account of the unliterary character of the traditional material one of the chief differences between oral and written traditions is lacking'.[22] This assumption of a continuity in the history of the transmission has recently been denied. Only within a written tradition, it is argued, does a normative authentic version exist; oral tradition exists only in variants and in it composition and transmission are identical. This is true when one compares texts which were composed from the beginning either in writing or orally. However, what is true in such a comparison of written literature and oral tradition is not therefore also true of the transition from previously oral literature to its written versions. When oral tradition has later been written down there has in practice continued to be great variability in the tradition; new oral versions were written down and affected the process of written transmission and written versions were also altered. The synoptic gospels are one example: Luke and Matthew certainly do not regard Mark as a normative model. Fairy tales are another: their different versions show great variation, although they may have been produced by the same author.[23] Where a previously oral tradition is committed to writing, the 'traditors' evidently feel less bound to take over the original text word for word than is the case with the transmission of a text deriving from a

---

[22] Bultmann, *HST*, 6, and 239, where the same reason is given – the non-literary character of the tradition. Criticism of the idea of 'regularities' is based on three main points:
  a) Neglect of the distinction between oral and written transmission. R. Jelke, *Die Wunder Jesu*, 1923, 34, objected long ago: 'It is never ever permissible to identify the regularities we find, for example, in the shaping of the material in the different New Testament sources, with regularities in the pre-redactional tradition.' This criticism was intensified by E. Güttgemanns, *Candid Questions*, 98, 124f., 208, passim. Güttgemanns insists that in oral transmission there is never anything but successive recreations: 'For an oral author the recital is the moment of creation' (50, A. Lord, *The Singer of Tales*, Cambridge, Mass., and London 1960, whom Güttgemanns follows here). It follows that the oral prehistory of a text must remain largely obscure.
  b) The neglect of the distinction between synchronous features of style and diachronous transmission tendencies, in other words the assumption that the beginning was pure form. This criticism is voiced by T. Boman, *Die Jesus-Überlieferung im Lichte der neueren Volkskunde*, 1967, 17, 20, 243, n. 49. E.P. Sanders, *Tendencies*, 16, has, however, rightly defended Bultmann against this criticism: as Sanders says, his language shows that he is well aware of the distinction between 'form' and 'style' and also 'regularities' of the tradition.
  c) Neglect of individual tendencies to modify shown by individual authors, which cannot be subsumed under general 'regularities' of the tradition: E.P. Sanders, *Tendencies*, 272.
[23] Cf. H. Bausinger, *Formen*, 161ff.

written original. There must therefore be a distinction between oral tradition, the written transmission of oral tradition and written tradition. This is the distinction Bultmann has in mind. He is not in any sense denying the great differences between oral and written literature, but he regards the distinction as overlaid by a more fundamental one, that between literary and non-literary texts. His distinction in fact is between non-literary oral composition, non-literary writing and literary writing, and in my view it describes precisely the phenomenon referred to here in the distinction between the written transmission of oral tradition and written tradition.

Agreeing with Bultmann on this point does not necessarily mean acceptance of the assumption of continuous transmission tendencies. Even in the observable process of the written transmission of oral tradition, we can detect only typical processes of change which point in various directions. To trace them back into the previous oral history of a text is an uncertain operation, even when we assume that the same tendencies existed in the process of oral transmission. It still remains difficult to decide whether a particular written version of a text was produced by processes of concentration, development or affinity unless it is possible to compare other versions or point to obvious clues (such as the boat in Mk 4.36 which plays no part in the story or the baroque overloading of detail in Jn 11). The prerequisite for a reasoned decision is always the 'transparency of the previous history' of a written version. If we directly compare the oral and written traditions, there is little room for this sort of transparency of previous oral history. On the other hand, if we assume that written versions of oral traditions are subject to particular conditions which link them partly with the oral and partly with the written tradition, we shall be more likely to regard cautious conclusions about the oral tradition as possible. After all, the very judgment that such and such texts transmitted in writing are versions of previous oral tradition now committed to writing assumes a 'transparency' of this previous oral history. It assumes that the written form must retain features of oral composition which make it possible to distinguish an originally oral text from an original written composition.[24] Traces at least must have survived. In this section three features of oral tradition will be discussed with reference to the Marcan miracle stories. The underlying assumption is not that there is a fundamental continuity

---

[24] Various writers have made efforts to establish such criteria: for the epic A. Lord, *The Singer of Tales*; for the Coptic legends W. Kosack, 'Der Gattungsbegriff "Volkserzählung"', *Fab* 12 (1971), 18-47.

between oral tradition and its transmission in writing, but that there are on the one hand continuous tendencies and on the other inevitable changes which appear with writing. The important thing is that both can still be detected.

(a) Narrative speech is different from a written work because the narrator and the listener are present together. This makes direct feedback possible: the listeners' reactions can be incorporated into the story as it goes on. Conversely, the story must be structured in such a way as to allow for this. The simple repetition of a motif may derive from this sort of feedback. The narrator notices that attention is flagging, his audience is puzzled, or that tension must be increased, so he says the same thing again with a variation, an interpretation or a development. This can turn into a fixed style. The repetitive style of Mk 1.40ff.; 5.25ff.; 6.45ff.; 14.32ff. is perhaps to be explained in this way,[25] though this does not exclude the possibility that this style is the result of affinity processes in which related motifs were incorporated into the story; the synchronous compositional structure 'repetitive style' must be distinguished from its diachronous emergence.

The direct link between narrator and listener may also produce an 'interlocking' of the content:[26] the listener's attitudes, his opposition or his agreement, may be incorporated into the story. The claim that to forgive sins is blasphemy in Mk 2.7f. may anticipate a response from the listener, and the same may be true of the disciples' questions in Mk 5.31b and the laughter in 5.39b. Wonder and acclamation may perhaps be regarded as anticipations of favourable reactions from the listeners; occasionally these concluding motifs may first have been incorporated into the story from the 'oral framework'.

Examples of such interlocking of course occur in written literature too, but the simultaneity of narrator and listener, their presence in the same place, makes it possible to indicate such interlocking more clearly. Storytelling is, of course, part of a context of expressive behaviour which includes inflections of the voice, silence, mimicry and gesture. These allow particular statements or remarks to be more clearly set apart from the story. The narrator can to some extent come out of the story and address the listeners directly. Examples of comments are the introductory formulae we

---

[25] For Mk 6.45ff; 14.32ff. this would mean that we should be sceptical about literary critical hypotheses (pace E. Lohmeyer, *Mk,* 130, and K.G. Kuhn, 'Jesus in Gethsemane', *EvTh* 12 (1952/53), 260-85).

[26] The existence of such 'dovetailing' in the parables has been demonstrated by E. Linnemann, *Parables of Jesus,* 1975, 4th ed., passim.

have postulated, also translations of foreign words ot healing (5.41 and 7.35b) and subsequent explanations (5.8; 6.50; 7.26b). Mk 2.10, about the authority of the Son of Man to forgive sins, a verse which has been much puzzled over, also becomes intelligible as a comment. A sudden change from the second to the third person has occasionally been explained as the insertion by Mark of a parenthetical remark to the reader.[27] However, to step out of the story in this way is difficult in written composition and would need to be indicated particularly clearly, whereas oral narration can use accompanying signs to set the verse more clearly apart from its context.[28]

All these are of course only traces of features of oral narrative, but they are enough to show a definite structural change during the transition from oral to written transmission. The features of oral narrative which depend on the immediate presence of the listeners do not disappear completely, but have to be incorporated into the compositional sequence of the text. The writer of a story can also of course address his readers directly, but then he interrupts his story. The oral narrator can do this within the story. In this way a story, by being written down, loses a range of expressive devices; but what it loses in one way it gains in another.

(b) Narrative speech takes place in time. Not only the events described, but also their linguistic presentation takes place in temporal sequence.[29] Since it is impossible to go back, as it is in reading, since the listener's attention (especially when there are many listeners) must be always alert, it is necessary to achieve a 'filling-out of the present moment' to hold the reader. This 'filling-out' can be compared with a spotlight moving across a series of connected pictures. A simply drawn segment which is easy to take in will stand out, while others will disappear and not be present in the moment of narration. In practice this means a concentration on essential characters, a single story-line, the unex-

[27] So G.H. Boobyer, 'Mark 2.10a and the Interpretation of the Healing of the Paralytic', *HThR* 47 (1954), 115-20. See also C.P. Ceroke, 'Is Mk 2.10a a Saying of Jesus?', *CBQ* 22 (1960), 369-90; W. Grundmann, *Markus,* 54f; L.S. Hay, 'The Son of Man in Mark 2.10 and 2.28', *JBL* 89 (1970), 69-74.

[28] See the examples of commentary in the oral tradition noted by H. Bausinger, *Formen,* 169. Other possible instances in the synoptic tradition are the 'sermon conclusions' of apophthegms (M. Dibelius, *TG,* 63ff.), where these stand up to critical examination. Additional items of information (e.g. the reference to 'the house' in Mk 7.17ff.; 9.28; 10.10) may go back to such commentaries. For a different view, cf. A.W. Mosley, 'Jesus' Audiences in the Gospels of St Mark and St Luke', *NTSt* 10 (1963/64), 139-49.

[29] For some general remarks on this see G. Müller, 'Erzählzeit und erzählte Zeit', *Festschrift P. Kluckhohn und H. Schneider* (1948), 195-212, and E. Lämmert, *Bauformen des Erzählens* (1955), 19ff., though the latter is more concerned with distinct literary forms.

plained appearance of persons and things (cf. the scribes in Mk 2.6, Jesus' sleeping in Mk 4.38, the bread and fishes in 6.38, the crowd in 7.33, the not previously mentioned nakedness in 5.15). The stylistic features of popular stories listed by A. Olrik can be largely explained as the result of the need for 'filling out the present moment'.[30]

This need, however, also has negative aspects which are even more obvious. These were identified by W. Kosack in an attempt to obtain criteria for deciding whether a text from the tradition was originally oral or written,[31] and demonstrated on the Coptic legends. The starting-point is the idea that the oral narrator is 'totally dominated by the event of the moment' and as a result can lose sight of the preceding and subsequent sections of a story. In the synoptic miracle stories, which are short, this danger is not particularly great, but comparable phenomena can be found. Kosack singled out four particular features of oral style:

i) The compresssion of essential elements of the story, making comprehension more difficult. We have seen an example in Mt 9.2, where the faith motif was retained while the expression of the faith (the entry through the roof) disappeared.

ii) Unprepared narrative, resulting in illogical structure. There is an example in Mk 5.34: an assurance of healing is given when it has already taken place. Mk 5.42 is also illogical: if the mourners have already assembled the raising can hardly be kept secret.

iii) The omission and later addition of important details. See the remarks which have the air of after-thoughts in Mk 5.8; 6.48; 7.26.

iv) Motif pressure. The narrator may lose the thread of his story and as a result be obliged to force the story to a conclusion – perhaps by a miracle. The only possible instance is the story of the Temple tax (Mt 17.24ff.), except that it is hardly plausible to suppose here that the narrator has lost the thread.

For our purposes the main point of interest is that even the written versions of the miracle stories continue to show structural features of oral narrative. However, the inconsistencies associated with the technique of instant input certainly become less and less noticeable. Luke's narrative is more coherent, more logical, better planned, and that must have something to do with the change to writing. A written work is not dependent on 'filling out the present moment': the context of the whole work and of individual episodes is always available to turn back to.

---

[30] A. Olrik, 'Gesetze der Volksdichtung', *Zeitschrift f. deutsches Altertum* 51 (1909), 1-12; Bultmann, *HST,* 187ff.

[31] 'Der Gattungsbegriff "Volkserzählung"', 33ff; the quotation is from p. 34.

(c) Finally, oral narrative is in a particular relation to time in yet a third way. It is dependent on the memories of the narrators and on a familiarity among the listeners with their stock of motifs and forms – everyone knows how difficult it is to follow a talk which contains a lot of unfamiliar themes and ideas. This is the reason for the predominance of typical motifs,[32] the recurrence of compositional sequences and the adherence to existing paradigmatic fields. The writing down of the miracle stories makes very little difference to these features. Matthaean and Lucan reproduction operates largely within the limits of existing genre structures. Nevertheless there is no doubt that the opportunity for individual composition is greater in writing than in oral narration. The difference is one of degree. In this connection it should be remembered that we have been able in the written medium to observe transmission processes which have abandoned the limitations of the existing possibilities of the genre, for example Matthew's incorporation of logia into miracle stories.

Our discussion leads to the following conclusion. The reproduction of narratives by writing them down cannot be treated generally in terms either of continuity or discontinuity. There is continuity, for example, in the following of motif fields and forms of composition characteristic of the genre (though allowances must be made for differences of degree). On the other side, a degree of discontinuity showing itself in certain tendencies to change cannot be ignored. Stylistic features deriving from the immediate presence in time and space of the audience at the narration recede, the repetitive style, comment in the narrative, the narrative mode of filling out the present moment. Even this disappearance, however, is not instantaneous. It can be observed. Even here discontinuity in the history of the transmission contains an element of continuity. The general distinction between writing and oral transmission – for all its legitimacy – has to be qualified in relation to the synoptic tradition: oral tradition written down shares in features of both writing and oral transmission. This applies to the written form of any tradition, but even more in the case of the synoptics because of two factors. First, we must reckon with the fact that after the first writing down of the tradition in Mark an oral tradition continued to exist and may have influenced the further process of writing in Matthew and Luke. Matthew, for example, may have retold the miracle stories according to patterns of composition familiar to

---

[32] In complete harmony with classical form criticism, A. Lord writes, *The Singer*, 130: 'Formula analysis . . . is able to indicate whether any given text is oral or 'literary'. An *oral* text will yield a predominance of clearly demonstrable formulas.'

him from oral tradition. Conversely, it would be wrong to project on to the oral tradition an 'inherent aversion' to committing things to writing. K. Ranke believes he can detect a tendency to fixation in writing in the particular case of applied forms, that is, forms which were not merely passed on for their narrative interest or entertainment value, such as genres used in teaching and preaching. As applied forms, he says, 'they must necessarily constantly be given fixed literary form because many of those who use them lack not only the capacities of the oral narrator to which we have referred, but also the narrator's naturally inherited stock of such traditions.'[33] There can be no doubt that the synoptic genres are applied forms. They were written down 'relatively' early – relatively that is, to the periods with which the study of popular oral traditions must deal.[34]

In conclusion it should be stressed once again that while many considerations may apply to all the synoptic genres, each genre must strictly be studied on its own. The typical transmission tendencies we have observed (compression, expansion and affinity), the changes introduced by writing, and the continuity in genre-specific motif fields and types of composition are initially features of miracle stories only. The relationship between variability and continuity must be determined for each genre specifically.[35]

---

[33] K. Ranke, 'Orale und literale Kontinuität', *Kontinuität?* (1969), 102-16, quotation from p. 113, who also discusses the interaction between written and oral literature and quotes (p. 112) E. Moser-Rath, *Predigtmärlein der Barockzeit* (1964), p. VII: 'There can be no doubt that in earlier times more was read, and more information derived from reading passed on orally, than was accepted for a long time. On the other hand, certain areas of popular tradition remain untouched by literary influences for long periods. There can be scarcely any piece of material which, in the constant give and take, was not affected by both literary and oral influences.' This applies equally to primitive Christian literature. The connections between the gospels of John and Thomas and the synoptic gospels cannot be explained solely by links of oral or written transmission, but by an interaction between the two.

[34] This is also a ground for caution in accepting suggestions from students of folk traditions, which often relate to longer periods of time. The scepticism expressed about the Finnish-geographical school's attempts to reconstruct original versions is undoubtedly justified. It is one thing to reconstruct the original version of a tale found in different countries, peoples and periods and another to reconstruct the original of a synoptic tradition.

[35] In the case of tales, jokes and anecdotes, J. Jech, 'Variabilität und Stabilität in der einzelnen Kategorien der Volksprosa', *Fab* 9 (1967), 55-62, has attempted to establish specific transmission tendencies, i.e. the proportion of variable and stable elements within a particular genre. L. Röhrich, 'Das Kontinuitätsproblem bei der Erforschung der Volksprosa', *Kontinuität?* (1969), 117-33, shows that even whole genres show a tendency of varying strength to turn into other genres. Legends often become sagas, while didactic genres and jokes are more likely to remain true to type. 'On the whole genres differ in their stability and variability' (128).

The type of genre must also be kept in mind in any application of statements from the general study of narratives to the synoptic traditions. The Serbo-Croatian heroic epic analysed by A. Lord, *The Singer of Tales*, is in a quite different genre from miracle stories, parables and apophthegms.

CHAPTER III

COMPOSITION WITHIN THE FRAMEWORK GENRE

The task of the diachronic section of this analysis is to demonstrate the significance of relatively continuous virtual genre structures for the transmission history of primitive Christian miracle stories. This is to adopt a position distinct both from recent redaction criticism and from classical form criticism, though close to the latter. Redaction criticism tended to some extent to make an exaggerated distinction between tradition and redaction and finally asserted a radical discontinuity within the transmission process,[1] whereas this study emphasises the continuity of genre structures. This is to re-establish links with classical form criticism, which postulated a relatively high degree of diachronous continuity in the history of the transmission of the tradition, but looked for this at the level of realised texts. Here, in contrast, we have emphasised that, while continuity exists, it exists at the level of virtual genre structures. This insight has its roots in classical form criticism: the real basis for the continuity it assumed in the history of the transmission process was the forms and their various 'life situations'.

Redaction criticism, however, has one argument on its side: the formation of the gospels was the creation of a new genre which has no parallel.[2] Even if it is admitted that in the reproduction of motifs and small units existing genre structures provide a framework for all changes, it may well be asked whether the combination of small units to form an inclusive genre does not result in the abandonment of these traditional genre structures. Is not the gospel form something new, which can no longer be treated as the actualisation of existing possibilities?

It must first be pointed out that even in the process of the transmission of individual pericopae every instance of reproduc-

---

[1] As in E. Güttgemanns, *Candid Questions*. While one may disagree with the author on many points, this book has the merit of forcing New Testament exegesis to re-examine assumptions which have come to be taken for granted.

[2] The classic study of this idea is K.L. Schmidt, 'Die Stellung der Evangelien in der allgemeinen Literaturgeschichte', *Eucharisterion* II, 2nd ed. 1923, 50-134.

tion is to some extent a new creation.[3] While the creative achievement of forming the gospels must be ranked much higher, the difference is perhaps only one of degree. Secondly, it can be argued that the formation of the gospels must be seen in a broader context. It represents only one possibility of combining various synoptic genres. Others are collections of sayings (Q, the Gospel of Thomas), which also found room for narrative genres (Mt 8.5ff.; parables in the Gospel of Thomas). It is obvious that the collections of sayings are based on the (restricted) compositional possibilities of didactic genres: one piece of teaching is attached to another, and the highest level of arrangement consists in a degree of systematisation. The gospels, on the other hand, are based on a narrative form of composition: one event is attached chronologically to another. It seems to me that the gospels undeniably draw on the compositional possibilities of the narrative genres, which gives rise to the assumption that the form of composition we find in the gospels rests on the genre structures of the narrative genres they have incorporated, those of the miracle stories and legendary narratives. We shall concentrate here on the miracle stories, even though this inevitably gives a partial view since the legendary narratives, especially the accounts of the passion, are of great importance for the formation of the gospels. The point can be made simply enough in the following way. Miracles and apophthegms can be arranged in almost any order, whereas the story of the passion has a fixed position at the end (just as the birth narratives belong at the beginning). The chronological order which underlies the gospels thus did not become necessary until the story of the passion came to be incorporated into the narrative.

By 'composition' in this chapter is meant not just the sequence of individual motifs within a small unit, but their sequence within a framework form. Our main interest here is in the typical devices used to produce such a form of composition. We distinguish four types of composition.[4]

---

[3] A. Lord, *Singer of Tales,* 13: 'For an oral poet the moment of composition is the performance.' L. Degh, 'Die schöpferische Tätigkeit des Erzählens', *Int. Kongress der Volkserzählungsforscher* (1961), 63-73; S. Lo Nigro, 'Tradition et Style', ibid. 152ff.

[4] These four categories, linking, typifying, analytical and overarching composition, are found in all stories of any length. Each of them has an analogue among the 'structures of narrative' (*Bauformen des Erzählens*), the title of the book in which E. Lämmert constructed a system of categories to cover all stories. With linking composition cf. 'gathering together and linking stories consisting of several strands' (43ff.), with analytical composition 'narrative phases' (73ff.), with typifying composition 'forms of compression' (82ff.), with overarching composition 'the spherical completeness of the narrative' (95ff.).

A. Linking Composition

(a) Mark

We call 'linking' any compositional arrangement which makes possible narrative transitions from one individual pericope to the next. We can distinguish five possible forms of linking composition:

i) The *time connection* makes the link with the previous pericope by a reference to the passage of time: the day (9.2; 14.1, 12), the time of day (1.32, 35; 4.35; 6.47; 11.12; 14.17; 15.1; 15.42; 16.1), the period of time ἐν ἐκείναις ταῖς ἡμέραις (1.9; 8.1) or the time sequence (μετά 1.14; 9.2; 14.1; εὐθύς 1.12, 21 (23); 14.43; 15.1). A number of variants of the time connection are combined in 9.2; 14.1; 15.1.

ii) The *place connection* starts as the actors have just left the scene of the previous events (1.29; 2.13; 3.7; 5.1, 21; 6.1, 34, 53; 7.24, 31; 8.10, 27; 9.30; 10.1, 17; 13.1; 14.26, 53; 15.16). Naturally the place and time connections may be combined (1.29; 11.12).

iii) The *action connection* mentions as an introduction elements of the preceding action. This link is very rare in Mark. (14.22, 43).

iv) The *motivation connection* is a reference to the preceding pericope(s) by the principal actor himself: he hears, sees or becomes aware of what has happened and lets it influence his subsequent action. This connection is also rare in Mark (6.14; 12.28).

v) A *circumstantial introduction* is a general remark which takes up the story after a longish interval with (καὶ) ἐγένετο (1.4, 9; 2.23), a periphrastic conjugation (2.18; 10.32), a genitive absolute (8.1; 14.3) or an imperfect (6.7; 10.13).

Mark prefers place and time connections, place connections in the middle section of the gospel (Mk 2-13 contains 16 of the 20 place connections) and time connections at the beginning and end (Mk 1-2.1; 14-16 contain 15 out of 20 time connections). This distribution is no accident. Time connections have greater linking force in the narrative, and at the beginning of the gospel there is a compositional need for a connected narrative. The impression created here continues to have an influence even if the narrative thread becomes looser in the middle. At the end, in the passion story, linking composition was to some extent already a feature of Mark's material.

Our thesis is that the types of linking composition can for the most part be explained by compositional link forms within small units. They actualise again in a new and creative way an existing stock of link forms. For our study the main interest in all this is the contribution made by the miracle stories to this stock.

The time connection can pick up datings of individual pericopes to the sabbath (Mk 1.23; 3.2), or specifications of the time of day within individual stories (Mk 6.48: 'the third watch of the night', or assumptions about periods (8.2: 'three days'); the main point of contact is linking adverbs of time. In Mark the motif (better: element) of suddenness, whose original position in the composition is the miraculous action itself or the pronouncement of success, moves five times into the introduction and otherwise occurs freqently in other positions within pericopae. In introductions it creates the impression that the action is taking its course in between two pericopae in just the same way as within a pericope. G. Rudberg has offered good reasons for supposing that εὐθύς in paratactic clauses is a characteristic of oral style – further evidence for Mark's closeness to the oral tradition.[5]

The place connection is the creation of the miracle stories insofar as many miracle stories (as opposed to apophthegms and logia) are localised. In Mark these place references are deliberate compositions. Until Mk 3.7ff. Jesus works in Galilee. The summary at 3.7ff. looks beyond into the surrounding regions, in which Jesus is later to work – except Idumaea. Mark may have mentioned this region in order to surpass the area of the Baptist's activity (Judaea and Jerusalem) on all sides: on the north with Galilee, Tyre and Sidon on the east with Transjordan, on the south with Idumaea. He is saying that the gospel is spreading from Capernaum through Galilee and the surrounding regions into the whole world (13.10; 14.9).

The action connection is rare in miracle stories. Within complete pericopae there is no need to recapitulate what has previously happened (but for some cases cf. Mk 2.4: ἐξορύξαντες, 4.39: διεγερθείς, 5.12: παρεκάλεσαν, cf. 5.10, 5.35: ἔτι αὐτοῦ λαλοῦντος, 9.20: πεσών). But the action connection is very rare in linking composition in general.

In contrast, the motivation connection is strikingly frequent. The retrospective perception appears as 'seeing' (2.5; 5.6, 22; 6.48, 49; 9.15, 20, 25), 'hearing' (5.27, 36; 7.25; 10.47), 'knowing' (2.8; 5.30, 33; 6.38), 'grief and fear' (3.5; 5.33).

The circumstantial introduction is conceivable within individual pericopae, but is in fact usually a redactional composition. Mark seems to have developed particularly the ὄχλος motif. This motif is

---

[5] G. Rudberg, 'ΕΥΘΥΣ' *CN* IX (1944), 42-46, J. Weiss, 'εὐθύς bei Markus', *ZNW* 11 (1910), 124-33, was right in saying that εὐθύς has a fixed position in miracle stories, but this does not mean that other texts are therefore post-Marcan. D. Daube, *The Sudden in the Scripture* (1964), 46-60, comes to the conclusion that Mark chooses this adverb for the following reasons: 'it does express the inevitable, one-after-the-other succession of events, from the first temptation to the final delivering over to Pilate' (60). Cf. also L. Rydbeck, *Fachprosa, vermeintliche Volkssprache und Neues Testament*, Uppsala 1967.

firmly rooted in a number of miracle stories (2.1ff.; 5.25ff.; 6.35ff.; 8.1ff.), and mark may have transferred it to other genres (2.13; 3.20; 4.1ff.; 10.1f.). The reader gets the impression that Jesus is always surrounded by a crowd. Here linking composition merges with typifying.

The miracle stories are thus involved in the linking composition found in the gospels. They themselves were linked by the two-part introductions which have already been discussed. Since the miracle-worker is in each case the first person to appear, the most prominent person in the introduction in each case is the one who remains constant through all the pericopae. This incorporation of the oral framework into the narrative is at the same time the incorporation of individual stories into the compositional framework. This incorporation of individual stories into a wider story has been given the name 'historicisation' by K. Kertelge, but this is a very broad term.[6] 'Compositional integration' would be a better one.

(b) Matthew

If we compare the linking forms found in Mark with those in Matthew, we find a difference in frequency.

i) The time connection is much more frequent than the place connection, whereas the relationship in Mark is exactly opposite. There is either an introductory τότε (2.16; 3.13; 4.1; 9.14; 12.38; 15.1; 16.24; 18.21; 19.13; 20.20; 23.1) or ἐν ἐκείνῳ τῷ καιρῷ (11.25; 12.1; 14.1; cf. 3.1; 13.1; 18.1; 22.23; 26.55). The increase in the number of time connections shows a greater degree of linking between individual pericopae, which makes it all the more striking that it is completely absent from the miracle stories.

ii) The time connection occurs 14 or 15 times: 8.1 (9.1); 9.9, 27, 32; 12.9; 13.1; 14.14, 34; 15.21, 29; 17.9; 20.29; 24.1; 26.30, whereas in the shorter Mark we found it 19 times.

iii) The action connection has become more frequent: 2.1, 13, 19; 9.18; 11.7; 12.46; 13.36; 14.34; 22.41; 26.47; 28.11.

iv) The motivation connection is very often made by 'seeing' (2.16; 5.1; 8.18; 9.36), 'knowing' (12.15) and 'hearing' (4.12; 11.2; 14.1, 13; 22.34).

---

[6] The term 'historicising' always implies an antithesis. The term has four shades of meaning: (a) chronological rather than thematically based composition (A. Meyer, *Entstehung*, 39); (b) a retrospective account rather than immediate kerygmatic appeal (W. Marxsen, *Introduction to the New Testament*, Oxford 1964, 120ff.); (c) a connected account instead of reports of individual episodes (K. Kertelge, *Wunder*, 186ff.); (d) an account emphasising historical fact as opposed to a naive narrative. The additional influence of the contrast between *Historie* and *Geschichte* (whatever may be meant by that) has not exactly contributed to the clarity of this term.

v) The circumstantial introduction is rare (3.1; 4.18; 8.23; 26.6), a feature accentuated by Matthew's removal of most of the summary notices in the Marcan introductions (cf. 9.1f.; 9.18; 12.22). Exceptions are 13.1f.; 14.13f. The summary introduction in 19.1f. has been made into a summary distinct from the following dispute by the mention of healings.

The characteristic connections in Matthew are thus those of time, action and motivation. As in Mark, a more compressed style can be seen at the beginning and end. The complex interlocking of elements in the infancy narrative also gives the sequel the character of a connected narrative. This enables Matthew to break up the coherence of the first day in Capernaum (Mk 1.21ff.). The relevant pericopae are left until after the Sermon on the Mount.

There is no sign of a specifically new contribution by the miracle stories to linking composition in Matthew, but there is a distinctive style of linking composition in the miracle stories. In Mark we observed a double movement: the appearance of Jesus and of his opposite number. Matthew constructs this type of introduction by using formulaic phrases, which show three main distinct forms.

i) Jesus' appearance is described in a participial construction while the main clause introduces his opposite number. If there is a change of subject between the participle and the main clause, we find a genitive absolute:[7]

a) εἰσελθόντος δὲ αὐτοῦ εἰς Καφαρναοὺμ
b) προσῆλθεν αὐτῷ ἑκατόνταρχος (8.5)
a) καὶ ἐλθὼν ὁ Ἰησοῦς εἰς τὴν οἰκίαν Πέτρου
b) εἶδεν τὴν πενθερὰν αὐτοῦ (8.14)
Cf. also 8.28; 9.27; 14.14; 17.14, 24.

ii) Jesus is introduced by a participial construction *a)*, the main verb gives a more detailed description of his coming *b)*, and the opposite number (or the storm on the lake) is introduced by καὶ ἰδού in a new independent sentence.[8]

a) καταβάντος δὲ αὐτοῦ ἀπὸ τοῦ ὄρους
b) ἠκολούθησαν αὐτῷ ὄχλοι πολλοί
c) καὶ ἰδοὺ λεπρός προσελθών (8.1)
a) καὶ ἐμβάντι αὐτῷ εἰς τὸ πλοῖον
b) ἠκολούθησαν αὐτῷ οἱ μαθηταὶ αὐτοῦ
c) καὶ ἰδοὺ σεισμὸς μέγας (8.23)
Cf. 12.9; 15.21; 20.29a.

---

[7] The introductory participial consruction corresponds to the Greek opening of chriae (G. Rudberg, 'Zur Diogenes-Tradition', *SO* 14 (1935), 22-43. Evidence from Plutarch is collected in H. Almquist, *Plutarch und das Neue Testament* (1946), 69.
[8] Cf. P. Fiedler, *Die Formel 'und siehe' im Neuen Testament* (1969).

iii) The middle element of the introduction may be omitted and the ἰδού sentence come immediately after the participial construction: in this case there is no καί before ἰδού.

a) ταῦτα αὐτοῦ λαλοῦντος αὐτοῖς

b) ἰδοὺ ἄρχων προσελθών (9.18). Cf. 9.32.

H.J. Held[9] has put forward the interesting thesis that the introductions to the Matthaean miracle stories have been assimilated to the introductions of the apophthegms, especially the controversies. He regards this as an argument for the apophthegmatic character of the Matthaean miracle stories. Our observations so far contradict this view. While the first type of introduction has some parallels in apophthegms, only one has the change of subject typical of miracle stories (Jesus/opposite number), 21.23. The opposite subject change (opposite number/Jesus) occurs twice (11.7; 22.41). Usually there is no change of subject: 4.18; 8.18; 9.9,36; 16.1; 16.5, 13. The second type of introduction has no parallel outside miracle stories. The third does occur outside miracle stories (2.1, 13, 19; 26.47), but only once in an apophthegm (12.46). On the other hand, features from introductions to apophthegms do not occur in miracle stories. A large number of apophthegms begin with the appearance of the opposite number, and there is often an introductory τότε: 9.14; 12.38; 15.1; 18.21; 19.13; 20.20 (19.3 has no τότε). This time connection never occurs in miracle stories, and the double stress characteristic of the introductions to miracle stories is, conversely, absent in apophthegms. The common features are reduced to the verb προσέρχεσθαι (and similar terms). In my opinion there is no basis for the view that Matthaean miracle stories have paradigmatic introductions. Even in Matthew the miracle stories have not lost their formal characteristics.

The stereotyped introductions give them a relatively self-contained appearance. This smoothness in the introduction to miracle stories is matched by the shape given to the conclusions by formulaic phrases (8.13; 9.22; 15.28; 17.18) and the omission of Marcan motifs pointing beyond individual miracle stories. Matthew removes the expansion of the dismissal conclusion into a missionary one (8.4, 34), and motifs of secrecy and incomprehension which indicate a revelation to come disappear. In Mark, for example, the reproach after the stilling of the storm provokes the question when the disciples will have faith. In Matthew (8.23-27)

---

[9] 'Matthew as Interpreter', 225-30. In my view, H.J. Held here gives a correctly observed phenomenon – the formal rounding off of a miracle story – a false interpretation.

the reproach is answered by the miracle. The story is complete in itself. Similar explanations apply to the disappearance of the reproach to the disciples after the walking on the lake (14.33) and the removal of the command to silence in 9.25. There is no longer any sign that the miracle stories are about truth not yet disclosed. While Matthew has generally strengthened the structural linking of individual pericopae, his treatment of the miracle stories makes them seem relatively self-contained narratives. They have an episodic character. Matthew is 'even more than Mark a book of pericopae' (K.L. Schmidt).[10]

(c) Luke

i) The time connection occurs ten times (1.26; 1.39, 57; 3.1; 4.42; 5.27; 10.1, 21; 13.1, 31).

ii) The place connection has become even less in evidence in Luke than in Matthew. It occurs only in 4.38 (=Mk); 9.57 (=Q); 19.1 (=Mk), and never in Lucan language.

iii) The action connection is not very frequent: 7.1 (=Q); 7.24 (=Q); 8.40; 9.43b; 10.38. The action conclusion in 9.43b is the only place in the gospels where a concluding motif of a miracle story acts as a transition to the next pericope: 'But while they were all marvelling . . .'.

iv) Motivation connections are even less numerous. Cf. 19.11; 20.45. Lk 14.15 is more of a transition within a connected unit. In other words, it is the very compositional linking forms preferred by Matthew which become less frequent in Luke.

v) The situation in the case of the circumstantial introduction is the reverse. It is found only four times in Matthew, but in Luke it becomes the typical link form with the stereotyped introduction (καὶ) ἐγένετο: a) circumstantial introductions without elements of other link forms: ἐγένετο δὲ ἐν τῷ τὸν ὄχλον ἐπικεῖσθαι (5.1; cf. 5.12; 9.18; 14.1; 17.11; 18.35). b) Circumstantial introductions with elements of an action connection: ἐγένετο δὲ ἐν τῷ βαπτισθῆναι ἅπαντα τὸν λαόν (3.21 cf. 9.28; 11.27). c) Circumstantial introductions with elements of a time connection: 1.5; 2.1; 5.17; 6.1, 6, 12; 7.11; 8.1, 22; 9.37, 51; 20.1. In addition to these 21 circumstantial introductions there are also a further five with a periphrastic construction or an imperfect (11.14; 13.10, 22; 14.25; 15.1). The frequency of the circumstantial introduction is reflected in the observation that Luke has taken over most of the summary notices in the Marcan introductions (4.31; 5.12; 8.4, 40; 9.10f.); only in 5.27 and 11.14 has he deleted them.

The circumstantial introduction with (καὶ) ἐγένετο is Luke's most important linking form. Bultmann has accurately described

---

its significance in his composition: '. . . it is even more characteristic of Luke that he can sense how false a picture is given if all the units are indifferently placed into one immediate temporal context, as happened in Mark at first, and was then further developed by Matthew. Luke knows that the few stories that have been passed on do not completely fit the course of events, but are only examples and illustrations; and so he frequently draws attention in some introductory phrase to the fact that the following section really occurs within a larger context. For this purpose he chooses a familiar formula from the LXX, καὶ ἐγένετο, which is particularly used in Luke for introducing many stories from Mark.'[11]

The process we have already seen in Matthew, the emergence of the episodic character of the miracle stories, can also be seen in Luke. The smoothing at the beginning of the miracle stories produced by the circumstantial introduction is matched by a smoothing at the end. Luke twice adds an acclamation conclusion to Marcan miracle stories (9.43a; 18.43) and twice has one – perhaps in Lucan language – in his special material (7.16; 13.17). He gives the decision of Jesus' enemies to seek his death (Mk 3.6) formal features analogous to those of an acclamation conclusion: 'But they were filled with incomprehension and discussed with one another what they might do to Jesus.' (6.11). The connection with Jesus' future end is much vaguer, whereas the connection with the miracle, as a result of the use of the conclusion style and the deletion of the note that the Pharisees left, is much closer. Although we would tend to expect a close interweaving from Luke, we have to admit here again that, while the miracle stories are indeed incorporated into the sequence of the narrative, they are not closely interwoven with it. They have an episodic character.

This study of linking composition has produced the following results. The evangelists have a stock of five linking devices. This stock comes from the compositional technique used in the small units and can also be found in the miracle stories. It is realised in the synoptic gospels to varying degrees. Mark prefers place and time connections, Matthew time, action and motivation connections, Luke circumstantial introductions. In Matthew and Luke the miracle stories become much more episodic than in Mark; they are more complete and finished.

---

[11] Bultmann, *HST*, 360. According to E. Lämmert, *Bauformen*, 84, the phrase 'At that time it came to pass . . .' is 'an example of iterative-durative compression combined with successive compression' – in our terminology, linking composition with typifying elements.

B. Typifying Composition

(a) Mark

Any narrative arrangement is typifying if it takes individual motifs from a few stories and makes them a constant feature of the whole story described in the framework form. The main typifying device is the summaries, which are – despite various arguments to the contrary[12] – redactional compositions based on miracle motifs. Certainly most of the individual features which find a place in the summaries occur in individual miracle stories. The summaries stress on the one hand that the miracle stories present only excerpts from Jesus' miracle-working activity, and on the other themselves give only a partial list: rescue and gift miracles are not mentioned.[13] They differ from Lucian's summaries[14] in mentioning only exorcisms and healings, i.e. miracles in which a human being is the object and the one addressed.

(b) Matthew

Matthew has produced five miracle summaries in addition to Mark's. If 11.2ff. is included, there are now two summaries between each of the five great discourses and in addition the introductory summary (4.23-25). Two of them replace Marcan miracle stories (4.23ff.; 15.29ff.), but take typifying features of those stories as a starting point (cf. the plural 'spirits', Mk 1.27, 'He has done *all* things well . . .', Mk 7.37).

In 4.23-25, the first summary, Matthew puts together motifs which in Mark are scattered across the early chapters: travelling around Galilee and preaching (Mk 1.21, 39), preaching of the 'gospel' (Mk 1.14f.), the spread of Jesus' fame (Mk 1.28), the bringing to Jesus of the sick (Mk 1.32-34), his large following from Galilee and the surrounding areas (Mk 3.7f.). For an understanding of Matthew's compositional intentions this summary is very important. In Mark we recognised the description of Jesus' activity spreading in concentric circles as an example of linking composition, but when statements are compressed into a summary this stylistic device disappears: in Matthew Jesus is from the beginning

---

[12] C.H. Dodd, 'The Framework of the Gospel Narrative', *ET* (1931/32), 396-400, regards the summaries as an existing outline used by Mark. H. Schürmann, 'Der "Bericht vom Anfang"', *TU* 87 (1964), 242-58, seeks to demonstrate that parts of Mk 1.32-34 are a reworking of a pre-Marcan composition; a similar view is advanced by R. Pesch, 'Ein Tag vollmächtigen Wirkens Jesu in Kapharnaum', *BL* 9 (1968), 114ff., 177ff., 261ff. L.E. Keck, 'Mark 3.7-12 and Mark's Christology', *JBL* 84 (1965), 341-58, looks for traditional material in 3.7 and 3.9, but this is rightly rejected by T.A. Burkill, Mark 3.7-12 and the Alleged Dualism in the Evangelist's Miracle Material', *JBL* 87 (1968), 409-17.

[13] Cf. R.H. Fuller, *Interpreting the Miracles*, London 1963, 35-36.

[14] Cf. H.D. Betz, *Lukian*, 145f.

a miracle worker known beyond Galilee. The Sermon on the Mount, which follows, acquires as a result more of a public character. It talks about 'the salt of the earth' (5.13) and the 'light of the world' (5.14), and is a proclamation of what the disciples are to teach to the whole world (28.19f.). The second summary (Mt 8.16f.), with its quotation from Isaiah, has been given the finish of an apophthegm which presents Jesus' saving activity as the fulfilment of Old Testament prophecy. The quotation replaces the confessions of the demons or their suppression. In the quotation Matthew does not follow the Septuagint, which refers to 'sins' and 'pains'; he needs the reference to diseases.[15] The third summary (9.35) repeats almost word for word the beginning of the first (4.23), and the reply to the question about the Baptist can be regarded as the fourth summary. In the fifth summary the link with the preceding pericope is made by means of a motivation connection: because Jesus knows about his opponents' plan to kill him, he disappears. In this context the command to silence is a precaution; it is addressed to human beings and is intended to keep secret not so much Jesus' christological status as his whereabouts. Matthew regards it as a fulfilment of Is 42.1ff.: the servant of God 'will not argue or cry out, and no-one in the streets will hear his voice'. Thus, in two places Matthew has introduced interpretative quotations into the Marcan summaries and so displaced the demons' confession. What is revealed in Mark by the mouths of demons – Jesus' status – is revealed for him by the Old Testament (Mt 12.15-21). The sixth summary contains no significant changes from Mark (Mt 14.34-36), while the seventh is a Matthaean composition, combining individual elements from Mk 7.31ff.; 8.22ff. with distinctive Matthaean motifs. It thus replaces Mk 8.22ff. – hardly because Matthew did not regard this as a suitable place to introduce the didactic story about faith. If that were the case, we would inevitably expect a stylised miracle summary on this theme.[16] The last

---

[15] Though the translation's independence of the LXX is not conclusive evidence of pre-Matthaean origin (pace G. Strecker, *Weg,* 66f.).

[16] H.J. Held, 'Matthew as Interpreter', 207-11, cf. 298, claims that Matthew left out Mk 7.32ff. because he could find no place to insert a didactic story about faith. However, the omission could have another reason. In Mark the crowd in the subsequent feeding miracle is introduced very abruptly. Matthew changes the preceding miracle story into a summary to give a reason for the presence of the crowd. The summaries in Mt 4.23-25; 9.35 and 14.14 have a similar function. The omission of 8.22ff. also has compositional reasons of this sort. The crowd is dismissed after the second feeding miracle (Mt 15.39) and does not reappear until after the transfiguration (17.14). Any intervening references to it, or any indications of any witnesses, have been consistently removed: the reference to the villages (cf. Mk 8.27), the summoning of the crowd (Mk 8.34), and similarly the healing of the blind man, which requires a stay in Bethsaida, and several bearers – in short, 'men' (Mk 8.24).

summaries are very short (19.2; 21.14), but important because they extend the impression that Jesus' typical form of activity was healing to cover his time in Jerusalem.

Matthew's typifying style of composition thus disproves the attempts to demonstrate that he distances himself from miracles. Nor is there any sign of a general subordination of miracle to word. The programmatic miracle summary in 4.23-25 precedes the Sermon on the Mount. In it teaching and healing are linked. What Matthew has joined, let not the exegete put asunder. Distinguishing between the two is a different matter.[17]

(c) Luke

It is characteristic of Luke that he includes not only narrative, but also a number of 'rhetorical' summaries, that is, surveys of Jesus' miracle-working activity in speeches. The best known example is Jesus' inaugural address in Nazareth: God's servant, anointed with the Spirit (Is 61.1f.) shows his power by freeing captives (exorcisms?) and healing the blind. Jesus' next summary reference to his work is his answer to the Baptist's question (7.18ff.), which Luke has expanded by means of a short narrative summary (v. 21): before the eyes of the messengers Jesus performs miracles and authenticates himself as 'Messiah'. The echoes of Is 61.1f. recall the inaugural address. There is another reference to Jesus' miracles in the reply to the Pharisees' warning about Herod: 'Behold, I cast out demons and perform cures today and tomorrow, . . .' (13.32).[18] Right up to the entry into Jerusalem performing miracles is a typical feature of Jesus' work. At the entry, Luke looks back over 'all' the miracles (19.37, a redactional phrase). Further examples of 'rhetorical' miracle summaries are 24.19; Acts 2.22; 10.38, where the miracles serve as an ἀπόδειξις for Jesus' authority.[19] Connected with this is Luke's practice of including christological titles, 'Son of God' and 'Christ' (4.41), in the narrative summaries he has taken from Mark, or stressing the 'power' which goes out from Jesus (6.19) and shows him to be God's anointed.

Typifying composition in the synoptic gospels rests largely on combinations of genre-specific miracle motifs. Where Matthew

---

[17] E. Trocmé, *La formation de l'Evangile selon Marc* (1963), 38, rightly challenges the view that 'le goût pour le merveilleux soit moindre chez Matthieu et Luc que chez Marc'.

[18] Lk 13.32 is probably tradition, 13.33 editorial. Cf. the analysis in O.H. Steck, *Israel und das gewaltsame Geschick der Propheten* (1967), 40-45.

[19] H. Conzelmann, *The Theology of Luke*, 1960, 191f.: 'The purpose of the miraculous proof is that of vindication.'

and Luke differ, they have expanded the original Marcan summaries, usually by adding further paradigmatically related motifs. It is interesting to note that the basic structure of the miracle stories is also reproduced in variations in the summaries: at the beginning there are usually expositional motifs, mainly motifs of approach, petition and insistence. At the end there are always final motifs: acclamatory confessions of demons (Mk 1.34; 3.12) or pronouncements of healings (6.56). The typifying compositional style of the synoptic gospels can thus be regarded to a large extent as the actualisation of genre-specific fields and sequences, with all the statements modified to make them apply not to individuals but to groups – except for the statements about the miracle-worker himself.

C. Analytical Composition

(a) Mark

We find analytical composition wherever pericopae are distinguished from other groups of pericopae by a common theme. Our question is: did Mark use motifs from miracles to form groups of pericopae? In my view we can distinguish four groups.[20] When Mark introduces the first miracle in the synagogue at Capernaum with the phrase, 'He taught them as one who had authority, and not as the scribes' (1.22, probably redactional), the theme of the following pericopae is stated: the confrontation with the Jewish authorities about Jesus' authority.[21] Its climax is in the Beelzebub controversy. The themes of this confrontation come from controversies and rule miracles. All the miracles in 1.21-3.1ff. (except 1.29f.) contain a tension between Jesus and his opponents.

The second group of miracles consists of 4.35-6.6. It is held together by the keywords πίστις or ἀπιστία, that is by a characteristic miracle motif (4.41; 5.34, 36; 6.6). The beginning and end of this section link belief in the miracles with the question of Jesus' identity: 'Who is this . . .? (4.41) and 'Is this not . . .?' (6.3).

A third group of miracles comprises 6.30-8.26. This makes the two feeding miracles the basis for the question about correct understanding. The relevant comments are probably redactional

---

[20] Cf. R. Pesch, *Naherwartungen* (1968), 48-73, for an account of scholarly attempts to analyse the structure of Mark.

[21] R.H. Fuller, on the other hand, *Interpreting the Miracles,* 70-71, distinguishes two groups: a) 1.9-39, confrontations with demonic opponents, b) 1.40ff., confrontations with human opponents. For what I believe is a correct view, see M.E. Glasswell, 'The Use of Miracles in the Markan Gospel', *Miracles* (1965), 151-62. K. Tagawa, *Miracles,* 82-92, regards Mk 1.21ff. as the programme of the whole gospel.

(6.52; 7.18; 8.17, 21). The motif of understanding comes from the tradition of the sayings (4.10ff.; cf. 12.24), but is here introduced into other genres. For Mark the miracles are διδαχὴ καινή recounted (1.28), which explains the call for understanding.

Mk 8.26ff. begins a new section in that Jesus' death comes more sharply into view. The disciples have to be prepared for the time when Jesus will be gone. Everything is dominated by the idea of discipleship which looks back to the cross (8.34). Accordingly, we now hear about the miracles of Jesus' disciples. 'Faith' is not only belief in miracles in the sense of receptivity, but also the active faith of prayer which can cast out demons (9.28f.) and move mountains (11.23f.). It is the miracle-working faith of the Christian community which follows Jesus. Miracles and discipleship go together (10.52); but not everyone who has been empowered by Jesus to work miracles follows the community (9.38-40).[22]

A general view of analytical composition shows that motifs are borrowed from other genres – the theme of conflict from controversies (though it occurs also in rule miracles), the theme of understanding from the sayings tradition – but miracle motifs always play a part in the process of analysis and grouping.

(b) Matthew

The main problem of analytical composition in Matthew is the integration of the discourse material into the narrative. The incorporation of the five great discourses sets up two conflicting tasks for the work of composition. If the narrative framework is not to be just a bare link between one discourse and another, references forward and back across the elaborately composed discourses must be used to give the narrative momentum. At the same time the passages between the discourses must be clearly marked off as separate sections, or the discourses will seem random insertions.

Narrative continuity across chapters of discourse is often secured by references to miracles. The introductory miracle summary ends with the note: 'and great crowds followed him . . .' (4.25). The narrative restarts with the same remark after the Sermon on the Mount, leading into the healing of the leper: 'great crowds followed him' (8.1). There is a similar bracket round the sending out of the Twelve (cf. 9.35 and 11.1). The discourse in parables is also followed by two reactions to miracles which refer back to events before the discourse, first Jesus' rejection by his

---

[22] K.G. Reploh, *Markus*, 87f. has shown that in 8.27-10.52 Mark is mainly addressing the community.

own town (cf. 13.54f.) and second Herod's belief that Jesus was John the Baptist risen from the dead because 'powers' were at work in him (14.2). After the community discourse Matthew takes up the story with a short reference to Jesus' miraculous activity (19.2). The placing of the discourses within this ongoing framework prevents them from disrupting the continuity of the narrative despite their length and the significance of the substance. This discharges the first task of composition.

The second task is to achieve by various groupings a due emphasis on the stories and pericopae between the discourses. In the process the Marcan structure completely disappears, and different ideas become the focus of the groupings. A variety of explanations has been offered for the particularly striking collection of miracles in between the Sermon on the Mount and the sending out of the Twelve (Chs 8-9).[23]

i) The grouping together of ten miracles is often explained by Matthew's wish to present Jesus in Chs 8-9 as the Messiah of action now that the Sermon on the Mount has shown him to be the Messiah of the Word. However, Chs 8-9 include not only miracles, but also apophthegms: 8.18-22; 9.9-13, 14-17. At least the insertion of the sayings on discipleship (8.18ff.) has a theological purpose, and it is unlikely that Matthew left the other apophthegms among the miracles accidentally either. The meal in the publican's house gives him an opportunity to interpret Jesus' saving activity as the work of a doctor and an act of mercy in terms of Hos 6.6. In the discussion on fasting he alters μὴ δύνανται . . . νηστεύειν (Mk 2.19) to μὴ δύνανται . . . πένθειν (Mt 9.15), which could be a reference to the mourning of 9.23: even the deepest grief must give way to the time of joy.

ii) A second explanation treats the grouping of the miracles in Chs 8-9 as a preparation for the situation which follows, notably Mt 11.2-6. Healing of the blind, the lame, lepers and the deaf and raisings of the dead are now to be expected. But not all Matthew's rearrangements can be accounted for in this way. It gives no explanation for the bringing forward of the stilling of the storm and the exorcism (8.23-34).

iii) Perhaps even a geographical consideration may be suggested. The reflexive quotation in 4.15f. mentions the sea, Transjordan and Galilee of the Gentiles. In Chs 8-9 we find precisely a journey across the 'sea', activity beyond the Jordan (8.28-34) and a Gentile (8.5ff.). The anticipation of the journey on the lake might be explained by Matthew's desire to make the prophecy of Is 8.23-9.1 come literally true. How important this is to him is shown by the change in the immediate context: there is an editorial reference to Zebulun and Naphtali in 4.13 to produce agreement between event and prophecy.

---

[23] Cf. H.J. Held, 'Matthew as Interpreter', 246ff.

In the second section, Chs 11-12, miracles are not so much described as present in the background. They settle the question whether Jesus is the Messiah or not (11.2ff.), the charge of failure to repent is linked with them (11.20ff.), they are the fulfilment of the prophecy of Isaiah (12.15-21). And on the other side the miracles (and the miracle-worker) run into abrupt dismissal, lead to the decision of his enemies to have him killed (12.14) and to the charge of an alliance with the devil (12.24).

The next section (Chs 14-17) takes things a stage further. The significance of the miracles is no longer merely posited in questions (11.2ff.; 12.23 and also 13.53ff.): firm positions are taken. Acclamation motifs increase in frequency: 'This is John the Baptist' (14.2), 'Truly you are the Son of God' (14.33), 'and they glorified the God of Israel' (15.31; cf. 16.17; 17.5). While there is no direct or indirect line from Jesus' miracles via reflection on the miracles to declarations about them, a certain gradation can nevertheless be clearly seen across the groupings. The miracles are very important to analytical composition in Matthew's gospel.

(c) Luke

Since H. Conzelmann's essay, *The Theology of Luke,* Luke has been almost universally regarded as the theologian of a salvation history consisting of distinct periods.[24] Nevertheless performing miracles is a relatively constant feature of Jesus' activity and contributes little to a division into periods. One might want to consider whether Luke makes a deliberate division between the story of the Passion and the period of miracles. According to 13.32 Jesus performs miracles and exorcisms up to the point of his journey to Jerusalem. At the entry into Jerusalem the crowd celebrates miracles of the past (19.37). It seems of a piece with this that Luke should leave out the cursing of the fig tree. On the other hand it would be a mistake to place too much weight on this: only in Luke does Jesus restore the ear cut off at his arrest (22.51), and the summary in Acts 10.39 also mentions miracles in Jerusalem.

D. Overarching Composition

1. Aretalogical Gospel Composition in Mark

'Overarching' is the name we give to the technique of composition which creates arches going beyond an immediate context to hold

---

[24] For criticism of Conzelman's periodisation, cf. W.C. Robinson, *Der Weg des Herrn* (1964).

together the whole gospel. Only overarching composition gives the gospels unity of form. The problem of composition is this. Originally every small unit contained its own focus within itself, and each could be transmitted on its own. But for the genre 'gospel' to be more than a stringing together and cumulation of small units, for these not just to be juxtaposed but also interconnected, in addition to the first focus a second is required which connects several units. How can this be superimposed without creating a tension within the individual sections, without destroying the narrative integrity of the individual forms? The solution was not merely to insert the small units into an overall structure external to them, but to build the overall structure out of them. Like the other types, overarching composition is creative realisation of field and compositional units of small genres. Our task here is to trace the contribution of the miracle stories to the formation of the overall structure, which we see taking place for the first time in Mark's gospel.[25]

The point of the miracle stories is the miracle, and based on this the recognition of the revelation which has taken place in the miracle in wonder and acclamation. The first point is part of every individual story; the second is common to all miracle stories and, in a sense, to all the synoptic genres. All the small units and the overall structure of the gospel can come together at this one point. Put in form critical terms, wonder and acclamation, together with the contrasting motif of secrecy, are structural motifs of overarching composition in Mark. Alongside this 'aretalogical arch' there stands both a mythical and a biographical one, but these are incomplete.

1. The aretalogical arch
The whole of Mark's gospel pushes towards acclamation, towards recognition of Jesus' true status. Except for the confessions of the

---

[25] The importance of the miracle stories for the composition of Mark's gospel has been emphasised by various scholars. According to A. Meyer, *RGG* V, 1st ed, 2151, 'strings of miracle stories, which in some cases originally had a different significance, were combined into a biography or travel narrative by the addition of references to time and place – and Mark was born.' G. Schille, *Wundertradition*, 45, sees a connection between affirmation of faith in the miracle-worker and the formation of the gospels: the miracles embody the memory of the earthly Jesus. Even if one assumes the existence of a pre-Marcan collection of miracle stories, one is still allowing the miracle stories a certain role in the composition of the gospel: cf. H. Köster, 'One Jesus and Four Primitive Gospels' in *Trajectories through Early Christianity*, 1971, 158-204. It is particularly noteworthy that Köster's four original gospel genres all derive their structure from a smaller genre. Logia lead to collections of sayings, miracle stories to an aretalogy, apocalyptic discourse to the literature of revelation and the passion narrative to the gospel form as we find it in Mark.

demons, which fall under the command to silence, in the early chapters this status of Jesus' remains in the background. Jesus talks about himself in veiled terms as the Son of Man (which for Mark was probably a mysterious title) (2.10), physician (2.17), bridegroom (2.19), Lord of the sabbath (2.23ff.). The demons' confessions indicate to the reader that all these phrases are the announcement of a truth which is still veiled. The question is not asked explicitly until the disciples ask after the stilling of the storm, 'Who is this?' Originally a concluding acclamation, in Mark's composition this question has taken on an expository role. Every time in the subsequent narrative there is a mention of people's amazement at Jesus' miracles, there is now an echo of this question (5.15, 20, 42). It is raised explicitly again in 6.1ff., provoked again by miracles which have occurred in the meantime. The reaction of the people of Jesus' home town may be negative, but nonetheless the necessity of the question about Jesus' status and identity as a result of the miracles has become clear: 'Is not this . . .?' (6.3).

This connection between miracles and the christological question is further emphasised by the popular views of 6.14f. Jesus' miracles lead to the supposition that he is John the Baptist, Elijah or a prophet. Mark says that his 'name had become known' (6.14). It is clear both that the miracles are pushing for a reaction of acclamation and that the reactions so far are inadequate, as the reader knows from the 'authentic' voice at the baptism and from the demons' confessions. The arch remains incomplete. In 6.52 it is given (redactional) reinforcement. The disciples were afraid during the storm on the lake 'for they did not understand about the loaves, but their hearts were hardened'. The criticism only makes sense on the assumption that Jesus' divine nature became recognisable in the miracle of the loaves and that properly a titular acclamation was to be expected at that point. The interesting point for Mark's technique of composition is that this is an example of retrospective composition: the criticism refers back to the miracle, passes over the narrative present (the walking on the lake) and goes back to a previous event. Also retrospective is the acclamation after the healing of the deaf and dumb man, which refers not just to the miracle but collectively to all Jesus' miraculous activity: 'He has done *all* things well.' Another retrospective comment is the renewed criticism of the disciples in 8.17, 21, which strengthens the charge of incomprehension of the miracle of the loaves.

The missing realisation breaks through for the first time in Peter's confession. Here too Mark is referring to miracles, since the popular opinions reported by the disciples correspond exactly to those expressed in 6.14. The disciples had heard about these views when they were sent out, and the views in turn had been prompted by Jesus' miracles. In this way Peter's confession is (in Mark's composition) indirectly prompted by miracles. It is not adequate, however, but still dominated by the secret; in the first place, it lacks the crucial title 'Son of God', and, secondly, as yet the Passion is not implicit in the confession. The arch is still incomplete. It is reinforced by the expectations of the people. Blind Bartimaeus calls on the 'son of David'. The crowd's acclamation at the entry into Jerusalem is the same, though these words are not used. In the parable of the tenants in the vineyard Jesus indirectly calls himself Son of God. The hearing before the Sanhedrin also brings the christological question to the fore. But it is the confession of the centurion by the cross which puts the last piece of the arch into place. Here for the first time a human being declares that Jesus is the Son of God.

The most important elements of this overarching compositional structure are on the one hand acclamations uttered (1.28; 2.12; 4.41; 7.37; 15.39) and on the other acclamatory titles now employed in the exposition (6.2; 6.14; 8.28). What in the smaller unit rounds off the miracle stories now in the overarching scheme forms the exposition of narrative units. And vice versa: while the acclamatory titles may occur in the exposition, in the overall context the acclamations whose position is in the conclusion of a miracle story also have expositional force. They transcend the 'narrative present' of the small unit and point beyond themselves.

If we are right in our supposition that Mark deliberately did not use acclamation conclusions containing christological titles, this would support the hypothesis of a composition based on the aretalogical acclamation. On this hypothesis, for the one central acclamation by the centurion at the cross Mark modified all the other acclamations and did not realise any titular acclamations although they were part of his (virtual) motif field. Even independently of this hypothesis, however, there is evidence of this delaying of acclamation within the observable text in the motifs of secrecy and incomprehension. The effect of the demons' confessions is to make them appear as opposed motifs to titular acclamations. Wherever the secrecy motif appears the reader is now aware of the unspoken presence of a titular acclamation. On two occasions the object of the secret is explicitly stated as the title 'Son of God', the very title which completes the aretalogical arch at the end of Mark's gospel. When, immediately before the centurion's confession, the veil of the Temple is torn in two, Mark is indicating that the secret which lay over the previous history of Jesus has now been revealed.

Mark extends the arch which is inherent in all the miracle stories, viz. between the miracle and the intended reaction of the audience, to the whole gospel. The compositional structure of the miracle stories is the basis of his overarching composition. A miraculous, mysterious event prompts a declaration. Miracle stories are used to create a miraculous story with a mysteriously delayed acclamation. For this reason we call Mark's gospel an 'aretalogical gospel composition', based on the realisation of motifs of secrecy and acclamation. Mark's art as an author lies precisely in retaining both the integrity of the small units and the form of the whole, in other words, in integrating the individual traditions in such a way that they remain self-contained but at the same time point beyond themselves, and, conversely, in structuring the whole so that it is held together by an inner dynamic without reducing the small units to the role of mere transitional stages.

2. The mythical progression

Projected on to the arch created by aretalogical acclamations is a mythical progression of baptism, transfiguration and cross, which P. Vielhauer has interpreted by analogy with ancient Egyptian enthronement ritual as adoption, presentation and enthronement (which pncludes acclamation). The distinctive position of these three scenes is unmistakable. They make the divine more immediately visible than usual in epiphanies and signs. 'To contemporary readers of Mark these cosmic miracles must have been particularly impressive, and the corresponding scenes must have seemed 'dramatic' high points of artistic composition.'[26] The composition is a mythical one because the story of a transcendent being is told as a story taking place between God and his Son.

The difficulty of this interpretation comes in the last act of the progression: did Mark mean to depict the enthronement as a crucifixion? The mockery scene certainly has features of an enthronement. Jesus receives royal insignia, the purple cloak and the crown of thorns. The soldiers acclaim him with the words χαῖρε · βασιλεῦ τῶν ᾿Ιουδαίων (15.18). But the royal purple is removed before the crucifixion, and there is no further mention of the crown of thorns. If Mark did intend to portray the crucifixion as a paradoxical enthronement, he has neglected uncommonly vivid images for his picture. What he does pick on by contrast are the acclamations. They appear again in the inscription and in the mockery of

---

[26] P. Vielhauer, *Erwägungen*, 213 n. 46a.

the high priests and scribes. Every group now declares its attitude to Jesus: pagan masters and servants, the Jewish people and its leaders. Rejection is the dominant reaction of the world; only the centurion recognises Jesus' true nature. The isolation of his confession indicates the isolation into which Christian faith leads. The only adequate titular acclamation in Mark's gospel is not a choral one. The community appears only at a distance, represented by women from Galilee (15.40f.).

Because of the dominant position of the acclamation at the end of Mark's gospel, we prefer to regard the gospel, not so much as a progressive realisation of Jesus' dignity,[27] but as the successive revelation and acknowledgement of that dignity. In baptism Jesus becomes the Son of God who has power to master all hostile powers (adoption). God reveals him to the disciples in the transfiguration (presentation). The cross is the place where Jesus makes a public appearance before the world to be rejected and acknowledged (acclamation). Such acknowledgement – which is still incomplete – is the goal of the preaching throughout the whole world. Not before the parousia will the world recognise his majesty (14.62).

We have thus slightly modified Vielhauer's interpretation by making the progression culminate, not in enthronement, but in acclamation. If Mark was familiar with an enthronement pattern (in the sense of a progressive revelation of Jesus' status), he modified it. On the other hand, it could equally well be argued that he has actualised a variant of the progression we find virtually contained in the familiar christological progressions. In 1 Tim 3.16 there is an example of a three-stage progression which contains within it an interesting parallelism. Corresponding to ἐδικαιώθη, ὤφθη, ἀνελήμφθη in the heavenly sphere (cf. pneuma, angels and doxa), in the earthly sphere we have ἐφανερώθη, ἐκηρύχθη, ἐπιστεύθη (sarx, Gentiles, cosmos). Set in parallel are a succession of gradual realisations of the path to glory and a succession of gradual acknowledgement (which would include the acclamation).[28] The successions constructed in parallel in 1 Tim 3.16 dominate variously in other progressions. Heb 1.5-13 contains what is mainly a progressive exaltation, in which proskynesis (1.6) forms only one element. On the other hand, the second verse of the hymn in Philippians leads unabiguously into proskynesis and acclamation. Here too three stages can be distinguished: exaltation and the giving of the name (Phil 2.9), proskynesis (2.10) and acclamation (2.11). Within New

---

[27] E. Best, *The Temptation and the Passion* (1965) and L.E. Keck, 'The Introduction to Mark's Gospel', *NTS* 12 (1965/66), 352-70, also tend to regard Jesus' full status as already achieved by the baptism.

[28] On the discussion of 1. Tim 3.16 cf. K. Wengst, *Christologische Formeln und Lieder des Urchristentums,* 1972, 156ff.

Testament progressions acclamation (or related motifs of acknowledgement) may appear either as an element or as the primary goal. Mark's decision to actualise the variant of the progression which ends in an acclamation is probably connected with the fact that the aretalogical arch leads to such an acclamation.

Both the mythical and the aretalogical arches are completed by the centurion's declaration, but even before that they are closely connected. What has already been revealed as a secret within the progression is revealed only gradually within Jesus' public activity. The reader is already aware of Jesus' status and so is waiting for the moment when that dignity will finally be seen by the human beings who appear in the gospel. His knowledge puts him in a position to recognise that all the hesitant attempts to interpret Jesus' identity are inadequate. He knows that only the title 'Son of God' does him justice. All other titles are approximations.

The mythical progression is designed to fit the aretalogical arch: it anticipates the final acclamation while the secrecy motifs delay it. On three occasions the mythical history (with the help of epiphanies and signs) gives crucial pointers, but on its own it does not give Mark's gospel unity. In itself it remains incomplete. In its treatment of the past the transcendent pre-history is missing, and for the future only the parousia could complete the mythical history. The only finished structure is the aretalogical tension of miraculous event, secret and acclamation; mythical anticipations intensify this tension, but are not its source.

The existence of a mythical arch could be taken as evidence against the view that the composition of the gospels can be treated as the actualisation of genre structures from small units. The mythical arch derives its structure from extra-synoptic traditions; it introduces a new element into the synoptic tradition. We shall therefore now discuss, from this point of view, the three most important attempts to locate the structural unity of Mark's gospel in a mythical event.

(a) Bultmann assumed that the Hellenistic Christ myth, as we find it in Phil 2.6ff., gave Mark's gospel, 'not indeed a biographical unity, but a unity based on the myth of the kerygma'.[29] It is true that Mark's gospel lacks biographical unity: Jesus' birth is not even mentioned. However, even the mythical unity is incomplete: Mark has 'not yet adopted' the pre-existence.[30] Not even in the parable of the vineyard can it be shown to be present: the pre-existence of the Son would entail the pre-existence of all the previous messengers.[31] But the reference to the parable of the

---

[29] Bultmann, *HST*, 371.
[30] *HST*, 349.
[31] Pace J. Schreiber, 'Die Christologie des Markusevangeliums', *ZThK* 58 (1961), 154-83.

vineyard shows one thing: to maintain this view of the composition of Mark one has to have recourse to an individual tradition.

(b) The mythical three-stage progression is also always connected in the New Testament epistles with the idea of pre-existence. To that extent the objection already raised against Bultmann applies here too. More important, however, is the fact that this progression is portrayed by means of two epiphanies, the vision at the baptism and the transfiguration. Connected with these is the legendary crucifixion account with its miraculous signs. This gives grounds for treating the progression also as a development of the idea of adoption contained in the baptism story.

(c) M. Dibelius regards the battle with the demons as the motif underlying the composition of Mark's gospel. Because of this idea the gospel is 'in the last analysis . . . a mythical book'.[32] This is undoubtedly right. The only point to correct is the view that this idea 'applies only to the framing which the Evangelist has given to tradition'.[33] In fact it is inherent in the exorcisms. Dibelius himself cites Mk 9.19. Here, in an exorcism, we hear of a divine being 'who appeared only temporarily in human form quickly to return to Heaven'.[34] Following Dibelius, J.M. Robinson has also sought to show that the battle with the demons is a constant feature of Mark's gospel.[35]

Mark's gospel cannot be imagined without mythical happenings, but it is only in John that the mythical elements become a complete myth. The Logos who exists with God before time becomes incarnate, works in this world, dies and goes back to his Father. The parousia has no significance. Here the unity of the gospel is created by the myth.[36] If Mark is a gospel built on aretalogy, John is a gospel built on myth.

3. The biographical arch

The goal of Mark's gospel is the declaration, 'Truly this man *was* the Son of God' (15.39). The imperfect looks back on a life which is over; the aretalogical arch is overlaid with a biographical framework. This framework is not forced on to the individual traditions from outside; the individual legends themselves presuppose it,[37] as is shown by the fact that for the most part they could

---

[32] M. Dibelius, *TG*, 278.

[33] *TG*, 278.

[34] *TG*, 278.

[35] *The Problem of History in Mark*, 1957.

[36] Bultmann, *HST*, 371. To that extent he is right to regard the Fourth Gospel as a 'development of the type of gospel created by Mark'.

[37] Bultmann, *HST*, 245: Legends 'are distinguishable from miracle stories chiefly by not being, as they are, unities, but gain their point only when set into a context. This context can be the life of some religious hero: that yields a biographical legend.' A. Jolles, *Einfache Formen*, 46f., also sees a necessary connection with the vita. The vita of a saint, he says, is the actualisation 'of the possibility present and contained in the legend' (46).

not be placed at any point one wished within a chronologically ordered narrative – unlike the miracle stories and apophthegms. Most of them occur in the passion narrative. Here, even before Mark, individual pericopae were placed in biographical or chronological order.[38] When this compositional structure was transferred to other material, when miracle stories and apophthegms too were seen as elements in a story which was moving towards a goal, the most important step towards the formation of a gospel had been taken. In this respect the Passion narratives and stories were crucial to the gospel form.[39] Where (as in Q and the Gospel of Thomas) they are absent, there is also no chronological order; where Christian faith treats collections of sayings as an adequate expression of itself, the very literary form rules out the incorporation of a Passion story.

In addition the decision to put Jesus to death and the prophecies of the Passion were used for overarching composition. The original context of the murder plan is probably the Passion story. It must be traditional there because the dating of the decision to put Jesus to death (14.1f.) contradicts the Marcan dating.[40] In 3.6 the change of scene (ἐξελθόντες), Jesus' original anonymity (3.2), the similarity of the wording with 11.8 and the identity of the characters with 12.12 all suggest a subsequent editorial appendix. In 11.18 and 12.12 the need to take account of the people is not explained by the context, and is more likely to come from 14.1f., making it plausible with Bultmann[41] to regard the repetition of the decision as redactional. Mark has probably quadrupled a single motif from the Passion story and moved it from its introductory position in 14.1f. to the end of controversies in order to extend to the whole gospel a tension inherent in the Passion story. The devices used for Mark's overarching composition here are alteration of original position and compositional position.

A similar process may be presumed to have taken place in the case of the prophecies of the Passion. H.E. Tödt[42] goes so far as to claim three independent pre-Marcan traditions, but none of his evidence, whether of semitisms (εἰς χεῖρας, 9.21), Old Testament

---

[38] Not so J. Schreiber, *Die Markuspassion*, 1969.

[39] The description of Mark and the gospels in general as 'passion narratives with lengthy introductions' (M. Kähler, *The so-called historical Jesus and the historic, biblical Christ*, 1964, 60) is intended to stress the discontinuous character of the gospels, but it is generally and rightly taken also as a statement about the internal structure of the gospels.

[40] M. Dibelius, *TG*, 180f.

[41] *HST*, 12, 36. Not so J. Roloff, *Kerygma*, 63-66, 89-110.

[42] H.E. Tödt, *The Son of Man in the Synoptic Tradition*, 1965, 141-283. Cf. the objections of F. Hahn, *Titles*, 37.

echoes (Ps 118.2 in 8.31) or of deviations in the order of events (10.33f.) is sufficient to establish pre-Marcan origin. The semitism appears also in 14.41, Ps 118.22 also in 9.12b, and the divergent order of the ill-treatment produces an intelligible climax: mockery, spitting, scourging. It is more likely that Mark has reproduced one tradition three times.

The arch erected by biographical legends is incomplete in Mark. The Passion narrative has no corresponding infancy narrative: not even in externals have we a *Vita*. Not until Matthew and Luke can we talk of biographical gospel composition. In Mark there are only occasional instances of legendary or biographical composition. It is not the beginning of the life of Jesus which interests him, but 'the beginning of the gospel' (1.1), not the unity of the *Bios*, but the unity of a miraculous story which calls for acclamation. Even if he drew inspiration from popular θεῖος-ἀνήρ lives,[43] they are not the model for his work.

The three arches all culminate in the centurion's confession. The mythical progression reaches a climax in the acclamation of the world (or, better, of an individual against the world), the aretalogical arch leads to the confession of the Son of God, and the biographical or legendary composition to a statement summing up his life. It is the aretalogical arch which dominates. It is no accident that there is an allusion to Jesus' miracles on the cross: 'He saved others; he cannot save himself' (15.31). It is no accident that the mockery contrasts the miracles with the cross. Cosmic signs give the answer and make possible the first profession of faith. The fact that it is phrased in the imperfect could imply an ultimate incompleteness in this profession,[44] but it could also have a deeper significance. By writing his gospel as a narrative of past events, Mark may be showing how important the past is to him. He may be trying to say that the Christian confession is possible in the light of this past history. His confession is a remembering. A miraculous story from the past is a permanent provocation to taking up a position in the present. The centurion is waiting for the reader of Mark's gospel to take his place beside him and repeat his words.

It is often argued that Mark wanted in some way to relativise the miracles. This view is based on his theory of secrecy and the Passion story, usually by connecting them closely. According to this view the purpose of the

---

[43] S. Schulz, 'Die Bedeutung des Markus für die Theologiegeschichte des Urchristentums', *TU* 87 (1964), 134-45. This theory will, however, remain implausible until we find comparable lives by which Mark might have been inspired. Cf. the careful remarks of D. Esser, *Formgeschichtliche Studien*, 168f.

[44] P. Vielhauer, *Erwägungen*, 209.

secrecy theory is to relativise the visible revelation of divine power in the miracles in order to emphasise the paradoxical revelation on the cross.[45]
i) This is certainly a misinterpretation of the theory of secrecy. To see it as having to do with the Passion is of course correct, but that by no means justifies setting it off against the miracles. How can one reduce their importance by plunging them into mysterious obscurity? How can failure to understand the miracles be a ground for complaint if understanding them is not vitally important? To be consistent, anyone who claims that the secret relativises the miracle must also accept a relativisation of the title 'Son of God': this title is no less surrounded by secrecy and is covered by the command to silence. Besides, the secrecy motif comes from the miracle stories themselves: secrecy belongs to miracles, gives them a particular emphasis. Insofar as secrecy belongs to revelation it is an indication that revelation is taking place at this point.[46]
ii) Nor can the Passion story be contrasted with the miracles. It is itself full of miraculous happenings. Jesus knows his end in advance, knows the betrayer and the hour. Cosmic signs are seen at his death. The empty tomb surpasses all previous miracles. Only the character of the miraculous has changed: 'Now the miraculous element is no longer related to others, but to Jesus himself.'[47] It has even been thought that Mark was combating a θεῖος-ἀνήρ christology, that his gospel arose out of the need to combat a heresy connected with belief in miracles.[48] Of course the opposite has also been maintained. It has been argued that Mark was engaged in a polemic against a Palestinian orthodoxy which denied the popular belief in miracles and Christian healing (E. Trocmé and K. Tagawa).[49] Neither can be proved, but this last theory comes closer to the phenomenon. It at least refrains from projecting the modern critique of miracles back on to the author of Mark's gospel.

2. The biographical gospel compositions of Matthew and Luke

In Matthew and Luke the biographical and legendary arch is completed and becomes the foundation for the overarching composition. Matthew and Luke supply the missing infancy legends. Mark's gospel composition becomes a gospel life. The overarching composition is constituted by the unity of a life. Since this can

---

[45] E. Percy, *Botschaft*, 286-99; E. Schweizer, 'Zur Frage des Messiasgeheimnisses bei Markus', *ZNW* 56 (1965), 1-8; U. Luz, *Geheimnismotiv*, 9ff.
[46] H.J. Ebeling, *Das Messiasgeheimnis und die Botschaft des Marcus-Evangelisten* (1939) gives a much better account of the situation, though the theory of secrecy is only indirectly concerned with the reader, insofar as it might reassure him that the secret is being revealed to him in particular. Its main relevance is to the object: the miracles and divine status of Jesus.
[47] H. Conzelmann, 'Historie und Theologie in den synoptischen Passionsberichten', *Zur Bedeutung des Todes Jesu*, 2nd ed. 1967, 35-53, quotation from p. 39, n. 6.
[48] T.J. Weeden, 'The Heresy that necessitated Mark's Gospel', *ZNW* 59 (1968), 145-58.
[49] E. Trocmé, *La formation*, 70-168; K. Tagawa, *Miracles*, 174-85.

lessen the importance of the miracle motifs for the structure of the gospel, these gospels will be discussed only briefly.

In Matthew the infancy legends present the whole history of Jesus in a new light, as the fulfilment of the Old Testament, as a stage in the coming of salvation to the Gentiles, as the deeds of a Son of God endowed all along with majesty. The introductory genealogy shows Jesus to be the son of David (1.1), and the thematic quotations confirm that his fate is the fulfilment of the Old Testament. The miracle stories are seen in terms of both ideas. Four times where Mark does not have it, Matthew introduces the title 'son of David' into miracle stories (9.28; 12.23; 15.22) or a miracle summary (21.15).[50] It is in the miracles that the son of David exercises his lordship over Israel: 'Never was anything like this seen *in Israel*' (9.33), 'And they glorified the God *of Israel*' (15.31). Both passages come from the Matthaean redaction. This is also a possibility in the case of the Old Testament thematic quotations in miracle summaries, which in both cases (8.14ff.; 12.17ff.) replace Marcan demon confessions. For Matthew the witness of the Old Testament is clearly more important than that of the underworld. The Old Testament evidence shows that the kingship of the son of David consists in carrying diseases and weaknesses (8.17), working in concealment without crying out (12.18-20), in being the humble king of Israel (21.5).

The shattering new idea of universal mission also begins in the infancy story. The Gentile magi come to see 'the king of the Jews' (2.2). The reflexive quotations see the Old Testament fulfilled precisely in Jesus' appearance in the 'Galilee of the Gentiles' (4.15) and the hope he brings for all the Gentiles (12.21). The Matthaean versions of 'The centurion of Capernaum' (8.5ff.) and 'The Syrophoenician woman' (15.21ff.) show that Jesus' miracles point beyond the boundaries of Israel. Faith appears as a crossing of the boundary between Jews and Gentiles.

The greatest difference between this and Mark's overarching composition is that Jesus' majesty is now no longer gradually acknowledged, but is clear from the beginning. The magi already know of his status, and the voice at the baptism proclaims it publicly by contrast with Mark (Mt 3.17). From the beginning Jesus is addressed as κύριος, from the beginning he is asked to quell storms (8.25) and raise the dead (9.18). Where the Marcan miracle stories move towards a constantly delayed acclamation,

---

[50] Cf. the fine study by C. Burger, *Jesus als Davidssohn* (1970), 72-91. Cf. also J.M. Gibbs, 'Purpose', *NTS* 10 (1963/64), 446ff.

Matthew's start with acclamatory cries. Jesus' majesty is not the climax, but the basis for what Matthew regards as the crucial sections of his gospel, the great discourses. The authority of the wonder-worker confirms the authority of the teacher; the omnipotence of the Risen One is the basis for the commission to preach the teaching of the earthly Jesus. There is no commission to proclaim his deeds. Where Mark referred to spreading miracle stories, Matthew abbreviates: in his gospel the cured leper (8.1-4) and the men of Gadara who have been freed from demons (8.28-34) do not proclaim the miracles they have experienced. Matthew has it is true written a biographical gospel composition, but the inner focus of his gospel life is Jesus' teaching. The miracles confirm the authority of the teacher. The gospel of Matthew can thus be described as a 'didactic gospel life'.[51]

Whereas in Matthew Jesus' teaching is integrated into the biographical and legendary framework of the gospel, in Luke this biographical framework is part of a larger work centred on salvation history. In Matthew the risen Lord gives orders that the world is to be instructed in Jesus' commandments; in Luke he shows that the Old Testament scriptures have been fulfilled (Lk 24.27, 44ff.). In the former case there is no mention of Jesus' history and in the latter none of his commandments. In Matthew Jesus' demands are the focus of the gospel, while salvation history slips into the background. In Luke salvation history comes to the fore and the ethical demands become an element in this history. Matthew writes a didactic gospel life, Luke a 'salvation history gospel life'.

Within salvation history the miracles mark Jesus out as sent by God (Acts 2.22); they prove that he was endowed with divine δύναμις. His conception took place through δύναμις ὑψίστου (1.35), the holy Spirit, who links himself with him in his baptism. From that point on Jesus is called πλήρης πνεύματος ἁγίου (4.1, redactional; cf. 4.18). On three occasions Luke mentions this endowment with δύναμις in connection with miracles. He prefaces the healing of the paralytic with the remark δύναμις κυρίου ἦν εἰς τὸ ἰᾶσθαι αὐτόν (5.17), in a summary (6.17-19) he adds: ὅτι δύναμις παρ' αὐτοῦ ἐξήρχετο (6.19); in the story of the woman with the issue of blood he transposes the comment about the loss of power into direct speech. *Dynamis* is at the same time *pneuma*: because Jesus has been anointed with Spirit, he can do miracles

---

[51] Similarly G. Schille, 'Bemerkungen zur Formgeschichte des Evangeliums' II, *NTS* 4 (1957/58), 101-14. It is, however, unlikely that Mark took the step from post-baptismal to pre-baptismal catechesis.

(4.18), an idea Luke repeats in a summary in Acts (10.38). This christological significance of the miracles must be qualified in three respects.

First, it is important to notice that the δύναμις is not imagined as static. The Spirit comes down on Jesus (3.21) at his baptism, a feature Luke stresses in contrast to Mark's text. In 5.16 Luke inserts a καὶ προσευχόμενος into the Marcan text and talks a few lines later of the 'power' which at that very moment is present to heal. Again in 6.12 a redactional reference to prayer precedes the δύναμις comment in 6.19.[52] In the story of the transfiguration the conferral of *doxa* takes place after a prayer (9.29, redactional). The constant renewal of the power corresponds to the subordinationist tendency of Lucan christology. God performs miracles 'through him' (Acts 2.22), liberation from Satan takes place 'because God was with him' (10.38). The acclamations are directed at God (9.43; 18.43).

The second important feature is the charitable character of Jesus' miracles. It is εὐεργετεῖν (Acts 10.38), is part of the message of salvation to the poor (Lk 4.18). Jesus uses miracles to console the father and mother who have lost their 'only child' (9.38; 8.42), and the summary stresses: he 'cured those who *had need* of healing' (9.11, redactional).[53]

A third characteristic of Luke's technique of composition is the insistence on the place of the miracles in salvation history: 'Today scripture has been fulfilled' (4.21), 'We have seen wondrous things today' (5.26), 'God has visited his people' (7.16). 'For him Jesus' deeds are the sign of the time of salvation which has "appeared" with Christ.'[54]

For both Matthew and Luke overarching composition consisted not so much in the creation of narrative tension as in the development of a number of basic ideas. As narratives the miracle stories are juxtaposed, complete and finished. The aretalogical and mythical arches are dismantled or reduced. It is the biographical unity of a life from beginning to end which provides the underpinning for overarching composition. This biographical and legendary arch reduces the need to interweave separate episodes. The interweaving is to some extent already there 'naturally'. In Mark the

---

[52] H. von Baer, *Der Heilige Geist in den Luksasschriften* (1926): 'Prayer is the inexhaustible source from which Jesus constantly drew new strength' (73). On Luke's idea of power, cf. also W. Grundmann, *Der Begriff der Kraft in der neutestamentlichen Gedankenwelt.*

[53] A. Friedrischsen, *Le problème du miracle,* 41, in particular, regards Luke as influenced by the Hellenistic image of the εὐεργέτης.

[54] H. Conzelmann, *Luke,* 191f.

miracle stories support the framework of the gospel, but in Matthew and Luke the framework supports the miracle stories.[55]

3. The mythical gospel composition of the Fourth Gospel (Excursus)

The structure of the overarching composition of the gospels is provided by small units: the miracle stories in Mark, the legends (and the biographical narrative presupposed by them) in Matthew and Luke, and the myth or, more accurately, the mythical Christ hymn in John. The self-contained narrative of divine fate which we call 'the Christ myth' appears in its most developed form in the New Testament in rhythmical hymns or hymn fragments, the best known example of which is Phil 2.6-11. It is no accident that such a hymn is prefixed to the Fourth Gospel and that its structure shows the divisions of the gospel. The revelation in the world (Jn 2-12) is followed by the revelation in the community (Jn 13-20). Only the return of the Logos to God is not anticipated in the prologue.

This mythical arch overlays the individual miracle stories and is in tension with them. The miracles are instances of particular crossings of boundaries with various this-worldly motivations, disease, poverty and so on. In contrast, the appearance of the creator in the world is such a fundamental boundary-crossing (grounded in God's love alone, 3.16) that any limited boundary-crossing justified on this-worldly grounds must be transfigured by it – or it will be misunderstood and we shall see in the miracles only the giver of bread and not the revealer. At the same time the myth transforms the biographical framework (only hinted at in John): that the divine Logos should have a human origin and die on the cross is a scandal.

L. Schottroff[56] has interpreted this tension as the co-existence of two realities in the Fourth Gospel, the this-worldly reality of miracle as well as of Jesus' origin and the heavenly reality of the revealer. The various interpretations of the Johannine understanding of miracles are various attempts to define this superimposition on the mythical, aretalogical and biographical structures. Schottroff suggests that there is a 'parallelism' of the two realities: both the miracles and Jesus' earthly origin are real, but 'the second, heavenly reality is the only one relevant for faith.' The step from the earthly world to the heavenly is taken in faith. This argument of Schottroff's is thus directed both against Bultmann's interpretation that both realities are paradoxically identical in the revealer and against E. Käsemann's opposing view that the heavenly reality is made manifest in the earthly.

However, with regard to the relationship of the mythical and biographical frameworks, Bultmann's interpretation is correct. It is scandalous and paradoxical that the Logos should become flesh (1.14), be

---

[55] D. Esser, *Formgeschichtliche Studien,* 169, rightly notes 'a clear proximity in Matthew and Luke to biographical forms'.

[56] L. Schottroff, Der Glaubende und die feindliche Welt (1970), 228ff. The next two quotations are on pp. 278 and 271.

descended from human parents (6.42), come, contrary to Messianic expectations, from Galilee (7.40-44; cf. 7.25-30) and die as a man (19.5): this historical man with specific biographical data is the Logos (and not just a parallel manifestation accompanying him). Käsemann's interpretation is correct as far as the relationship of the mythical framework and miracles is concerned: in the miracles the *doxa* of God is made manifest in fact – not just in sign or symbol, but in solid reality.[57] Both aspects must be upheld, the manifestation of the Logos in the miracles and the paradoxical identity of the Logos with the historical Galilean. Faith sees the revelation of God in the miracles; *despite* the revealer's earthly origin he insists on his unity with God. If he sees in the miracles and in the earthly origin no more than the earthly history he falls victim to a misunderstanding – Schottroff has described this particularly well.

But the mythical history is not superimposed on the miracle stories like an alien framework; rather, the stories are told in such a way that they fit easily into the mythical story. A brief comparison of the form-critical field of motifs in John and the synoptics will make this clear.

i) All motifs associated with demons are absent in John. Human beings are not placed in between a divine and a demonic world, but solely in confrontation with revelation: the cosmos and God are the crucial opposites. It is not the underworld, but this world itself, which is in opposition to God insofar as it remains closed to revelation. In other words, human beings in their subservience to the world take the place of the demons.

ii) Motifs associated with human beings are retained, but the contrast between boundary-stressing and boundary-crossing motifs is sharpened into an opposition of faith and unbelief. The miracle stories bring about a *krisis* (9.39), provoke faith (2.11; 4.53; 9.35ff.; 11.45) and rejection (5.9ff; 9.13ff.; 11.46ff.). John makes the decision to put Jesus to death a consequence of the Lazarus miracle.

iii) The boundary-crossing motifs associated with the miracle-worker are emphasised and intensified. Almost all miracles are the result of an initiative by Jesus (4.46ff. is an exception); where there are requests they are at first rejected. Jesus' intervention is not prompted by distress; rather, miracles occur 'that the works of God might be made manifest' (9.3; cf. 11.4). A corollary of this is that Jesus' word of assurance acquires greater significance. In the story of Lazarus it appears five times in a baroque cumulation. (11.4, 11, 15, 23, 25f.). Argument is extended into whole revelatory discourses and the controversies are prolonged (5.17ff.; 6.22ff.; 9.8ff.). In short, the miracles are presented primarily as crossings of the boundary from the revealer's side and as a result fit well into the mythical framework of an incarnation and epiphany of the Logos in the world. There is no relativisation of miracles in John; on the contrary, they

---

[57] Cf. the summary in R. Bultmann, *New Testament Theology*, II, 49ff. Bultmann is criticised by E. Käsemann, *The Testament of Jesus*, 1968, esp. pp. 4ff. For discussion see also J. Becker, 'Wunder und Christologie', *NTS* 16 (1969/70), 130-48, and W. Wilkens, *Zeichen und Werke* (1969).

are a continuation of God's work of creation (5.17), and indeed surpass it (5.20). They are unique. No-one else can perform them (15.24; 3.2). The absolute revelation is matched by unique miracles. The mythical framework has raised them to a peak of intensity.

The investigation of overarching composition leads to the conclusion that the four gospels actualise in an almost systematic way the possibilities inherent in the framework genre 'gospel': they can be regarded as aretalogical, mythical or biographical compositions. In every case possibilities are realised which are part of the structure of smaller units, miracle stories, hymns, legends, of which only the hymns are a non-synoptic genre. In Mark the mythical and biographical arches are subordinate to the aretalogical and in themselves remain incomplete. In the subsequent development the completed mythical and biographical arches become in turn the basis of the composition, the biographical arch in the gospel lives of Matthew and Luke and the mythical one in John's mythical gospel composition. Now the miracle stories no longer support the framework, but are supported, as episodes, by it. When Irenaeus, in his speculative approach, recognised the necessity of a gospel in four forms,[58] he was certainly going too far. A form-critical morphology comes to more modest conclusions, but does not totally refute him.

At the end of the diachronic consideration of miracle stories we can discuss the problem raised by redaction criticism of the relation between tradition and redaction. There are four distinct models, from a preponderance of tradition over redaction to the 'absorption' of tradition by redaction. We shall label them compilation, interpretation, mediatisation and creation.

1. Compilation
Classical form criticism tended to regard the evangelists as 'principally collectors, vehicles of tradition, editors'.[59] Since the composition of the gospels 'involves nothing in principle new, but only completes what was begun in the oral tradition, it can only be considered in organic connection with the history of the material as it lay before the evangelists'.[60]

2. Interpretation
Moderate redaction criticism attributes a generous measure of autonomy to the editors, but stresses the continuity from tradition to redaction. H.J. Held formulates this position as follows: 'The interpreter is . . . also a

---

[58] Cf. H. von Campenhausen, *Die Entstehung der christlichen Bibel* (1968), 230ff.
[59] M. Dibelius, *TG*, 3.
[60] Bultmann, *HST*, 321.

traditor. He does not strictly add a new idea to the tradition, but rather proves himself to be in the precise sense of the word its exegete, one who brings out what is contained in it.' It is readily admitted that in this process the interpreter may critically extend the tradition.[61]

3. Mediatisation

Another current in redaction criticism in contrast stresses the discontinuity between tradition and redaction. The unity of the gospel is 'the result of deliberate planning and can in no sense be treated as the culmination of the anonymous stage of the transmission process. That ends in final incoherence. Redaction sets itself against this natural development' (W. Marxsen).[62] The eschatological kerygma uses the individual traditions as 'illustrations'. Here the redactor is the master of his 'material'.

4. Creation

Finally, the process of redaction can be assessed totally without reference to a prior tradition as an original act of creation which seeks to be treated as a whole and must be analysed primarily by synchronic methods. The mediatisation of tradition then becomes complete assimilation in an object which must be interpreted as a whole. This is the conclusion of E. Güttgemanns, who has developed an idea of Marxsen's. The gospel then comes to be seen as an 'auto-semantic linguistic form'.[63]

If the diachrony of the history of transmission is regarded as the reproduction of virtual genre structures, these four definitions of the relationship of tradition and redaction can be combined. Continuity exists primarily on the level of virtual genre structures. Every actualisation of these genre structures can be regarded as a new creation. If one then compares different successive actualisations, one can discover either a development or a transformation. Moderate redaction criticism is interested primarily in developments, 'consistent' redaction criticism in transformations.

---

[61] H.J. Held, 'Matthew as Interpreter', 296. It is interesting to note that A. Friedrichsen, *Le problème,* already uses the methods of redaction criticism (p. 34). He devotes his attention in particular to the editorial elements in order to show in them the extent to which miracles had already become a problem within primitive Christianity.

[62] W. Marxsen, *Der Evangelist Markus,* 2nd ed. 1959, 9. On p. 146 Marxsen talks about 'illustration', and on p. 87 about 'material': 'The fact that reports *also* appear here (i.e. in Mark) is almost accidental from this point of view. They are anyway only material.'

[63] Cf. the summary in E. Güttgemanns, *Candid Questions,* 407ff.

Part Three

Miracle Stories as Symbolic Actions (Functionalist Approach)

CHAPTER I

THE SOCIAL FUNCTION OF PRIMITIVE CHRISTIAN MIRACLE STORIES

Traditions can be understood only in terms of the real context of social and historical life. Primitive Christian miracle stories are symbolic interactions on the part of groups within ancient society. Their social dimension can be explored in two directions. First, they reflect social factors which unconsciously influenced both story-tellers and audiences and, second, they project a particular form of social relationship. The first section of this chapter will situate them in the general network of conditions and influences which composed ancient society and the second will examine the structure of social life they project. The aim of the study is to explore their social function from the two sides.

A. The Social Conditions of Primitive Christian Miracle Stories

Miracle stories are an expression of belief in miracles. We shall examine this belief first from a sociological point of view for two reasons. First, an evaluation of sources for the history of religion requires a prior understanding of the connections between social position and belief in miracles. Second, a history of belief in miracles must distinguish between different forms of belief in miracles, which is impossible without sociological categories. Both points must be briefly discussed.

Our sources come mainly from the upper classes and may give a one-sided picture.[1] If, for example, we find in our literary sources some decline in belief in miracles and superstition in the Hellenistic period,[2] we must limit our judgment to the narrow stratum of the educated. It is indeed plausible to assume that they indicate seismographically movements in society as a whole, but it is

---

[1] This difficulty is stressed by M. Smith, 'Prolegomena to a Discussion of Aretalogies, Divine Men, the Gospels and Jesus', *JBL* 90 (1971), 174-99: 'our knowledge is limited by the snobbishness of the literary tradition of antiquity. Ancient literature is almost entirely upper-class and rationalistic' (179).

[2] R.M. Grant, *Miracles and Natural Law* (1952), 41.

equally plausible to suppose that less educated groups showed an increasing tendency to belief in miracles and superstition.[3] Even this supposition, however, cannot be generalised; there may be periods in which educated people *en masse* take up irrational attitudes far removed from good commonsense. We never know in advance the degree or the direction of bias in literary sources. Occasionally we are able to check their statements against archaeological finds (imprecatory tablets, ostraca, amulets and papyri), but such finds, which inform us of the ideas of groups which left no literary expression, depend on a variety of accidents. Even more important is the second point. It is totally impossible to describe belief in miracles and superstition without reference to sociological categories unless one simply calls superstition anything which is obscure to oneself.[4] Historical analysis, however, requires a term which does not make value judgments, but describes the value judgment contained in the term 'superstition'. On such a definition, 'superstition' is a belief rejected in a society, and 'religion', to put it ironically, the officially recognised superstition. Where to draw the line is the decision of the dominant groups, the groups, for example, which in the Roman Empire were unanimous in regarding Christianity as an eccentric superstition: 'nihil aliud inveni quam superstitionem pravam, immodicam' writes Pliny the Younger (ep. X, 96). Similar judgments were made by Suetonius (*Nero* 16) and Tacitus (*ann.* XV.44.2). The Christians for their part thought of paganism as superstitious and rejected its magical practices, oracles and healing sanctuaries. In order to understand this conflict between Christians and pagans we must distinguish different forms of belief in miracles.[5] For example, the desire to obtain more than the normal measure of knowledge about the unknown leads to various forms of divination. The desire for increased power leads to various forms of miracle-working activity. Both phenomena, however, can be distinguished only as ideal types. In reality there are many connections between soothsayers

---

[3] G. Mensching, Soziologie der Religion, 2nd ed. 1968, 172ff.

[4] R. Herzog, *Epidauros,* 140, puts it very well: 'Superstition is always other people's beliefs. For the Roman state it was the Christians; for the Christians it was the adherents of the old religion. . . .'

[5] There is a survey in G. Haufe, 'Hellenistische Volksfrömmigkeit', in *Umwelt des Urchristentums* I (1965), 68-100; see also K. Prümm, *Religionsgeschichtliches Handbuch für den Rahmen der altchristlichen Umwelt* (1943), 357-464.

and magicians, oracles and healing sanctuaries, prophets and charismatic miracle-workers.[6] More important is a second distinction between institutionalised, charismatic and 'technical' forms of miraculous activity. Healing sanctuaries and oracles are recognised institutions of social and religious life. Their legitimation is traditional and achieved by means of foundation legends. Their power is based on the action of the gods. Their charisma is attached to the institution. It is a charisma of office and is passed down through generations. This sort of legitimation is not available to individual prophets or miracle-workers. They are inspired. Their charisma is attached to their person and generally disputed by the public. Distinct from the charismatic is the 'technician': soothsayers and magicians exercise their activities as the result of a skill they have learned.[7] They have a 'technical' legitimation and can transmit their skill without any consideration of persons. Anyone who knows the correct magic formulas and rituals can produce the desired results. This is why the instructions for spells have to remain secret, but it is also what enables magical lore to be systematised: there are extensive bodies of knowledge relating to astrology and the interpretation of dreams. The Neoplatonists have a carefully differentiated philosophy of magic. In their view the arts of divination and magic are accessible to any individual and can therefore be used for completely individual and anti-social purposes. Whereas oracles and healing sanctuaries fulfil exclusively social functions and are publicly encouraged, magicians and soothsayers are in a twilight area. Their skill is often regarded as a 'black art' and is sometimes even banned. The Roman emperors attack astrology and divination, but are for the most part themselves believers in them. What was a dangerous instrument in the hands of subjects (we need think only of political oracles, prophecies about the date of the emperor's death, and so on), was a valuable aid to preserving one's own power. This gives us six forms of miraculous activity.

---

[6] Some institutions are devoted almost exclusively to medicinal, others exclusively to divinatory purposes, but even so there is overlap. Of 70 cures preserved from Epidaurus three (Nos. 24, 46, 63) can be classified as divination (cf. R. Herzog, *Epidauros*, 112ff.). Conversely, Alexander of Abonuteichos occasionally gave medical advice at his oracle.

[7] The ancient world also distinguished within divination between a gift and a facility, between *divinatio naturalis* and *divinatio artificiosa* (Cic. *de divin.* I, 49). We hear of a τέχνη μαγική or an *ars magica*. Cf. T. Hopfner, art. 'Mageia', PW 14, 1, 301-93, esp. col. 367.

	Skill (τέχνη) Soothsaying	Institution Oracles	Charism Prophets
Divination			
Miraculous Activity	Magic	Healing Sanctuaries	Charismatic Miracle- Workers

The decisive criterion for distinguishing miraculous activities is sociological. The crucial factor is the social position of divination and miraculous activity, their legitimation and the different roles of their practitioners. Without such distinctions it is difficult to specify differences; for example, the same motifs can be found in all forms of divination and miracle-working.

What functions do these various forms of belief in miracles and superstition perform? Why did ancient society attach so much importance to these abnormal forms of coping with life? In an attempt to answer these questions we shall employ integration and conflict models, which we shall first illustrate with the help of the phenomena of divination. After this we shall ignore divination.

In an integration model in the sociology of religion the function of divinatory activities can be described as that of stabilising people in the face of a chronic boundary situation, for example, uncertainty about the obscure future particularly when important decisions are required or unusual events occur. The art of reading signs ensures that the individual and society are not destroyed by fear and panic, that no-one gets false ideas, that decisions remain within the recognised rules. This does not always succeed. Theophrastus, in his character portraits, describes how the 'superstitious man' is constantly misled by signs into inappropriate behaviour (*Char.* XVI).[8] 'If a mouse has gnawed through the flour sack he goes to the interpreter of signs and asks him what should be done in this case. When the interpreter of signs replies that he should take the sack to the saddler to have it stitched, he does not act accordingly but brings an expiatory offering to ward off evil.' Here a social institution designed to give individuals stability seems to have failed, though the problem is trivial.

However it is easy to imagine that a person might feel confirmed by signs in attitudes which went beyond the bounds of the legitimate, and in these cases it is important that 'experts' guard against misinterpretations. When the banished Spartan king Cleomenes was crucified in Egypt, a snake wound itself round the dead man's head, at which the people began to call him 'the son of the gods', but the Egyptian sages gave a completely

---

[8] Cf. H. Bolkestein, 'Theophrastos' Charakter der Deisidaimonia als religionsge-schichtliche Urkunde', *RVV* 21, 2 (1929). Our term 'superstition' does not coincide exactly with Theophrastus'.

natural interpretation of the phenomenon. Cleomenes had unsuccessfully attempted social reform in Sparta and it would no doubt have been inexpedient if an aura of divinity had become associated with him and the ideas associated with him had continued to be influential.

Other phenomena may be better explained in terms of conflict models. Josephus reports numerous signs which preceded the destruction of Jerusalem. A sword-shaped star was seen over the city, chariots and bands of armed men appeared in the sky, the door of the Temple opened of its own accord, etc. (*bell.* VI, 5, 3). Josephus regards all this as signs of the coming disaster, but originally the signs could have been given a quite different interpretation, as signs announcing God's intervention on behalf of the Jews.[9] In disputes interpretations of signs were certainly controversial. Often only the interpretations of the victors have survived. Consequently anyone who wanted to be victorious or to remain in power needed to be in control of the divinatory institutions from the outset. The Romans were very skilled at this. Hardly a move was made in Rome without enquiries being made of the augurs, who, however, were subject to subtle political control.[10]

Generally we favour an interpretation in terms of conflict models where religious phenomena have a clear link with one social group. Where such links are less apparent integration models are more appropriate. We shall follow this approach in analysing the three social forms of miraculous activity.

Religious healing sanctuaries enabled society to put its sick in places where they would be less of a burden but without being totally excluded. In this way sanctuaries ensured at least a minimum of integration for the sick. A god was specially present for them; there was advice on treatment and hope. The ancient healing sanctuaries were unquestionably there for all. Rich and poor visited them. Fear of death and pain knows no social boundaries. The sanctuaries seem not to have taken much notice of the social status of the sick. In the inscriptions from Epidaurus the suppliants are mentioned merely by name, often with their place of origin added. Even a queen is treated no differently: the Andromache mentioned in Inscription 31 is in all probability identical with the wife of King Arybbas (c. 350 BC).[11] The refer-

---

[9] Cf. S.V. McCasland, 'Portents in Josephus and in the Gospels', *JBL* 51 (1932), 323-335.
[10] On this cf. A. Gehlen, 'Über die Verstehbarkeit der Magie', in *Studien zur Anthropologie und Soziologie* (1963), 79-92.
[11] Cf. R. Herzog, *Epidauros*, 73f. R. Herzog thinks that consideration for the social status of the queen has influenced the form of the report: 'For the sake of our distinguished clientele the miraculous dream is described in the most discreet form: A handsome boy uncovered her, the god touched her with his hand. . . .' In the case of other women sleeping in the sanctuary in the hope of conceiving the references to a sexual approach are much more direct (Nos. 42 and 77).

ence to her refutes the view occasionally expressed that only
uneducated people would have come to Epidaurus.[12] Further evidence comes from the presence of other prominent worshippers of
Asclepius alongside the queen of Epirus: the famous orator Aeschines, Demosthenes' political opponent, was cured in Epidaurus
(AP VI, 330). An Athenian woman named Ambrosia is instructed
to donate a silver pig as a thank-offering (4) – she can hardly have
been poor. One Thersandros of Halieis (33) is brought forward in a
chariot. From late antiquity in particular we have the names of
educated worshippers of Asclepius:[13] Aelius Aristides (2nd century AD), Libanius (ep. 607, 759, 1382) and the Emperor Julian
(4th century AD). Strabo says explicitly of the sanctuary at
Canopus that well-known people sought to sleep within the pre-
cincts because of its healthy effects (XVII, 1, 17). Nevertheless,
despite this evidence, there is no mistaking an affinity between the
cult of Asclepius and the lower social classes. Asclepius was the
friend of the humble folk.[14] In the documents by which slaves
acquired their freedom no gods appear so often as Asclepius and
Serapis.[15] The slaves were particularly likely to rely on them to
protect their rights. On the other hand, the inscriptions from
Epidaurus give few indications of low social status among visitors.
There is a slave among them (10) and a poor boy, who has to offer
no more than ten knuckle-bones as a dedication (8), and the
fish-seller Amphimnestus (47), who will hardly have belonged to
the highest social circles. More illuminating are the rebukes
addressed to the visitors about ἀμαθία (4) and εὐηθία (9), lack of
culture and simpleness. If the editors of the inscriptions found it
necessary to defend visitors against this charge by means of
appropriate stories, it is a reasonable conclusion that there were
people who ridiculed the uneducated and simple people. Can it be
an accident that this mockery is put into the mouth of none other
than the (presumably) well-to-do Ambrosia of Athens (4)? Of

---

[12] Also questioned by R. Herzog, *Epidauros*, 63, who cites the large buildings in
Epidaurus, the inscriptions 4 and 33 and also the establishment of offshoots in Sicyon,
Athens, Pergamum and Naupactus.

[13] J. Geffcken, *Der Ausgang des Griechisch-römischen Heidentums* (1920), 102 believes
that 'until a late date' Aclepius 'remained the particular refuge of the educated'. O.
Weinreich, *AH*, 30f., sees a development: during the Roman Empire faith in Asclepius
spread increasingly among the educated classes.

[14] F. Böhmer, *Untersuchungen über die Religion der Sklaven in Griechenland und Rom*,
II, (1960), 62: 'Asclepius was not a great, shining and all-ruling deity like Zeus or Apollo,
but a human god and the god of the afflicted.' On the other hand he was not specifically a
deity of slaves like Silvanus or Fortuna in Rome (*Untersuchungen* III (1961), 478; on the
cult of Asclepius in general, cf. 302-09.

[15] F. Bömer, *Untersuchungen* II, 61f.

another prominent visitor, the orator Aeschines, we are told Θνητῶν μὲν ἀπορούμενος . . . (AP VI, 330); only despair of human skill had brought him to Epidaurus. Remarkably, the theme that the doctors have failed never appears in the actual inscriptions from Epidaurus; possibly most of the visitors were unable to consult (and pay) a doctor as could the wealthy Aeschines. And, finally, on closer inspection Strabo's report reveals the direct opposite of what it might first have been taken to imply:[16] the sanctuary of Serapis was so celebrated that *even* the most distinguished men believed in it and sought healing sleep within the sanctuary (ὥστε καὶ τοὺς ἐλλογιμωτάτους ἄνδρας πιστεύειν καὶ ἐγκοιμᾶσθαι Strabo XVIII, 1, 17). The social groups the suppliants normally came from are reasonably clear.

It is indeed open to doubt whether rich people had many inducements to seek out the healing cults. The reasons emerge from Pausanias' very realistic description (II, 27, 6): 'The Epidaurians in the sanctuary were in a very sorry state because their wives had no roof over them when they gave birth and the sick had to wait for death under the open sky. However, Antonius improved matters when he erected a building.' It was certainly not an attractive prospect to tend one's ailments among the dying, and women in childbirth, and possibly in the open air. The impression given is rather that this was a place where society could dump individuals who had become useless. Some slave-owners were able to get rid of their sick slaves in this way, and the Emperor Claudius was forced to take action to stop this: 'Because certain persons were leaving their sick and disabled slaves on the island of Aesculapius in order to avoid having to care for them, he ordered that all those left there were to count as free and were not obliged to return to the service of their masters when they recovered' (Suet. *Claud.* 25).

Among visitors to the sanctuaries the lower classes will have predominated. The members of the higher social classes were in any event fewer in number, so that even on the assumption that all classes were equally affected by illness and all visited cultic sanctuaries to the same extent, they would inevitably remain a minority. If we then take into account the fact that illnesses resulting from inadequate food and overexertion will have been less numerous among them, their proportion among the suppliants falls, and it is further reduced by their ability to turn first to doctors, and not

---

[16] Not so R. Herzog, *Epidauros*, 63.

only because they could pay better fees.[17] Only they were sufficiently economically independent to tend their ailments. For ordinary people in this situation there was often simply the alternative of either working or going to the wall (economically, if not physically). Plato makes this starkly clear. In his ideal state (*Rep.* 406c) no-one is to have time 'to be ill all their life and recover by themselves, as we ridiculously find happening among common workers, but do not notice among the rich and those who are congratulated on their good fortune.' An ordinary worker must either quickly recover in order to work or work to total physical destruction (*Rep.* 406e). As E. and L. Edelstein rightly remark: 'Under these circumstances it seems safe to say that in a world in which the poor were left to their fate by the communities at large, where laical medicine did not know of any special provisions for the needy, the Asclepeia and religious medicine were of the greatest importance for the medical welfare of the lower classes.'[18] Indeed, Asclepius was a refuge for the poorest and most wretched, and anyone, rich or poor, could soon join the poorest, except that even then the poor were often still a little poorer than the others. In general it is true to say that the cultic healing sanctuaries can be seen as performing the function of socially integrating the sick from all social classes. Even these institutions, however, bear the marks of a society in which privileges are most unequally distributed.

The feature which distinguishes the magic arts from healing sanctuaries is not the absence from the latter of magic.[19] Most rituals and religion contain magic features. The difference is that, as part of a religion they constitute social acts in which the community participates. It is precisely this link with the community and its rules which is missing from ancient magic, and especially that of late antiquity. Its three main features are cosmopolitanism, individualism and 'optimism'.[20]

---

[17] Pliny (ep. VIII.24) puts the problem discreetly: 'Take the example of doctors. It is true there is no difference for them between slaves and free men when they are ill, but they do treat a free man more gently.' On the care of the sick, cf. H. Bolkestein, *Wohltätigkeit und Armenpflege im vorchristlichen Altertum* (1939), 274f. There were public doctors in Greece (Plato *Rep.* 259). The first evidence of them in Rome is from the 4th century AD (Bolkestein, 379).

[18] *Asclepius* II, 178.

[19] The standard work is still T. Hopfner, *Offenbarungszauber* (1921-1924); cf. also his article 'Mageia', *PW* 14, 1, 301ff. There is a survey of the literary evidence for magic in S. Eitrem, 'La magie comme motif littéraire', *SO* XXI (1941), 39-83.

[20] On the three features of magic in late antiquity, cf. esp. P. Derchain, 'Die ägyptische Welt nach Alexander dem Grossen', in: *Der Hellenismus und der Aufstieg Roms* (1965), 212-44, esp. 241-44. Also A.A. Barb, 'The Survival of Magic Arts', in H. Momigliano (ed.), *The Conflict Between Paganism and Christianity in the Fourth Century* (1963), 100-125.

The cosmopolitan attitude of magic appears in the thorough-going syncretism of the magical papyri. In the papyri every possible name of the one God is mentioned. There are no gods tied to particular groups or peoples.[21] All are subject to the magician. The appearance in the Egyptian papyri of even the Jewish God Yahweh or Yao – despite tensions between Egyptians and Jews – shows a certain lack of prejudice. The magician has freed himself from the shackles of his community. Anything that has power is recognised. Anything that contributes to the magic is useful. The result is a considerable degree of individualism. Ideas which origi-nally may have been associated with official religion are individual-ised. They no longer contribute to the social stabilisation of an 'interpreted world', but serve very practical ends, which sometimes may have a distinct anti-social character. In general four ends can be distinguished: attack and inflictive harm, defence and protec-tion, obtaining love and power, knowledge and revelation.[22] Magic used to attack or harm in particular violates the rules of social life, though revelation magic may also have explosive effects (as when someone wants to know the date of death of an emperor, an official or a master). We consequently find regular attempts to criminalise magic wholly or partly. In Israel there was a strict prohibition on magic (Dt 18.9ff). Plato discusses the problem in detail in his *Laws* (*leg.* 909b; 932e-933).[23] The Romans took action on several oc-casions against magic and divination. Quite early, the Twelve Tables make the damaging of another person's property by magic an offence. The emperors opposed magic, despite having more than a passing interest in it.[24]

The third notable feature of magic in late antiquity was its 'technical optimism': 'Given the conditions of the time, of a demoralised world, . . . magic, strange though it may seem to our modern ideas, represented an optimistic current. While the adher-ents of traditional religion were predicting the collapse of the world in which they lived and with it of the whole universe, the magicians believed in the power of word and of ritual, the power on

---

[21] Cf. M.P. Nilsson, *Die Religion in den grieschischen Zauberpapyri* (1948).

[22] The classification is from T. Hopfner, 'Mageia', 378.

[23] Cf. S. Eitrem, 'La magie', 51-53.

[24] Cf. the expulsion of astrologers and magicians (Dio Cass. 49.43.5) and the burning of books of oracles under Augustus (Suet. *Aug.* 31), a *senatus consultum* under Tiberius (Dio Cass. 57.15), a trial at the same date (Tac. *ann.* IV.22). Cf. also the trial of Apuleius of Madaura (cf. A. Abt, *Die Apologie des Apuleius von Madaura und die antike Zauberei*, 1907). Eusebius knows of trials of educated people (*praep. ev.* IV. 2.10). On the legal status of magic cf. T. Hopfner, 'Mageia', 384-87.

which the old world was based, and were able to create new rituals, designed for the new needs and based on a new view of man.'[25]

Magic is a sign of social disintegration and also intensifies it. It takes place mainly in secret so that there is no possibility of accusations. Since it is thus by definition not a part of the official order protected by the state, it attracts particularly those groups who are on the edges of that order. Elsewhere they may have been victims of discrimination, but in the marginal areas of magic and the occult all are equal.[26] Here it was possible, albeit with ghostly weapons, to fight on a level on which the more powerful did not automatically possess better weapons. Destructive magic must often have been the recourse of the defenceless. Revelation magic was probably practised by those who could not determine their own futures, but were exposed to daily risks: soldiers, gladiators, racing drivers, wrestlers and boxers, as well as all those who had to live from hand to mouth.[27] F. Bömer, who has made a detailed study of the problem of the class-relatedness of magic, comes to the conclusion that its world is, 'not exclusively, but certainly in the main, that of these (sc. the lower) strata of a population. The *infimum genus* does not generally possess the outward resources to ward off the unpleasantnesses of everyday life in the normal way (and here again the line runs not between free and unfree, but between poor and rich)'.[28] Magic is a survival technique used by marginal social groups.

For precisely this reason it is not limited to the lower classes. Where people from all social classes find no place in society (as in the great social crises of the 3rd century),[29] magic also finds its way into the upper ranks of society. In the process, however, it changes its character, and this very process of change confirms the class-specific nature of magic in late antiquity. The Neo-platonic philosophy of magic distinguished between several levels of magic:

---

[25] P. Derchain, 'Die ägyptische Welt', 243.

[26] This aspect is emphasised particularly by F. Bömer, *Untersuchungen* IV, 957-94, in a study in sociology of religion called 'Zauberei und Magie': 'In this area of personal belief which is not regulated by civil society, free and unfree as "religious persons" are in a sense on the same level, without significant differences between them.' (974).

[27] T. Hopfner, 'Mageia', 382, supported by G. Haufe, 'Hellenistische Volksfröm-migkeit', 82.

[28] F. Bömer, *Untersuchungen* IV, 983f.

[29] The connection between this crisis and the growth of sorcery is stressed by T. Hopfner, 'Mageia', 387ff., though no general connection can be deduced from this between situations of social crisis and irrational survival strategies. The riddle of the belief in magic and miracles in late antiquity is rather that it grew steadily from the 1st century onwards, that is to say precisely in a period of remarkable political stability. However it must certainly have been given added stimulus by the crisis of the 3rd century.

there was the humble *goetia* and the sublime *theourgia* (and some-times in between 'magic' in the narrower sense).[30] What the edu-cated practised was *theourgia*. It differed from *goetia* first in the type of spirits influenced. *Goetia* was directed to the lower, ma-terial demons, while *theourgia* addressed the higher-ranking, spiritual beings. It will be observed that even in their dealings with the world of the occult the upper classes insist on dealing only with the higher orders. The social hierarchy is projected into the world of the demons. A second difference concerns the effects sought. The aim of *theourgia* is the vision of God, a mystical experience of the presence of God, a goal raised far above the everyday prob-lems with which the magical speculations of the simple people grapple. Thirdly, the picture is completed by the more refined techniques of *theourgia,* which rejects material pressures and sum-mons the deity through the immaterial medium of speech, by com-mands, not through the use of material objects. In spite of what seem to me socially determined differences between *goetia* and *theourgia,* the inner structure of both types of magic is the same. Augustine was right to reject theoretical distinctions. He despises indiscriminately

'what is called magic or by the repellent name of *goetia* or by the honourable name of *theourgia.* Those who use these names want to distinguish among those who engage in these prohibited arts be-tween those who must be condemned, and whom the people call witchmasters, – these are the so-called *goetai* – and others, who are said to be praiseworthy, the practitioners of *theourgia*' (*civ.* X, 9).

The position is clear. The 'prohibited arts' had to change their form before they became respectable for the educated.[31] And con-versely: the educated classes required the pressure of an unsettled social, economic and political situation before they abandoned more rational survival strategies.[32] The rise of magic into the

---

[30] Cf. T. Hopfner, 'Mageia', 373-384. On *theourgia* cf. S. Eitrem, 'La théurgie chez les Néoplatoniciens', *SO* 22 (1942), 49-79. On the specific social features of the religion of the educated, cf. M. Weber, *Wirtschaft und Gesellschaft,* 3rd ed. 1947, 288ff.

[31] As belief in miracles rises in society, other aspects change. The miraculous becomes a topic of smart shocking conversation. In Lucian's *Philopseudes* the representatives of the main philosophical movements vie with each other to tell unlikely miracle stories. They become so involved in this *jeu d'esprit* that the only representative of ordinary common sense leaves the gathering in confusion. One sees Lucian shaking his head over the new fashion, but he is also clearly well aware of the entertainment value of his miraculous tales.

[32] The social rise of belief in miracles is confirmed by archaeological finds. C. Bonner, *Studies in Magical Amulets* (1950), VIII and 5, emphasises that most magic amulets come from the lower classes. This situation does not change until late antiquity: 'The expense of making the more elaborate amulets shows how important a part magic had come to play in the lives of the wealthier classes' (13).

higher strata of post-classical society does therefore not refute the class-specific character of ancient magic, but confirms it. It would be false to explain this 'social rise' of the occult in terms of purely religious reasons, such as the absence of a powerful high religion to check popular beliefs.[33] Instead, sociological investigation of religious practices excluded by the official cult throw a significant light on the 'higher' forms of worship and religion, as F. Bömer rightly emphasises:

'Magic . . . finally, allows us to gain an insight into an area of religious behaviour which, by its very nature, escapes the influence of the civil order, even though the state, for its part, has a natural interest in bringing magic under its control or at least in not allowing it to threaten its public order. When it turns out that in the area of magic – and the evidence is quite conclusive – slaves were the active subjects and affected objects in magical practices over a very wide area, this is further confirmation of the earlier conclusions of this study, that vital forces in the area of the practice of Greek and Roman worship were not of a religious nature, but of a different, perhaps political kind.'[34]

Magic is an individualistic reaction to social disintegration. The magician has no need to be integrated into society. He remains in the dark. It is quite different with the charismatic miracle-worker. He seeks followers quite openly, starts up missionary movements or founds 'schools' – not because he wants to be integrated into the existing pattern of social life (this is what distinguishes him from the healing sanctuaries), but because he is looking for new patterns of life applicable to society. Charismatic miracle-working and a rejection of magic are thus quite logically found side by side. Primitive Christianity boasted of the many miracles and exorcisms of its apostles and at the same time had books of magic burnt (Acts 19.19). Apollonius of Tyana is said (by Philostratus) to have rejected the title of *goetes*. The charismatic miracle-workers and their followers feel themselves to be distinct from magicians.[35] They are looking for new forms of social integration, expressing a

---

[33] Cf. the otherwise correct observation of A. von Harnack, *Mission und Ausbreitung* I, 154: 'The main characteristics of belief in demons in the 2nd century are, first, that it pushes up from the obscure lower classes into the higher, even into literature and becomes a much more important affair than previously, and secondly that it no longer has a powerful public religion alongside it to keep it down.'

[34] F. Bömer, *Untersuchungen* IV, 959.

[35] R. Otto, *Kingdom of God*, 342: 'This distinction of charismatic activity from magical activity or from technical miracle working belongs to the very category of the real charismatic.' *Vita Apoll.* VII.38 is instructive on the attitudes within the charismatic movement, and see D. Esser, *Formgeschichtliche Studien*, 85f.

new social awareness, and thus come unavoidably into conflict with their world, whereas a magician would tend to avoid this conflict. This becomes particularly clear where they play a role in political conflicts and their miraculous power is used to legitimate political claims and intentions. The best example here is the instigator of the Sicilian slave revolt (136-32 BC), King Eunus.[36] As a slave, he had already prophesised kingship for himself and given his prophecy force by a miracle: he put a glowing substance into a nut which had a hole in either side and with his breath made fire spurt out. The rebellious slaves chose him as king, 'not because of his valour and generalship, but, as they said, because of his miraculous powers and because he had begun the revolt, and also because his name was a good omen for kindness to subjects' (Diod. 34.2.14). It is possible that Eunus was inspired by the Maccabean rebellion.

Here, in Palestine, we find in the 1st century AD a series of messianic prophets who prophesy a miraculous end to Roman rule and lead their followers to the place of the promised miracle, where they are usually brutally crushed by the Roman occupying power.[37] Theudas promised a new parting of the Jordan (*ant.* 20.97ff.), a prophet from Egypt a repetition of the miracle of Jericho at the walls of Jerusalem (*ant.* 20.167ff.; cf. *bell.* 2.261ff.). Jonathan the Sicariam prophesised miracles and apparitions in the wilderness (*bell.* 7.437f.). It may be doubted whether Eunus and the messianic prophets were the only miracle-workers of this type. Resistance movements are crushed and their history is written by the victors. We may assume that miracles and miracle-workers played a role in other disorders and resistance movements.

These political resistance movements, or those that have political effects, make it clear that miraculous power can play a part in social conflicts. This is also true, however, of those charismatic miracle-workers who were less proponents of political change than of a general doctrine of salvation or new religious ideas. Almost all are in conflict or in a state of tension with their world. Symptomatic of this is the charge of magic brought against them: Jesus was accused of being in alliance with the devil (Mt 12.24) and magic (*Sanh.* 107b; Orig. *c. Cels.* I.28). Apollonius had to face a trial on a

---

[36] Cf. J. Vogt, 'Struktur der antiken Sklavenkriege', *AbhMainz* (1957), 1-15, esp, 18ff., 32ff. The connection between political legitimation and miraculous power was also used by the emperors. Suetonius begins his story of Vespasian's miracle with the words: 'Vespasian still lacked the necessary respect, what might be called the divine confirmation of his authority, since he had been raised to the throne unexpectedly, and only a short time before. But this too was granted to him' (Suet. *Vesp.* 7). Vespasian had no dynastic legitimacy.
[37] Cf. R. Meyer, *Der Prophet aus Galiläa* (1940), 82ff.

charge of *goetia* (*vita* VII). The Samaritan Simon Magus is described as a 'magician' (Acts 8.9). These accusations are inaccurate. The rejection of charismatic miracle-workers has deeper reasons. They were religious reformers and propagated new ideas and impulses. They confronted the accepted pattern of life with a different one. This inevitably led to conflict. Pythagoras emigrated from the scene of his activity in Croton, Empedocles was banished, Apollonius of Tyana may have been a victim of a persecution of philosophers, Eliezer ben Hyrcanus was excommunicated, Jesus crucified. Miraculous power develops in a social process in which a revolution in religion, sensibilities and society takes place amid conflict. The social function of miraculous power is constituted by its power to legitimate and motivate in various types of social conflict.

This function of miraculous powers can be seen in miracle-workers in both resistance and religious movements. The two types of charismatic miracle-worker must be distinguished, though there are some points of contact: Apollonius of Tyana should probably be seen in the context of the philosophical opposition movement which led to the repeated expulsion of philosophers from Italy.[38] Points of contact can also be found between the messianic prophets and Jesus: in Acts 5.34ff. he is mentioned in the same breath as Theudas.[39] A comparison can be made on four points. It shows that the points of contact are not found in Jesus' miracles, but in his prophecy of the miraculous destruction and rebuilding of the Temple.

i) All the miracles announced by messianic prophets have a typological link with Israel's saving history, with the Temple, the occupation of the land (the parting of the Jordan, Jos. *ant.* 20.97ff.; the capture of Jericho, ibid. 20.167ff.) and the Exodus, Jos. *bell.* 7.437f. Jesus' miracles were brought into association with saving history externally, as when he was regarded as Elijah (Mk 6.14f.), but otherwise this connection with saving history is absent. It appears only in the promise of a new Temple.

ii) The messianic miracles were only promised, not carried out, the correspondence between the prophecy and the sign is what matters. In the Jesus tradition miracles are not merely announced; they are also performed, with the exception of the destruction and rebuilding of the Temple. Jesus prophesies this miracle and goes with his followers to the scene, just as the messianic prophets did. All other prophetic signs are rejected (Mk 8.11f.).

---

[38] In 74 AD Vespasian expelled all philosophers from Rome and in 89 and 95 Domitian expelled all philosophers from Rome and then Italy. Apollonius of Tyana may have been killed in Domitian's persecution. Cf. D. Esser, *Formgeschichtliche Studien*, 36f.

[39] R.M. Grant, *Miracles and Natural Law*, 166f., has stressed this connection, but the distinction between Jesus and the messianic prophets needs to be given more emphasis than it is by Grant.

iii) The miracles are performed by God, even if also by the messianic prophets. The prophets, however, do not regard themselves as the source of the miraculous activity; their work is only to 'show' the miracles. Δείκνυμι and σημεῖον are technical terms:

bell. 2.259   προῆγον εἰς τὴν ἐρημίαν ὡς ἐκεῖ τοῦ θεοῦ δείξοντος αὐτοῖς σημεῖα ἐλευθερίας.

bell. 6.285   ὡς ὁ θεὸς ἐπὶ τὸ ἱερὸν ἀναβῆναι κελεύει δεξομένους τὰ σημεῖα τῆς σωτηρίας.

bell. 7.438   προήγαγεν εἰς τὴν ἔρημον σημεῖα καὶ φάσματα δείξειν ὑπισχούμενος.

ant. 26.168f.   δείξειν γὰρ ἔφασαν ἐναργῆ τέρατα καὶ σημεῖα κατὰ τὴν τοῦ θεοῦ πρόνοιαν γινόμενα.

In the case of Jesus there is only one parallel to this, the destruction of the Temple. In the Fourth Gospel we even find in this connection the terms δείκνυμι and σημεῖον (2.18f.).

iv) Almost all messianic miracles were treated as a declaration of war on the Romans, who usually acted swiftly to destroy the movements. Similarly, in the case of Jesus, their action was not directed against his exorcisms and miracles in themselves. His imprisonment and execution took place in connection with the prophecy about the Temple: it was not until he came to Jerusalem that he was imprisoned – away from the Temple (Mk 14.49) – and the Temple prophecy appeared in the accusation. When, a little later (AD 35), the Samaritan appeared and found the Temple vessels on Mount Garizim (*ant.* 18.85), Pilate crushed this harmless movement so brutally that he was successfully prosecuted. The word 'Temple' was evidently enough to make Pilate intervene. There is, of course, disagreement about the genuineness of the Temple prophecy.[40] In its favour is the fact that it was not fulfilled. Where it can be interpreted as a *vaticinium ex eventu,* only its negative part is reported (Mk 13.2).[41] The positive half, the building of a new Temple, had to be reinterpreted: in Acts 6.14 in ethical terms (Jesus will change the customs of Moses), in Jn 2.19 as christological (Jesus will rise from the dead), and in Mk 15.38 perhaps in ecclesiological terms (as a reference to the new Church of the Gentiles?). It seems to me likely, though I cannot discuss it here, that the crowd which followed Jesus into Jerusalem came in expectation of a miraculous cosmic transformation and a new Temple. The Romans interpreted the incident as a messianic movement and intervened accordingly.[42]

---

[40] Cf. Bultmann *HST*, 120, and note, p. 399.

[41] This is in fact a *vaticinium ex eventu*. The fact that the Temple was destroyed by fire is not a counter-argument (as maintained by W.G. Kümmel, *Promise and Fulfilment*, 1957, 99-102). The Temple was subsequently rased to the ground, as pointed out by W. Nikolaus, 'Tempelzerstörung und synoptische Apokalypse', *ZNW* 57 (1966), 38-49.

[42] Political considerations were behind Jesus' execution (cf. the discussion in M. Hengel, *Charismatic Leader,* 38-42). The most important arguments can be listed here without discussion:

Our thesis that miraculous charismatic powers have a legitimating and motivational function in social conflicts leaves open the question which social conditions are involved in these conflicts. The situation in the Sicilian slave rising was certainly quite different from that of primitive Christianity. Each conflict must be studied on its own from this point of view, and a single factor can rarely be shown to have been decisive, quite apart from the fact that our tradition is far too fragmentary to be able to give satisfactory answers to our questions. Nevertheless it is useful to set out the questions and collect together such evidence as is relevant to an answer.

1. Socio-Ecological Factors

Primitive Christian miracle stories are rooted in the predominantly rural world of Galilee. In the light of this E. Trocmé has suggested that they are the expression of a quasi-animistic rural attitude from the border areas of Syria and Palestine, in contrast to the heavily ethically oriented sayings tradition, which comes from the urban world of Jerusalem.[43] Not that Trocmé intended to make the sociological point that there is a structural connection between belief in miracles and a rural environment. Such a view would be easy to disprove. The whole of the synoptic tradition, including the

---

a) Jesus was 'marked' as a native of Galilee, which was also the home of the Zealots, whose message of the rule of God alone could easily be confused with the preaching of the imminent arrival of God's kingdom. He was also 'marked' by having been a disciple of John the Baptist, who was executed for political reasons.

b) The prophecy of the new Temple involves Jewish political history, or could be taken to do so. The Temple was politically significant.

c) The opponents in the Passion story are not so much the Pharisees, who were interested in religious issues, as the forces of political stability, the Sanhedrin and the Roman administration. One reason for their intervention seems to have been fears of disorder among the people (Mk 14.2).

d) Jesus was arrested as a 'robber' (Mk 14.48) and ended on the cross. The method of execution is Roman. Even if the inscription on the cross is unhistorical (which is not certain), it may have contained an element of truth in that the authorities were afraid of messianic movements and wanted to nip them in the bud.

e) The Jesus movement was in fact interpreted as a messianic movement (cf. Acts 5.34-37). The Christian *testimonium Flavianum* (Jos. *ant.* 18.63) was inserted into a list of disorders and may have supplanted a corresponding reference and condemnation by Josephus.

Whether it was Jewish or Roman authorities who had more reason to get rid of Jesus is less important than the fact that all the authorities interested in political and social peace had sufficient reasons for taking action against him. Even if Jesus was not a political revolutionary, his movement could quickly have become politically relevant. Whatever the truth, we should be cautious about implying that his religious opponents acted deceitfully by denouncing him for political crimes when the real reason for his execution was his attitude to the Law.

[43] E. Trocmé, *La formation*, 37-44. For criticisms see T.A. Burkill, 'The Formation of St Mark's Gospel', in: *New Light on the Earliest Gospel* (1972), 180-264.

sayings, is rural in character: the parables take us into the world of farmers and fishermen, vine-growers and shepherds. Many sayings contain images from a rural setting (e.g. Mt 6.25ff.; 7.6, 15; 11.7ff.). Conversely the miracle stories of Acts take place in the great cities of the Roman Empire, Lystra (14.7ff.), Philippi (16.16ff.), Troas (20.7ff.) and so on. Apollonius of Tyana does miracles in Tarsus (*vita* VI.43), Athens (IV.20), Ephesus (IV.10) and Rome (IV.45). There is no basis for a general assumption that a rural population at this period would be more susceptible to belief in demons and forces than an urban one. While there is no structural connection, it is not impossible that there was an actual one. After all, the synoptic tradition does come from a predomin-antly rural area surrounded by two series of Hellenistic cities: the cities on the coast of the Mediterranean and those to the east of the Jordan, the so-called 'Decapolis',[44] and it is quite possible that this background has had some effect on the character of the miracle stories.

Most of the miracle stories are set in Galilee. It is indisputable that this is the origin of the miracle tradition as a whole, but there is disagreement about the tightness of the connection of the tradition history with the area. Did the miracle stories also continue to be transmitted and preached in Galilee? G. Schille takes the place references in the miracle stories as evidence of this. He thinks they are indications that miracle stories were originally foundation stories of primitive Christian communities in Galilee.[45] Against this view the following arguments may be brought:

i) There is little basic difference between localised and nonlocalised miracle stories. For example, the missionary commission – according to Schille an indication of missionary activity – appears in non-localised as well as localised stories (e.g. Mk 5.25ff.).

ii) Several miracle stories set in one place would have to correspond to several communities or several first converts. In Capernaum alone four miracles take place: Mk 1.21ff.; 1.29ff.; 2.1ff; Mt 8.5ff. On the Decapolis see Mk 5.1ff; 7.31ff.

---

[44] On the urbanisation of Palestine cf. A.H.M. Jones, *Cities*, 248ff. 'Many parts of Syria were too backward for republican government, and it was better to leave the simple villagers or wild tribesmen of the mountains and deserts under the authority of dynasts whom they respected than to attach them to cities which would be too weak to control them, or to convert them into republican communities which would soon break down' (258). The synoptic tradition comes from this rural world, whereas the tradition of the epistles is largely a product of urban society (cf. A. Deissmann, *Licht vom Osten*, 210f.). The relative independence of the two lines of tradition probably has sociological reasons as well as others.

[45] The Galilee hypothesis is advanced in a number of variants particularly by G. Schille, *Anfänge der Kirche*, 1966, 39-98, and *Die urchristliche Wundertradition*, 1967, E. Trocmé, *Formation*, 37-44, and K. Tagawa, *Miracles*, 15-36.

iii) Woes over Chorazim, Bethsaida and Capernaum (cf. Tyre and Sidon) in Mt 11.20-34 show that attempts to found communities failed in these places. Nevertheless the tradition contains miracle stories about these places, either set in them (Mk 8.22; 2.1ff.) or stories in which the suppliants come from there (Mk 7.24ff.). Chorazim is an exception.

iv) Aetiologies usually contain something still present or familiar in the present. Schille has in mind the first converts. If that were so, however, we should expect more proper names in the miracle stories. These are absent even where there is a definite setting as in Mk 5.1ff.; 7.31ff.; 8.22ff.

v) It is true that in Acts miracle stories are told in connection with the foundation of communities. However the miracle stories 9.32ff. and 9.36ff. assume that communities already exist (cf. vv. 32, 36), and in 16.11ff. the community is founded before the miracle. Foundations are also 'confirmed' by miraculous revelations: 10.1ff.; 8.26ff.; 16.9.

An aetiological use of miracle stories is not excluded, but it was probably not the general rule. Nevertheless this does not disprove the thesis of a connection between the miracle stories and Galilee. K. Tagawa, for example,[46] suggests that Mark sets the miracle stories in the places where he learned them, and the references to the spread of Jesus' fame do give the impression that miracle stories were told in particular localities (cf Mk 1.28; 5.20). Even this view, however, probably goes too far. Essentially we are not justified in supposing more than that place references presuppose a certain familiarity in narrators and audience when – as in most cases – they are introduced without explanation. Luke is the first writer who is clearly addressing an audience for whom Palestine is a 'corner' of the Roman Empire (Acts 26.26). He is the first to give occasional explanations of place references. He describes Nazareth as the place where Jesus had been brought up (4.16), and Capernaum as 'a city of Galilee' (4.31). He introduces 'the country of the Gerasenes' (Mk 5.1) with the words 'which is opposite Galilee' (Lk 8.26). Once he even writes from the point of view of someone introducing the unfamiliar: 'a city called Nain' (7.11). Otherwise such features are totally absent from the miracle tradition. This perhaps allows the inference that the stories were told for a long time in Palestine and its immediate neighbourhood, but it does not justify limiting them to Galilee.

This rather general familiarity with the area of Galilee is matched by a certain distancing from the large cities and villages. Some of the marginal comments in the miracle stories stress that Jesus did not stay in the villages but in lonely places (Mk 1.45;

---

[46] K. Tagawa, *Miracles*, 20ff., though he is aware of other reasons for attributing a setting.

6.30-33), or that, for example, he was in the region of Tyre and Sidon but did not enter these cities (7.24; cf also 7.31). Even if these comments in the framework have been worked over redactionally, it is probably true that Jesus worked in the countryside.[47] This feature has also survived in the miracle stories independently of the redactional framework. They often take place in open country, outside towns and villages (Mk 1.40ff.; 5.1ff.; 5.25ff.; 6.34ff.; 8.1ff.; 7.24ff.; 7.31ff.; 9.14ff.; Lk 17.11ff.). In Mk 8.22ff. the blind man is taken out of the village specially to be healed. In addition Mk 5.1ff. shows a certain reserve towards the urban Hellenistic cities of the eastern bank of the Jordan: Jesus is rejected there. The same applies to the larger cities of Galilee, Chorazim, Bethsaida and Capernaum, which were not brought to repentance by miracles (Mt 11.20-24).

While we may not wish to assume any inherent connection between belief in miracles and a rural mentality, in the case of primitive Christian miracle stories it is reasonable to suppose that they acquired their character in a rural environment and were told in that environment for a time but soon left it. According to Mk 5.20 the story of the exorcism at the lake was told in the Decapolis.

2. Socio-Economic Factors

The movement inaugurated by Jesus was certainly not an affair of the upper classes. In Galilee Jesus turned to the social and political outcasts. The summaries leave no doubt about the sort of people who flocked to him; it was the ὄχλος, the 'crowd', the humble people.[48] It is true that primitive Christianity soon had members from higher classes (the οὐ πολλοί of 1 Cor 1.26), but the miracle stories in particular present themselves as forms of expression of lower classes, in the simplicity of their theology, the simplicity of their narrative, but above all in their subject matter. Belief in miracles is concentrated here on specific situations of distress, on possession, disease, hunger, lack of success and danger, in other words on situations which do not strike as hard in all social groups.

The problem revealed by the exorcisms is – whatever class-specific features it may have – a general social problem, the breakdown in interpersonal communication, a profound alienation in social relations. 'Possession' certainly occurs in all social groups,

---

[47] W. Bauer, 'Jesus der Galiläer': *Aufsätze und kleine Schriften*, 1967, 91-108, esp. 106.

[48] The 'crowd' is probably the common people. The permissibility of a sociological evaluation of the term is seen also by T.A. Burkill, 'Theological Antinomies': *New Light*, 173ff. In the towns primitive Christianity very soon penetrated the higher levels of society. Cf. E.A. Judge, *Christliche Gruppen in nichtchristlicher Gesellschaft*, 1964, 48ff.

but, if we are to believe the gospels and Acts, primitive Christianity was accompanied by a massive upsurge of this phenomenon. It is as though 'a particularly strong wave of demonism had overflowed the world of Palestine' at this time.[49] Nor was Jesus the only successful exorcist. The whole of primitive Christianity is an exorcistic movement; its charismatics and missionaries regard themselves as exorcists (Mk 3.15; Lk 10.17ff.). While possession as such could not be class-specifically conditioned, its mass appearance could be. In a society which expresses its problems in mythical language groups under pressure may interpret their situation as threats from demons. Symptoms of possession may be socially learned.[50] If these symptoms are accepted as expressions of insoluble conflicts and the possibility of solving the problems so expressed is offered through exorcism, they may become a public language successfully used by many. The appearance of exorcists thus generally brings an increase in the amount of possession requiring exorcism.

This general remark can be supported by an analogy from the present. In Ethiopia the Christian Church is still successfully exorcising demons.[51] An interesting feature of the situation is that possession appears only in the lower social classes and there almost exclusively in women. In this society those threatened by demons are people exposed to situations of particular pressure. That social and psychological problems may be converted into somatic ones can hardly be denied, but it should be stressed that 'possession' represents a serious threat to the affected person which may lead to his or her death. It is not just imagination.

Apart from the summaries, which describe the crowd flocking to Jesus from fear of demons, the New Testament has one indication of a connection between social class and possession. In Acts 16.16ff. Paul and his companions expel a spirit from a girl who is a soothsayer and from whom her master derives a considerable income. As a result the exorcists are brought before the city magistrates on a charge. The accusation is that Paul has propagated unlawful customs. If we remember that soothsaying had an important social function and that an attack on the practice would have produced a far-reaching change in ancient social life, this is not untrue. As the story shows, these forms of ancient problem-solving were closely involved with upper-class financial and social

---

[49] R. Otto, *Kingdom of God,* 43.

[50] P. Berger and T. Luckmann, *The Social Construction of Reality,* 175-76.

[51] For information about Ethiopian exorcisms I am indebted to Frau Dr M. Renner, who had the opportunity of observing these exorcisms herself.

interests. Miracles and exorcisms challenged more than a slave-girl's possession. Not only exorcisms, but also healings, are class-specific. Illness is of course universal, but even without recourse to modern social criticism we can find a connection between socio-economic status and belief in miracles in an unprejudiced consid-eration of the story of the woman with the issue of blood (Mk 5.25ff.). As long as the woman had money she tried doctors. Only when her money was spent did she come to Jesus, with the most irrational kind of belief in miracles. Many poorer people must have seen themselves in that story. For a person without any resources illness meant exposure to immediate economic distress (the woman at least had some 'reserves'). 'The economic threat . . . of disease to the lower and middle class was grave, graver perhaps than at any later time.'[52] Illness meant inability to work. This is brought out in an apocryphal version of the 'healing of the with-ered hand' (Mk 3.1ff.). In this the sick man has become a mason. He makes his request in these words: 'I was a mason and earned (my) living with (my) hands. Jesus, I beg you to give me back my health so that I no longer have to beg for food' (Jerome, Commen-tary on Mt 12.13).[53] The important point is that the primitive Christian communities did not meet such fears merely with miracle-stories, but saw to it that no sick person needed to go hungry because of lack of work; the important point is that they looked after the sick. For illness is, of course, not just a physical and economic problem, but a social one. The sick fear isolation, being abandoned by others, becoming a burden. Here the miracle stories assured even the sick person whose case was hopeless that he or she will not be abandoned – even if their illness lasts years (Jn 5.1ff.). Were not the vicarious petitioners in the miracle stories like members of the community interceding for the sick? Were they not ready to overcome resistance in the process – including internal resistance to contact with someone incurably ill? The healings must be seen against the background of the community which recounted them, as collective symbolic actions by which distress was remedied and in which the members found strength to combat it in their ordinary lives by actions which were not merely 'sym-bolic'.

This is true of gift miracles too. The miraculous distribution of loaves is definitely connected with the support of the members of the community for each other. The apologist Aristides writes,

---

[52] Edelstein, *Asclepius* II, 175.
[53] Cf. Hennecke-Schneemelcher, *Apokryphen* I, 96.

'When there is someone among them who is in need or poor, and they have nothing to spare, they fast for two or three days to provide the poor person with sustenance' (*Apologia* XV.9). Is not such fasting a miracle? It at least recalls an apocryphal miracle story:[54]

'When Christ . . . was invited to a meal and went, we went with him. A loaf was set before each of us, and he too received a loaf. He blessed the loaf and divided it among us, and that small amount filled all of us. Our own loaves remained uneaten, and the other guests were amazed' (*Act. Ioh.* 93).

Another gift miracle, the miraculous draught of fishes, addresses the situation of fruitless labour (Lk 5.1ff.). The wine miracle at Cana is anything but a 'luxury miracle'. Where there is not enough wine for a celebration, means must be limited. Celebrations are occasions when poor people are particularly afraid of having their poverty exposed. When A. Deissmann praises the primitive Christian miracle stories for showing 'such popular simplicity, such childlike piety, such naive charm,' he is directing a gentle beam of social romanticism on the culture of the lower classes.[55] Not the least important aspect of the popular character of these stories is that in them people whose social and economic position left them no other outlet articulate their hopes.

The other themes of the miracle stories also allow us to make inferences about their social setting. The synoptic sea rescue miracles take us into the world of simple fishermen, exposed to danger from wind and waves in their small boats. It is true that in Acts we also find the sea trade between the cities of the Roman Empire, but distress and rescue are experienced from the lowest possible position, that of a prisoner (Acts 27). This view 'from below' is also characteristic of the stories of liberation from prison. Stories like Acts 12.1ff.; 16.23ff. will have been particularly appreciated where people knew from experience what it was to be defenceless and have no rights.

It seems to me that a degree of class correlation in the primitive Christian miracle stories can hardly be denied. In no sense is this an assertion that ancient miracle stories in general originate in the lower classes or that this statement 'explains' the primitive miracle stories. I claim merely that this is the social setting of the particular themes and motifs of the stories, that in them an imagination which

---

[54] Cf. R. Otto, *Kingdom of God*, 348.
[55] *Licht vom Osten*, 330.

believed in miracles is coming to grips with problems which were more remote from the upper classes. If it is true that belief in charisms and miracles generally originates in a conflict between old and new ways of life, in the particular case of these miracle stories the new way of life they legitimate belonged mainly to lower social groups. Of course this is not a complete description of the social dynamic expressed in the miracle stories. Primitive Christianity sought adherents by means of its miracles in higher circles too. People of status appear in the miracle stories: the centurion from Capernaum (Mt 8.5ff.), a synagogue superintendant (Mk 5.21ff.), a Syro-Phoenician woman, who was probably a member of the Hellenised upper class (Mk 7.23ff.). The 2nd century apologists addressed their miraculous proofs to educated people. Belief in miracle-workers certainly went right up the social scale in this period. The history of the Apollonius traditions illustrates this process. At the beginning of the 3rd century the somewhat controversial figure of Apollonius became the object of a religious and aesthetic cult in the circle of the Empress Julia Domna from Syria and a leading writer of the time wrote his *Life*. This one example shows that other social factors may have been at work.

3. Socio-Cultural Factors

Of the miracle-workers of early antiquity, the most distinctive examples appeared in Greek Italy (Pythagoras, Empedocles, Menecrates) or Israel (Elijah and Elisha). In the later period we find that charismatic miracle-workers come mainly from the east. The slave Eunus was a Syrian. Apollonius came from eastern Asia Minor and on his travels visited the Indian miracle-worker Jarbas (*vita* III.39). Simon Magus and Jesus worked in Palestine. The Neo-Platonists Porphyrius and Iamblichus, who were open to the cult of miracle-workers, came from Phoenicia and Syria. In Rome, by contrast, such figures are largely absent.[56] Vespasian is the first figure to whom miracles are attributed. The story is told that Serapis sent two sick men to him in Alexandria (!) to be cured. Vespasian first refused to perform the healing gestures requested, but a medical report testified that he nevertheless performed the cure (Tac. *hist.* IV.81; Suet. *Vesp.* 7). The tradition shows how strange the Romans found the phenomenon of the miracle-

[56] Cf. G. Delling, 'Zur Beurteilung des Wunders durch die Antike', in: *Studien zum NT*, 1970, 54, n. 7; R.M. Grant, *Miracles and Natural Law*, 58. Both refer to R. Lembert, *Der Wunderglaube bei Römern und Griechen*, 1905, but I was unfortunately unable to obtain a copy of this.

worker. They encountered it first in the east, and it was in the east that a Roman first performed miraculous healings. In the appearance of charismatic miracle-workers there is undoubtedly a great variation between east and west, but that should not be used as a basis for one of those dubious attempts to attribute fixed characteristics to particular nations, in this case greater belief in miracles to the Orientals than the Romans. If there are differences here, if, from its origin in the east, belief in miracles grows in late antiquity, this process must be studied historically and sociologically and not in terms of dubious national psychologies. It is useful in this context to remember that the fiercest critics of belief in miracles, Lucian of Samosata and Oenomaus of Gadara, came from Syria. Analysis must start with those features in the miracle stories which focus directly on a contrast between different cultures and ethnic groups, the appearance of pagan petitioners, 'foreign' words of power and the Elijah typology.

a) Non-Jewish petitioners appear in Mk 7.27ff.; Mt 8.5ff.; Mk 5.1ff.; and Lk 17.11ff. The contrast between Jews and Gentiles is particularly prominent in 'The centurion from Capernaum' and 'The Syro-Phoenician woman'. In both stories the motif of resistance overcome is given unusual stress. In one case the resistance comes from Jesus (Mk 7.24ff.); in the other the Gentile himself emphasises his 'unworthiness' (Mt 8.5ff.). Matthew has introduced logia into both stories dealing with the transition of missionary work from the Jews to the Gentiles. The miracle stories themselves show that they are reaching out beyond socio-cultural boundaries, but they also articulate a clearly perceived awareness of the boundaries, a tension between different cultures. Gentiles appear in them in an ambivalent position, now worthless (Mk 7.27; Mt 8.7f.), now the model (Mk 7.29; Mt 8.10; Lk 17.11ff.), now close, now far off (Mk 5.19f.). Overall the resulting dynamic between the different ethnic groups tends to be expansive and missionary.

b) The 'foreign' words of power belong to the same context. They make sense only in a confrontation between different languages and cultures. No doubt the Aramaic words in Mk 5.41 and 7.35 are intended to demonstrate the superior power of eastern words of healing. There is a slight resemblance to the opponents of the apostle Paul who appear in 2 Corinthians. They perform miracles (2 Cor 12.12), boast of their religious and cultural heritage as Hebrews, Israelites and descendants of Abraham (2 Cor 11.22). As so often, the idea of wisdom and power from the east is being used for propaganda.[57] Here a missionary element can be seen within the tension between two cultures; another example of ῥῆσις βαρβαρική emphasises the antagonistic character of this tension. In Mk 5.9 we hear a Latin word in the mouth of the demon. His name is 'Legion'; there is not just one demon but a host of 2000. The allusion to the Roman occupation is unmistakable. The hostility towards the Roman occupiers is made clear when the demons clearly express their wish to be allowed to remain in the country (5.10). This is precisely what the Romans also want. They are not concerned with forcing particular individuals into submission, but with controlling the whole country.[58] The story symbolically satisfies the desire to drive them into the sea like pigs. It becomes clear why the successful exorcist is sent away: his presence is a real threat to social peace. This is not to say that this miracle story contains a deliberately encoded political message. Within the society of this time political and religious factors did not exist separately. The two were intertwined from the beginning. The struggle was carried out in both spheres. Roman domination, like any foreign rule, had from the outset a religious aspect: with the foreigners came their gods. Judaism could see in them only idols and demons (Dt 33.17; Ps 95.5; Eth.En. 19.1; 99.7; Jub 1.11). The presence of a foreign political power was always the presence of a threatening numinous power, a pollution of the land. Roman rule could thus be interpreted as a threat from a demonic power – for all the Romans' tolerance in religion and politics. This made the activity of the exorcist a 'sign' of future liberation.

c) In Mk 5.7 there is a verbal allusion to a miracle of Elijah: τί ἐμοὶ καὶ σοί;. These are the words used by the widow of Sarepta to reject the man of God (1 Kings 17.16). The same formula of resistance appears in the mouth of the demons (Mk 1.24). According to Mk 6.14f., the people regard Jesus as Elijah come again because of his miracles. The source of this Elijah typology may be a belief that the battle against demons was a renewal of the battle against foreign idols. It is the 'unclean' spirits which proclaim the secret of Jesus: he is 'the Holy One of God'. Is this not an allusion to the messianic task of freeing the land from all uncleanness and restoring its holiness, now impaired by foreign demons (cf. the task

---

[57] Cf. D. Georgi, *Die Gegner des Paulus im 2. Korintherbrief,* 1964.

[58] I may perhaps be allowed here to put forward a (totally unprovable) hypothesis. The possessed are clearly in the power of spirits of the dead which have not found rest, which is why they stay by the tombs. Could they have been fallen fighters who lost their lives in the resistance?

of the Messiah in PsSol 17)? This context also makes sense of Jesus' statement, 'If it is by the Spirit of God that I cast out demons, then the kingdom of God has come upon you' (Mt 12.28). The rule of demons is alien rule. The casting out of demons restores the rule of God, and this also means the end of Roman rule, though not of that only.

Within a society which can express its problems and intentions in mythical language, social and political pressure can be expressed as the rule of demons. Or, to put it more carefully, political control by a foreign power and the resulting socio-cultural pressure can intensify the experience expressed in belief in demons and lead to the spread of possession on the vast scale which we must assume existed in the world of primitive Christianity. W.E. Mühlmann has placed this phenomenon in a broader context:

> 'In messianic movements of the charismatic type one of the most important elements of the social functions of shamanism, if not the most important, recurs, the exorcism of evil spirits. . . . From the shamanism of Siberian tribes we know that phenomena of possession by spirits are particularly important in a situation of interethnic pressure. "Oppression" by a foreign ruling people sometimes appears in code as "possession" by a foreign spirit (i.e. a spirit from a different tribe): the emphasis of the shaman's task may be connected with this. The situation of Judaism at the time of Jesus is somewhat similar. There had been centuries of foreign rule and oppression. The revolt of the Maccabees against alien Hellenistic culture lay only a few generations in the past. Roman rule was even more recent. Such a situation creates demons. . . .'[59]

In these terms a cult of exorcism would be an act of liberation transposed into the mythical realm. Miracle stories involving exorcism can be understood as symbolic actions which break the demonic spell of all-pervading dependence. Inter-ethnic tensions and political pressure are certainly only one factor in this dependence. And to prevent misunderstandings let it be explicitly stated that there is no suggestion here that the miracle stories which involve exorcism were political in intent. We are simply placing them in the functional context which formed the background to their intentions. The beginnings of a conscious awareness of this connection are to be found in primitive Christianity itself. It is given expression in Mk 5.1ff. To deny it would be to slip below the level of consciousness of the primitive Christian belief in miracles.

The miracle stories show that their social setting is the tension

---

[59] W.E. Mühlmann, *Chiliasmus und Nativismus*, 1961, 252.

between different cultures and peoples, and it is perhaps therefore less important to attribute them to a particular socio-cultural environment and to show their dependence on Jewish Christianity, Gentile Christianity or Hellenised Jewish Christianity.[60] What is more important is the fact that they bear witness to a dynamism which pushes beyond these socio-cultural boundaries. One of the roots of the ambivalence between boundary-crossing and boundary-stressing which is characteristic of their structure is thus a social one.

It was not only for the primitive Christian belief in miracles that socio-cultural tensions between subject and dominant peoples were an important factor. The fact that the charismatic miracle-workers of the 1st century AD were invariably from the east which was firmly under Roman domination invites the hypothesis that belief in charismatic miracle-workers can be treated as a reaction of subjugated Hellenistic and eastern cultures: the politically inferior proclaims and propagates his superiority on the level of miraculous activity. It is characteristic that in each case elements of the subject culture are revived. This is a general feature of the period. Apollonius revives Pythagoreanism, the second Sophistic movement is a renaissance of classical rhetoric and Neo-Platonism is a rediscovery of Plato. The Stoa becomes orthodox and turns its attention to the founders of the school.[61] The miracle-working prophets of Palestine go back to Moses and Joshua and seek to renew the miraculous charism of early Israel. Jesus is hailed as Elijah returned from the dead,[62] even though primitive Christianity and its belief in miracles, taken as a whole, are more than a renaissance. Christianity offered a genuinely new way of life, and rightly measured itself against the 'never yet' of the eschatological future. These revivals (or attempts to revive) elements of one's own culture must be placed in a larger context; it is a reaction to politically superior foreign cultures which can be observed frequently.[63] Naturally it is not a necessary reaction. When it occurs its course is different in each case. Belief in miracles is also by no means a necessary component of such a reaction, but it can form part of it. A comparable example is the

---

[60] Cf. H.W. Kühn, *Ältere Sammlungen im Markusevangelium*, 1971, 191ff.

[61] K. Praechter, *Die Philosophie des Altertums*, 14th ed. 1957, 486ff.

[62] The 'theory of prophetic connection' attacked by K. Koch, *The Rediscovery of Apocalyptic*, 1972, 36ff. certainly contains an element of truth.

[63] Ethnologists have described and analysed these processes as 'nativism'. Primitive Christianity is occasionally cited as an example, as in W.E. Mühlmann, *Chiliasmus und Nativismus*, 1961. See also R. Linton, 'Nativistische Bewegungen' in: *Religionsethnologie*, ed. C.A. Schmitz, 1964, 390-403; R.F. Wallace, 'Revitalisations-Bewegungen', ibid. 404-27. Even though historians have to look for more precise distinctions, the attempts of the ethnologists to find typical features and stages in charismatic movements of the sort that appear in a confrontation between different cultures are useful to an analysis of primitive Christianity. On the tension between Rome and the east see H. Fuchs, *Der geistige Widerstand gegen Rom in der antiken Welt*, 2nd ed. 1964.

confrontation of Greek and eastern cultures in Hellenism. There are some similarities. Both apocalyptics and Maccabeans go back to the Israelite past, but there are no charismatic miracle-workers. And in other respects the confrontation between the peoples and cultures developed differently. In Hellenism the intellectual culture of the victors was clearly superior. Even the resistance movement had to adopt elements of the culture against which it fought. This produced creative syntheses; the Stoa, astronomy and astrology, mystery religions and Hellenistic Judaism. The advance of the Romans was not a comparable intellectual challenge. The subject peoples were not first forced to bring their traditions up to the level of the 'dominant' culture. Here it could be enough to revive elements of one's own culture, even such naive phenomena as belief in charismatic miracle-workers.

To sum up, belief in charismatic miracle-workers is a source of legitimation and motivation in social conflicts. These may be conflicts of political claims (Eunus and the Palestinian miracle-working prophets) or between new understandings of salvation and the accepted ways of life in a society; the two cannot always be sharply distinguished. In primitive Christianity the conflict between a new understanding of salvation and existing ways of life was influenced by three social factors, the opposition between town and country, though this was not of primary importance, the differences between various strata of society and the tension between different cultures and ethnic groups. All three factors interact. The important development is that in primitive Christianity the charismatic miracle cult becomes the only one; all other forms of miraculous activity are excluded and opposed. This points to a far-reaching change in the attitude to the future and to the fundamental risks of life, to a new way of dealing with existential anguish, a new understanding of existence. Those who mistrust such sociological reflections (perhaps because they are insufficiently 'theological') may put more faith in the explanations of Origen. In them we find aspects of the situation we have analysed formulated with remarkable clarity:

'And in the case of the Christians, who have formed an association in a remarkable way, we shall see that in the beginning they were influenced more by the miracles than by exhortations to abandon the customs and practices of their fathers and adopt others totally different from these. And if we are asked for the probable reason for the beginning of the Christian community, we shall have to say that it is unlikely that the apostles of Jesus, *men from the common people and without education,* were inspired to proclaim the teaching of Christ to people by anything other than (confidence in) the power given to them and the grace which gave their words the power to account for these events. *It is equally inconceivable that their hearers would have rejected the immemorial customs and practices of their fathers unless they had been influenced by some considerable power and by miraculous events* to accept teachings which were so strange and totally different from the teachings with which they were familiar' (*c. Cels.* VIII.47).

Here Origen has clearly identified the social function of belief in miracles: it contributes to the establishment and legitimation of a new way of life. This takes place under social conditions to one of which Origen gives particular emphasis: belief in miracles is kept alive by the lower social groups, by 'men from the common people and without education'. (The fact that it is influenced by confrontations between different socio-cultural groups is implicit in the reference to the 'customs of the fathers'). In different terms, primitive Christian miracle stories are collective symbolic actions of lower social classes in which traditionally legitimated ways of life are abandoned. This social function of primitive Christian miracle stories is not identical with their social conditions. It is a fact that primitive Christian belief in miracles also spread in different conditions. It penetrated higher classes and became the common property of different socio-cultural groups. This cannot be understood without some consideration of its social intention.

B. The Social Intention of Primitive Christian Miracle Stories

Primitive Christian miracle stories have a social intention and there is no better description of that intention than the doctrinal formula 'Your faith has saved you.' The miracle stories promise rescue, salvation, redemption. The men and women to whom they are addressed are intended to be moved to join the community which has escaped perdition. Unlike paraenesis, hymns, liturgical formulas and letters, forms whose main function is within the community, they are directed beyond it. They have a missionary intention. This intention can be reconstructed from the analogy of miracles and miracle-workers. It is the task of the apostles to preach and heal (Lk 10.8f.; Mt 10.7.; Mk 3.15; 6.15ff.). Miracles are associated with missionaries (Mk 6.12; 2 Cor 12.12; Heb 2.4). Acts bears witness to this throughout. Origen repeatedly emphasises the missionary significance of miracles (*c. Cels.* I.38; I.46; VIII.47). The absence of a command to perform miracles from the missionary commission in Matthew is one of the striking exceptions. This missionary intention of miracles makes it very probable that the miracle stories have a similar intention. Miracle stories can replace miracles. Acts shows that conversions resulted, not directly from miracles, but from the spread of news of them in narratives: 'It became known throughout all Joppa, and many believed in the Lord' (9.42; cf. 19.17f.). Similar remarks about the dissemination of knowledge of miracles (κηρύσσειν Mk 1.45; 5.20; 7.36; ἀκοή Mk 1.28; λόγος Mk 1.45; Lk 7.17) can be found in the gospels; no conversions are reported, but the language is clearly primitive Christian missionary terminology (cf. Rom 10.10-17; Acts 2.41), which enables us to say that the tellers of miracle stories perform missionary activity. Miracle stories were probably part of primitive Christianity's καινὴ διδαχή. Sergius Paulus believes as the result of a miracle: he is amazed at 'the teaching of the Lord' (Acts 13.12). People acclaim the 'new teaching' (Mk 1.27). 'New teaching' is the label given to Paul's preaching in Athens.

Analytical procedures come to the same conclusion. The culmination of the miracle stories in acclamation, whether this appears in the text or is merely an implicit component of the 'oral framework', gives them a missionary, recruiting character. The demonic confessions are illuminating in this respect. A place which had been missionised had been annexed for the ruler of the universe; other numinous powers had to give way and acknowledge the new lord. Even in defeat they are forced to proclaim, 'These men are servants of the Most High God, who proclaim to you the way of salvation' (Acts 16.17). 'Jesus I know and Paul I know . . .' (Acts 19.15). Their confessions signal a transfer of power. The power of the gods and of the techniques of soothsaying and magic associated with them is at an end (Acts 16.19; 19.18f.). The *most high* God has appeared, who is superior to all other gods and demons. It is no accident that this title appears in two exorcisms (Mk 5.7; Acts 16.17). The demons give way before the power 'which Paul preaches' (Acts 19.13); they give way before the 'new teaching' (Mk 1.27). An equivalent to the casting out of demons in the name of Jesus is baptism in his name.[64] This sets the seal on liberation from demonic power. The important thing is not the power displayed in exorcism but the fact that 'your names are written in heaven' (Lk 10.20).

The missionary use of miracle stories is confirmed further by an analogical reconstruction of their *Sitz im Leben*. Ancient belief in

---

[64] On the connection between baptism and protection against demons cf. O. Böcher, *Dämonenfurcht*, passim.

charismatic miracle-working in many cases has a propagandist character. Vespasian's miracle was used as propaganda for the legitimacy of his title. Philostratus, in his *Vita Apollonii,* makes propaganda for his holy man and his teaching.[65] The miracle stories in Lucian's *Philopseudes* are told to bring a sceptic to 'faith'. It is only the narrative framework which overlays this intention with irony. There is also propaganda in the stories from healing cults: the inscriptions from Epidaurus are as much propaganda for Asclepius as the sacred discourses of Aelius Aristides. A 'missionary' slant in miracle stories is not a unique feature of the New Testament.

Primitive Christian miracle stories are the symbolic actions of a religious minority in ancient society which has set out to conquer the whole world. Mission is their *Sitz im Leben,* the winning of new members their purpose. But this does not take us very far. All Christians were missionaries in the wider sense. All sought adherents for their faith. Only a few were missionaries in the narrower sense, charismatics moving from city to city, founding new communities and reinforcing existing ones. These missionaries were miracle-workers. This raises the question whether these travelling missionaries were the bearers of the miracle tradition. This is occasionally assumed to be the case with Paul's opponents in 2 Corinthians.[66] In 2 Corinthians Paul says in his polemic, 'The signs of a true apostle were performed among you in all patience, with signs and wonders and mighty works' (12.12). This is part of his claim to have worked miracles just like his opponents. Does this mean that their preaching of 'another Jesus' (2 Cor 11.4) included the spreading of miracle stories? Were the synoptic miracle stories contrasted with Paul's preaching? For our purposes the important question is not so much the dispute in Corinth as the general question whether travelling primitive Christian charismatics engaged in missionary work were bearers of the miracle stories? The following arguments are relevant.

i) Unlike the transmission of sayings narrative transmission requires no special charism for its continuation. Words of Jesus, for example, are

---

[65] The missionary, 'kerygmatic', character of the Apollonius traditions has been established most notably by G. Petzke, *Die Traditionen über Apollonius von Tyana und das Neue Testament,* 1970.

[66] D. Georgi, *Gegner,* 210f., 213ff, asserts this indirectly in ascribing to Paul's opponents a θεῖος-ἀνήρ christology, citing the synoptic miracle stories as evidence. His view has been widely accepted. The reader is referred to H.W. Kuhn's comprehensive essay, 'Der irdische Jesus bei Paulus als traditionsgeschichtliches und theologisches Problem', *ZThK* 67 (1970), 295-320, which contains a bibliography.

frequently phrased in the first person. The transmitter here takes the place of Jesus. He identifies himself with him. Jesus speaks through him and gives his human words authority. We may think of the 'Amen' formula. When, according to 2 Cor 13.3, Paul's opponents boast that Jesus is speaking through them, this is unlikely to be a reference to miracle stories. We should probably think instead of sayings in the 'I' style. Stories are told in the third person. The narrator distances himself from the narrative. He can establish the distance in introductory and accompanying remarks. He speaks about Jesus. Jesus does not speak through him. Anyone with a gift for storytelling can retell such stories. It does not require a special religious charism.

ii) A further consideration is that the miracle stories are not permeated by the ethos of the primitive Christian wandering charismatics. They lack the idea of discipleship and the ethical demands connected with it. They lack an eschatology. This cannot be just the influence of the genre. It would be perfectly possible to call the cured to discipleship and place them under an obligation to preach. Instead they are usually sent back into their former world. There is scarcely a trace of a radical change of life or of the strict ethical demands to which the primitive Christian missionaries were subject (cf the commissioning discourse in Mt 10 and the Didache). E. Trocmé was so impressed by the absence of specifically Christian ideas that he was prepared to postulate that even non-Christians may have been the disseminators of many of the miracle stories.[67] It is a fact that the miracle stories are in many respects ordinary popular tales and show no signs of being connected with such an unusual way of life as that of the first Christian missionaries.

iii) There is also little indication that the miracle stories were spread by miracle-*workers*. True, it has been suggested that they served as instructions for Christian miracle-workers.[68] The instructions for exorcisms (Mk 9.28f.), however, were given, not through the public miracle, but after it, away from the public eye: the disciples asked Jesus κατ' ἰδίαν about the technique of exorcism. A striking feature of this incident is that the means of exorcism recommended is prayer, which does not occur at all in the preceding miracle story. The most important miracle-working techniques, prayer (Mk 9.28; 11.23f.; cf. Jas 5.15; Acts 9.40) and the name of Jesus (Mk 9.39; Mt 7.22; Lk 10.17; Acts 3.6 etc.), do not appear in the miracle stories. If miracle-workers and the tellers of miracle stories had been the same people, we would expect a greater assimilation of Jesus' miracle-working techniques to the procedures of primitive Christian miracle-workers.

In addition to these analytic arguments we have the fact that the positive evaluation of explicit comments about the spreading of

---

[67] E. Trocmé, *Formation*, 37-44. M. Dibelius, *TG*, 79, also stresses the secular character of the novellas.
[68] Cf. M. Dibelius, *TG*, 83ff.

miracle stories also tells against the identification of miracle-workers and tellers of miracle-stories. Nowhere do the miracle-workers describe their miracles. It is always other people who appear as the disseminators of the new 'reports'. The statement after the raising of Tabitha by Peter, 'and it became known throughout all Joppa' (Acts 9.42), implies that all sorts of people talked about the miracle. Miracle-workers do not talk about miracles; they perform them. They leave propaganda to others. This is made clear in a very attractive way in the apocryphal Abgar saga. In this Abgar writes to Jesus:

> 'I have heard about you and your healings, and how you perform them without drugs or herbs. For according to the reports, you make the blind see, the lame walk, cleanse lepers, drive out unclean spirits and demons, cure those suffering from chronic illnesses and raise the dead. And when I heard all these things about you, I came to the conclusion that you are either God himself and have come down from heaven to do this or the Son of God if you do it. For this reason I am writing.' (Euseb. *hist. ecc.* I.13.6-7).

The missionary intention of the stories of Jesus' miracles is clear. As a result of them Abgar believes. We are not told who he heard them from, but missionary charismatics seem not to be envisaged since Abgar is not confronted with them until later. After the ascension the apostle Thaddaeus is sent to him. He performs healings.

> 'And Abgar was amazed that he saw the same things as he had heard ascribed to Jesus performed before him by his disciple Thaddeus, who cured him without drugs or herbs, and not only him, but Abdus son of Abdus, who had gout. Abdus came too, fell at his feet and was cured by prayer with the laying on of hands. And he cured many other people of the town in the same way, performing mighty miracles and proclaiming the word of God' (Eus. *hist ecc.* I.13.18).

It is certainly possible that miracle stories formed part of the preaching of miracle-workers. But the stories clearly preceded them. They are missionary in character, but belong to the preliminaries of mission; they prepare for the appearance of the primitive Christian wandering and miracle-working charismatics. They might be compared with the posters and leaflets used to announce an evangelical meeting. Of course the posters display the same message as is later proclaimed at the meetings, but it is quite possible to distinguish missionary work and publicity for the work. Publicity for primitive Christian missionary work was spread by Christians who were not themselves missionaries. Occasionally they may have been only sympathisers with Christianity.[69] Miracle stories were told before and after the appearance of primitive Christian missionaries. They created the climate of tense expectations without which the charism of working miracles would not have been able to unfold.

We may here briefly summarise our investigations of ancient and primitive Christian belief in miracles by means of the sociology of religion and the sociology of literature. Whereas healing and oracular sites are concerned with the maintenance of the accepted order and way of life and sorcery and magic represent an individualistic reaction to growing social disintegration, belief in charismatic miracles embodies the claim of a new way of life. This process is on the one hand shaped by social forces and on the other fuelled by social intentions. The intention of the primitive Christian miracle stories is to bear witness to a revelation of God which is directed to the whole world and seeks to bring all human beings to recognise that revelation. At the same time, however, they are influenced by the concerns of the lower classes in society. Between the intention and the conditioning there exists a hermeneutical conflict. A functionalist analysis cannot solve this conflict, but can go beyond it. If we define miracle stories as collective symbolic actions in which a new way of life is opened up, this function transcends both the social conditions in which the primitive Christian belief in miracles was moulded and the intentions it attributes to itself.

---

[69] M. Dibelius, *TG*, 70ff., postulated 'narrators' for the novellas, whom he distinguished from the preachers, the guardians of the paradigms. He realised, in my view correctly, that the tradition of the word and the narrative tradition were probably transmitted in different social settings.

CHAPTER II

THE FUNCTION OF PRIMITIVE CHRISTIAN MIRACLE STORIES IN THE HISTORY OF ANCIENT RELIGION

When we treat primitive Christian miracle stories as symbolic actions in which a new way of life is opened up our analysis acquires a historical aspect. We are now no longer examining their function in a society conceived of as relatively static, but their significance in a process of historical transformation which profoundly restructured ancient society and its culture. In this section this transformation will be studied in terms of religious developments. The question is: what is the place of belief in miracles and miracle stories in this process of transformation? To what extent are they continuous with earlier developments and to what extent do they embody something really new? The question opens a further dimension of the hermeneutical conflict. According to their own self-understanding, primitive Christian miracle stories were created by an incomparable event, but the techniques of comparative religious studies subject them to analogies and contexts of development which relativise this self-understanding.

A. Religious Influences on Primitive Christian Miracle Stories

Primitive Christian miracle stories are undoubtedly conditioned by their time. But in this context everything depends on what is meant by 'time'. It may be the time of the 1st century AD or the whole of antiquity, the Hellenistic period or the Roman. There is far too little differentiation here, as when the 'rampant jungle of ancient credulity with regard to miracles' is invoked,[1] or when it is apparently accepted that 'miracle-workers were a normal phenomenon' in the ancient world and that 'miracle stories were thoroughly familiar to the ancient world in general'.[2] Assertions of this sort are problematic in this broad form. Graeco-Roman antiquity comprises a whole millennium, and within this period there was

---

[1] G. Klein, 'Wunderglaube und Neues Testament', *Ärgernisse* (1970), 13-57, quotation from 28.
[2] W. Schmithals, *Wunder und Glaube*, 1970, 9.

undoubtedly a history of belief in miracles. There was a change in its form and intensity. This change of form will at least be outlined in order to bring out the position of primitive Christian belief in miracles within the religious developments of ancient society. Three periods can be distinguished, the archaic and classical period (until c. 300 BC), the Hellenistic period (until about the birth of Christ) and late antiquity, which is divided into two periods by the crisis of the 3rd century. Belief in miracles has a characteristic profile in each period.[3]

It is relatively easy to distinguish between the θεῖοι ἄνδρες of the archaic and classical periods and the God-men of the Hellenistic world. The oldest θεῖοι ἄνδρες resemble ecstatic shamanism (comparable figures in Palestine are the miracle-working prophets Elijah and Elisha).[4] Some of these are now little more than shadowy figures: Melampas and Abaris, Epimenides (7th century BC) and Aristeas (6th century BC). These miracle-workers and expiatory priests sent their souls on journeys, performed healings and acted as seers. They acquired historical significance in Pythagoreanism. Pythagoras (6th century BC) and Empedocles (5th century BC) continued this type. They held a philosophico-religious doctrine of salvation and expiation and sought to liberate people from their unsaved condition. There are miraculous traditions attached to both. Pythagoras[5] possessed miraculous knowledge (for example about the form of the previous existence of himself and others), he had power over animals, commanded wind and waves, could transport himself over great distances in an instant, banished an epidemic and performed cures by means of music and song. Crowds of people seeking help flocked to Empedocles. He healed them and is even said to have raised the

---

[3] R.M. Grant, *Miracles and Natural Law*, 41, assumes that ancient belief in the miraculous rose and fell cyclically: 'The credulity of the Greeks and Romans has often been exaggerated in modern times, and we shall see that credulity not only varies from person to person and from group to group, but also has a cyclical history of its own like the fever chart of a sick man.' The Athenian enlightenment and Hellenism are, according to Grant, the least superstitious periods. In between and afterwards credulity about miracles increases. M.P. Nilsson, *Griechischer Glaube*, 1950, 210, on the other hand, sees a great change, 'from rationalism to mysticism, from the clear logical line of Greek thought to belief in the miraculous, the supernatural, the incomprehensible'.

[4] Cf. M.P. Nilsson, *Geschichte* I, 582-87. W. Burkert, 'ΓΟΗΣ. Zum griechischen "Schamanismus"', *RhM* 102 (1962), 36-55; M. Hengel, *Charismatic Leader*, 25.

[5] Pythagoras' miracles are in Iambl. *vita Pythag*. 60-67; 134-36; 140-44 and Porphyr. *Vita Pythag*. 23-31. On the sources cf. I. Lévy, *Recherches sur les sources de la légende de Pythagore*, 1926, and *La légende de Pythagore de Grèce en Palestine*, in which Lévy undoubtedly overestimates the influence of the Pythagoras legend on Judaism and Christianity. On this see M.J. Lagrange, 'Les légendes pythagoriciennes et l'évangile', *RB* 45 (1936), 481ff.; 46 (1937), 5ff.

dead. He regarded himself as a human being resembling the gods. No more than in the case of Jesus should the miracles here be seen as isolated phenomena. They are part of a new understanding of salvation: the superiority of the soul over the physical is demonstrated by its miraculous power. The transition to the Hellenistic type of the θεῖος ἀνήρ is marked by the doctor Menecrates of Syracuse (second half of the 4th century BC),[6] who believed himself to be Zeus, cured epileptics and made disciples of them. In him the sense of divinity reaches a peak. However, while it may be a pathological case, it is nonetheless characteristic that his 'superhumanity' had successors – notably among politicians and generals. Nicostratus of Argos, his disciple, went into battle as Heracles; the tyrant Nicagoras got himself up as Hermes, and so on.[7] The miracle-working 'God-man' becomes the historically active superman. It is now kings and mercenary captains who are regarded as 'divine'. Ultimately anyone can count as 'divine' if their superhuman gifts create a numinous aura round them: statesmen, poets, philosophers, athletes, doctors.[8] The only charismatic miracle-worker of this period, the slave king Eunus, can be clearly distinguished from comparable miracle-workers of other periods. His activity is political and military. He thought of himself as a Hellenistic monarch; the Seleucid model is still recognisable in many features of his administration. We previously placed him in the same class as the messianic miracle-working prophets of the 1st century AD. Now we must stress the differences. Eunus legitimated his political claims with 'miracles', but he established his claims by realistic means. He did not wait for the intervention of the gods; he fought. He did not prophesy miracles. On the whole he is closer to the Maccabees than to the miracle-working prophets of the 1st century AD, whose concerns were primarily religious. The Hellenistic 'Godmen' are a living example of euhemerism. Extraordinary human abilities are overlaid by a divine aura.

At the same time a structural change took place in the area of

---

[6] Cf. O. Weinreich, *Menekrates, Zeus und Salmoneus,* 1933; M.P. Nilsson, Geschichte II, 131.

[7] Cf. M.P. Nilsson, Geschichte II, 131. H. Bengtson, *Griechen und Perser,* 1965, 260: 'Phenomena such as Clearchus and Menecrates render intelligible the establishment of Hellenistic divine kingship by Alexander and the Hellenistic princes.'

[8] Cf. H. Windisch, *Paulus und Christus,* 1934, 25-59. The popular reference to a universally found type, the θεῖος ἀνήρ is not enough to reduce the uniqueness of the miracle-worker Jesus. A charismatic miracle-worker may be called a θεῖος ἀνήρ, but this does not make every θεῖος ἀνήρ a miracle-worker. And all too disparate figures are classed as examples of this type: Plato and Eunus, Hannibal and Jesus, Augustus and Antonius. Cf. the survey in M. Smith, *Prolegomena,* 174-99. L. Bieler's classical study of the 'divine man' makes too few historical distinctions.

divination. The oracles which had been powerful in the classical period lost their (political) influence.[9] Plutarch, himself a priest of Apollo at Delphi, complains at the end of the Hellenistic period of their decline (*de def. orac.*): originally two priestesses were on duty at Delphi, with a third in reserve, but in the 1st century AD one was enough. The decline of the oracular shrines was connected with the rise of an art of divination which flourished alongside scientific astronomy; this was astrology,[10] the fascination of which derived from its 'scientific' character. The charisma of office associated with the oracles was increasingly replaced by the techniques of 'research into the future'. Just as in the field of the traditions of the 'Godman' the historically effective man now came into prominence, the typical figures in divination were the professional 'researchers'. Even Jewish apocalyptic betrays the influence of its period in this respect: charismatic prophecy gives way to higher wisdom and learning.[11]

There is a comparable change in the field of sorcery. Naturally sorcery had always existed. Plato's *Laws* (932e-933e) and the imprecatory tablets from the 5th-4th centuries BC are evidence of its existence in classical Greece. All this survived into Hellenism. What is new is the permeation of these magical practices by science. They were now systematised and given a speculative basis by a pre-scientific physics of force.[12] Around 200 BC Bolus of Mendes wrote περὶ τῶν συμπαθειῶν καὶ ἀντιπαθειῶν and investigated the 'forces' of various things, animals, plants and stones. Popular magic acquired a veneer of 'physics' from this doctrine of sympathy. Here again irrational belief in miracles combined with rational elements.

Such a combination is always at the same time an individualisation of charismatic or institutionally based extraordinary methods of coming to terms with existence. What can be achieved more or less by means of a given method is in principle accessible to anyone. This shift towards individualism can also be seen in the healing cults, although they are among the most constant phenomena in the history of religion. Archaeological finds testify to their existence in the 2nd millennium BC and Lourdes demonstrates their vitality in the present. In the Hellenistic period the healing gods came into sharper prominence. The inscriptions from

---

[9] On this cf. M.P. Nilsson, *Geschichte* II, 97ff.; 447ff.

[10] On the emergence of astrology and in particular on the influence of Greek rationalism on it, cf. M.P. Nilsson, Geschichte II, 256-67.

[11] Cf. M. Hengel, *Judaism and Hellenism*, I, 1974, 202-254.

[12] Cf. M.P. Nilsson, *Geschichte* II, 512ff.

Epidaurus date from the second half of the 4th century BC. Here votive inscriptions have been skilfully turned into a presentation of the healing cult. This is a sign of increased self-confidence. It is characteristic that at the beginning of the 3rd century BC Ptolemy I should have wanted to unite Greeks and Egyptians in the cult of Serapis and chose for this purpose a god whose reputation was for healing,[13] and whose central sanctuary in Canopus flourished throughout the Hellenistic period. In the Ptolemaic sphere of influence in the Aegean subsidiaries were soon established (for example in Delos).[14] The rise to prominence of Asclepius and Serapis is undoubtedly connected with the individualistic tendencies of the time. The old gods had become too much representations of states and cities and were remote from the needs of individuals. Though the Epicureans criticised the religious healing cults, both they and the followers of Asclepius had a common link in the individualistic trend of the Hellenistic period.

This period may well have been the least superstitious period of antiquity,[15] even if we have to allow for the continued existence in concealment of an undercurrent of the usual superstitions and belief in miracles. However that may be a change sets in with the beginning of late antiquity. Popular belief in miracles and superstition revived. Whereas in Hellenism belief in miracles was permeated with rational elements, now the relationship was reversed. 'Scientific' astrology and dynamics made all sorts of belief in miracles respectable even in educated circles, while the new speculations were at the same time popularised. An increasing irrationalism began to flood in to Romano-Greek culture.[16]

We shall sketch this change first in the field of religious healing cults. Despite all the continuity of religious development, there are four points here at which new emphases can be detected:

i) There is a change of literary style. The Epidaurus inscriptions are curt and popular. The testimonies from the imperial period become increasingly detailed. The account of the healing becomes literary. In the Apellas stele (SIG[3] III, 1170 = Herzog No. 79) the various cures are listed in

---

[13] Cf. M.P. Nilsson, *Geschichte* II, 147ff.
[14] Cf. O. Weinreich, *Neue Urkunden zur Sarapis-Religion,* 1919; M.P. Nilsson, *Geschichte* II, 115ff.
[15] R.M. Grant, *Miracles and Natural Law,* 41.
[16] Cf. R.M. Grant, 'Miracles and Mythology', *ZRGG* 3 (1951), 124f.: 'Nevertheless we can, I think, distinguish between the Hellenistic age and the period of the Roman empire. In the earlier period there was considerable scientific progress, some diffusion of the results of science, and widespread belief in relatively scientific explanations of the working of the universe. In the first century BC the tide begins to turn, and we find much greater emphasis on irrational and religious factors more than on divine laws as expressed in nature.' He refers to 'the changing attitude towards miracles'.

detail. The Imhotep aretalogy is literary in character (*Pap. Ox.* XI.1381), as is the suppliant's diary incorporated into Aristides' 'Sacred Discourses' (*or.* 47-52).

ii) This stylistic change is a symptom of the increasing frequency of educated people among the adherents of the Asclepius cult. Claudius' decree that slaves abandoned in the Roman Asclepium should be set free after being cured shows the sociological composition of the healing cult in the early Empire. This is reflected in the terse Roman inscriptions (SIG, 3rd ed. 1173). Then there comes a change. 'While in this period it is indeed people from the lower classes who follow him (Asclepius), this soon changes in the course of the 1st century of our era and it is the most educated and the most significant intellectual figures who now turn to Asclepius.'[17] The most famous pagan orators of late antiquity, Aelius Aristides (2nd century AD) and Libanius (4th century AD) were followers of Asclepius.

iii) Simultaneously with the stylistic and sociological change there comes a change in religious attitude. The Asclepius cult becomes increasingly permeated by a mystical piety. Aelius Aristides describes his relationship with Asclepius in terms taken from the mystery religions.[18] He describes the reception of medical advice in the following words: 'The revelation was beyond doubt, just as in a thousand other cases the manifestation of the god could be felt with complete certainty. We felt his touch and were aware of his coming in a state in between sleep and waking . . . What human being could describe this state in words? Those who are initiates know it and recognise it.' (*or.* 48.32). Aristides is a representative of a paganism which has become pietistic.[19] One sees how an Asclepius worshipped in this way could become a rival of Christ. The religious assimilation to the mystery religions reflected an institutional link between the healing cult of Epidaurus and the Eleusinian mysteries in the 3rd-4th centuries: we know of some priests of Asclepius in this period who simultaneously held office in Eleusis.[20]

iv) Finally, a point relating the history of medicine. In classical Greece and in Hellenism there had been a form of empirical medicine. This science of medicine increasingly declined in the Roman Empire;[21] though there continued to be doctors using empirical methods (for example the sceptic Sextus Empiricus). It is nonetheless symptomatic that the physician Galen received his training in the Asclepium in Pergamum, where

---

[17] O. Weinreich, *AH*, 31.

[18] Cf. M.P. Nilsson, *Geschichte* II, 539. On Asclepius in late antiquity cf. F.J. Dölger, *Der Heiland*, 1950, 241-72; H. Lietzmann, *Geschichte der alten Kirche* II, 3rd ed. 1961, 14f.

[19] On this change in religious sensibility which appears in Aelius Aristides, cf. C. Bonner, 'Some Phases of Religious Feeling in Later Paganism', *HThR* 30 (1937), 119-40.

[20] Cf. M.P. Nilsson, *Geschichte* II, 321.

[21] I cite just two comments. H. Sigerist, 'Die historische Betrachtung der Medizin', *Archiv für die Geschichte der Medizin* 13 (1926), 1-19, speaks of a 'period of decadence. . . . One highly significant phenomenon is . . . that in this last period religious medicine comes into great prominence' (18). E. Stemplinger, *Volksmedizin*, 2: 'From the time of the Roman Empire popular medicine completely swamped medical science.'

at the same time Aelius Aristides was cultivating diseases and pious feelings.

Despite the considerable continuity within these developments in the healing cults, they too show change. They flourished once more in the Empire and acquired growing religious importance.

The change through time in the field of divination is also unmistakable. Some oracles experienced new popularity, especially in Asia Minor. The oracle of Colophon seems to have been abandoned, but in the 2nd-3rd century AD it once more became famous.[22] Another instructive example is the success of the 'lying prophet' Alexander of Abonuteichus in the 2nd century AD, who opened a profitable oracle business in his native town.[23] According to the estimates of his enemy Lucian (*Alex.* 23f.) he made 70,000-80,000 drachmas a year, the more remarkable in view of the fact that oracles had to compete with other divinatory techniques. It was not until this period that astrology became popular. Unusually, this can be precisely dated, since the popularisation of astrology became possible only with the introduction of the Julian calendar in 46 BC, when now even non-specialists could make astrological calculations.[24]

The growth of magic fits into the general picture. As early as the end of the Roman Republic the circle around Nigidius Figulus, which cultivated Pythagorean traditions and which had connections with Cicero became prominent.[25] Another sign of a general increase in belief in magic, and not just among the upper classes, is the strikingly sudden increase in the 1st century AD of simple amulets, which must come from people in the lower classes. C. Bonner, in his survey, speaks of a 'marked change'.[26]

The clearest example of this change through time, however, is the charismatic miracle-workers. The last representative of this type, Menecrates, lived in the 4th century BC. If we except King 'Eunus', who is more like a Hellenistic mercenary captain than the charismatic miracle-workers, for 300 years we hear nothing of charismatic miracle-workers. Our sources may of course be incomplete, but even if we assume that there were more charismatic miracle-workers than we know of, they can hardly have had a very large following. In the 1st century AD this changes. Particularly in the eastern part of the Roman Empire charismatic

---

[22] Cf. M.P. Nilsson, *Geschichte* II, 455ff.
[23] Cf. M.P. Nilsson, *Geschichte* II, 452ff.
[24] M.P. Nilsson, *Geschichte* II, 465ff.
[25] Cf. M.P. Nilsson, *Geschichte* II, 235, 400.
[26] C. Bonner, *Studies in Magical Amulets*, 6.

miracle-workers appear. Apollonius of Tyana comes from eastern Asia Minor. Jarbas is an Indian sage whom he met on his travels (*vita* III.39). Plutarch tells of a miracle-worker on the Red Sea who existed almost without food, lived with nymphs and demons and possessed the gift of prophecy (*Mor.* V, 421 Aff.). The only one of any historical importance is Apollonius of Tyana,[27] a reviver of Pythagoreanism, a religious reformer, who believed in a monotheistic religion, unbloody sacrifices and an ascetic life. His claim to be a follower of Pythagoras, more than 400 years before him, reflects the religious situation of the time. There was no example of a combination of the charism of miracle-working and a doctrine of salvation in the previous 400 years. At roughly the same time as him Simon Magus was active in Samaria. We have no reliable information about his intellectual environment, but the Church fathers' treatment of him as the leader of the Gnostics and the claim of later Gnostics to be his disciples implies that he must have been more than a 'sorcerer', which is what he is presented as in many Christian writings (cf. Acts 8).

In Palestine at this time there were a number of charismatic miracle-workers in addition to Jesus. The messianic prophets promised a return of the great miracles of Israel's early period. Miracle-working rabbis emphasised their teachings by miracles. Rabbi Ḥanina ben Dosa (c. 70-100 AD), performed healings and proved himself immune to snake-bite. Rabbi Eliezer ben Hyrcanus (c. 90-130 AD) reinforced one of his doctrinal decisions with miracles: he made a carob tree uproot itself and take root again. The charismatic miracle-worker Jesus appeared at a time when miracle-workers of various types were unusually active in Palestine. However in examining this situation various types of phenomena must be carefully distinguished.

i) Literary evocations of the miracle-workers of Israel's past must be distinguished from the appearance of new miracle-workers. Hellenistic Judaism in particular portrayed these classical miracle-workers of Israel as 'divine men': Artapanus makes Moses perform a door-opening miracle (Euseb. *praep. ev.* IX.27),[28] Philo in his *vita* presents Moses as a prophet endowed with divine power, demonstrating his divine power in his miracles.[29] The much more general ancient idea of the θεῖος ἀνήρ (θεῖος

---

[27] From the extensive literature I shall mention only two more recent works, G. Petzke, *Die Traditionen über Apollonius von Tyana und das Neue Testament*, 1970. On the miracle stories and form-critical issues, and on the position of Apollonius in the history of religion, D. Esser, *Formgeschichtliche Studien*, 1969, esp. 35-111, is useful.

[28] Cf. O. Weinreich, *Türöffnung*, 298ff.; L. Bieler, *Theios Aner* II, 30ff.

[29] L. Bieler, *Theios Aner* II, 34-35. For details D. Georgi, *Gegner*, 145ff.

referrred to anything which produced a superhuman, divine aura) was here firmly reconnected with miracles, not because miracles were an essential part of the conception, but because they occurred frequently in the Israelite tradition being interpreted. No doubt this evocation of previous ages is part of the transformation of belief in miracles at the end of the 1st century BC: Apollonius returns to Pythagoras, the messianic prophets to Moses and Joshua. It would however be a mistake to take it for granted that the interest of Hellenistic Judaism in the miracle-workers of the past was due to the appearance of comparable figures in the Hellenistic Judaism of the period.

ii) A distinction must also be made between charismatic miracle-working and traditions of exorcism or healing. The latter traditions are close to popular medicine. True, they were traced back to great charismatic figures of the past: Solomon was regarded as a great exorcist (Jos. *ant.* VII.2.5; *Test. Sal.*); in Qumran reports were current of exorcisms performed by Abraham and David (*Genesis Apokryphon* XX.16-32; *Prayer of Nabonid*). This, however, does not justify assuming the existence of charismatic exorcists, but only of methods of exorcism[30] which were attributed to the great charismatics of the past because in the present the charism was absent. The absence of any reference to exorcists in the major Qumran writings shows how slight their religious significance was. This is a 'scholastic' tradition. Josephus reports (*bell.* 8.6) that the Essenes cured the sick and for this purpose had studied ancient books. Jub 10.12f. confirms the existence of such books: they were said to have been written by Noah after he had been enlightened by angels about drugs and roots. Therefore books were studied and teaching given about remedies. 'Disciples' of the Pharisees cast out demons (Mt 12.27). These exorcists and healers can be distinguished from charismatic miracle-workers.

iii) Among the Jewish charismatic miracle-workers we must distinguish between miracle-working prophets and miracle-working rabbis. P. Fiebig's view that in the time of Jesus rabbinic teachers were regarded as miracle-workers and that 'miracle stories were common' has encountered justified opposition.[31] A. Schlatter went so far in his opposition as to date the earliest miracles by rabbis to a period no earlier than the end of the 2nd century AD. This is refuted by the miracles of Ḥanina ben Dosa and Eliezer ben Hyrcanus, but he is right when he says, 'From the beginning of the 3rd century on there was a steady increase in miracle stories, both

---

[30] A. Dupont-Sommer, *Exorcismes*, 246ff.

[31] P. Fiebig, *Jüdische Wundergeschichten*, 72. His view is criticised independently by A. Schlatter (*Das Wunder in der Synagoge*, 1912) and M. Smith (*Tannaitic Parallels to the Gospel*, 1951), who points out that miracle stories are almost completely absent from the Tannaitic literature (84). The assumption of particular credulity for miracles among the Jews is criticised also by L. Blau (*Das altjüdische Zauberwesen*, 1898, repr. 1970, 28) and C.G. Montefiore, *Rabbinic Literature and Gospel Teachings*, 2nd ed. 1970, 240: 'I see no adequate evidence that the Jews in the age of Jesus or the Rabbis suffered from *Wundersucht*, an exaggerated or unseemly desire for miracles and signs.'

in number and in elaboration, parallel to the phenomena we find in ecclesiastical literature.'[32] In Babylonian Judaism the rabbis were regarded as miracle-workers in the Sassanid period.[33] This branch of the miracle tradition is still alive today. One type of Jewish joke is about the 'miracles' of the rabbis. The rabbis were thus slow to accept belief in miracles, but miracles were part of the idea of a prophet at a very early date. Prophets promising miracles appear in Judaism before miracle-working rabbis.

The end of the 1st century BC is marked by a general increase in the intensity of belief in miracles. The belief takes on a new form. The balance of rational and irrational elements in Hellenistic belief in miracles tips towards the irrational. The 'divine man' is no longer the one who distinguishes himself by extraordinary achievements in the historical field. He performs paradoxical miracles. In his whole manner he resembles the charismatic miracle-workers of the archaic period.[34] He often deliberately takes the early period as a model. One could speak of a renaissance of belief in miracles. It is as though the ancient world were turning back to past ages in order to follow new impulses. The charismatic miracle-workers of the 1st century AD undoubtedly signal the beginnings of a change in attitudes to life. They pave the way for the most important currents in religious developments in late antiquity. Apollonius stands at the beginning of Neo-Pythagoreanism, which continues in Neo-Platonism. Simon Magus is revered in Gnostic circles. Jesus paves the way for Christianity. About historical conditions which brought about this change to a new irrationalism there can be no more than conjecture. The spread of the Roman Empire across the whole of the Mediterranean world may have been a factor. R.M. Grant suggests, 'Perhaps one factor in the process was the concentration of power at Rome, combined with a decline in individual initiative as the republic gradually developed into the empire.'[35] This is compatible with the suggestion made above that belief in the miraculous was a reaction of subjugated peoples. Nonetheless the rise of the new irrationalism remains a riddle. The early Roman Empire was one of the most

---

[32] A. Schlatter, *Das Wunder in der Synagoge*, 57.

[33] On this development cf. J. Neusner, *A History of the Jews in Babylonia*, vol. 3, 102ff.; vol. 4, 334ff.; vol. 5, 174ff.

[34] L. Bieler, *Theios Aner* I, 3, refers in this connection to 'late antiquity, which resembled early Greece in more than one respect'. This impression is naturally in part the result of the fact that the evidence for the early Greek miracle-workers comes partly from late antiquity, which 'also depicted the lives of the ancient sages after the pattern of those of their own θεῖοι φιλόσοφοι' (3).

[35] R.M. Grant, *Miracles and Natural Law*, 61.

stable and peaceful periods in the history of Europe. It would be short-sighted to interpret the new irrationalism as a phenomenon of crisis.

On the other hand it must be admitted that in the relatively peaceful and stable period of the first two centuries the irrationalism which first appeared at the beginning of the 1st century was unable to strike roots. There continued to be rationalist movements alongside it. In his dialogues Lucian mocked his contemporaries' belief in the miraculous. Oenomaus of Gadara mocked the oracles, and Sextus Empiricus once more brought together all the arguments of scepticism. Even where increased irrationalism was notable – for example in Plutarch's development[36]– it remained within bounds, without eccentricity or fanaticism. There was no decisive change before the great social and political crisis of the 3rd century AD.[37] Within this century the multiplicity of intellectual currents was reduced to Neo-Platonism and Christianity, both currents in which the new irrationalism had become the determining factor. The Neo-Platonists Porphyry, Iamblichus and Proclus were *theourgoi*. Their philosophy of magic sublimated the idea of putting pressure on the gods into a mystical way of salvation. Porphyry (3rd century) is still very restrained in his attitude: he believes that true mystical ecstasy takes place without *theourgia*. In the 4th century these reservations disappear. Philosophy becomes totally identified with occult theosophy. Nevertheless, despite the mysticism, a specifically philosophical element is preserved, the idea of self-redemption. While the longing for redemption might be equally strong in Neo-Platonism and Christianity, in 'philosophy' it was brought about through human knowledge and ability, by *theourgia*. In Christianity, on the other hand, the charismatic element of belief in the miraculous remained decisive[38]– all the more because all other forms of belief in the miraculous were rejected.

---

[36] Cf. M.P. Nilsson, *Geschichte* II, 383ff.

[37] On this crisis cf. M. Rostovzeff, *The Social and Economic History of the Roman Empire*, 2nd rev. ed. Oxford 1957, I, 494-501, who explains it as the result of antagonism between town and country. F. Millar, *The Roman Empire and its Neighbours*, 1967, considers various social and political factors. The crisis of the 3rd century is placed in a general historical context by F. Altheim, *Gesicht vom Abend und Morgen*, 1955. See also A. Alföldi, *Studien zur Geschichte der Weltkrise des 3. Jahrhunderts nach Christus*, 1967. On the intellectual situation in paganism in this period cf. J. Geffcken, *Der Ausgang des griechisch-römischen Heidentums*, 1929.

[38] There is a survey of developments up to the victory of Constantine in J. Speigl, 'Die Rolle des Wunders im vorkonstantinischen Christentum', *ZKTh* 92 (1970), 287-312. Cf. also H. Schlingensiepen, *Die Wunder des Neuen Testaments. Wege und Abwege ihrer Deutung in der alten Kirche bis zur Mitte des fünften Jahrhunderts*, 1933.

The process thus led to an intellectual alternative of Neo-Platonic *theourgia* and the Christian gift of miracles. Christianity prevailed, but in the process took over many elements from Neo-Platonism. Conversely, the development of Neo-Platonism was influenced by its duel with Christianity. Iamblichus' omission or even refutation of Porphyry's criticisms of religion is certainly in part a consequence of that struggle by late paganism to assert itself against the rising Christianity: opponents must not be given any arguments against one's own position.[39] Primitive Christian belief in the miraculous thus has a crucial role in the religious development of late antiquity. It stands at the beginning of the 'new' irrationalism of that age. Our brief outline of this development may have done something to correct the widespread picture of an ancient belief in the miraculous which has no history. What we have found here is not a rampant jungle of ancient credulity with regard to miracles, but a process of historical transformation in which forms and patterns of belief in the miraculous succeed one another. If we accept this picture, we must firmly reject assertions that primitive Christian belief in the miraculous represented nothing unusual in the context of its period. What is genuinely unusual is the general intensification and expansion of belief in the miraculous around the end of the 1st century BC. Another unusual phenomenon is the growth of belief in the miraculous in primitive Christianity and the polemic against other forms of ancient belief in the miraculous. The period itself cannot be held solely responsible for this belief in the miraculous. Conversely, we must consider the responsibility of primitive Christianity for the period's belief in the miraculous. For primitive Christian belief in the miraculous was one of the catalysts of the general belief in the miraculous in late antiquity.

B. The Historical Intention of Primitive Christian Miracle Stories

The primitive Christian miracle stories regard themselves as testimonies to a unique event in the past. They have a 'historical' intention.[40] They are aware of the uniqueness of the miracles they recount. The narrators know that where all doctors not only have failed (this is a familiar trope), but have even done harm, Jesus heals. The uniqueness of the miracles is claimed when the crowd

---

[39] J. Geffcken, *Ausgang*, 103ff.
[40] As J. Roloff, *Kerygma*, 111ff, has rightly emphasised, though one may disagree with the detail of his argument.

shouts in acclamation, 'We have never seen anything like this' (Mk 2.12; cf. Mt 9.33). The Fourth Gospel insists, 'From eternity it has been unheard of that anyone should open the eyes of a blind man' (9.32). It makes Jesus speak of his miracles as feats 'which no-one else does' (15.24; cf. 3.2). The intensification of the miracles in the course of their transmission could also be connected with this sense of uniqueness, as could the development of analogies and comparisons with non-Christian miracle stories. In Jn 5.1ff. the contrast implied with ancient healing shrines is unmistakable.[41] Jn 2.1ff. is probably trying to outdo other wine miracles.[42] Lk 7.11ff. could be modelled on similar ancient miracle stories (*vita Apoll.* IV 45; Apuleius, *flor.* 19). The stories of liberation from prison in Acts (12.3ff.; 16.22ff.) may be setting out to rival similar liberation miracles in Dionysus traditions.[43] In order to do full justice to this sense of being something unique as regards miracles, primitive Christianity had to tell new miracle stories, elaborate old ones and outdo any rivals. The stories which may perhaps be regarded as attempts to outdo rivals only appear in the later tradition, but all these developments show a sense of the uniqueness of Jesus' miracles.[44] Only retrospective study can relativise this uniqueness by setting them within a larger historical context, and this relativistic approach is in the sharpest possible conflict with the historical intention of the miracle stories. They set out to be evidence of an absolutely valid revelation. Although historical study can in no sense either legitimate or establish this claim, it must nonetheless take note of it as a datum present in the texts. It can do more: it can allow it relative legitimacy. The primitive Christian miracle stories stand out from their historical context as something new, unique and individual. This newness can in no sense substantiate their claim, but it makes it intelligible. This new element must be examined first in Jesus and then in primitive Christianity.

1. Jesus' Miracles

There is no doubt that Jesus worked miracles, healed the sick and cast out demons, but the miracle stories reproduce these historical events in an intensified form. However, this enhancement of the historical and factual begins with Jesus himself. For Jesus too the

---

[41] K.H. Rengstorf, Die Anfänge der Auseinandersetzung zwischen Christusglaube und Asklepiosfrömmigkeit, 1953. I was unable to obtain A. Duprez, *Jésus et les Deux Guérisseurs. A Propos de Jean V*, 1970.

[42] For critical comments on this, H. Noetzel, *Christus und Dionysos*, 1960.

[43] O. Weinreich, *Türöffnung*, 309-41.

[44] For a different view, W. Schmithals, *Wunder und Glaube*, 13: 'They claim neither originality nor uniqueness.'

miracles were not normal events, but elements in a mythical drama: in them the miraculous transformation of the whole world into the βασιλεία θεοῦ was being carried out. As an apocalyptic charismatic miracle-worker, Jesus is unique in religious history.[45] He combines two conceptual worlds which had never been combined in this way before, the apocalyptic expectation of universal salvation in the future and the episodic realisation of salvation in the present through miracles. This thesis has both an historical aspect relating to the development of religious traditions and a substantive one.

The historical aspect presupposes that before Jesus there was no comparable combination of apocalyptic and the charism of miracle-working. Of course there are miracles in apocalyptic texts and contexts, but they are different in character.

i) The book of Daniel contains a combination of two different traditions.[46] The legends of the miraculous rescues in the first part are not apocalyptic, and the visions in the second part contain no miracles which take place in the present. This combination of miraculous rescues and apocalyptic visions must naturally be taken seriously as a combination, but in contrast to primitive Christianity we find no charismatic miracle workers active on earth. The miracles are always performed by God.

ii) In Qumran exorcisms were performed. Abraham and Daniel were regarded as exorcists (*Genesis Apokryphon* XX.16-32; *Prayer of Nabonid*). This, however, is an art of exorcism and healing based on ancient traditions (cf. Jos. *bell*. II.8.6; Jub 10.12f.). There is no intrinsic connection between the future end of the world and the miracles in the present.

iii) Finally we must look again at the messianic prophets active at the same time as Jesus.[47] With them too there were no miracles in the present as initial realisations of the future transition. In addition their view of the future change was different from Jesus'. The messianic prophets expected an Israel freed from foreign rule; Jesus and the genuine apocalyptics looked for a cosmic reversal.

---

[45] The eschatological view of miracles is generally and rightly held to be a peculiarity of Jesus' preaching. See R.M. Grant, *Miracles and Natural Law*, 172; R. and M. Hengel, *Heilungen*, 352; R. Pesch, *Taten*, 151ff.; H. Baltensweiler, 'Wunder und Glaube im NT', *ThZ* 23 (1967), 241-56; R.H. Fuller, *Miracles*, 44ff. Cf. also W. Grundmann, *Kraft*, 65-68; A. Oepke, *TWNT* III, 213; G. Delling, 'Das Verständnis des Wunders im Neuen Testament', *Studien zum NT und zum hellenistischen Judentum*, 1970, 146-59; A. Richardson, *Miracle Stories*, 54.

[46] O. Plöger, *Theokratie und Eschatologie*, 1959, 18ff.

[47] R.M. Grant, *Miracles and Natural Law*, 166f, here gives insufficient emphasis to the difference from the miracles of Jesus.

On the other hand, these two tendencies in Judaism, the particularist and the universalist, are much less distinct than is frequently assumed.

Even before Jesus, then, there were various combinations of apocalyptic ideas with miracles, but they were miracles performed by God, traditions of exorcism or miracles announced but not brought about. The elements were there. Jesus combined them in a new way. Nowhere else do we find miracles performed by an earthly charismatic which purport to be the end of the old world and the beginning of a new one.

At the same time, however, the combination of the charism of miracles with apocalyptic creates a substantive problem. Apocalyptic pessimism, as shown in the assumption that the whole universe is in the grip of evil, is in conflict with the hope of a salvation brought about here and there by individual miracles. It is not that the present history is empty of promise in apocalyptic, but that the promise is tied to a fulfilment of the divine will which confers an entitlement to future salvation.[48] Only because apocalyptic and miracles in Jesus' work modify each other can they form a genuine combination: Jesus gives future expectation a root in the present and his miracles become signs of a universal change.[49] This understanding of Jesus' miracles appears only in the sayings-tradition.

The statements of present eschatology are clearest in dualistic contexts. Satan has fallen from heaven (Lk 10.18); his kingdom is disintegrating (Mk 3.24-26), his house being plundered (3.27). The casting out of demons is the first sign of the arrival of the rule of God (Mt 12.28). The end of the negative has already come; the web of evil around this passing world has already been torn. That is why there are no apocalyptic speculations about this web of evil, its duration and its stages. And yet the full establishment of the positive is still to come.

Similarly, the starting point for an eschatological interpretation of the miracles is the exorcisms – that is, miracles with a pronounced dualistic, conflictual character. All four dualistic and present-centred statements appear in the context of exorcism. Because Jesus casts out demons he can proclaim that the end has entered into the present. There is a close connection between present eschatology and the eschatological interpretation of the miracles. Apocalyptic and miracles have modified each other.

---

[48] W. Harnisch, *Verhängnis und Verheissung der Geschichte*, 1969.
[49] R. Otto, *Kingdom of God*, 53f., 117f., has drawn attention to this connection.

Because the negative web of evil has already been broken it is possible for salvation to come in individual instances. Because individual instances of salvation occur, the presence of the end can be proclaimed here and now.[50] Even the Qumran texts provide no parallel for this combination of present and future eschatology.

In a fine study,[51] H.W. Kuhn has shown that present and future eschatology were combined in Qumran, the present deriving from a spiritualised liturgical tradition, the future from an apocalyptic and dualistic tradition. Entry into the community's cultic saving area meant salvation in the present, the expectation of the eschatological battle between God and Belial future salvation. The following differences from Jesus' eschatology should be stressed:

i) In Qumran the two 'eschatologies' coexist without connection. Where God battles with Belial there is no present eschatology. Conversely, 'the community songs, whose interweaving of future and present we have examined, never use the dualism of God and devil.'[52] In Mt 12.28, however, present eschatology and the dualism of God and Satan's kingdom are coherently combined in a single saying.

ii) In the case of Jesus the dualistic sayings themselves are evidence of present eschatology: the power of Satan is already broken. The references to the Temple, on the other hand, belong to future eschatology. In Qumran it is the exact opposite.

iii) For Jesus the end which has aready come is given a cosmic interpretation: demonic and satanic powers give way. In Qumran present eschatology rests on an individual act, entry into the community.

The combination of eschatology and miracle in Jesus' activity is distinctive. This combination is no less characteristic than that of eschatology and wisdom. Jesus sees his own miracles as events leading to something unprecedented. They anticipate a new world. They seek to be 'already here and now a microcosm of a new heaven and a new earth'(Ernst Bloch).[53] The new world has not come, and yet its expectation is intelligible. The primitive Christian charism of miracle-working in fact began a far-reaching restructuring of the ancient world. The cosmic world was not turned upside down, but the world as interpreted by symbolic actions was.

---

[50] On Jesus' eschatology, cf. W.G. Kümmel, *Promise and Fulfilment*, 1957; E. Grässer, *Das Problem der Parusieverzögerung in den synoptischen Evangelien und in der Apostelgeschichte*, 1957, 3-75; J. Becker, *Das Heil Gottes*, 1964, 197-217; H.W. Kuhn, *Enderwartung und gegenwärtiges Heil*, 1966, 189-204.

[51] *Enderwartung*, esp. 176-88.

[52] *Enderwartung*, 202.

[53] E. Bloch, *Prinzip Hoffnung*, 1959, 1544.

2. The Primitive Christian Miracle Stories

If we move from the sayings tradition, which talks about the miracles, to the miracle stories themselves, it is impossible not to be struck by the complete disappearance of the eschatological interpretation of the miracles. The distinctive feature of Jesus' miracles has disappeared; the eschatological framework is missing. In only one place is the casting out of demons associated with the final judgment: Jesus is said to torment the demons 'before the time', that is, before their final destruction at the judgment (Mt 8.29). Only at this secondary point in the developed miracle stories are the miracles presented as signs of the eschaton, nowhere else – a fact which is often overlooked.[54] The development which can be seen here from Jesus to primitive Christianity consists of two contrary tendencies. On the one hand there is a tendency to smooth out characteristic features, a 'popular adaptation', which can be observed in other traditions. On the other hand there is a tendency to intensify, to make the miraculous even more striking, which goes well beyond the historical and factual. The process is marked both by a disappearance of distinctive features and at the same time by the appearance of a new character. Both tendencies will be briefly described.

The 'popular adaptation' is easier to appreciate when comparable processes are considered. Take for example the traditions about Paul in Acts and about John the Baptist in Mk 6.17ff. In both cases all the unusual and provocative features of these eschatological preachers have been smoothed out. There is no more than a vague echo of what gave their presence distinctiveness and power. What would we learn from Acts about Paul's teaching on justification, its crucial importance and its polemical character? It appears only in Acts 13.38, watered down into an addition to justification by the Law, robbed of its provocative force, the Law-Christ dichotomy. What would we know about Paul's eschatology? In Acts it is 'moved from the centre of Pauline belief to the end and turned into a treatise on the last things'.[55] John the Baptist appears

---

[54] G. Delling, 'Botschaft und Wunder im Wirken Jesu', in *Der historische Jesus und der kerygmatische Christus*, 1964, 389-402, admits that the miracle stories show 'scant interest' in the eschatological significance of the miracles (401).

[55] P. Vielhauer, 'Zum Paulinismus der Apostelgeschichte', *Aufsätze*, 18ff., quoted from 23. Cf. H. von Campenhausen, *Entstehung*, 57, who suggests that the author of Luke was a travelling companion of Paul's. He admits: 'However, the Pauline ideas in their Lucan version are all more muted; they have lost not only their abstruseness but also their original profundity, and seem paler, more ordinary, as though they had been smoothed out for easier assimilation and something had been lost' (57). It is this process that is here called 'popular adjustment'.

in Mk 6.17-29, made unrecognisable by a popular adaptation. There is no reference to his preaching of repentance, no reference to the threatening, imminent judgment. We see the courageous critic of an Oriental despot, attacking blatant sins, but not the complacency of the religious. That there is little left of historical truth either is shown by a comparison with Jos. *ant.* 18.116-19, where the Baptist's execution is politically motivated. Is there not a similar popular adaptation in operation when the eschatological interpretation of Jesus' activity is completely written out of the miracle stories? To attempt to reconstruct a vivid picture of the historical Jesus from the miracle stories would be as nonsensical as to attempt to reconstruct the Pauline teaching on justification from Acts 13.38f. or the Baptist's preaching of repentance from Mk 6.17ff.

This is not an argument for radical historical scepticism. Of course Acts 13.28f. contains an echo of the doctrine of justification. Undoubtedly the Baptist's preaching of repentance lies behind Mk 6.17ff. Even Paul's miracles in Acts cannot be explained as simply travel motifs, transferred stories or inventions.[56] After all, we know from the Pauline letters, if only from passing remarks, that Paul had charismatic powers: action at a distance (1 Cor 5.1ff.),[57] visions (2 Cor 12.1ff), miracles (2 Cor 12.12; Rom 15.18f.), speaking with tongues (1 Cor 14.18), rescue from distress at sea (2 Cor 11.25), survival of a stoning (2 Cor 11.25), miraculous escape (2 Cor 11.32f). The relevant accounts in Acts undoubtedly have a historical background. But the popular image of the historical kernel is misleading. It suggests that the kernel was transmitted. The truth is that the historical shell was transmitted, all that Paul boasts about in his folly. Applied to the Jesus tradition, this means that, reduced though the eschatological framework may be, the historical background to the miracle stories cannot be denied. Primitive Christian miracle stories are symbolic actions provoked by the historical Jesus in which the historical figure has been intensified out of all proportion. We can still put forward hypotheses about where we have echoes of historical truth:

i) Just as Jesus' exorcisms were closely connected with his eschatological

---

[56] Cf. R. Otto, *Kingdom of God*, 346ff., who, however, starts from the problematic assumption that Luke was an eye-witness. On Paul as a charismatic cf. also H. Windisch, *Paulus und Christus,* passim.

[57] K. Thraede, *Grundzüge griechisch-römischer Brieftopik,* 1970, 93-106, esp. 98, sees no more than a traditional trope here, but any trope can be filled with new life in a specific context.

view of miracles, so it was the exorcisms which were the stimulus to primitive Christianity to attach christological titles to Jesus: 'Holy One of God' (Mk 1.24) and 'Son of the Most High' (5.7). The banishment of unclean demons and idols gave messianic hopes their greatest purchase.[58]
ii) In the rule miracles, the conflicts about the sabbath, there is undoubtedly an echo of Jesus' freedom with regard to the sacred institutions of his environment.
iii) The idea of faith gained such prominence in the miracle stories because 'faith' was a central concept in primitive Christianity. It is not impossible that this is directly or indirectly connected with Jesus.

The development from Jesus' understanding of miracles to the interpretation of miracles in the primitive Christian miracle stories cannot be treated just as a process of displacement, smoothing out, toning down and softening of original features. There is rather a simultaneous process of stylisation, enhancement and heightening. In any case it would be one-sided to take isolated motifs and examine their originality and unmistakability. What gives the primitive Christian miracle stories their character is the whole form-critical field of motifs, characters and themes. In the framework of the genre-specific structure of the miracle stories Jesus is seen in a new light. He appears as the miraculously enhanced figure of the historical Jesus. His miracles become increasingly more paradoxical, more miraculous. Their contradiction of normal experience becomes more and more prominent. This enhancement certainly has popular features, but it cannot be treated simply as an assimilation to popular expectations and ideas. Traditional miracle motifs are, on the contrary, developed into an exceptionally striking miracle structure which far exceeds any other contemporary phenomenon. From the miracle-working prophets of the Old Testament to the Coptic legends of the saints, from the inscriptions of Epidaurus to the miracles of the later Neo-Platonists, from the divine men of early Greece to the miracles at Christian shrines, little comparable material has survived. Comparison is possible only at a few points.

The language in which the motifs and structure of the miracles of Epidaurus are presented is terse and brittle. The stories lack internal drama; their religious expressiveness is slight. We have to bear in mind their purpose: they are intended to give suppliants comfort and confidence, to increase expectations and cushion disappoint-

---

[58] R.H. Fuller, *Interpreting the Miracles*, 75-76, interprets this feature of exorcisms as a transition from an implicit to an explicit Christology.

ments. In this respect they are skilful compositions.[59] Everywhere one sees the hand of an experienced shrine bureaucracy, cleverly managing hope and hopelessness. The mood in the primitive Christian miracle stories is quite different. Where the priests of Epidaurus seem to insist, 'Miracles are an everyday event here,' in the Christian stories the miracle is presented as something completely improbable: 'We never saw anything like this' (Mk 2.12). Miracles are not the object of expectation and hope supported by permanent institutions, but paradoxical events which fly in the face of all experience. In contrast to the miracle stories of Epidaurus, which radiate confidence, in which the accents of fear and despair are silent, we find an often defiant will to live which has to surmount obstacles. In the case of the ancient healing cults, it was left to the Cynic Diogenes to point to other sides of the picture. When someone was admiring the mass of votive tablets in Samothrace, he said, 'There would be even more if those who were not saved had put up tablets' (Diog. Laert. VI.59). The inscriptions from Epidaurus are about 300 years older than the primitive Christian miracle stories. It is also interesting to compare the primitive Christian stories with later miracle stories, which we owe to the writers of the second Sophist movement, Aelius Aristides, Lucian and Philostratus. In Lucian the miracles are part of satirical dialogues, partly the object of ridicule, partly a device for intellectual entertainment.[60] Lucian's stories derive their vitality from the narrator's ironical distance from his stories. They are parodies. Miracle stories appear in a quite different form in the 'Sacred Discourses' of Aelius Aristides,[61] the great orator of the second Sophist movement, which contain a re-working of an 'invalid's diary' composed by Aristides. It is all written in perfectly classical style, but pervaded by a rather cloying sentimentality. The closest parallel to the gospels is Philostratus' *vita Apollonii*, a biography with novelistic features and propagandist intentions.[62] Even here, however, there are large differences. Philostratus' work has a taste for the exotic derived from travellers' tales and an embarrassment about miracles both of which are foreign to the gospels. Philostratus goes to considerable lengths to present Apollonius, not as a

---

[59] On the purpose of the inscriptions cf. R. Herzog, *Epidauros*, 59ff; M. Dibelius, *TG*, 166ff.

[60] On the form of Lucian's dialogues cf. W. Schmid and O. Stählin, *Geschichte der griechischen Literatur*, 1924, 710ff.

[61] On these discourses in their literary and historical context, cf. Schmid and Stählin, 698ff.

[62] On this characterisation of the genre cf. D. Esser, *Formgeschichtliche Studien*, 98ff. He defines the *vita Apollonii* as 'a novelistic biography of a "divine man" written for purposes of religious politics' (⁰8).

possessor of magical powers, but as a sage who can do the most amazing things by virtue of his miraculous knowledge. His description of the raising of the dead bride is typical: He ends it with the words, 'And whether he had found a spark of life in her which had remained hidden from those who had treated her . . . or whether he rekindled and brought back life which had been extinguished . . .' (*vita* IV.45). He refers previously to the 'apparent death' of the young woman, so discreetly hinting at his own view. In his writings miracles are, wherever possible, eliminated by apologetic. The attitude of all the writers of the second Sophistic movement towards miracles is similarly cut through by reflection, irony, sentimentality or apologetic. In them members of educated classes are reproducing popular traditions in different ways. They lack naivety. The repeated assertion that miracles are only ever described outside the New Testament for their own sake should therefore be abandoned. The truth is more nearly the reverse. The attractiveness of primitive Christian miracle stories is due in no small part to their wholehearted appreciation of miracles and to their radical enhancement of them.

This enhancement may have popular features, but its main source is the tension between boundary stressing and boundary crossing which becomes visible in the form-critical field of motifs, characters and themes. It is as if traditional miracle motifs have moved into a new field of force which has brought the potentialities immanent in the genre to their highest development. Here the light falls more sharply than elsewhere on the transcending of human expectations and ordinary logic. In contrast to Epidaurus, we hear the voices of despair and resignation. In contrast to Philostratus, there is not a trace of educated, cautious apologetic. Even the most impossible things appear as quite simply possible. The miracle stories will sooner deny the truth of all human experience than the claim of human distress to be overcome. In contrast to Aelius Aristides, no personal relationship to the saving God is cultivated. 'Faith' may be central, but it does not mean a personal relationship with Jesus, but that unconditional desire which receives the promise πάντα δυνατά (Mk 9.23). The miracle itself is the revelation, the manifestation, of the sacred in fascinating otherness and total unconditionality. In the face of such a power interference from irony, emotion and apologetic is silenced. Most typical of all is the absolute denial of experience, and in this the primitive Christian miracle stories are an extension of Jesus' own understanding of miracles. Jesus too saw his miracles in the context of a universal turning point which burst the bounds of experience. This eschatological orientation has faded in the miracle stories, but the contradiction of experience, in the form of the miraculous and paradoxical, has been pushed to an extreme.

This internal heightening of charismatic belief in miracles is combined with a rejection of all other forms of belief in the miraculous current in the ancient world. The two are closely connected. Charismatic belief in miracles is probably heightened to such a degree because it now has to absorb all the expectations which otherwise led to magic and soothsaying and were institutionalised in oracles and healing sanctuaries. Primitive Christianity was not just a part of the general movement of the age, which led to increased irrationality; within this movement it offered an alternative which, as the ancient world drew to a close, took the form of a choice between Neo-Platonic *theourgia* and the Christian charisma of miracles. However much we must place primitive Christianity within a general religious development, it nonetheless towers above it. The paradoxical feats of charismatic miracle-workers are here given an aura of religious significance without parallel elsewhere. If we may use for purposes of illustration a periodisation usual in other contexts, we could say that the primitive Christian miracle stories form the 'classical' pinnacle of the genre, between the archaic brittleness of the Epidaurus inscriptions and the baroque embellishments of the later Empire. No historical assessment can make good their absolute claim, but it can make it intelligible: the new way of life which established itself in symbolic actions distinguished itself from all existing ways of life by its claim to absoluteness.

The analysis of contemporary religious influences on primitive Christian miracle stories and the interpretation of their historical intention leads to a hermeneutical conflict. Functional analysis cannot resolve this conflict, but it can make it intelligible. Primitive Christian miracle stories are part of a wider process, and this relativises their claim. However, they were able to give this process a new impetus only because they enhanced the historical figure of Jesus in symbolic actions out of all proportion. Only a figure enhanced in symbolic transformation could radiate the totally motivating force which was able to bring about the profound change in ancient consciousness which we associate with the name of Christianity.

CHAPTER III

THE EXISTENTIAL FUNCTION OF PRIMITIVE CHRISTIAN MIRACLE STORIES

Primitive Christian miracle stories are symbolic actions in which a new understanding of existence is opened up. Our final task is to examine this understanding of existence in its own right. Method requires us to start from the genre-specific fields of characters, motifs and themes. These are, of course, not just static structures. What we find in them as a finished structure is the result and record of a symbolic transformation and mastering of reality.

The opposition between boundary-stressing and boundary-crossing motifs shows that miracle stories are symbolic actions in which the limits of the world of ordinary living are transcended. The process takes place within the framework of the specific problems which give the thematic field of the genre its structure. It takes place through the characters which appear in the genre. The character field is crucial to an understanding of the inner dynamic of the miracle stories. It indicates the forces which bring about the crossing of the boundary. In the centre stands the figure of Jesus, God's Holy One (Mk 1.24). There are also other transcendent powers: demons, who often act only in the background but are always present as part of the form-critical field. Does the dynamic of the miracle stories come perhaps, not just from the power of the holy, but also from unconscious forces which dominate human beings? These need not be demonic forces; they could be human wishes. Certainly attempts have been made to understand the miracle stories in those terms.

A. Existential Influences on Primitive Christian Miracle Stories

Feuerbach regarded the miracle stories as the imaginary fulfilment of wishes in fantasy: 'Miracle is as rapid as wish is impatient! Miraculous power realises human wishes in a moment, at one stroke, without any hindrance. That the sick should become well is no miracle; but that they should become so immediately, at a mere word of command, that is the mystery of miracle.'[1] The power of a miracle is 'the sorcery of the imagination, which satisfies without contradiction all the wishes of the heart'.[2] Freud took interpretations of this sort further:[3] for him the 'omnipotence of thought' is infantile narcissism. This rather complicated theory can only be summarised here. At an early stage of childhood the libido has its own body as its object, an object which is constantly available. In later relationships with objects too, the objects remain something like emanations of the libido. If this narcissistic libido dominates thought, it attributes to itself an omnipotence in which the outside world, as an emanation of the ego, appears as constantly under its control. In this view belief in miracles is a regression to a narcissistic world of childhood. Whatever scepticism may be felt about such psycho-analytic interpretations, the question remains: do the miracle stories compensate for childish wishes? Can miracles be understood in terms of wishes? The reductionist interpretation of Feuerbach and Freud probably had a true insight. Paul Ricoeur's view must in essence be accepted. According to Ricoeur, 'Reductionist hermeneutics is today no longer a private event, but a public process, a cultural phenomenon; whether we call it demythologisation, when it takes place within a specific religion, or demystification, when it comes from outside, the process is always the same: the death of the metaphysical, religious object. Freudianism is one path to this death. . . . Today we can read and understand the signs of the absolutely other – and this is our impotence and perhaps our opportunity and our good fortune – only through the mercilessness of reductionist hermeneutics.'[4] However, in order to understand the miracle stories a few correctives are necessary even if one does not want to deny the force of wishes in them.

First, in my view, there is no need of complicated psychoanalytical theory to explain how miracle stories go back to a world of childhood experience. For the child food and drink are simply there. Omniscient and omnipotent adults have 'conjured them up'. The child learns that it can influence these adults by its will and this makes it tend to regard 'its will as independent and relatively omnipotent'.[5] The child's very helplessness and powerlessness

---

[1] Ludwig Feuerbach, *The Essence of Christianity* (1841), trans. George Eliot, New York 1957, 129. On miracles see pp. 125-135 For further detail see H.J. Klimkeit, *Das Wunderverständnis Ludwig Feuerbachs in religionsphänomenologischer Sicht* (1965).

[2] Feuerbach, *Essence*, 134.

[3] S. Freud, *Totem and Taboo*, Standard Edition, vol. XIII, London 1955, 1-162.

[4] Ricoeur, *Interpretation*, 542.

[5] This and the following quotation come from D.P. Ausubel, *Das Jugendalter*, 1968, 171.

encourages him to think, 'My will must be really powerful if a tiny, helpless creature like me can force omniscient adults to satisfy my desires.' Since the internal and external worlds are not yet separate and the world is perceived in terms of faces, a magical picture of the world can arise (as a secondary stage) in which things can be determined by thoughts.[6] If we discover fantasies of omnipotence in our children, should we be surprised to find them in the past too? To understand something of this requires no psychological unmasking. Anyone who refuses to dismiss the phenomena of childhood as 'infantile' need feel no hesitation in accepting the idea that the primitive Christian miracle stories are made from the archaic material of childish experience. They are the expression of a human race in its 'childhood'.

This return to a world of childish experience is not a regression which takes place without the knowledge of human subjectivity. Rather, miracle stories can be understood as symbolic actions of an adult subject reaching back to his childhood. Their world is not the childish world in which the boundaries of inner and outer are blurred. Wishes are certainly not fulfilled in the miracle stories 'without any hindrance' and 'without contradiction'.[7] On the contrary, a field analysis of motifs, themes and characters shows that the central feature of the miracle stories is an experience of limitation which challenges the human being with all his or her 'powers' (will, sensibility, intellect). The whole of a person's subjectivity is involved in the attempt to transcend this limitation – not just a force of desire cut off from the personality. Miracle stories are symbolic actions of human subjectivity in which the real negativity of existence is transcended.

Very different views may be taken of this subjectivity. V. Gardavsky says that the miracles of Jesus reveal 'the subjective action which imprints a new order, a new law, on to the chain of cause and effect.[8] He goes on to describe it as love, which he regards as 'the radically subjective element in history':[9] love, he says, transcends the distress imposed by material limitations and humanises nature which seeks to thwart men. In the same phenomenon Feuerbach can see only the arrogance of desire, which he criticises as 'unlimited, extravagant, fanatical, supernaturalistic subjectivity'.[10] As his model is the natural order as seen by Greek philosophy,

[6] Cf. O. Kroh, *Die Psychologie des Grundschulkindes,* 4th to 6th ed. 1930. On perception through physiognomy, p. 69; on magical thinking, pp. 226f.

[7] Feuerbach, *Essence,* 129.

[8] V. Gardavsky, *God is not yet dead,* London 1973, 47.

[9] Gardavsky, 49.

[10] Feuerbach, *Essence,* 133.

he is bound to reject this 'world of unlimited subjectivity'.[11] In contrast, R.M. Grant sees both a positive and a negative side:

'From one point of view the first centuries of our era represent the triumph of superstition. From another, they mark the rediscovery of "passionate subjectivity". In the first sense, the miracle stories of the gospels are examples of human self-deception. In the second, they are myths which express the Christian's freedom from the world of nature, from fate, from destiny, from any chain of material causation.'[12]

This subjectivity, which comes up against its material and physical limitations and seeks to overcome them, is quite different from the world of the child in which the internal and external world are still confused. Miracle stories do go back to childhood experience, but they reformulate it in the light of 'adult' experience.

The human desires structured in this way are historical. R.M. Grant spoke of a rediscovery of passionate subjectivity in late antiquity. As examples autobiographical reflections (those of Marcus Aurelius and Augustine), the novel of the early Empire and portraits could be cited. The disclosure of new dimensions of the subject goes in very different directions. Marcus Aurelius is impressive in his lack of illusions, by the way in which, though fully aware of his frailty and mortality he yet accepts reality. The Gnostics distanced themselves radically from this world in mythical speculations. In comparison the primitive Christian miracle stories are naive. Human wishes are not sacrificed to reality in Stoic ἀταραξία, nor do they retreat to a higher world of light. In the miracle stories desires rebel against reality and insist on tangible changes in it, insist that sick people are cured, the hungry filled and the blind made to see. Reality is opposed, and this opposition to reality is so thorough-going that it can hardly be called 'naive'. It seems more like the completely un-naive radicality of Parmenides,[13] who pressed the logical proposition of identity with ruthless logic against all the multiplicity and change of the visible world of experience. In both cases the normal world of human logic is radically transcended, in the one case by the internal coherence of thought and in the other by desire, by logical operations on the one hand and by passionate subjectivity on the other. The primitive Christian miracle stories in their radical outlook are an authentic reflection of the ancient world and especially of that first

---

[11] Feuerbach, *Essence*, 128.
[12] R.M. Grant, *Miracle and Mythology*, 132.
[13] See K. Heinrich, *Parmenides und Jona*, 1966, 61-128.

century in which the variety of human possibilities was plumbed within a culture for the first time.

The primitive Christian miracle stories clearly bear the imprint of wishes, but not of infantile wishes asserting themselves while human subjectivity is off its guard. They are much more historical embodiments of wishes in symbolic actions. It may of course be quite rightly asked whether this is more than an impotent protest which refuses to accept its futility, whether it is an illusion which has to be 'unmasked', which must be stripped of its sacred aura. This is clearly how it is seen by those who speak of the 'anticipation of the now customary speculative Ash Wednesday on which all masks fall'.[14] Is there no more behind the mask of the sacred than human wishes? It can hardly be denied that the conflict between wish and reality is one of the existential sources of the miracle stories, but does it fully comprehend their existential meaning?

B. The Existential Meaning of the Primitive Christian Miracle Stories

Primitive Christian miracle stories testify to a revelation of the holy, to its power to break into the normal course of the world. That is their only message. A large part of the exegetical labour expended on them, however, is devoted to denying or minimising this. The attempt is made from various positions. In this section we shall look in turn at attempts to minimise the importance of the miraculous in the miracle stories associated with the history of religions, redaction criticism and tradition history, and with historical and interiorising interpretations.

A popular method of minimising the importance of the New Testament miracles comes from *the history of religions*. Sometimes it is asserted that they represented nothing at all unusual in the ancient world and sometimes there is an insistence that they are less miraculous or magical than other miracles. In other words, the miracles are sometimes assimilated to their period and sometimes contrasted with it. Assimilation and contrast need not, of course, be contradictory, but it is unacceptable for exegesis (and sometimes the same exegetes) to treat the same features now as conventional and now as a break with convention. This can be illustrated under three heads.

---

[14] H. Plessner, in the introduction to P. Berger and T. Luckmann, *Konstruktion*, XVI. Cf. also the fine chapter, 'Science smiling into its beard, or first full dress encounter with Evil,' in R. Musil, *The Man without Qualities*, 1953 (ch.72).

W. Grundmann for example argues: 'The New Testament miracles of Jesus have no connection with magic, or with magic means and processes like the majority of miracles outside the New Testament.'[15] Others admit the existence of magical features – ῥῆσις βαρβαρική, the laying on of hands, healing with spittle and so on – but attempt to excuse them by means of references to the standards of the time: 'Phenomena which today are clinging tenaciously to life as "superstitions" were an accepted element in ancient society. Magical features in New Testament miracle stories . . . told the ancient reader nothing unfamiliar or strange.'[16] This certainly brings us nearer to the truth, but we may still ask why the enemies of Christianity accused Jesus of being a sorcerer if magical features in his miracles were 'an accepted element of ancient society'. The Jewish scholar L. Blau is much more objective on this matter: 'In the eyes of the Romans and the Greeks . . . the miracles of the New Testament and its adherents were nothing other than sorcery, which will be quite comprehensible when one considers the following definition, offered by a Christian scholar: "Miracles are legitimate sorcery; sorcery is illegitimate miracles"!'.[17]

Other historical comparisons bring in ethics. A. Oepke, for example, feels able to say, 'At Epidauros egoism is the central force; in the gospels love.'[18] The occurrence of homosexual activity in the dreams from the Epidaurus sanctuary prompts him to remark, 'Such things would be quite unthinkable in the Gospels. There everything takes place in a state of wakefulness, in the clear light of day, and the air is pure.'[19] The 'pure air' can be ignored, but not the unjustified charge of egoism. Less biased interpreters have rightly stressed the 'social concern' of the Asclepius circle,[20] while per contra the humanitarian emphasis of the primitive Christian miracle stories has even been challenged: '. . . what we must say emphatically is that the Evangelists do not relate the miracle-stories primarily in order to illustrate the compassion of Jesus. They lived in an age unaffected by the humanistic approach and the humanitarian attitude . . .'[21] Of course this judgment is also unjust with regard both to the period of primitive Christianity and to the miracle stories.

Another popular argument makes use of the form and intention of the miracle stories. It seems impossible to eradicate the view that ancient miracles outside the New Testament were described for their own sake, but that the New Testament miracles are in the service of an intention which includes more than miracles. G. Klein writes, for example, 'I have

[15] W. Grundmann, TDNT II, 302, rightly criticised by Grant, *Miracles and Natural Law*, 172f.

[16] W. Schmithals, *Wunder und Glaube*, 12.

[17] L. Blau, *Zauberwesen*, 28f.

[18] A. Oepke, TDNT III, 208.

[19] A. Oepke, TDNT III, 209.

[20] A. von Harnack, *Mission und Ausbreitung*, 134; J. Leipoldt, *Von Epidauros bis Lourdes*, 13f.; E. & L. Edelstein, *Asclepius* II, 178.

[21] A. Richardson, *Miracle Stories*, 32.

come across no instance in which a miracle is described – as so frequently in contexts outside the New Testament – for its own sake; it always points beyond itself; it always 'means' something.'[22] Dibelius long ago showed, with rare clarity, that miracle in the miracle stories (which he called 'novellas') was an 'end in itself which stands in the centre of the picture and dominates everything'.[23] True, Dibelius felt obliged to apologise for this by referring to the audience of the time. The novellas were 'a substitute for a sermon among hearers already accustomed to miraculous acts of gods and prophets'.[24] Were the miracle stories in primitive Christianity really only a substitute?

The method of argument is always the same. The features modern theology finds undesirable are blamed on the period, while the positive ones are assigned to the credit of Christianity. In the process valid observations are certainly made, but it is hard to escape the impression that the argument is prompted by apologetic opportunism, marshalling the arguments to meet its needs. It is true that the miracle stories belong to their time. They contain unique features and conventional elements. However, this gives no-one the right to play uniqueness off against conventionality, as though the first Christians, in order to make themselves intelligible, had simply slipped on the costume of their period, as though the period was no more than an outer covering. And the idea that originality was the only quality esteemed by an author makes it impossible to understand almost any ancient writer,[25] let alone the primitive Christian writings. Nevertheless if uniqueness – even contrary to the intentions of ancient authors – is set up as an objective criterion, one condition may be stipulated. Such uniqueness must be assessed with the greatest fairness we can muster, without in any way devaluing the utterances of others. In my opinion, for example, the uniqueness of the primitive Christian miracle stories is not a minimising of miracles but their inner magnification.[26]

The many attempts to use the techniques of *redaction criticism* to reduce the importance of the miracles also carry little conviction.

---

[22] G. Klein, *Wunderglaube*, 50.
[23] M. Dibelius, *TG*, 80.
[24] M. Dibelius, *TG*, 76.
[25] U. Hölscher, *Die Chance des Unbehagens*, 1965, 61ff.
[26] See the religio-historical section of the book. The intensification of the miraculous is not only qualitative but also quantitative. Nowhere else do we have traditions of so many miracles by a single miracle-worker (with the exception of cult sanctuaries). The gospels have 29 miracles of Jesus – not counting summaries and dual traditions, the *vita Apollonii* only nine (*vita Apoll.* I,4; IV,10. 13. 20. 25. 45; VI, 27. 43; VIII,38). *Vita Apoll.* V,18 is a varient of IV,13.

Even so this view admits that Christian traditions before their redaction had a firm belief in miracles and that it was only the redaction that corrected this.[27] According to G. Klein, it was the intention of Mark and John 'emphatically to warn readers against belief in miracles'.[28] According to K. Kertelge the Marcan miracles have a tendency 'to make themselves superfluous'.[29] Some doubts about these claims must surely be allowed, doubts whether the biblical authors dealt so unfeelingly with their traditions as many modern theologians with the biblical traditions, whether they transmitted them only to dissociate themselves from them immediately, to make them fundamentally superfluous. Can Mark really have told sixteen miracle stories solely in order to warn against belief in miracles? It seems a rather clumsy way of doing it.

The main evidence cited in support of the alleged underplaying of miracles by the gospel redaction is the motifs of secrecy and misunderstanding in Mark and John: 'And so we see that John incorporates a brake into the miracle stories in just the same way as Mark and applies it even more sharply than he.'[30] It is true that the Johannine miracles point beyond themselves to a greater degree than the synoptic ones, but this is true of the Revealer himself in John: 'He who believes in me believes not in me but in him who sent me. And he who sees me sees him who sent me' (Jn 12.44). The miracles are no more criticised in John than the revealer is criticised or underplayed, not even by being constantly misunderstood. The word of Jesus is also misunderstood (cf. Jn 3.1ff.; 7.31ff.), but that is far from making it an inadequate mode of revelation.

The same is true of Mark. If the secret reduces the importance of the miracles, then it also relativises that of the divine sonship, since it is the divine sonship which underlies the secret. If misunderstandings express reservations about miracles, they are also an expression of reserve about the Passion – the prophecies of the Passion are also misunderstood. In my opinion a reading of Mark suggests a different conclusion: what underlies the secret is of special importance, what is misunderstood of special significance. If Mark wanted to warn against belief in miracles, it is hard to see why he should emphasise Jesus' miraculous activity in redactional summaries. A second argument relates to the Passion story. 'Obviously, Mark radically criticises and corrects the Christology of his sources, which present, as it were, Jesus as the Divine Man and Messiah in a rather "naive" way . . . it is only through his death and resurrection that Jesus'

---

[27] See, for example, H.D. Betz, 'Jesus as Divine Man', in *Jesus and the Historian*, 1968, 114-33, esp. 121.

[28] G. Klein, *Wunderglaube*, 56.

[29] K. Kertelge, *Wunder*, 206.

[30] G. Klein, *Wunderglaube*, 56.

messianic and divine nature can be fully revealed.'[31] Now it is quite true that everything in Mark's gospel leads into the Passion. But that is no argument against the preceding miracles. Miracles occur during Jesus' crucifixion, a darkening of the sun and the tearing of the Temple curtain. The resurrection and empty tomb are miracles which dwarf anything that has gone before. There is no need to deny that the Passion sets a new tone: miraculous power is now confronted with lack of power. The two act in mutual tension, but the tension increases both power and impotence, just as revelation and veiling, grace and wrath, salvation and damnation are in tension. This ambivalence is a basic feature of every revelation of the sacred.

Finally we may consider attempts at an 'allegorical' interpretation of the miracles. Matthew introduces the story of the storm on the lake with the words, 'And when he got into the boat, his disciples followed him' (8.23). Just before in Matthew we have discipleship sayings.[32] Does this mean that the boat has become a sign of the 'disciple' Church exposed to the storm of the ages? In the first place the miracle story simply means that as a disciple of Jesus one has no need to fear storm and waves. The preceding discipleship sayings refer plainly to homelessness and breaking with one's family. There is no sign that the subsequent unit is intended to be less direct.

The alleged reservations of New Testament redactors about the miracles turn out on closer examination to be almost always reservations by modern exegetes about the New Testament authors. Once one stops looking at the relationship between tradition and redaction as a relationship between archaeological strata, and sees both as actualisations of a virtual genre structure, it becomes impossible to make a simple opposition between redaction and tradition. Every redaction does indeed place new emphases, but new emphases are not in themselves criticism; new emphases highlight what is emphasised.

The importance of the miracles is frequently minimised by reference to traditions in the New Testament 'critical of miracles'. This minimising of miracles in terms of *the history of the tradition* can be found, for example, in G. Klein associated with arguments from the history of religions: 'We have to keep in mind the rampant jungle of ancient credulity about miracles to assess the provocation represented by the New Testament in such surroundings. Not that it denies the possibility of miracles.' The New Testament writers, as men of their time with the conventional attitudes of their time, were completely incapable of that. Rather, precisely

---

[31] H.D. Betz, 'Jesus as Divine Man', 124.
[32] See G. Bornkamm, 'Stilling of the Storm', 52-57.

because that possibility in itself remained unquestioned, the development of a concept of miracle which was critical of miracles must inevitably have been felt as an unprecedented attack. The New Testament concept of miracle in its pure form is in fact abruptly dismissive of miracles.'[33] Klein's evidence for this view comes mainly from Pauline sources, but we may ignore these here as they have nothing to contribute to an understanding of the traditions of the gospels.[34] The synoptic miracle stories have to be understood on their own terms. Whether there is a single New Testament concept of miracle is a priori not at all certain. Only the criticism of miracles contained in the gospels themselves is relevant to the interpretation of the miracle stories.

Rejection of the demand for signs is not a rejection of signs (Mk 8.11f. parr.). On the contrary, refusal of a sign is a punishment for unbelief, which would be nonsense if it were accepted that signs were valueless. What is criticised is unbelief, not miracles. In fact, miracles are given added importance, since the reverse of the refusal of a sign is the giving of signs to faith.[35] This is certainly not an unprecedented attack on ancient credulity about miracles, as can be seen from Apollonius of Tyana's refusal of a sign. At his trial he was challenged by Domitian to turn himself into water or an animal and so free himself from his bonds to prove that he was not a sorcerer, but he refused (*vita* VIII.2). It is true that Philostratus is cooler about miracles than other New Testament writers, but his concept of miracles in the vita Apollonii can hardly be called 'dismissive of miracles'.

---

[33] G. Klein, *Wunderglaube,* 28.

[34] It is well known that Paul knows very little about Jesus' preaching or actions, but this cannot be used as an objection to the Sermon on the Mount, even if Paul says of himself that in future he will not think of Christ 'according to the flesh' (2 Cor 5.16). If 2 Cor 12.12 is directed at an idea of the θεῖος ἀνήρ which reflects the christology of the synoptic miracle stories (which need not be decided here), Paul would hardly have found the concept of the miraculous contained in these miracle stories 'abruptly dismissive of miracles'. As a general principle we need to keep on reminding ourselves that the theological unity of the canon is a dogmatic postulate. Historically, in fact, it is often plausible to suppose that much of the polemic contained in the New Testament writings is directed at ideas in other writings. Each work and each tradition has to be understood in its own terms. There is no single New Testament concept of the miraculous.

[35] It is questionable whether the 'sign' in Mk 8.11f. can possibly refer to a miracle of Jesus of the sort described in the synoptic miracle stories. If it refers to something quite different, this tradition cannot simply be cited as an example of the relativisation of synoptic miracles.

a) The sign is to come 'from heaven'. It is a cosmic sign (cf. the terminology in Mt 24.30; Lk 21.11, 25; Rev 12.1). In Paul too 'sign' and 'cosmos' go together (1 Cor 1.21f.).

b) The miracle is presumably to be worked by God (cf. K. Kertelge, *Wunder,* 26). This is indicated by the passive δοθήσεται (on the language see also Is 7.14 LXX: διὰ τοῦτο δώσει κύριος αὐτὸς ὑμῖν σημεῖον.

c) The miracle will be the fulfilment of an expectation: O. Linton, 'The Demand for a Sign from Heaven', *StTh* 19 (1965), 112-29.

The Johannine criticism of miracles is directed against the linking of seeing and believing: 'blessed are those who have not seen and yet believe' (20.29). 'Unless you see signs and wonders you will not believe' (4.48). Believing without seeing – it is the problem of every later generation. This is not criticism of belief in miracles, but criticism of a scepticism which refuses to believe what it cannot see (cf. Lucian *Philopseudes* 15). It is criticism of the unbelieving Thomas, not an admonition to a credulous age but an attempt to transform a faith based on miracles into a faith which does not need to see.

The conversation about Beelzebub (Mt 12.22ff. par.) is often cited as evidence that 'miracles not only *should* not be a basis for faith; they *cannot* be. They cannot be, not only once the human understanding of reality leaves no room for miracles; even in the midst of an environment which believes in miracles they lack the power. They lack it because they are in their essence profoundly ambivalent. An observer can scent God or the devil behind them as he chooses. The fact that he has a view of the world in which miracles are possible is no advantage to him at all. Miracles can lead to amazement, but not commitment.'[36] In my opinion, the reason exorcisms are discussed is that in them it is impossible to see either God or the Satan at work 'as one chooses', but that one thing is beyond question, that here superhuman, numinous powers are at work and that it is therefore impossible to avoid taking a stance. Miracles in the New Testament invariably force one to choose. Σκανδαλίζειν can be connected with miracles (Mk 6.1ff.; Mt 11.2ff.), the call to repentance can be linked with miracles (Mk 11.20ff.). The fact that the miracles in Chorazim and Bethsaida do not lead to repentance is not evidence against this: does the word automatically lead to repentance?

There can be no doubt that the New Testament does contain a critique of a false understanding of miracles, a desire to see miracles, a demand for signs. There is criticism of many forms of miracle (cf. the story of the Temptation), but this criticism follows logically from the synoptic belief in miracles itself. This belief is a radical crossing of boundaries which challenges a human being's whole existence. This faith must reject signs which allow a person to avoid this step, signs which do not involve this faith which crosses boundaries. But criticism of particular views of miracles is not criticism of miracles. On the contrary, one criticises where one is committed. Lines have to be drawn where closeness is undeniable. And even if there were somewhere in the New Testament traditions critical of miracles, an unhistorical opposition of quite different traditions, such as Paul against the synoptics, John against Luke, and so one, would be unacceptable. The old

---

[36] G. Klein, *Wunderglaube*, 53.

theologians defended the absence of contradictions in the Bible on dogmatic grounds, whereas today people leap on the contradictions which it undoubtedly contains, but the aim is often no less dogmatic than in the past. In both cases passages and traditions which do not fit are underplayed. Historical scholarship is turned into a tool of modern apologetics.

A less current tendency to minimise the importance of the miracles is based on a confusion of historical criticism and interpretation. This 'historical' underplaying of the miracles takes place in attempts to interpret the miracles in terms of their 'historical kernel'. It is claimed that the historical element in them is natural and that only interpretation turns this into miracle.[37] This may well be true, but the whole intention of the miracle stories is to proclaim the end of the natural, 'historical' system of the world. They may be responses to historical events, but they reach far beyond them. This method reveals not their meaning, but only their origin.

There remains only the minimising of the miracle stories in an interiorising approach. In this view the miracles themselves are not the point of the stories, which always carry a reference to something else. This is usually said to be either to the wonders of creation or to a redemption thought of as something inward. The real miracle is found in the opening of blind human eyes to creation. Schleiermacher gave this view its classical formulation: '"Miracle" is merely the religious word for "event".'[38] But is it really true that in the New Testament only closed eyes refuse to see God's marvellous creation? Why is this creation itself changed in the miracles? In John's gospel they are regarded as a continuation of the creation (5.17). Jesus' mightier works are greater than the Father's (5.20). They would not be necessary if there was not a world in distress. No, the miracles do not belong to the creation but to the redemption. It is therefore more accurate to say that the essence of the miraculous is the forgiveness of sin (Bultmann).[39] The radical discontinuity between sin and grace is indeed a miracle – but that is not the phenomenon with which the miracle stories are concerned, which always has a physical or material substratum.

---

[37] For example, E. Hirsch, *Frühgeschichte des Evangeliums*, 1941; see the critical account of his view of miracles in M. Lehmann, *Synoptische Quellenanalyse und die Frage nach dem historischen Jesus*, 1970, 33-54.

[38] D.F. Schleiermacher, *Über die Religion*, ed. H.J. Rothert, 1961, 118f. (2nd ed., p. 65f.). On modern variants of this view of miracles, cf. E. & M.L. Keller, Miracles in dispute: a continuing debate, 1969, 293ff.

[39] R. Bultmann, 'The Question of Wonder', *Faith and Understanding* I, London 1969, 247-61. Bultmann is followed by G. Klein, *Wunderglaube,* passim.

The miracle stories point to Jesus' redemptive action. This redemptive action is specific: Jesus defeats disease and demons. It is illegitimate to bring the redemptive action of the Pauline Christ into the interpretation here – even if the Pauline Christ is much more fascinating than the figure of Jesus in the miracle stories. The miracle stories point to something, but the object to which they point has to be read off the stories themselves. Can we really say, 'The stories of the healings of blind people are not telling us that God can, in certain circumstance, restore sight to the blind. The account of the stilling of the storm does not console the victims of shipwreck with the information that God can save people from distress at sea. The exorcisms do not invite us to believe that God has the power to save from possession and madness. Rather, Jesus' various individual signs and deeds of power reflect, in the form of a parable, the message of the gospel *as a whole*.'?[40] Have we really so firmly suppressed the elemental fears of disease, hunger and death as to deny their existence in the past too? Anyone who has preserved any objectivity in reading the Bible is often perplexed by the interpretations of 'modern' exegetes. They say things like, 'Thus miracles are perhaps happenings where the time for the word of God has come, as the *time* to believe, to surrender *immediately* to that word, which is the announcement of a time, the inauguration of a present. Is not this what the miracle stories of the gospels are saying?'[41] Perhaps I misunderstand this interpretation, but I would suggest that it is quite easy to distinguish between the epiphany of a language elevated to the status of an enduring subject and the miracles of the gospels.

Where Goethe could still assert that the miracle was faith's favourite child,[42] modern exegetes instead give the impression that the miracle is faith's illegitimate child, whose existence they try embarrassedly to apologise for. The ancient Church's pride in the miracles has turned into its opposite. A 'philological cultural Protestantism' finds them too primitive; hermeneutical profundity suspends them, 'explains' them and buries them with praise. Orthodox insistence on their factual reality has been as little able to prevent this as the apodictic simplicity of fundamentalists. Their impotent objections to modern exegesis are quite justified but have to be thought through, purged of all anti-intellectualism, before they become valid. But then it turns out that the minimising

[40] W. Schmithals, *Wunder und Glaube*, 25.
[41] E. Fuchs, 'Über die Aufgabe einer christlichen Theologie', *ZThK* 58 (1961), 245-67. The quotation is from p. 267.
[42] *Faust* I, Night.

of miracle by modern restorative hermeneutics is often only somewhat more respectful (and also vaguer) than their disillusioned reduction. In the one case they are minimised from above, in the other from below. All these profound interpretations often reveal all too clearly 'how much store the theologians set by the miracles they defend, and how far from anxious they really are that our world should be disturbed by these alien visitors'.[43] It is quite true. The miracle stories are alien visitors in our world. Should we not therefore pay them great attention? Should we not try to love them as they are, in all their distinctiveness and strangeness? The point of the miracle stories is the revelation of the sacred in miracles, in tangible, material, saving miracles. Respect for the men and women of primitive Christianity, who told them and were attached to them, obliges us to make this admission and not all the modern perplexities about these texts justify modifying it.[44]

Their existential meaning can be described as follows. Primitive Christian miracle stories are symbolic actions in which the experienced negativity of human existence is overcome by an appeal to a revelation of the sacred. Their action transcends the limits of what is humanly possible. They claim to derive the power for this transcendence from the 'Holy One of God', who casts out demons, multiplies bread, walks on the water and raises the dead. The historical charismatic wonder-worker Jesus appears in symbolic intensification as a divine miracle-worker. It would be far too easy to see this symbolic intensification as the projection of a wish. It is more a shaping and transformation of human wishes. In the miracle stories this wish is certainly aware of its hopelessness in the 'normal' course of events. It realises that it is exposed to a hostile reality, elevated in symbolic actions to the status of demonic forces. It rebels against these limitations.

But is it only the intensity of the wish that overcomes resistance? Is it not truer to say that human wishes are challenged to reach out 'beyond hitherto absolute limits' only by an experience whose source does not lie within itself?[45] If that is true, the miracle stories are not just symbolic *actions,* in which human beings come to terms

---

[43] F. Overbeck, *Über die Christlichkeit unserer heutigen Theologie,* 1903 (=1963), 52. Overbeck criticises a no longer current variant of the minimising of miracles: they happened, but soon became superfluous.

[44] Among writers who have criticised the tendency of modern exegesis to underplay miracles are J. Roloff, *Kerygma,* 111ff.; J. Kallas, *The Significance of the Synoptic Miracles,* 1961; E. Gutwenger, 'Die Machterweise Jesu in formgeschichtlicher Sicht', *ZKTh* 89 (1967), 176-90; J.M. Court, 'The Philosophy of the Synoptic Miracles', *JThS* 23 (1972), 1-15. Cf. also K. Tagawa, *Miracles,* 12: 'Mais enfin, les miracles sont des miracles!'

[45] V. Gardavsky, *God is not yet dead,* 47.

with their existence. They also possess a *symbolic* dimension which points beyond any human mastery of existence. This is what we find: they point to a revelation of the holy which can be described phenomenologically in terms of its main features.

1. Pregnancy
The miracle-worker Jesus is unlike anything in ordinary experience. He arouses amazement and wonder. Where he appears, a gap is made in the fabric of ordinary, everyday experience: 'We never saw anything like this' (Mk 2.12).

2. Competition
The miracle-worker Jesus is not an isolated figure. Particularly in the later strata of the miracle stories, conflict with others become important. This competition is one reason for the symbolic intensification of the earthly charismatic miracle-worker. His miraculous power is superior to that of healing cults (Jn 5.1ff.), of divination (Acts 16.16ff.) and doctors (Mk 5.25ff.). However, even in the earliest tradition the miracle-worker Jesus stands in opposition to another form of the sacred, the law. The sabbath disputes show that a person has to choose between two different forms of the sacred.

3. Dominance
Jesus appears as the powerful conqueror of disease and distress. He commands demons (Mk 1.27), wind and waves (Mk 4.41). His power is presented both as the personal authority of his word (Mt 8.5ff.) and as a fluidlike emanation (Mk 5.25ff.), but it always leads to an encounter with another person who addresses and lays claim to people.

4. Transparency
Jesus' miracles reveal divine power: 'God has visited his people' (Lk 7.16). The epiphanies make this aspect of miracles their sole theme. In them Jesus is transformed into a superhuman figure or appears in a heavenly aura. On the other hand, where something becomes transparent there is also concealment. Secrecy is structurally immanent in the miracle stories and is given particular stress by Mark.

5. Ambivalence
Jesus' miracles can be viewed in various ways. They can be seen as the result of either Satanic or divine action (Mt 12.22ff.). Even where positive attitudes predominate, however, the fascination always includes an element of fear and repulsion. Revelation of the sacred always makes the negative side of the sacred appear more clearly, whether in the form of hostile demons or in the form of human sin (Lk 5.8). Above all, however, the revelation of the sacred in Jesus' miraculous power throws the helplessness of the man on the cross into sharper relief. It is the enormous

contradictions embraced by this revelation of the sacred which gives it the power to illuminate and transform existence.

The structure of the sacred has left its mark on the miracle stories, on them and on the human wishes given form in them. It is important to be clear that these wishes can have quite different articulations. The Christian miracle stories as a genre are not the necessary result of that life-wish which is undoubtedly at work in them. No, the wish acquires a new element here: not just a shaping by human historical subjectivity, but an element of obligation. Where a protest against human suffering takes place through a revelation of the sacred, the elimination of that suffering is not just desirable; it is no less than an obligation. This remains true even when that obligation contradicts all previous human experience. This is the final implication of the miracle stories: they will rather deny the validity of all previous experience than the right of human suffering to be eliminated. They proclaim this right as a sacred law, as something absolute. In symbolic actions they make a radical refusal to submit to the experienced negativity of human existence, a protest which cannot be justified by the visible world of experience alone. The protest is absolute because evoked by an absolute appeal, by a revelation of the sacred in tangible form. The miracle stories are thus a 'radical answer to an appeal uttered in the accents of necessity' (V. Gardavsky).[46]

---

[46] Gardavsky, 47.

Bibliography

Abt, A.: *Die Apologie des Apuleius von Madaura und die antike Zauberei*, Diss. Gießen = Naumburg 1907.

Acquavia, S.S.: *Der Untergang des Heiligen in der industriellen Gesellschaft*, Essen 1964.

Allemann, B.: 'Strukturalismus in der Literaturwissenschaft', in: *Ansichten einer zukünftigen Germanistik*, Munich 1969, 4th ed., 1970, 143-152.

Almquist, H.: *Plutarch und das Neue Testament, ASNU* 15, Uppsala 1946.

Altheim, F.: *Gesicht vom Abend und Morgen*, Fischer Bücherei 79, Frankfurt 1955.

Apel, K.O.: 'Szientistik, Hermeneutik, Ideologiekritik', in: *Hermeneutik und Ideologiekritik*, Frankfurt 1971, 7-44.

Ausubel, D.P.: *Theory and problems of adolescent development*, New York 1954.

Baer, H.v.: *Der Heilige Geist in den Lukasschriften, BWANT* 3, 3, Stuttgart 1926.

Baltensweiler, H.: 'Wunder und Glaube im Neuen Testament', *ThZ* 23 (1967) 241-256.

Bammel, E.: ' "John did no Miracle" ', in: *Miracles. Cambridge Studies in their Philosophy and History*, ed. C.F.D. Moule, London 1965, 2nd ed., 1966, 181-202.

Barb, A.A.: 'The Survival of Magic Arts', in: *The Conflict between paganism and christianity in the fourth century*, ed. A. Momigliano, Oxford 1963, 100-125.

Bauer, W.: 'Jesus der Galiläer', in: *Aufsätze und kleine Schriften*, Tübingen 1967, 91-108.

Bauernfeind, O.: *Die Worte der Dämonen im Markusevangelium, BWANT* 3, 8, Stuttgart 1927.

Baumann, H.: 'Mythos in ethnologischer Sicht', *StudGen* 12 (1959) 1-17. 583-597.

Bausinger, H.: *Formen der 'Volkspoesie', Grundlagen der Germanistik* 6, Berlin 1968.

– 'Strukturen des alltäglichen Erzählens', *Fab* 1 (1958) 239-254.

Becker, J.: *Das Heil Gottes. Heils- und Sündenbegriffe in den Qumrantexten und im Neuen Testament, StUNT* 3, Göttingen 1964.

– 'Wunder und Christologie', *NTS* 16 (1969/70) 130-148.

Behm, J.: *Die Handauflegung im Urchristentum*, Leipzig 1911 = Darmstadt 1968.

Bengtson, H.: *Griechen und Perser. Die Mittelmeerwelt im Altertum*, Fischer Weltgeschichte 5, Frankfurt 1965.

– 'Syrien in der hellenistischen Zeit', in: *Der Hellenismus und der Aufstieg Roms. Die Mittelmeerwelt im Altertum II*, Fischer Weltgeschichte 6, ed. P. Grimal, Frankfurt 1965. 244-254.

Berger, P., Luckmann, T.: *The Social Construction of reality: a treatise in the sociology of knowledge*, London 1966.

Bertram, G.: 'θαῦμα' *ThW* III, 27-42 (*TDNT* III, 27-42).

Best, E.: *The Temptation and the Passion. The Markan Soteriology*, Cambridge 1965.

Betz, H.D.: 'Jesus as Divine Man', in: *Jesus and the Historian, Essays Written in Honor of Ernest Cadmann Colwell*, Philadelphia 1968, ed. F. Th. Trotter, 114-133.

– *Lukian von Samosata und das Neue Testament, TU* 76, Berlin 1961.

– 'Ursprung und Wesen des christlichen Glaubens nach der Emmauslegende (Lk 24, 13 bis 32)', *ZThK* 66 (1969) 7-21.

Bieler, L.: ΘΕΙΟΣ ΑΝΗΡ. *Das Bild des 'Göttlichen Menschen' in Spätantike und Frühchristentum*, Wien 1935/36 = Darmstadt 1967.

Bierwisch, M.: *Strukturalismus. Geschichte, Probleme und Methoden*, Kursbuch 5 (1966) 77-152.

Bitter, W. (Ed.): *Magie und Wunder*, Stuttgart 1959.

Blau, L.: *Das altjüdische Zauberwesen*, Budapest 1898 = Westmead, Farnborough 1970.

Bloch, E.: *Prinzip Hoffnung*, Frankfurt 1959.

Böcher, O.: *Dämonenfurcht und Dämonenabwehr. Ein Beitrag zur Vorgeschichte der christlichen Taufe, BWANT* 10, Stuttgart und Berlin 1970.

Bogatyrev, P.G., Jakobson R.: 'Die Folklore als eine besondere Form des Schaffens', in: *Donum Natalicium Schrijnen*, Nijmegen-Utrecht 1929, 900-913.

Bolkestein, H.: *Wohltätigkeit und Armenpflege im vorchristlichen Altertum*, Groningen 1939 (= 1967).

– *Theophrastos' Charakter der Deisidaimonia als religionsgeschichtliche Urkunde*, RVV 21, 2, Gießen 1929.

Boman, T.: *Die Jesus-Überlieferung im Lichte der neueren Volkskunde*, Göttingen 1967.

Bomer, F.: *Untersuchungen über die Religion der Sklaven in Griechenland und Rom*, AbhMainz I 1957, II 1960, III 1961, IV 1963.

Bonner, C.: 'Some Phases of Religious Feeling in Later Paganism', *HThR* 30 (1937) 119-140.

– *Studies in Magical Amulets*, University of Michigan Studies, Humanistic Series XLIX 1950.

– 'The Technique of Exorcism', *HThR* 36 (1943) 39-49.

– 'Traces of Thaumaturgic Technique in the Miracles', *HThR* 20 (1927) 171-181.

– 'The Violence of Departing Demons', *HThR* 37 (1944) 334-336.

Boobyer, G.H.: 'The Gospel Miracles: Views Past and Present', in: *The Miracles and the Resurrection*, London 1964, 31-49.

– 'Mark 2. 10a and the Interpretation of the Healing of the Paralytic', *HThR* 47 (1954) 115-120.

Bornkamm, G.: 'Die Sturmstillung im Matthäusevangelium', in: G. Bornkamm, G. Barth, H.J. Held: *Überlieferung und Auslegung im Matthäusevangelium*, WMANT 1, 4th ed., Neukirchen 1965, 48-53 ('The Stilling of the Storm in Matthew' in G. Bornkamm, G. Barth, H.J. Held, *Tradition and Interpretation in Matthew*, 52-57).

Bornkamm, K.: *Wunder und Zeugnis*, SGV 251/252, Tübingen 1968.

Bousset, W.: *Kyrios Christos*, 6th ed., Göttingen 1967 (Nashville 1970).

Braumann, G.: 'Jesu Erbarmen nach Matthäus', *ThZ* 19 (1963) 305-317.

– 'Die Schuldner und die Sünderin in Luk. vii. 36-50', *NTS* 10 (1963/4) 487-493.

– 'Der sinkende Petrus', *ThZ* 22 (1966) 403-414.

– 'Die Zweizahl und Verdoppelungen im Matthäusevangelium', *ThZ* 24 (1968) 255-266.

Breymayer, R.: 'Vladimir Jakovlevič Propp (1895-1970) – Leben, Wirken und Bedeutsamkeit', *LB* 15-16 (1972) 36-66.

– 'Bibliographie zum Werk Vladimir Jakovlevič Propp und zur strukturalen Erzählforschung', *LB* 15/16 (1972) 67-77.

Bultmann, R.: *Das Evangelium des Johannes*, MeyerK, 10th ed., Göttingen 1964 (*The Gospel of John*, Oxford 1971).

– *Die Geschichte der synoptischen Tradition*, FRLANT 12, Göttingen 1921, 8th ed., 1970 with supplement, 4th ed. (*The History of the Synoptic Tradition*, Oxford 1963).

– 'Neues Testament und Mythologie', in: *Offenbarung und Heilsgeschehen*, Munich 1941 ('New Testament and Mythology', in: *Kerygma and Myth*, ed. H.W. Bartsch, vol. 1, London 1964, 1-44).

– 'πιστεύω' *ThW* VI, 174-230 (*TDNT* VI, 174-228).

– *Theologie des Neuen Testaments*, 4th ed., Tübingen 1961. (*Theology of the New Testament*, London 1952-53).

– 'Zur Frage des Wunders' in: *Glauben und Verstehen* I, 5th ed., Tübingen 1964, 214-228 ('The Question of Wonder' in: *Faith and Understanding*, London 1969, 247-261).

Burger, Ch.: *Jesus als Davidssohn*, FRLANT 98, Göttingen 1970.

Burke, K.: *Language as symbolic action*. Berkeley and Los Angeles 1966.

Burkert, W.: 'ΓΟΗΣ. Zum griechischen "Schamanismus" ', *RhM* 102 (1962) 36-55.

Burkill, T.A.: 'The historical Development of the Story of the Syrophoenician Woman', *NovTest* 9 (1967) 161-177.

– 'The Syrophoenician Woman: The congruence of Mark 7, 24-31', *ZNW* 57 (1966) 23-37.

– 'Mark 3, 7-12 and the alleged Dualism in the Evangelist's Miracle Material', *JBL* 87 (1968) 409-417.

– *Mysterious Revelation. An Examination of the Philosophy of St. Mark's Gospel*, Ithaca N. Y. 1963.

– *New Light on the Earliest Gospel*, Ithaca/London 1972.

– 'The Notion of the Miracle with special Reference to St. Mark's Gospel', *ZNW* 50 (1959) 33-48.

Buschan, G.: *Über Medizinzauber und Heilkunst im Leben der Völker*, Berlin 1941.

Cairns, D.S.: *The Faith that Rebels. A Re-examination of the Miracles of Jesus*, London 1928.

Campenhausen, H.v.: *Die Entstehung der christlichen Bibel, BHTh* 39, Tübingen 1968 (*The formation of the Christian Bible,* London 1972).

Canaan, T.: *Aberglaube und Volksmedizin im Lande der Bibel, Abhandlungen des Hamburgischen Kolonialinstituts* XX Series B, 12, Hamburg 1914.

Cassirer, E.: *Was ist der Mensch? Versuch einer Philosophie der menschlichen Kultur,* Stuttgart 1960 (*An essay on man: an introduction to a philosophy of human culture,* New York and London 1970).

– *Philosophie der symbolischen Formen,* 4th ed., Darmstadt 1964 (*The philosophy of symbolic forms,* New Haven 1953-57).

– *Wesen und Wirkung des Symbolbegriffs,* 4th ed., Darmstadt 1969.

Ceroke, C.P.: 'Is Mk 2. 10 a Saying of Jesus?' *CBQ* 22 (1960) 369-390.

Clavier, H.: 'La multiplication des pains dans le ministère de Jésus', *TU* 73, Berlin 1959, 441-457.

Conzelmann, H.: *Die Apostelgeschichte, HNT* 7, Tübingen 1963.

– 'Historie und Theologie in den synoptischen Passionsberichten', in: *Zur Bedeutung des Todes Jesu,* 2nd ed., Gütersloh 1967, 35-58.

– *Die Mitte der Zeit, BHTh* 17, 5th ed. Tübingen 1964 (*The theology of St. Luke,* London 1960).

Court, J. M.: 'The Philosophy of the Synoptic Miracles', *JThSt* 23 (1972) 1-15.

Cullmann, O.: *Die Christologie des Neuen Testamentes,* Tübingen 1957 (*The christology of the New Testament,* London 1959).

Daube, D.: *The Sudden in the Scripture,* Leiden 1964.

Degh, L.: 'Die schöpferische Tätigkeit des Erzählens', in: *Internationaler Kongreß der Volkserzählungsforscher,* Berlin 1961, 63-73.

Deissmann, A.: *Licht von Osten,* 4th ed., Tübingen 1923 (*Light from the ancient East,* rev. ed. London 1927).

Delling, G.: *Antike Wundertexte, KlT* 79, Berlin 1960.

– 'Zur Beurteilung des Wunders durch die Antike', in: *Studien zum Neuen Testament und zum hellenistischen Judentum,* Göttingen 1970, 53-71.

– 'Botschaft und Wunder im Wirken Jesu', in: *Der historische Jesus und der kerygmatische Christus,* ed. H. Ristow and K. Matthiae, 3rd ed., Berlin 1964, 389-402.

– 'Josephus und das Wunderbare', in: *Studien,* 130-145.

– 'Das Verständnis des Wunders im Neuen Testament', in: *Studien,* 146-159.

– 'Wunder – Allegorie – Mythus bei Philon von Alexandreia', in: *Studien,* 72-129.

Derchain, Ph.: 'Die ägyptische Welt nach Alexander dem Großen', in: *Der Hellenismus und der Aufstieg Roms. Die Mittelmeerwelt im Altertum* II, Fischer Weltgeschichte 6, ed. P. Grimal, Frankfurt 1965, 212-244.

Dibelius, M.: *Die Formgeschichte des Evangeliums,* 2nd ed., Tübingen 1933, 4th ed., 1961 (*From Tradition to Gospel,* London 1934).

Dobschütz, E.v.: 'Zur Erzählkunst des Markus', *ZNW* 27 (1928) 193-198.

Dodd, C.H.: 'The Appearances of the Risen Christ. An Essay in Form-Criticism in the Gospels', in: *Studies in the Gospels. Essays in Memory of R.H. Lightfoot,* Oxford 1955.

– 'The Framework of the Gospel Narrative', *ET* 43 (1931/2) 396-400.

Dölger, F.J.: 'Der Heiland', in: *Antike und Christentum. Kultur- und religionsgeschichtliche Studien,* Vol. IV, Münster 1950, 241-272.

Dundes, A.: 'From etic to emic Units in the structural Study of Folktales', *JAF* 75 (1962) 95-105.

Dupont-Sommer, A.: 'Exorcismes et Guérisons dans les écrits de Qoumrân', *Supplementum VT* VII, Leiden 1960, 246-261.

Duprez, A.: 'Jésus et les Dieux Guérisseurs. A Propos de Jean V', in: *Cahiers de la Revue Biblique* 12, 1970.

Ebeling, H.J.: *Das Messiasgeheimnis und die Botschaft des Markus-Evangelisten, BZNW* 19, Berlin 1939.

Edelstein, E. and L.: *Asclepius. A Collection and Interpretation of the Testimonies I. II., Publications of the Institute of the History of Medicine.* The John Hopkins University, 2nd Series Vol. II, Baltimore 1945.

Eitrem, S: 'La magie comme motif littéraire', *SO* XXI (1941) 39-83.
– 'Some Notes on the Demonology in the New Testament', *SO* Fasc. Suppl. XII, Oslo 1950.
– 'La théurgie chez les Néoplatoniciens', *SO* 22 (1942) 49-79.
Eliade, M.: *Le sacré et le profane*, Paris 1965 (*The Sacred and the profane*, New York and Evanston 1961).
– *Mythes, rêves et mystères*, Paris 1957 (*Myths, dreams and mysteries*, London 1960).
– *Traité d'histoire des religions*, Paris 1949.
Erman, E.: *Die Literatur der Ägypter*, Leipzig 1923.
Esser, D.: *Formgeschichtliche Studien zur hellenistischen und zur frühchristlichen Literatur unter besonderer Berücksichtigung der vita Apollonii des Philostrat und der Evangelien*, Diss. Bonn 1969.

Fascher, E.: *Die formgeschichtliche Methode*, *BZNW* 2, Berlin 1924.
– *Kritik am Wunder, Eine geschichtliche Skizze*, Stuttgart 1960.
Fenner, F.: *Die Krankheit im Neuen Testament*, *UNT* 18, Leipzig 1930.
Feuerbach, L.: *Das Wesen des Christentums*, in: *Sämtliche Werke* 6, eds. W. Bolin and F. Jodl, Stuttgart 1903-11 (*The essence of Christianity*, London 1854).
Fiebig, P.: *Antike Wundergeschichten*, *KlT* 79, Bonn 1911.
– *Jüdische Wundergeschichten des neutestamentlichen Zeitalters*, Tübingen 1911.
– 'Neues zu den rabbinischen Wundergeschichten', *ZNW* 35 (1936) 308-309.
Fiedler, P.: *Die Formel 'und siehe' im Neuen Testament*, Munich 1969.
Frankfort, H. and H.A., u.a.: *Frühlicht des Geistes*, Stuttgart 1954, 9-16.
Freud, S.: *Neue Folge der Vorlesungen zur Einführung in die Psychologie, Gesammelte Werke* XV, London 1940 (*New series of Introductory Lectures on psychoanalysis*. Standard ed. vols. 15 & 16, London 1963).
– *Totem und Tabu, Ges. Werke* IX, 3rd ed. London 1961. (*Totem and taboo: some points of agreement between the mental lives of savages and neurotics*, London 1950).
Fridrichsen, A.: *Le problème du miracle dans le Christianisme primitif*, *EHPhR* 12, Strasbourg – Paris 1925 (*The problem of miracle in primitive Christianity*, Minneapolis 1972).
Friedrich, H.: 'Strukturalismus und Struktur in literaturwissenschaftlicher Hinsicht', in: G. Schiwy: *Der französische Strukturalismus*, rde 310/311, Hamburg 1969, 219-227.
Fuchs, E.: 'Über die Aufgabe einer christlichen Theologie', *ZThK* 58 (1961) 245-267.
Fuchs, H.: *Der geistige Widerstand gegen Rom in der antiken Welt*, 2nd ed., Berlin 1964.
Fügen, H.N.: *Die Hauptrichtungen der Literatursoziologie, Abhandlungen zur Kunst-, Musik- und Literaturwissenschaft* 21, 4th ed., Bonn 1970.
Fuller, R.H.: *Interpreting the Miracles*, London 1963.
Fürstenberg, F.: *Religionssoziologie, Soziologische Texte* 19, Neuwied 1964.

Gadamer, H.G.: *Wahrheit und Methode*, 1st ed., Tübingen 1960, 2nd ed., 1965 (*Truth and Method*, London 1975).
Gardavsky, V.: *Gott ist nicht ganz tot*, Munich 1968 (*God is not yet dead*, London 1973).
Geckeler, H.: *Strukturelle Semantik und Wortfeldtheorie*, Munich 1971.
Geffcken, J.: *Der Ausgang des griechisch-römischen Heidentums, Religionswissenschaftliche Bibliothek* 6 (1929) = Darmstadt 1963.
Gehlen, A.: 'Über die Verstehbarkeit der Magie', in: *Studien zur Anthropologie und Soziologie*, Neuwied 1963, 79-92.
– *Urmensch und Spätkultur*, Frankfurt-Bonn 1964.
Georgi, D.: *Die Gegner des Paulus im 2. Korintherbrief. Studien zur religiösen Propaganda in der Spätantike*, *WMANT* 11, Neukirchen 1964.
Gerber, W.: 'Die Metamorphose Jesu', *ThZ* 23 (1967) 385-395.
Gerhardson, B.: *Memory and Manuscript. Oral Tradition and Written Transmission in Rabbinic Judaism and Early Christianity*, *ASNU* XXII, Lund 1961.
– *Tradition and Transmission in Early Christianity*, *CM* XX, Lund 1964.
Gibbs, J.M.: 'Purpose and Pattern in Matthew's Use of the Title "Son of David" ', *NTS* 10 (1963/4) 446-464.
Glade, D.: 'Zum Anderson'schen Gesetz der Selbstberichtigung', *Fab* 8 (1966) 224-236.

Glasswell, M.E.: 'The Use of Miracles in the Markan Gospel', in: *Miracles. Cambridge Studies in their Philosophy and History*, ed. C.F.D. Moule, London 1965, 151-162.

Glombitza, O.: 'Der dankbare Samariter', *NovTest* 11 (1969) 341-346.

Grasser, E.: 'Jesus in Nazareth', *NTS* 16 (1969) 1-23.

– *Das Problem der Parusieverzögerung in den synoptischen Evangelien und in der Apostelgeschichte, BZNW* 22, Berlin 1957.

Grant, R. M.: 'Miracle and Mythology', *ZRGG 3* (1951) 123-133.

– *Miracles and Natural Law in Graeco-Roman and Early Christian Thought*, Amsterdam 1952.

Greimas, A.J.: *Sémantique structurale, recherche de méthode*, Paris 1966.

Gressmann, H.: *Altorientalische Texte und Bilder zum Alten Testament*, 2 Vols., 2nd ed., Leipzig and Berlin 1926/27.

Greverus, I.M.: 'Thema, Typus und Motiv. Zur Determination in der Erzählforschung', in: *Vergleichende Sagenforschung*, ed. L. Petzoldt, *WF* CLII, Darmstadt 1969, 390-401.

Grobel, K.: *Formgeschichte und Synoptische Quellenanalyse, FRLANT* 53, Göttingen 1937.

Grundmann, W.: *Der Begriff der Kraft in der neutestamentlichen Gedankenwelt, BWANT* 4, 8, Stuttgart 1932.

– 'δύναμαι' *ThW* II, 286-318 (*TDNT* II, 284-317).

– *Das Evangelium nach Lukas, ThHK* 3, Berlin 1961.

– *Das Evangelium nach Markus, ThHK* 2, Berlin 1959, 4th ed., 1968.

– *Das Evangelium nach Matthäus, ThHK* 1, 2nd ed., Berlin 1971.

Güttgemanns, E.: *Offene Fragen zur Formgeschichte des Evangeliums, BEvTh* 54, Munich 1970 (*Candid Questions concerning Gospel form-criticism*, Pittsburgh 1979).

– 'Linguistisch-literaturwissenschaftliche Grundlegung einer Neutestamentlichen Theologie', *LB* 13/14 (1972) 2-18.

– 'Struktural-generative Analyse des Bildwortes "Die verlorene Drachme" (Lk 15, 8-10)', *LB* 6 (1971) 2-17.

– et al.: 'Theologie als sprachbezogene Wissenschaft', *LB* 4/5 (1971) 7-41, abbrev. in: E. Guttgemanns: 'studia linguistica neotestamentica. *BEvTh* 60, Munich 1971, 184-230.

Guttmann, A.: 'The Significance of Miracles for Talmudic Judaism', *HUCA* 20 (1947) 363-406.

Gutwenger, E.: 'Die Machterweise Jesu in formgeschichtlicher Sicht', *ZKTh* 89 (1967) 176-190.

Habermas, J.: *Zur Logik der Sozialwissenschaften, PhR Beiheft* 5, Tübingen 1967.

– 'Der Universalitätsanspruch der Hermeneutik', in: *Hermeneutik und Ideologiekritik*, Frankfurt 1971, 120-159.

Haenchen, E.: *Die Apostelgeschichte*, MeyerK, 13th ed., Göttingen 1961 (*The Acts of the Apostles*, Oxford 1971).

– 'Johanneische Probleme', in: *Gott und Mensch*, Tübingen 1965, 78-113.

– *Der weg Jesu. Eine Erklärung des Markus-Evangeliums und der kanonischen Parallelen*, Berlin 1966.

Hahn, F.: *Christologische Hoheitstitel, FRLANT* 83, 3rd ed., Göttingen 1966 (*The titles of Jesus in christology*, London 1969).

Hand, W.D.: 'Curative Practice in Folk Tales', *Fab* 8 (1966) 264-269.

– 'The Curing of Blindness in Folk Tales', in: *Volksüberlieferung. Festschrift für K. Ranke zur Vollendung des 60. Lebensjahres*, eds. F. Harkort, K.C. Peeters and R. Wildhaber, Göttingen 1968, 81-87.

Harkort, F.: Volkserzählungstypen und -motive und Vorstellungsberichte', *Fab* 8 (1966) 208-223.

Harnack, A.v.: *Die Mission und Ausbreitung des Christentums in den ersten drei Jahrhunderten*, 4th ed., Leipzig 1924 (*The expansion of Christianity in the first three centuries*, London 1904-5).

– *Lukas der Arzt. Beiträge zur Einleitung in das NT 1*, Leipzig 1906 (*New Testament Studies* I, *Luke, the Physician*, London 1907).

Harnisch, W.: *Verhängnis und Verheißung der Geschichte, FRLANT* 97, Göttingen 1969.

Haufe, G.: 'Hellenistische Volksfrömmigkeit', in: *Umwelt des Urchristentums* I, ed. J. Leipoldt and W. Grundmann, Berlin 1965, 68-100.

Hay, L.S.: 'The Son of Man in Mark 2. 10 and 2. 28', *JBL* 89 (1970) 69-74.

Headlam, A.C.: *The Miracles of the New Testament*, London 1923.

Heinemann, I.: 'Die Kontroverse über das Wunder im Judentum der hellenistischen Zeit', in: *Jubilee Volume in Honor of Prof. Bernhard Heller*, Budapest 1941, 170-191.

Heinrich, K.: *Parmenides und Jona. Vier Studien über das Verhältnis von Philosophie und Mythologie*, Frankfurt 1966.

Held, H.J.: 'Matthäus als Interpret der Wundergeschichten', in: G. Bornkamm, G. Barth, H.J. Held: *Überlieferung und Auslegung im Matthäusevangelium*, WMANT 1, 4th ed., Neukirchen 1965, 155-310. ('Matthew as Interpreter of the Miracle Stories' in G. Bornkamm, G. Barth, H.J. Held, *Tradition and Interpretation in Matthew*, 165-299).

Hempel, J.: *Heilung als Symbol und Wirklichkeit im biblischen Schrifttum*, 2nd ed., Göttingen 1965.

Hengel, R. and M.: 'Die Heilungen Jesu und medizinisches Denken', in: *Medicus Viator, Festschrift R. Siebeck*, Tübingen und Stuttgart 1959, 331-361.

Hengel, M.: *Judentum und Hellenismus. Studien zu ihrer Begegnung unter besonderer Berücksichtigung Palästinas bis zur Mitte des 2. Jh. v. Chr.*, WUNT 10, Tübingen 1969. (*Judaism and Hellenism: Studies in their encounter in Palestine during the Early Hellenistic Period*, London 1974).

– *Nachfolge und Charisma*, BZNW 34, Berlin 1968 (*The charismatic leader and his followers*, SNTW 1, Edinburgh 1981).

Hennecke, E., and W. Schneemelcher: *Neutestamentliche Apokryphen* I, Tübingen 1959.

Herrmann, W.: 'Das Wunder in der evangelischen Botschaft. Zur Interpretation der Begriffe "blind" und "taub" im Alten und Neuen Testament', *Aufsätze und Vorträge zur Theologie und Religionswissenschaft* 20, Berlin 1961.

Herzig, O.: *Lukian als Quelle für die antike Zauberei*, Diss. Tübingen 1933 = Würzburg 1931.

Herzog, R.: *Die Wunderheilungen von Epidauros. Ein Beitrag zur Geschichte der Medizin und der Religion*, Philol. Suppl. XXII, vol. 3, Leipzig 1931.

Hirsch, E.: *Frühgeschichte des Evangeliums* I, Tübingen 1941.

Höfler, A.: *Der Sarapishymnus des Aelios Aristeides*, Tübinger Beiträge zur Altertumswissenschaft 27, Stuttgart und Berlin 1935.

Hölscher, U.: *Die Chance des Unbehagens. Zur Situation der klassischen Studien*, Göttingen 1965.

Holtzmann, H.J.: *Die Synoptiker*, HNT 1, 3rd ed., Tübingen und Leipzig 1901.

Honko, L.: 'Genre Analysis in Folkloristics and Comparative Religion', *Temenos* 3 (1968) 48-66.

Hopfner, Th.: 'Mageia', *PW* 14, 1, 301-393.

– 'Μαντική', *PW* 14, 1258-1287.

– *Griechisch-ägyptischer Offenbarungszauber I.II.*, Studien zur Palaeographie und Papyruskunde XXI.XXIII, Leipzig 1921. 1924.

Humboldt, W.: *Schriften zur Sprachphilosophie, Werke* III, eds. A. Flitner and K. Giel, Stuttgart and Darmstadt 1963.

Iber, G.: 'Zur Formgeschichte der Evangelien', *ThR* 24 (1956/7) 283-338.

Iersel, B. von: 'Die wunderbare Speisung und das Abendmahl in der synoptischen Tradition', *NovTest* 7 (1964/5) 167-194.

Jakobi, J.: *Komplex, Archetypus, Symbol in der Psychologie C. G. Jungs*, Zürich and Stuttgart 1957.

Jahnow, H.: 'Das Abdecken des Daches Mc 2, 4 Lk 5, 19, *ZNW* 24 (1925) 155-158.

Jakobson, R., and J. Tynjanow: 'Probleme der Literatur und Sprachforschung', reprinted in *Kursbuch* 5 (1966) 74-76.

Jayne, W.A.: *The Healing Gods of Ancient Civilization*, New York 1925, 2nd ed., 1962.

Jech, J.: 'Variabilitat und Stabilität in den einzelnen Kategorien der Volksprosa', *Fab* 9 (1967) 55-62.

Jelke, R.: *Die Wunder Jesu*, Leipzig 1923.

Jeremias, J.: *Die Gleichnisse Jesu*, 7th ed., Göttingen 1965 (*The parables of Jesus*, London 1963).

Jolles, A.: *Einfache Formen*, Tübingen 1930, 3rd ed., 1965.

Jones, A.H.M.: *The Cities of the Eastern Roman Provinces*, Oxford 1937.
Judge, E.A.: *The Social Pattern of Christian Groups in the First Century*, London 1960.
Julicher, A.: *Die Gleichnisreden Jesu II*, 2nd ed., Tübingen 1910.
Jung, C.G.: *Psychologische Typen*, 7th ed., Zürich 1950 (*Psychological Types. Collected Works*, vol. 6, London 1972).

Kasting, H.: *Die Anfänge urchristlicher Mission*, Munich 1969.
Kähler, M.: *Der sogenannte historische Jesus und der geschichtliche biblische Christus*, new ed. by E. Wolf, *ThB* 2 2nd ed., Munich 1956 (*The so-called historical Jesus and the historic, biblical Christ*, Philadelphia 1964).
Käsemann, E.: 'Begründet der neutestamentliche Kanon die Einheit der Kirche' in: *Exegetische Versuche und Besinnungen* I, Göttingen 1960, 214-223 ('The Canon of the New Testament and the Unity of the Church' in *Essays on New Testament Themes*, London 1964, 95-107).
– *Jesu letzter Wille nach Johannes 17*, Tübingen 1966 (*The Testament of Jesus: a study of the Gospel of John in the light of chapter 17*, London 1968).
– 'Das Problem des historischen Jesus' in: *Exegetische Versuche und Besinnungen* I, 187-214 ('The Problem of the Historical Jesus' in *Essays on New Testament Themes*, 15-47).
– 'Zum Thema der Nichtobjektivierbarkeit, in: *Exegetische Versuche und Besinnungen* I, 214-236 ('Is the Gospel Objective? in *Essays on New Testament Themes*, 48-62).
Kallas, J.: *The Significance of the Synoptic Miracles, Biblical Monographs* 2, London 1961.
Keck, L.E.: 'The Introduction to Mark's Gospel', *NTS* 12 (1965/6) 352-370.
– 'Mark 3, 7-12 and Mark's Christology', *JBL* 84 (1965) 341-358.
Kee, H.C.: 'The Terminology of Mark's Exorcism Stories', *NTS* 14 (1967/8) 232-246.
Keller, E. and M.L.: *Der Streit um die Wunder*, Gütersloh 1968 (*Miracles in Dispute: a continuing debate*, London 1969).
Kertelge, K.: *Die Wunder Jesu im Markusevangelium, StANT 23*, Munich 1970.
Klatt, W.: *Hermann Gunkel, FRLANT* 100, Göttingen 1969.
Klausner, Th.: 'Akklamation', *RAC* I, 216-233.
Klein, G.: 'Wunderglaube und Neues Testament', in: *Ärgernisse*, Munich 1970, 13-57.
Klimkeit, H.J.: *Das Wunderverständnis Ludwig Feuerbachs in religionsphänomenologischer Sicht. Untersuchungen zur allgemeinen Religionsgeschichte N.S.* 5, Bonn 1965.
Klostermann, E.: *Das Markusevangelium, HNT* 3, 4th ed., Tübingen 1950.
– *Das Matthäusevangelium, HNT* 4, 3rd ed., Tübingen 1938.
– *Das Lukasevangelium, HNT* 5, 2nd ed., Tübingen 1929.
Kock, K.: *Ratlos vor der Apokalyptik*, Gütersloh 1970 (*The Rediscovery of apocalyptic*, London 1972).
Kosack, W.: 'Der Gattungsbegriff "Volkserzählung" ', *Fab* 12 (1971) 18-47.
Köster, H.: 'One Jesus and Four Primitive Gospels' in: *Trajectories through Early Christianity*, (with J.M. Robinson) Philadelphia 1971, 158-204.
Kramer, W.: *Christos Kyrios Gottessohn, AThANT* 44, Zürich and Stuttgart 1963.
Kraus, S.: 'Das Abdecken des Daches Mc 2, 4 Lc 5, 19', *ZNW* 25 (1926) 307-310.
Kroh, O.: *Die Psychologie des Grundschulkindes*, 4th-6th eds., Langensalza 1930.
Kümmel, W.G.: *Verheissung und Erfüllung, AThANT* 6, 2nd ed., Zürich 1953 (*Promise and Fulfilment*, London 1957).
– *Die Theologie des Neuen Testament, NTD* Ergänzungsreihe 3, 1969 (*The Theology of the New Testament*, Nashville 1973).
Kuhn, H.W.: *Enderwartung und gegenwärtiges Heil, StUNT* 4, Göttingen 1966, 189-204.
– 'Der irdische Jesus bei Paulus als traditionsgeschichtliches und theologisches Problem', *ZThK* 67 (1970) 295-320.
– *Ältere Sammlungen im Markusevangelium, StUNT* 8, Göttingen 1971.
Kuhn, K.G.: 'Jesus in Gethsemane', *EvTH* 12 (1952/3) 260-285.

Lagrange, M.J.: 'Les légendes pythagoriciennes et l'évangile', *RB* 45 (1936) 481ff., 46 (1937) 5ff.
Lämmert, E.: *Bauformen des Erzählens*, Stuttgart 1955.
Langer, S.K.: *Philosophy in a New Key: A Study in the Symbolism of Reason, Rite and Art*, 3rd ed., Harvard 1957.

Lampe, G.W.: 'Miracles in the Acts of the Apostles', in: *Miracles. Cambridge Studies in their Philosophy and History,* ed. C.F.D. Moule, London 1965.

Laubscher, A.: 'Betrachtungen zur Inhaltsanalyse von Erzählgut', *Paideuma* 14 (1968) 170-194.

Leach, E. (Ed.): *The Structural Study of Myth and Totemism,* London 1967.

Leeuw, G.v.d.: *Phänomenologie der Religion,* 2nd ed., Tübingen 1956 (*Religion in essence and in manifestation,* Gloucester (Mass.) 1967).

Lehmann, A.: *Aberglaube und Zauberei,* Stuttgart 1925 = Aalen 1969.

Lehmann, M.: *Synoptische Quellenanalyse und die Frage nach dem historischen Jesus, BZNW* 38, Berlin 1970.

Leipoldt, J.: *Von Epidauros bis Lourdes,* Leipzig 1957.

– 'Gebet und Zauber im Urchristentum', *ZKG* 54 (1935) 1-11.

– 'Von Übersetzungen und Übersetzern', in: *Antike und Orient, Festschrift W. Schubart,* ed. S. Morenz, Leipzig 1950.

Lembert, R.: *Der Wunderglaube bei Römern und Griechen,* Augsburg 1905.

Lévi-Strauss, C.: 'Die Sage von Asdiwal', in: *Religionsethnologie,* ed. C.A. Schmitz, Frankfurt 1964, 154-195 (French 1958).

– 'Die Struktur der Mythen', in: *Strukturale Anthropologie,* Frankfurt 1967 (French 1958), 226-254.

Lévy, I.: *La légende de Pythagore de Grèce en Palestine, Bibliothèque de l'école des hautes études. Sciences historiques et philologiques* 250, Paris 1927.

– *Recherches sur les sources de la légende de Pythagore, Bibliothèque de l'école des hautes études. Sciences religieuses* 42, Paris 1926.

Lietzmann, H.: *Geschichte der alten Kirche,* 4 vols., 3rd ed., Berlin 1961.

Lindars, B.: 'Elijah, Elisha and the Gospel Miracles', in: *Miracles. Cambridge Studies in their Philosophy and History,* ed. C.F.D. Moule, London 1965, 63-79.

Lindblom, J.: *Gesichte und Offenbarungen. Vorstellungen von göttlichen Weisungen und übernatürlichen Erscheinungen im ältesten Christentum, Acta Reg. Soc. Hum. Litt. Lundensis* LXV, Lund 1968.

Linton, O.: 'The Demand for a Sign from Heaven (Mk 8, 11-12 and Parallels)', *StTh* 19 (1965) 112-129.

Linton, R.: 'Nativistische Bewegungen', in: *Religionsethnologie,* ed. C. A. Schmitz, Frankfurt 1964, 390-403.

Linnemann, E.: *Gleichnisse Jesu,* 4th ed., Göttingen 1966 (*Parables of Jesus: introduction and exposition,* London 1975).

Littleton, G.S.: 'A Two-Dimensional Schema for the Classification of Narratives', *JAF* 78 (1965) 21-27.

Lohmeyer, E.: *Das Evangelium des Markus, MeyerK,* 16th ed., Göttingen 1963.

– '"Und Jesus ging vorüber" ', in: *Urchristliche Mystik,* Darmstadt 1955, 57-79.

– 'Die Verklärung Jesu nach dem Markus-Evangelium', *ZNW* 21 (1922) 185-215.

Lo Nigro, S.: 'Tradition et Style du Conte populaire', in: *Internat. Kongreß der Volkserzählungsforscher,* Berlin 1961, 152-160.

Loos, H.v.d.: *The Miracles of Jesus, Supplem. NovTest* 8, Leiden 1965.

Lord, A.B.: *The Singer of Tales,* Cambridge (Mass.) 1960.

Lorenzer, A.: *Kritik des psychoanalytischen Symbolbegriffs,* edition suhrkamp 393, Frankfurt 1970.

Lüthi, M.: 'Aspekte des Volksmärchens und der Volkssage', *GRM* NS 16 (1966) 337-350.

– *Das europäische Volksmärchen,* Bern 1947, 2nd ed., 1960.

– 'Urform und Zielform in Sage und Märchen', *Fab* 9 (1967) 41-54.

Luz, U.: 'Das Geheimnismotiv und die markinische Christologie', *ZNW* 56 (1965) 9-30.

Maisch, I.: *Die Heilung des Gelähmten,* Diss. Freiburg 1970.

Malinowski, B.: 'The Role of Myth in Life', in: *Myth in Primitive Psychology,* London 1926, 11-45.

Marxsen, W.: *Einleitung in das Neue Testament,* Gütersloh 1963 (*Introduction to the New Testament,* Oxford 1968).

– *Der Evangelist Markus, FRLANT* 67, 2nd ed., Göttingen 1959 (*Mark the Evangelist,* Nashville 1969).

McCasland, S.V.: *By the Finger of God*, New York 1951.
– 'Signs and Wonders', *JBL* 76 (1957) 149-152.
– 'Portents in Josephus and in the Gospels', *JBL* 51 (1932) 323-335.
McDonald, A.H.: 'Herodotus on the Miraculous', in: *Miracles. Cambridge Studies in their Philosophy and History*, London 1965, 95-111.
McGinley, L.J.: 'Form-Criticism of the Synoptic Healing Narratives', *ThSt* 2 (1941) 451-480, 3 (1942) 47-68, 203-230, 4 (1943) 53-99, 385-419.
MacRae, G.: 'Miracles in the Antiquities of Josephus', in: *Miracles. Cambridge Studies in their Philosophy and History*, London 1965, 129-147.
Mead, R.T.: 'The Healing of the Paralytic – a Unit?' *JBL* 80 (1961) 348-354.
Meletinskiy, E.: 'Zur strukturell-typologischen Erforschung des Volksmärchens', in: W. Propp: *Morphologie des Märchens*, Munich 1972 (Russ. 1928), 179-214.
Mensching, G.: *Soziologie der Religion*, 2nd ed., Bonn 1968.
– *Das Wunder im Glauben und Aberglauben der Völker*, Leiden 1957.
Meyer, A.: 'Die Entstehung des Markusevangeliums', in: *Festgabe für A. Jülicher*, Tübingen 1927, 35-60.
Meyer, R.: *Der Prophet aus Galiläa*, Leipzig 1940 = Darmstadt 1970.
– 'Προφήτης' *ThW* VI 813-828 (*TDNT* VI, 812-828).
Millar, F.: *Das Römische Reich und seine Nachbarn. Die Mittelmeerwelt im Altertum IV*, Fischer Weltgeschichte 8, Frankfurt 1966 (*The Roman Empire and its Neighbours*, London 1967).
Minette de Tillesse, G.: *Le secret messianique dans l'évangile de Marc, Lectio Divina* 47, Paris 1968.
Monden, L.: *Le miracle signe de salut*. n.p. 1960.
Montefiore, C.G.: *Rabbinic Literature and Gospel Teachings*, New York 1930, 2nd ed., 1970.
Moore, G.F.: *Judaism in the first centuries of the Christian Era. The Age of the Tannaim*, 2 vols., Cambridge 1927.
Mosley, A.W.: 'Jesus' Audiences in the Gospel of St. Mark and St. Luke', *NTS* 10 (1963/4) 139-149.
Moule, C.F.D.: 'The Classification of Miracles', in: *Miracles. Cambridge Studies in their Philosophy and History*. London 1965, 239-243.
– 'The Vocabulary of Miracle', in: *Miracles. Cambridge Studies in their Philosophy and History*, London 1965, 235-238.
Moulton, J.H.: *A Grammar of New Testament Greek*, Edinburgh 1963.
Mühlmann, W.E.: *Chiliasmus und Nativismus, Studien zur Psychologie, Soziologie und historischen Kasuistik der Umsturzbewegungen. Studien zur Soziologie der Revolution* vol. 1, Berlin 1961.
– 'Umrisse und Probleme einer Kulturanthropologie', in: W.E. Mühlmann: *Homo Creator*, Wiesbaden 1962, 107-129, reprinted in: W.E. Mühlmann and E.W. Müller: *Kulturanthropologie, Neue Wissenschaftl. Bibliothek* 9, Köln and Berlin 1966, 15-49.
Müller, G.: 'Erzählzeit und erzählte Zeit', in: *Festschrift P. Kluckhohn und H. Schneider*, Tübingen 1948, 195-212.
Müller, H.P.: 'Die Verklärung Jesu. Eine motivgeschichtliche Studie', *ZNW* 51 (1960) 56-64.
Mussner, F.: *Die Wunder Jesu. Eine Hinführung, Schriften zur Katechetik* 10, Munich 1967.

Nathhorst, B.: 'Genre, Form and Structure in Oral Tradition', *Temenos* 3 (1968) 128-135.
Neil, W.: 'Expository Problems: the Nature Miracles', *ET* 67 (1955/6) 369ff.
Neusner, J.: *A History of the Jews in Babylonia*, vols. 3-5, Leiden 1968, 1969, 1970.
Nikolaus, W.: 'Tempelzerstörung und synoptische Apokalypse', *ZNW* 57 (1966) 38-49.
Nilsson, M.P.: *Geschichte der griechischen Religion*. I: *Bis zur griechischen Weltherrschaft, AW* 5, 2, 1, Munich 1941, II: *Die hellenistische und römische Zeit, HAW* 5, 2, 2, Munich 1950.
– *Die Religion in den griechischen Zauberpapyri, Bulletin de la societé royale des lettres de Lund* 1947-1948, Lund 1948.
Noetzel, H.: *Christus und Dionysos, Arbeiten zur Theologie* 1, Stuttgart 1960.

Oepke, A.: 'ἰάομαι' *ThW* III, 194-215 (*TDNT* III, 194-215).

Olrik, A.: 'Gesetze der Volksdichtung', *Zeitschrift f. deutsches Altertum* 51 (1909) 1-12.

Ortutay, G.: 'Begriff und Bedeutung der Affinität in der mündlichen Überlieferung', in: *Internat. Kongreß der Volkserzählungsforscher* Berlin 1961, 247-252.

— 'Principles of oral Transmission in Folk Culture', *Acta Ethnographica* 8, Budapest 1959, 175-221.

Otto, R.: *Das Heilige*, Breslau 1917 (*The idea of the holy*, rev. ed., London 1929).

— *Reich Gottes und Menschensohn*, Munich 1934 (*The Kingdom of God and the Son of Man*, rev. ed., London 1943).

Otto, W.F.: *Die Gestalt und das Sein*, Düsseldorf 1955.

— *Theophania*, rde 15, Hamburg 1956.

— *Die Wirklichkeit der Götter*, rde 170, Hamburg 1963.

Overbeck, F.: *Über die Christlichkeit unserer heutigen Theologie*, Leipzig 1903 = 3rd ed., Darmstadt 1963.

Pax, E.: ΕΠΙΦΑΝΕΙΑ. *Ein religionsgeschichtlicher Beitrag zur biblischen Theologie, MThS* I, Hist. Abt. 10, Munich 1955.

— 'Epiphanie', *RAC* V, 832-909.

Perels, O.: *Die Wunderüberlieferung der Synoptiker in ihrem Verhältnis zur Wortüberlieferung, BWANT* IV, 12, Stuttgart and Berlin 1934.

Pesch, R.: *Jesu ureigene Taten? Quaestiones Disputatae* 52, Freiburg 1970.

— *Naherwartungen. Tradition und Redaktion in Mk 13*, Düsseldorf 1968.

— *Der reiche Fischfang (Lk 5, 1-11/Jo 21, 1-14), Wundergeschichte — Berufungserzählung — Erscheinungsbericht*, Düsseldorf 1969.

— 'Ein Tag vollmächtigen Wirkens Jesu in Kapharnaum (Mk 1, 29-34, 35-39)', *BL* 9 (1968) 114-128, 177-195, 261-277.

Pfister, F.: 'Beschwörung', *RAC* II, 169-176.

Percy, E.: *Die Botschaft Jesu*, Lund 1953.

Peterson, E.: 'Die Einholung des Kyrios', *ZSTh* 7 (1930) 682-702.

— εἷς Θεός, *FRLANT* 41, Göttingen 1926.

Petzke, G.: *Die Traditionen über Apollonius von Tyana und das Neue Testament, Studia ad Corpus Hellenisticum Novi Testamenti* 1, Leiden 1970.

Plöger, O.: *Theokratie und Eschatologie, WMANT* 2, Neukirchen 1959.

Pop, M.: 'Aspects actuels des recherches sur la structure des contes', *Fab* 9 (1967) 70-77.

Popkes, W.: *Christus traditus, AThANT* 49, Zürich 1967.

Praechter, K.: 'Die Philosophie des Altertums', in: *F. Ueberwegs Grundriß der Geschichte der Philosophie*, 14th ed., Basel and Stuttgart 1957.

Preisker, H.: 'Wundermächte und Wundermänner der hellenistisch-römischen Kultur und die Auferweckung des Lazarus im 11. Kap. des Johannesevangeliums'. *Wissenschaftl. Zeitschrift der Martin-Luther-Universität Halle–Wittenberg, Gesellschafts und sprachwissenschaftliche Reihe No. 6 11* (1952/3) 519-523.

Preisigke, F.: *Die Gotteskraft der frühchristlichen Zeit. Papyrusinstitut Heidelberg Schrift 6*, Berlin and Leipzig 1922.

Preisendanz, K.: *Papyri Graecae Magicae. Die griechischen Zauberpapyri*, 2 vols., Leipzig 1928. 1931.

Preuss, H.R.: *Galiläa im Markus Evangelium*, Diss. Göttingen 1966.

Propp, W.: *Morphologie des Märchens*, Munich 1972 (Russ. 1928).

Prümm, K.: *Religionsgeschichtliches Handbuch für den Raum der altchristlichen Umwelt*, Freiburg 1943.

Ranke, K.: 'Betrachtungen zum Wesen und zur Funktion des Märchens', *StudGen* 11 (1958) 647-664.

— 'Orale und literale Kontinuität', in: *Kontinuität? Geschichtlichkeit und Dauer als volkskundliches Problem*, eds. H. Bausinger and W. Brückner, Berlin 1969, 102-116.

— 'Einfache Formen', in: *Internat. Kongreß der Volkserzählungsforscher*, Berlin 1961, 1-11.

— 'Kategorienprobleme der Volksprosa', *Fab* 9 (1967) 4-12.

Reitzenstein, R.: *Hellenistische Mysterienreligionen*, 3rd ed., Stuttgart 1927 = Darmstadt 1966 (*Hellenistic mystery-religions*, Pittsburgh 1978).

— *Hellenistische Wundererzählungen*, Leipzig 1906 = 2nd ed., Darmstadt 1963.

Rengstorf, K.H.: *Die Anfänge der Auseinandersetzung zwischen Christusglaube und Asklepiosfrömmigkeit*, Münster 1953.
Reploh, K.G.: *Markus – Lehrer der Gemeinde, SBM* 9, Stuttgart 1969.
Richardson, A.: *The Miracle Stories of the Gospels*, London 1941, 3rd ed., 1948.
Richter, W.: *Exegese als Literaturwissenschaft*, Göttingen 1971.
– 'Formgeschichte und Sprachwissenschaft', *ZAW* 82 (1970) 216-225.
Ricoeur, P.: *De l'Interpretation*, Paris 1965 (*Freud and philosophy: an essay on interpretation*, London 1970).
– *La symbolique du mal*, Paris 1960 (*The symbolism of evil*, Boston 1969).
Riesenfeld, H.: 'Tradition und Redaktion im Markusevangelium', in: *Neutestamentliche Studien für R. Bultmann, BZNW* 21 (1954) 157-164.
Robinson, J.M.: *Das Geschichtsverständnis des Markusevangeliums, AThANT* 30, Zürich 1956 (*The problem of history in Mark*, London 1957).
Robinson, W.C.: *Der Weg des Herrn, ThF* 36, Hamburg-Bergstedt 1964.
Rohde, E.: *Psyche. Seelencult und Unsterblichkeitsglaube der Griechen*, 5th & 6th eds., Tübingen 1910.
Röhrich, L.: 'Das Kontinuitätsproblem bei der Erforschung der Volksprosa', in: *Kontinuität? Geschichtlichkeit und Dauer als volkskundliches Problem*, eds. H. Bausinger and W. Brückner, Berlin 1969, 117-133.
Roloff, J.: *'Das Kerygma und der irdische Jesus'*, Göttingen 1970.
– 'Das Markusevangelium als Geschichtsdarstellung', *EvTh* 27 (1969) 73-93.
Rostovtzeff, M.: *Gesellschaft und Wirtschaft im römischen Kaiserreich*, 2 vols., Leipzig 1931 (*The social and economic history of the Roman Empire*, Oxford 1926).
Rüschemeyer, D.: 'Einleitung zu T. Parsons: Beiträge zur soziologischen Theorie', *Soziologische Texte* 15, Neuwied 1964, 9-29.
Rudberg, G.: 'ΕΥΘΥΣ', *CN* IX (1944) 42-46.
– 'Zur Diogenes-Tradition', *SO* 14 (1935) 22-43.
Rydbeck, L.: *Fachprosa, vermeintliche Volkssprache und Neues Testament*, Uppsala 1967.

Scheler, M.: *Die Wissensformen und die Gesellschaft*, 2nd ed., Bern and Munich 1960 (*Problems of a sociology of knowledge*, London 1979).
Schenk, W.: 'Tradition und Redaktion in der Epileptiker-Perikope Mk 9, 14-29', *ZNW* 63 (1972) 76-94.
Schenke, L.: *Auferstehungsverkündigung und leeres Grab, SBS* 33, Stuttgart 1968.
Schick, E.: *Formgeschichte und Synoptikerexegese, NTA* 18, 2-3, Münster 1940.
Schille, G.: *Anfänge der Kirche. Erwägungen zur apostolischen Frühgeschichte, BEvTh* 43, Munich 1966.
– 'Bemerkungen zur Formgeschichte des Evangeliums II', *NTS* 4 (1957/8) 101-114.
– 'Das Leiden des Herrn', *ZThK* 52 (1953) 161-203.
– 'Die Seesturmerzählung Markus 4, 35-41', *ZNW* 56 (1965) 30-40.
– 'Die Topographie des Markusevangeliums', *ZDPV* 73 (1957) 133-166.
– *Die urchristliche Wundertradition. Ein Beitrag zur Frage nach dem irdischen Jesus. Arbeiten zur Theologie* I, 29, Stuttgart 1967.
Schiwy, G.: *Der französische Strukturalismus*, rde 310/311, Hamburg 1969.
Schlingensiepen, H.: *Die Wunder des Neuen Testaments. Wege und Abwege ihrer Deutung in der alten Kirche bis zur Mitte des fünften Jahrhunderts, BFChTh* 2, 28, Gütersloh 1933.
Schlatter, A.: *Das Wunder in der Synagoge, BFChTh* 16, 5, Gütersloh 1912.
Schmid, W., O. Stählin: Geschichte der griechischen Literatur, HAW VII, 2, 2, Munich 1924.
Schmidbauer, W.: *Mythos und Psychologie. Methodische Probleme, aufgezeigt an der Ödipus-Sage*, Munich and Basel 1970.
Schmithals, W.: *Wunder und Glaube, BSt* 59, Neukirchen 1970.
Schnider, F., W. Stenger: *Johannes und die Synoptiker*, Munich 1971.
Schottroff, L.: Der Glaubende und die feindliche Welt. WMANT 37, Neukirchen 1970.
Schrage, W.: 'τυφλός' *ThW* VIII, 270-294 (*TDNT* VIII, 270-294).
Schreiber, J.: 'Die Christologie des Markusevangeliums', *ZThK* 58 (1961) 154-183.
– *Die Markuspassion*, Hamburg 1969.
Schreuder, O.: 'Die strukturell-funktionale Theorie und die Religionssoziologie', *IJR* 2 (1966) 99-134.

Schubert, P.: 'The Structure and Significance of Luke 24', in: *Festschrift R. Bultmann*, *BZNW* 21, Berlin 1954, 165-186.

Schulz, S.: *Die Bedeutung des Markus für die Theologiegeschichte des Urchristentums, TU* 87, Berlin 1964.

Schürmann, H.: 'Der "Bericht vom Anfang" ', *TU* 87, Berlin 1964, 242-258.

– *Das Lukasevangelium. Erster Teil, HThK* III, 1, Freiburg 1969.

Schütz, C.: 'Die Wunder Jesu', in: *Mysterium Salutis* III, 2, Einsiedeln 1969, 97-123.

Schütz, H.J.: *Beiträge zur Formgeschichte synoptischer Wundererzählungen, dargestellt an der vita Apollonii des Philostratus*, Diss. Jena 1953.

Schweizer, E.: 'Anmerkungen zur Theologie des Markus' in: *Neotestamentica*, Zürich and Stuttgart 1963, 93-104.

– 'Zur Frage des Messiasgeheimnisses bei Markus', *ZNW* 56 (1965) 1-8.

– *Das Evangelium nach Markus, NTD* 1, Göttingen 1968 (*The good news according to Mark*, London 1971).

Sherwin-White, A.N.: *Roman Society and Roman Law in the New Testament*, Oxford 1963.

Sigerist, H.E.: 'Die historische Betrachtung der Medizin', *Archiv f. Gesch. d. Medizin* 13 (1926) 1-19.

Smith, M.: 'Prolegomena to a Discussion of Aretalogies, Divine Man, the Gospels and Jesus', *JBL* 90 (1971) 174-199.

– *Tannaitic Parallels to the Gospel, JBL Monograph Series* 6, Philadelphia 1951.

Smitmans, A.: *Das Weinwunder von Kana*, Tübingen 1966.

Speigl, J.: 'Die Rolle des Wunders im vorkonstantinischen Christentum', *ZKTh* 92 (1970) 287-312.

Stählin, G.: 'Die Gleichnishandlungen Jesu', in: *Kosmos und Ekklesia, Festschrift für W. Stählin*, Kassel 1953, 9-22.

Steck, O.H.: *Israel und das gewaltsame Geschick der Propheten, WMANT* 23, Neukirchen 1967.

Steinleitner, F.: *Die Beichte im Zusammenhang mit der sakralen Rechtspflege in der Antike*, Diss. Munich 1913 = Leipzig 1913.

Stemplinger, E.: *Antike und moderne Volksmedizin, Das Erbe der Alten*, 2 Series H. 10, Leipzig 1925.

Strack, H.L.: *Einleitung in Talmud und Midraš*, 5th ed., Munich 1921.

Strecker, G.: 'Zur Messiasgeheimnistheorie im Markusevangelium', *TU* 88, Berlin 1964, 87-104.

– *Der Weg der Gerechtigkeit, FRLANT* 82, 2nd ed., Göttingen 1966.

Sundwall, J.: *Die Zusammensetzung des Markusevangeliums, Acta Academiae Aboensis, Humaniora* IX, Abo 1934.

Suhl, A.: *Die Wunder Jesu. Ereignis und Überlieferung*, Gütersloh 1968.

Sweet, J.P.M.: 'The Theory of Miracles in the Wisdom of Solomon', in: *Miracles. Cambridge Studies in their Philosophy and History*, ed. C.F.D. Moule, London 1965, 115-126.

Sydow, C.W.v.: 'On the Spread of Tradition', in: *Selected Papers on Folklore*, Copenhagen 1948, 11-43.

– 'Folk-Tale Studies and Philology', in: *Selected Papers on Folklore*, Copenhagen 1948, 189-219.

Tambornino, J.: *De antiquarum daemonismo, RVV* 7, Giessen 1909.

Taylor, V.: *The Formation of the Gospel Tradition*, 6th ed., London 1957.

– *The Gospel according to St. Mark*, 6th ed., London 1952.

Thraede, K.: *Grundzüge griechisch-römischer Brieftopik, Zetem.* 48, Munich 1970.

– Art. Exorzismus, *RAC* VII, 44-117.

Tillich, P.: *Symbol und Wirklichkeit*, Göttingen 1962.

– *Systematische Theologie*, 3 vols., Stuttgart 1956ff. (*Systematic Theology*, London 1953-64).

Tödt, H.E.: *Der Menschensohn in der synoptischen Überlieferung*, Gütersloh 1959 (*The Son of Man in the Synoptic Tradition*, London 1965).

Traub, G.: *Die Wunder im Neuen Testament, RV* 5, 2, Tübingen 1907.

Trilling, W.: *Das wahre Israel, StANT* 10, Munich 1964.

Trocmé, É.: *La formation de l'Évangile selon Marc, ÉHPhR* 57, Paris 1963 (*The formation of the Gospel according to Mark,* Philadelphia 1975).

Vernon, G.M.: 'The Symbolic Interactionist Approach to the Sociology of Religion', *IJR* 2 (1966) 135-155.

Vielhauer, Ph.: 'Erwägungen zur Christologie des Markusevangeliums', in: *Aufsätze zum Neuen Testament, ThB* 31, Munich 1965.

– 'Zum Paulinismus der Apostelgeschichte', in: *Aufsätze zum Neuen Testament, ThB* 31, Munich 1965.

Vogt, J.: 'Struktur der antiken Sklavenkriege', *AbhMainz* 1957, 1, 1-57.

Vögtle, A.: 'Jesu Wunder einst und heute', *BL* 2 (1961) 234-254.

Waagenvoort, H.: 'Contactus', *RAC* III, 404-421.

– *Roman Dynamism,* Oxford 1947.

Walker, W.O.: 'Post-crucifixion Appearances and Christian Origins', *JBL* 88 (1969) 157-165.

Wallace, R.F.: 'Revitalisations-Bewegungen', in: *Religionsethnologie,* ed., C.A. Schmitz, Frankfurt 1964, 404-427.

Wallace, R.S.: *The Gospel Miracles,* Edinburgh–London 1960.

Waugh, B.: 'Structural Analysis in Literature and Folklore', *Western Folklore* 25 (1966) 153-164.

Weber, M.: 'Wirtschaft und Gesellschaft' in: *Grundriss der Sozialökonomik,* Section III, 3rd ed., Tübingen 1947 (*Economy and Society: An Outline of Interpretive Sociology,* California 1979).

Weeden, T.J.: 'The Heresy that necessitated Mark's Gospel', *ZNW* 59 (1968) 145-158.

Weinreich, O.: *Antike Heilungswunder. Untersuchungen zum Wunderglauben der Griechen und Römer, RVV* 8, 1, Berlin 1909 (= 1969).

– *Menekrates Zeus und Salmoneus, Tübinger Beiträge zur Altertumswissenschaft,* Tübingen 1933.

– 'Türöffnung im Wunder-, Prodigien- und Zauberglauben der Antike, des Judentums und Christentums', in: *Genethliakon W. Schmid zum 70. Geburtstag, Tübinger Beiträge zur Altertumswissenschaft* H. 5, Stuttgart 1929, 200-264.

– *Neue Urkunden zur Sarapis-Religion, SGV,* 86, Tübingen 1919.

Weisgerber, L.: *Die Vier Stufen der Erforschung der Sprachen,* Düsseldorf 1963.

Weiss, J.: 'εὐθύς bei Markus', *ZNW* 11 (1910) 124-133.

Wellek, R., Warren, A.: *Theorie der Literatur,* Ullstein Buch 420/21, Frankfurt and Berlin 1963.

Wengst, K.: *Christologische Formeln und Lieder des Urchristentums, StNT* 7, Gütersloh 1972.

Wheelwright, P.: 'Notes on Mythopoeia', in: J.B. Vickers (ed.): *Myth and Literature,* Lincoln 1966, 574-591.

– 'The Semantic Approach to Myth', in Sebeok, T.A. (ed.): *Myth. A Symposium,* Bloomington 1958, 95-103.

Wilckens, U.: *Auferstehung,* Stuttgart 1970.

Windisch, H.: *Paulus und Christus, UNT* 24, Leipzig 1934.

Wrede, W.: 'Zur Heilung des Gelähmten (Mc 2, 1ff.)', *ZNW* 5 (1904) 354-358.

– *Das Messiasgeheimnis in den Evangelien,* 3rd ed., Göttingen 1963 (*The messianic secret,* Cambridge 1971).

Subject Index

Index of References